The Story of
Percy Main Amateurs FC
2009/10 season

Ian Cusack

Ian Cusack Publishing

First published in the UK in 2010 by Ian Cusack Publishing

A CIP catalogue record for this title is available from the British Library

ISBN: 978-0-9565736-0-5

Typeset by Andrew Searle

Cover design: Ian Cusack Publishing

Printed and bound in the UK by Anthony Rowe Ltd

IAN CUSACK PUBLISHING
52 River View, Tynemouth, NE30 4AF
Tel: 0191 2099284 Email: iancusack@blueyonder.co.uk

Contents

To all players, supporters and committee members at Percy Main Amateurs, but especially for Norman de Bruin, who introduced me to this wonderful football club, Laura Huntley, who provided unflagging support throughout the whole project and for the memory of my dad, Eddy Cusack, who would have loved to have held a copy of this book

Introduction: *Village People*

ON MAY 24th 2009 Newcastle United, a professional football team I'd wasted most of my life supporting, lost 1-0 away to Aston Villa, courtesy of Damien Duff's unwitting deflection of a hitherto harmless Gareth Barry effort that had, prior to Duff's crucial, catastrophic intervention, been drifting woefully wide of a predictably static Steve Harper's left hand post. The significance of this own goal was not lost on the estimated 4,000 travelling Geordie fans in a sold-out crowd of 42,585; after 16 years in the top flight, their team had been relegated, with barely a whimper of protest or a shot in anger during a tortuous second half of mute inaction. During the intervening time between promotion and demotion, their team had gone from being known as Kevin Keegan's Entertainers to a shambolic ragbag of underachieving has-beens and no-hopers that had managed to win only two games out of their final 23 Premiership fixtures. Even then these victories were only against fellow relegation casualties West Brom and Middlesbrough; a truly shocking statistic, which bore tribute to their complete ineptitude and deserved demotion.

As a metaphor for their team's decline, Duff's uncomprehending bafflement as his accidental complicity in his team's ultimate demise resulted in an unconvincing and ineffective dive by the slow moving Harper as the ball almost crawled apologetically in to the net, could not be bettered in a season during which time Newcastle had reeled impotently from one self-inflicted wound to another. Unscientific on-line surveys had indicated 77% of neutral fans had wanted Newcastle relegated; just how many of those indicating a preference were actually clandestine Newcastle supporters, sick of the indignities they had been forced to endure by their team, was not clear.

At the same time as this morbid charade was unfolding in front of a sickened and unbelieving fanbase, most of whom had travelled to the Midlands still clinging to the forlorn hope that, somehow, the single, crucial point that would maintain top flight status could be accrued by whatever unlikely method, Byker Key Club were beating Osborne's Bar 4-0, courtesy of two goals apiece by Paul McCutcheon and Darren Turnbull, in the final of the Newcastle Central Sunday Afternoon League Malcolm Turner Memorial Trophy. The game took place at Purvis Park, home of the club I am proud to support, Northern Alliance Division 1 side Percy Main Amateurs. This book will tell the story of a small yet proud club from the north east of England during our wildly successful and deeply enjoyable 2009/10 season. Newcastle United may have clambered out of the Championship with over 100 points, but their achievements are dwarfed by the Main's triumphant return to the Northern Alliance Premier Division after 4 years away, not to mention the capturing of the Pin Point Recruitment Combination Cup.

Percy Main Amateurs were probably reformed in the 1919/20 season by ex servicemen returning from World War 1. It's impossible to accurately state when the club was actually formed as a football team bearing the name Percy Main AFC had been in existence prior to the First World War, possibly from as early as 1885, but no concrete information about this club or its achievements has come to light. Somewhat mysteriously and eerily, a perfectly preserved framed team photograph of the anonymous players who made up the team in

1912 hangs on the pavilion wall at Purvis Park. It is a cause of sober speculation for all those who pause in front of the photo to wonder which if any of those players made it back to the banks of the Tyne after the Great War.

The ground was then known as Middle Row Park, in reference to three sets of pitmen's cottages that stood near the site: Low Row situated where Percy Main Cricket Club now stands, Middle Row, where the football club is now, and High Row, which was North of the Railway line, while the Percy Main Colliery which gave the village its name was some 200 yards East, just past St John's Church.

A Primitive Methodist Chapel stood on the current site of the club's pavilion from the mid 1800s and may be responsible for one or two of the alleged unexplained noises and strange sightings that have been said to occur in the changing room area every now and again. St John's Green, the road on which the football club is situated, is built on the site of the Backworth Wagonway, historically one of the busiest coal-bearing railway lines down to the River Tyne, while the pitch is situated on what was once the Coble Dene, a stream whose waters also flowed in to the murky Tyne.

The Villagers, as Percy Main are nicknamed, began life playing in the Northern Amateur League and finished their first season as league champions, also lifting the Northumberland Minor Cup in 1920; a feat we almost repeated this year. The club went on to win the Championship in four consecutive seasons, between1925 and 1928. During the 1929/30 campaign, Percy Main reached the Quarter Finals of the FA Amateur Cup, defeating such notable opponents as Cleethorpes Town, Rawmarsh Welfare and Yorkshire Amateurs before going down to eventual finalists Bournemouth Gasworks Athletic. This game produced The Main's then greatest payday in their history, as the share of the gate money was a huge £105 12 shillings and 9d. At a quid entrance and 50p for a programme, an average Villagers home game these days makes about £30 on the door.

Between 1931 and the immediate post War years, the club played in the Tyneside Senior League before rejoining the Northern Amateur League. The Villagers subsequently joined the Northern Alliance in 1968 and enjoyed Northumberland Amateur Cup successes in 1968, 1970 and 1971, and also lifted the Northern Alliance League Cup by beating Bedlington Terriers at St James' Park the following season.

In 1978 The Villagers won the Northumberland Senior Bowl for the first time with a 1-0 win over West Allotment at North Shields' now-defunct Appleby Park ground in front of a crowd of over 500. The Northern Alliance League Championship was won in consecutive seasons, 1981 and 1982, while the club finished runners up in 1983. The 1981/82 season was Percy Main's only foray into the FA Cup, when a plucky Villagers side were defeated 3-1 at Lancaster City. The following season saw The Main have their best run in the FA Vase, when wins over Darlington RA, Boldon CA, Heaton Stannington, Wingate, Tadcaster Albion, Seaham Red Star, Peterlee, Easington and Brandon United saw the club reach the Fifth Round Proper of the national competition.

Percy Main were relegated to Division 1 of the Northern Alliance in 1991. The installation of a new committee in 1993 took place with the club penniless, bottom of the league and with no players or points. However, the committee of current treasurer and former Manager Bob Rodgerson, Honorary President Graham Marsh, who died in April 2010, John Humberstone and Gary Hull, who died in 2002 and in whose memory an annual pre-season game with local rivals North Shields takes place, set about the arduous task of putting the club back on an even keel both on and off the pitch. Their hard work was rewarded as The Villagers were promoted as league champions in 1998/99. After an encouraging seventh place Premier League finish, the club went on to lift the League Cup, with victory over Carlisle City in the final at Ponteland's Leisure Centre ground in their first season back in the top flight.

The Village Ground was renamed Purvis Park in 1996 in recognition of 50 years dedicated service by the late Alan Purvis as player, secretary and chairman, while a new perimeter fence was erected around the ground in 2003 with help from the Football Foundation. In 2004 The Villagers ended their Premier League season in fourth place and won the Northumberland Bowl once more, defeating Cramlington Town at Whitley Park 2-1, but two years later the team were once again relegated.

The first two seasons back in the Northern Alliance first division were a struggle, but in Summer 2008, the club appointed the then 21 year old Jason Ritchie as player manager and in a vastly improved campaign, the club rose from 12th place to finish 5th, having been in contention for promotion until the last fortnight of the season, as well as reaching the final of the Northumberland Senior Bowl, only to come up short 2-0 against Blyth Town. Unlike St. James Park, where Newcastle won only 5 games and lost 7, Purvis Park was a fortress in 2008/09, with the Villagers boasting an impressive 10-2-2 record. In fact, the best game I saw that season was Percy Main 3 Chopwell Officials' Club 2 on January 17th, when Jason Ritchie thumped home the winner in the dying minutes in a superb free-flowing contest. Purvis Park is a beautiful little ground and a cracking place to watch football, regardless of who is playing, which is why I headed there on May 24th instead of enduring the inevitable recriminations surrounding Newcastle's failure in a packed pub with bad-tempered drunks.

In fact, the Malcolm Turner Memorial Trophy wasn't a bad game and Byker Key Club were worthy winners; the hundred or so pub regulars, family members, drinking buddies and fake-tanned teenage WAGs who'd turned up with about a dozen cans each, had seen a bunch of honest young blokes playing the game for the love of it on a glorious, sunny, early summer afternoon, as a prelude to a serious Sunday night out down Tynemouth Front Street or the Quayside, with the added bonus of a Bank Holiday Monday bender in the local to follow for both winners and losers. At full time, there were no replica-shirted followers of Osborne's weeping crocodile tears in the hope of being captured on camera and seeing themselves on endless looped re-runs on Sky Sports News. The losers took it on the chin and then headed off for a pint.

Back in October 1993, at the fourth attempt, Newcastle United collected their first ever away victory in the Premiership, ironically at Villa Park, by two goals to nil, courtesy of a Malcolm Allen penalty and a late Andy Cole tap-in. I was there that day; indeed it was one of 61 away games I attended during Newcastle's sojourn amongst the English game's top brass. While that's a fair number of days and weekends spent away from home wasting money I didn't have on tickets, train fares and beer, not to mention squandering precious time I should have spent with my family in the company of people whose only connection with me was the team we followed, it is an awfully long way from the unending fanaticism displayed by some of my friends and acquaintances, many of whom are late 40s and older, who plan their holidays, and in some cases sick days, to allow them the freedom to travel to Spurs for a midweek game in January. My mate Gary spent his 48th birthday driving back from a Sunday game at Portsmouth in December 2008; he didn't mind as Newcastle had won 3-0. While I was never that committed, I did used to make it to about eight to ten away games a season, despite the escalating cost and the fact my son was born in June 1995, when Newcastle had only been up two seasons, until about the turn of the millennium.

I'd love to say it was simply because I was a good father, or more prosaically that the cost of match attendance and Sky TV tinkering with fixtures caused me to reduce my travelling to one or two away games a season maximum in the last decade, but it was none of those things. I simply fell out of love with the professional game and Newcastle United in particular. Frankly, for years I would be delighted when Newcastle home games were moved from 3pm on a Saturday, as it meant I could get to see proper football instead. Watching non-league football is cheap and it's generally enjoyable. Admittedly, if your side loses, it still hurts like hell, but a defeat isn't seen by dozens of media commentators and print journalists as a potential lead story on ***Newsnight***. Now I've broken the bond with Newcastle United that was first sealed on New Year's Day 1973 when I attended a 2-2 draw with Leicester City with my dad, my Uncle and my cousin John, the timings of their games are of minimal interest to me. Perhaps the saddest part is that even ten years ago, I would never have believed I could even think such a thing, much less express it in public.

The greatest enjoyment I ever had out of watching football was Newcastle's promotion in 1992/93, closely followed by the unexpected joy of finishing third in The Premiership the year after. However, that's when the pressure to win started to overtake the simple joys of the game, as Newcastle United, who only three years previously had been a joke of a club, suddenly became contenders for the major prizes; of course, they never won any of them! In my mind, the tragic near miss of winning the title in 1995/96 isn't remembered for the glorious football Newcastle played, but for the eventual anguish of defeat as Keegan ranted, the team imploded and Cantona led Manchester United inexorably to the crown. While Bobby Robson's intervention in making Newcastle credible contenders again in 2002, after the bemusing false starts under Dalglish and Gullit, and Glen Roeder's unexpected window of adequacy in early 2006, following the unspeakable bilge dished up under Souness, were other refreshing incidents in an unremitting decade of tedious frustration, the vast majority of time I've spent watching Newcastle has left me with the distinct feeling that I've been cheated, if not defrauded, both financially and emotionally.

The Ashley era, trumpeted by so many as a fresh start, reinforced the gloom around the club: Allardyce with his bluetooth headset and team of quack doctors, Keegan, the discredited populist looking for a cushy pre-retirement sinecure, Tourette's Kinnear and seemingly sinking Hughton, before Shearer was left with the impossible task of motivating players on anything up to £110,000 a week to take more than five points from the last 24. Pathetic. Disgusting. Shameful.

After 20 years as a season ticket holder and 36 years as a fan, I had made the decision long before the first, never mind final, whistle at Villa Park that no longer would I waste money, time or affection on a club that cared little for me other than as one of the 40,000 plus mugs who sent them a cheque each June for my seat. That cheque had grown from £130 in 1989 to £780 in 2008, to include mine and my son's seats; if the club had offered free renewals for 2009/10, we still wouldn't have bothered. My son Ben is 15; he plays prop forward for Wallsend Eagles XIII and rugby league - a game I've had no exposure to, nor comprehension of, in my life - and this is what he does with his weekends and I'm proud of him. Personally, I'm happy that my energies as a supporter are now channelled in to Percy Main, because I know both players and committee appreciate that. Frankly, I can't imagine saying the same about Newcastle United's attitude to me. Ever.

Having effectively retired as a Newcastle fan, I was as likely to have attended Sunderland's home game with Chelsea (a fixture between two sides I have the utmost and abiding loathing for) on May 24th, as I was to have travelled to Villa Park. Hence, Duff's costly intervention at approximately 4.45 coincided with me collecting in the corner flags and helping to put the goalposts away at Purvis Park as Byker Key Club showered each other in Carling and Fosters at the end of the 103rd and final game I'd attended in 2008/09, during which time I'd visited 12 new grounds following Percy Main.

Fairly obviously, I like football and I watch games whenever I have the opportunity. In my defence, I'm not really a groundhopper, as I actually support a particular team or teams in my case. Whenever possible I go and watch one of the sides I follow; if, for reasons of geography or other commitments, that doesn't prove possible, I go and watch a game that I may have an interest in, often governed as much by location as participants. However, it is important to keep an eye on the opposition in Northern Alliance Division 1, or so I told myself after cycling to watch Newcastle East End entertain Cullercoats on a blustery spring evening. East End won 2-1 incidentally; not a bad game either.

In 2008/09, I attended 21 Newcastle United first team games (and half a dozen Reserve games), 31 Percy Main Amateurs fixtures, including a phantom contest against Westerhope, who subsequently resigned from the league and had their records expunged (which was a relief as they'd done us 6-3 at Purvis Park), and 41 other local non-league games, not to mention playing 36 games in goal in the North East Over 40s League 4th Division for Heaton Winstons and a bit of groundhopping in Ireland and Scotland, when opportunities arose. Consequently, I spent 2008/09 supporting one team (Percy Main), playing for a second (Heaton Winstons), checking the results of third (Hibernian) and enduring the home games of a fourth (Newcastle United). In a season when Whitley Bay won the FA Vase, Gateshead were promoted to the Conference and Blyth Spartans hosted Blackburn Rovers in the third round of the FA Cup live on television, non-league football was, without question, the best version of the game available in the North East.

Where do these allegiances come from? With Newcastle United, I had no choice as my support for the Magpies had been mapped out from birth; my maternal grandfather had held a season ticket from the end of World War II and kept it until his death in 1967, while my dad had first set foot in St James' Park in 1946, aged 13, to see Len Shackleton score six goals on his debut as Newcastle beat Newport County 13-0. Even my mam had attended the 1955 Cup Final, seeing Newcastle win 3-1 at Wembley, a feat I will never match. From first attending games with my dad, where he'd perch me on one of the unique concrete crush barriers in the Gallowgate as a small child, I graduated to attending games with mates as a teenager and penniless student (after my dad stopped going in his 40s, sickened by the sacking of Joe Harvey, the sterile non-football of Gordon Lee and the sale of Malcolm MacDonald), to celebrating Newcastle's relegation in 1989 by purchasing a season ticket, initially in the Milburn Stand, and then, without any choice in the matter as a victim of creeping commercialism and the lure of corporate cash, again in the Gallowgate from 1994 onwards as my original seat was transformed in to a corporate hospitality revenue stream.

Perhaps it was that enforced move to the Gallowgate that started to sour my relationship with the club. Perhaps it was just the huge amount of free Saturdays caused by the Premiership fixture list, but it was around that time I began to search elsewhere for footballing delights. Inspired by Harry Pearson's marvellous account of North East football in 1993/94, ***The Far Corner***, I began to seek out Northern League football, not so much as a fan, just as an interested observer.

I quickly formed allegiances with both Shildon and Ashington; two clubs a long way from where I lived and from places that I had no connection with, other than the fact I liked Dean Street and Portland Park as places to watch football. At that time we lived near the centre of Newcastle, in the marvellously named district of Spital Tongues, where my local side played at St. James Park. It was only when we moved in 1998 to High Heaton when I actually had a local club on my doorstep; former Northern League side Heaton Stannington, who are long time members of the Northern Alliance and in 2010/11 will be rivals of Percy Main.

As an indication how far removed teams like Heaton Stannington are from the heights of the Premiership, it would take them nine straight promotions, as well as the construction of an entirely new ground of course, to be able to play Wigan or Stoke City. And Percy Main were a division below them in 2009/10. Fans of the Northern League, which has historically drawn its clubs from County Durham, point out it was formed in 1889 and is only a year younger than the Football League. However, the Northern Alliance is a strong and proud league with a history stretching back to 1890. What is equally important is that the Alliance is primarily Tyneside and Northumberland's competition; a proper Geordie football league.

Although the Alliance was at one time absorbed by the North Eastern League and on another occasion closed down through lack of entries, it is still in existence 120 years later. The founder members in 1890/91 were Birtley, Bishop Auckland, Elswick Rangers, Gateshead North Eastern Railway, Rendel, Sunderland 'A' and Whitburn.

Newcomers in 1891/92 were Mickley, Shankhouse, Southwick, Sunderland Olympic and Willington Athletic, with Birtley, Bishop Auckland and Elswick Rangers dropping out. Further additions in 1892/93 were Ashington, Blyth, Newcastle United 'A' and Seaham Harbour. The turnover in clubs during the early years was eye-wateringly high, a phenomenon that has continued to this day. The Northern Alliance was initially dominated by Sunderland 'A', who won the championship on five occasions during the first six seasons between 1890 and 1896, the exception being 1892/93 when Shankhouse were champions. They are still in the Northern Alliance Premier Division today, but had to wait until the 2004/05 season for their second title. During 1896/97, Axwell Park became the first club to resign in mid-season. In 1902/03, the 'A' sides of Football League clubs Middlesbrough (who had joined in 1899/1900), Newcastle United and Sunderland transferred their allegiance to the Northern League. At the end of the 1905/06 season, the Northern Alliance decided to exclude some of the Durham clubs to reduce travelling costs for the bulk of the membership. Clubs to leave for this reason were Consett Swifts, Leadgate Park, who joined the Northern League, and Stanley. Newcomers in 1906/07 were

Rutherford, who remain to this day (you'll read about us beating them on three separate occasions, even if they still had the last laugh), and Scotswood, as the Northern Alliance operated with 13 clubs.

Blyth Spartans joined the Northern Alliance in 1907/08 and managed two championship wins before transferring to the North Eastern League in 1913/14. Ashington joined the North Eastern League in 1914/15 after winning the Northern Alliance championship in 1913/14. The Northern Alliance closed down from 1915 to 1919 because of the First World War. When the league resumed in 1919/20, it comprised of 16 clubs, with several newcomers including Chopwell Institute, Consett Celtic, Felling College, Hebburn College, Lintz Institute, Prudhoe Castle and Walker Celtic, but one of the established clubs, Annfield Plain Celtic, were champions. At the end of the 1925/26 season, the Northern Alliance amalgamated with the North Eastern League, with the Northern Alliance clubs forming Division Two. This situation continued until1935, when the North Eastern League's Division Two was disbanded and the Northern Alliance reformed in 1935/36.

Membership was increased to 16 clubs in 1936/37 by the inclusion of Alnwick Town, Ashington Reserves, Blyth Spartans Reserves, Chopwell Colliery, Crookhall Colliery and Morpeth Town. Consett returned to the North Eastern League in 1937/38, but the Northern Alliance added Newcastle United 'A' and South Shields Reserves to their ranks. Newcastle United 'A' were champions in the1938/39 campaign. Soon after, the Northern Alliance closed down because of the Second World War. Five clubs, Ashington Reserves, Chopwell Colliery, East Cramlington Colliery Welfare, Mickley and Newburn, competed in 1939/40, before the Northern Alliance closed down until the 1946/47 season. Membership in 1946/47 comprised 18 clubs, including many newcomers: Blyth Spartans, Burradon Welfare, Gosforth & Coxlodge, Hexham Hearts, Jarrow, Lynemouth Welfare, North Shields Reserves, Prudhoe East End, Seaton Burn Welfare, Shilbottle Welfare, and West Sleekburn Welfare.

During the late 1950s and early 1960s the Northern Alliance lost many of its regular members. By 1963/64, only 10 clubs were in membership and some of those intimated that they would not be competing in

1964/65. As adequate replacements could not be found the Northern Alliance closed down at the end of the 1963/64 season, presumably to enter a period of solemn mourning as I had made my entry in to the world on August 11th 1964. Alnwick Town, who had been Northern Alliance champions in 1962/63 and again in 1963/64, managed a belated hat trick of championship wins in 1965/66 when the Northern Alliance reformed with 14 clubs.

The Northern Alliance has continued to have a large turnover of clubs. Wallsend Athletic joined in 1966/67, Newcastle University in 1967/68, Chopwell St.John's, Wallsend Gordon United and Winlaton Mill in 1968/69. Other newcomers in the early 1970s were Alston, Bede College (Durham), Northumberland College, Throckley Welfare and Workington Reserves. Most of these clubs had left by 1975 without getting amongst the honours. Later additions were more successful. Marine Park were Northern Alliance champions in 1972/73 and 1973/74 before dropping to a lower grade of football. South Shields Mariners spent two seasons between 1974 and 1976 in the Northern Alliance, winning the championship on both occasions before joining the Wearside League. Brandon United and Guisborough Town joined the Northern Alliance in 1977/78. Both clubs spent three seasons in the Northern Alliance, with Brandon United winning two championships and Guisborough Town one, in 1979/80, when they were unbeaten throughout the campaign. These two clubs also won the Northern Alliance Cup in those three seasons. Guisborough Town transferred to the Midland League in 1980/81. Brandon United had also sought to improve their status but were unsuccessful. Unfortunately, they had anticipated being accepted into another league and had tendered their resignation to the Northern Alliance and consequently found themselves in limbo and without a league in 1980/81. They were accepted into the Wearside League in 1981/82. Another recent newcomer, Carlisle City, have finished runners-up on four occasions since joining the Northern Alliance in 1975/76. Darlington Cleveland Bridge, who joined the Northern Alliance in 1981/82, were champions in 1982/83.

Although several recent additions have mainly been successful, the Northern Alliance still has its list of failures. Throckley Welfare were expelled from the Northern Alliance during the 1975/76 season for failing to fulfil fixtures. Northumberland College found the competition too exacting and transferred to the Northern Amateur League in 1974/75. Other losses included Durham University, Newcastle University, Sunderland Greenwells and Sunderland Pyrex. Peterlee Newtown and Seaham Colliery Welfare joined the Wearside League in 1979/80, where they were more successful.

At the end of the 1981/82 season, the Northern Alliance lost Alnwick Town, Bedlington Town, Esh Winning and Ryhope C.A. to the newly-formed Northern League Division Two. At the same time Cramlington Newtown resigned and Cramlington High Pit disbanded. This left only 11 clubs in membership, but with the addition of Prudhoe and the newly-formed Seaton Terrace, the Northern Alliance was able to function with 13 clubs in 1982/83. Darlington Cleveland Bridge and Shotton Comrades joined the Northern League in 1983/84. In the 1983/84 season the Northern Alliance was sponsored by Scottish and Newcastle Breweries and known as the McEwan's Lager Northern Alliance. The champions in that season were Morpeth Town, who took the title to the market town for the first time in more than eighty years.

In later years the Northern Alliance has suffered from more comings and goings and a decision was made to re-form in a three-division format. Agreement was reached with the Northern Combination League and the Northern Amateur League for an amalgamation of the three competitions under the Northern Alliance banner, with the 'new' competition kicking off in the 1988/89 season, which was ten years before I first experienced Northern Alliance football. In the intervening dozen years since I first saw Alliance football, there has continued to be a fairly substantial turnover of clubs, and of the 45 kicking off the three-division constitution in 1989, no less than 30 have disappeared from the Alliance's membership lists.

However, the league's management has continued with its recruitment of teams, resisting calls to shrink the set-up to two divisions, and the Alliance remains the more powerful feeder to the Northern League, as demonstrated by the successes of Benfield and West Allotment when moving up a step. Presumably, this is why teams from Durham and Cumbria are also currently in membership

My local side Heaton Stannington had joined the Northern Alliance in 1952/53 after a spell in the Northern League, though I wasn't to know this when I first watched them defeat Spital Rovers from Berwick by 2-0 on a warm August afternoon in 1998. My son, ex-wife and myself had just moved round the corner from the Stann's Grounsell Park in the summer of 1998 and, with Newcastle playing away to Chelsea, in a match that ended 1-1 and was the final one under the managership of Kenny Dalglish, I wanted to get Ben out of the house and hopefully to see a game.

At the age of three my son was already showing an interest in kicking footballs, running after them and throwing them at his daddy. To try and encourage this I'd taken him to see a couple of non-league games in the local area, mainly so he could run around and get some fresh air. At St. James' Park I'd long been aware of the phenomenon at cup games in early rounds, especially at the subsequently abolished two-legged affairs in the League Cup, whereby young kids were taken by their parents for their first experience of football. Unfortunately, these kids had grown up in the Sky generation, where the television coverage includes constant re-runs of action and gimmicky camera angles meaning it is very difficult for the average viewer to get bored, such was the showbiz element essential to the presentation of games. Sadly, real life matches are often dull and mundane, especially in the second round of the League Cup. Hence the youngsters get irritable, start playing on their phones or agitating for fizzy drinks and hot dogs. To avoid this, I started to take Ben to see amateur football at a very young age, just so he'd be aware that he may well be cold, bored and disappointed by the experience of live football.

On August 22nd 1998, Ben certainly wasn't cold as a glorious, still August afternoon lazily slipped past. While I'd only been watching non-league facilities for about three years at that time, I was aware of the basic requirements for grounds at Northern League level, in the shape of floodlights, 100 covered seats, hard standing on all sides and perimeter fencing, all of which bar the perimeter fencing were missing at Grounsell Park. Initially I was taken aback by how basic the facilities were, though not by the football, which was of a comparable standard to Northern League Division 2. However, the Alliance is a lower league in terms of its place in the non-league Pyramid and many of the clubs, Percy Main included, have no realistic aspirations of climbing higher, generally for economic reasons, as it costs a fortune to upgrade a ground, but often also for social reasons.

It has become clear to me over the years that the Alliance is reminiscent of club rugby union of the 1970s; players playing a game they love for the sake of it are at the heart of the matter, with officials drawn very much from the ranks of former players and the odd smattering of spectators being seen as an oddity rather than an expectation. On Cup Final Day 2005, while Arsenal and Manchester United played out a sterile, drab 0-0 draw, I was in the company of several groundhoppers who had travelled from Leeds, London and the West Midlands, happily taking in Seaton Burn's comfortable 5-0 win over Sport Benfield in Alliance D2, when a league official approached and asked, with a note of incredulity that could have been mistaken as menace by those unfamiliar with the cadences of the Geordie dialect, "What are you lot doing here?"

Perhaps such attitudes and the impossibility of getting a bit of craic going with the other spectators when only a dozen people are watching the game, most of them being substitutes, injury victims and the committee, as opposed to the welcoming and expansive clubhouses of much of the Northern League, where many teams have vociferous and tireless supporters' clubs who raise more money for the side than sponsorship could ever hope to, led me to remain as an observer rather than a fan of Alliance football. That, however, was all to change following the events of Saturday February 11th 2006.

For the casual supporters, groundhopper and football addict, the Northern Alliance provides a source of great joy in the early summer. The lack of floodlights at almost all grounds means that midweek matches between mid September and early April are a complete non-starter. Hence, while the Northern League wraps up its fixtures by the May Day

Bank Holiday, the Alliance continues on until Whit weekend. This is why my first experience of Percy Main Amateurs came with a visit to Purvis Park on May 14th 2005, to witness the visit of Heaton Stannington, who I was nominally supporting, having watched them intermittently since my first visit back in August 1998. Whenever Newcastle were away or inactive and my local Northern League sides West Allotment and Benfield were away, I'd watch Heaton Stannington to ensure I got to see a game each Saturday, though this was something new; an away trip!

The game finished 3-2 to Heaton Stannington and I've no real recollection of it, other than standing near the corner flag with Ben and admiring the scenic privet hedge that acts as a barrier between the football ground and the adjoining cricket pitch. Thankfully, the Internet exists to preserve accounts of even the most minor of football matches and make these reports permanently accessible. This game was reported on the Percy Main website in the following terms :

An end of season game with nothing at stake for either side it may have been but Percy Main and Heaton Stannington served up an entertaining game for the sizeable crowd at Purvis Park for this Northern Alliance Premier Division game.

Percy Main started the game in the ascendancy as John Amos and Robbie Livermore linked up to threaten Lee Campbell in the Heaton goal, but it was the visitors who opened the scoring on the quarter hour mark as a long ball from defence caught The Main rearguard napping and Andrew Weeks slipped the ball over the head of the advancing goalkeeper Ian Hall.

The visitors, with the bit between their teeth, enjoyed the bulk of the possession as Hall saved well from Paul Hodgson and Daryl Leach while Geoff Walker and Gary Donaldson combined to play in Jon Finlay, but his shot was inches wide of the target. Percy Main rallied and John Hunt's quick free kick found Livermore, who brought a spectacular diving save from Campbell, but just before the break the visitors doubled their lead as Weeks' long ball from the left found Hodgson, who rose unchallenged to head home.

A minute into the second half The Villagers were handed a glimmer of hope as Heaton's Richard Kerr was adjudged to have handled in the area and Livermore stepped up to despatch the kick. As the game swung from end to end The Main's

John Hunt flashed a shot across the face of goal, while at the other end Hall palmed Geoff Walker's effort behind for a corner and was relieved to see Hodgson fire over from the subsequent kick.

On 79 minutes it looked as though the visitors had the game sewn up as substitute Chris Johnson headed home Josef McAnespie's left wing cross to claim his side's third of the game. As the full time whistle approached Livermore's through ball found Rob Herman, pitched into the fray, who headed over Campbell into an empty net to once again give his side hope, but the Heaton defence held out in the remaining few minutes to claim the points.

The two sides next met on a cold Saturday in February 2006. It was, in retrospect, a momentous day; Newcastle won 2-1 at Aston Villa, I met my partner Laura for the first time that night and, perhaps most importantly, I discovered the beauty that is Percy Main Amateurs. The club website carries only a brief outline of the day's events. In its entirety, the match report consists of the following statement: "By all accounts an even game with chances at both ends and a good performance by Percy Main." To say the least, that doesn't tell the full story.

It was a cold but clear afternoon, with temperatures pegged slightly above freezing by a biting wind and ready to decline as the shadows lengthened; the day before my ex wife's sister had given birth to twins and she'd hurried down with Ben to see the new arrivals in Yorkshire. Leaving in something of a hurry, Sara, my ex, had forgot to cancel the milk, so I'd gone round to take it in from the front step. With Newcastle away to Villa and Benfield at Squires Gate in Blackpool in the FA Vase, I had resigned myself to not seeing a game, but walking past Grounsell Park, I saw the goal nets were up and corner flags in place. Having attended to my domestic responsibilities at my former place of residence and purchased a cup of hot brown liquid of indeterminate provenance from the ATS garage next door to Grounsell Park (this being the sole source of sustenance available near the ground), I was ready to make up approximately 15% of the crowd for this crucial Northern Alliance Premier Division game.

The opposition was immaterial to me as I was simply thankful to be able to see a game, but the claret and blue strips of the away team immediately told me it was Percy Main I'd be watching. 2005/06 was a rancid season for the Main; a final playing record of won 4, drawn 4, lost 26; goals conceded 94, goal difference minus 65 led to a fairly predictable last place finish. As Heaton Stann were to finish in fourth place, a comfortable home win was to be expected. In fact, this was one of only about half a dozen games I've ever seen fail to finish; the other non-completers have been a couple of times for fog, three times because of a deteriorating pitch in monsoon conditions and once, in an Over 40s league game I played in for my team Heaton Winstons at home to Southwick WMC, because of high winds. None of those reasons applied here.

Heaton Stannington versus Percy Main Amateurs is the only game I've seen abandoned because of fighting. This wasn't just a couple of players pushing and shoving, or any of the proverbial handbags, this was 21 blokes having a full-scale brawl that wouldn't have looked out of place in a Wild West Saloon during the Goldrush, or the Bigg Market taxi rank at closing time on Christmas Eve.

It was an incredible spectacle to watch; with the game goalless and only a few minutes remaining, a disputed throw-in on the touchline led to a swift and frank exchange of opinions that soon escalated in to a no-holds barred fight as Alan Ryder, a stalwart defender for Percy Main, lost his temper. Subsequent to this I've seen Alan launch corner flags like javelins in the direction of referees and kick footballs over the roof of clubhouses after having been sent off, so I know he's got anger management issues. However, this was the first time I'd seen him in action, so I wasn't to realise taking on the entire Heaton Stannington team, plus substitutes and management, was all in a typical afternoon's work for him.

Rather like those staged wrestling bouts that Kent Walton would commentate on at the end of ***World of Sport***, where half the audience at the Fairfield Hall, Croydon or Wolverhampton Civic Theatre would climb through the ropes and do their best to launch a few shots at whoever was available, seemingly everyone from both clubs were windmilling, gesticulating and snarling on the touchline about 10 yards from where I stood, with no sign that it would all be over with a few handshakes and rueful smiles any time soon.

The elderly referee and callow linesmen beat a tactical retreat as the melee continued unabated for several minutes, until Alan was eventually calmed down by Main's manager Bob Rodgerson, who spoke soothingly and put him in a bear hug. Looking on from the sidelines were about eight spectators, which was a typical crowd for the Stann. One fella, earphones in, surveyed the damage and said, "Toon are winning 2-1; Given's saved a penalty and Babayaro's been sent off. Mind, it seems boring compared to this."

As I turned to leave, a bloke about my age who had only arrived as the fireworks were going off, turned to me and said "football eh? Bloody hell!" The person who appropriated Sir Alex Ferguson's immortal words following the 1999 Champions League Final was Villagers secretary Norman de Bruin. He, more than anyone else, even Alan Ryder, built upon the fascination I had with this club following that astonishing introduction and is the reason why I started to write for the programme and do the best I can, as Assistant Secretary, to help out at Purvis Park.

But this book isn't about me or about Norman; it's about Percy Main Amateurs Football Club and the interesting times that were promised in the club press release from the end of May 2009 :

> *For the season 2009/10 a new look Percy Main Amateurs Football Club will be observed. With the introduction for the first time in our history, a competitive Ladies Team will be seen in the Percy Main colours. The Club has affiliated itself to the worthy Charity of St Oswald's Hospice for the foreseeable future and will raise funds and awareness for people less fortunate than themselves.*
>
> *An Honorary President, Mr Graham Marsh, has returned and appointed, and the Club has applied for FA Charter Status. Percy Main are indeed moving with the times and making huge strides to promote and integrate with both local Community Groups of all ages and Business. The long term strategy will be reviewed at the end of every season and added to as the club moves forward, ensuring our long term sustainability is maintained for the years to come.*

This is their story and I'm honoured to be able to tell it.

June & July: *Postscript & Preparation*

THE START OF each new season is an occasion eagerly anticipated by all football fans, regardless of the level their club plays at. Every year the summer provides supporters and players with the chance to start afresh and the attendant charming, perhaps naïve, rush of optimism that greets the first whistle shows yet again that football fans are always willing to delude themselves on the flimsiest of pretexts. In 1987/88, League Division 1, as it was known back then, had the decidedly unwieldy number of 21 teams in it, which meant that one side would necessarily be left kicking their heels on the opening day; predictably it was Newcastle who were the odd team out. I recall watching the final scores come in that Saturday afternoon on the ***Grandstand*** teleprinter with a bemused sense of detachment; it felt similar to watching the clear-up after a brilliant party to which we'd not been invited. Thankfully, things got belatedly underway on the Wednesday following with a poor 3-1 loss at White Hart Lane, but no matter, at least we'd started playing at last. Back then, that enforced blank weekend had been an expected blight on the sporting calendar since the publication of fixtures in early

June. However, to be left at a loose end because of a waterlogged pitch on the opening day is quite another matter.

The summers of 2007 and 2008 were consecutively the wettest in Britain since records began. Incredible thunderstorms in July are not uncommon and groundsmen, wary of having their lovingly prepared turf churned up by a meaningless kickabout, often get the last word. Hence on July 12th 2008, Percy Main's away friendly at Gosforth Bohemians was cancelled to save the pitch from unnecessary hammer. However, that particular weekend's downpour was only a mild shower compared to August 9th. I'd played in the Over 40s that morning in a squalling monsoon, augmented by gale force winds, as we'd won 7-4 in a farcical contest away to Southwick WMC in Sunderland. Returning to civilisation around noon, I was astonished to pick up a text message from Norman saying Percy Main's opening fixture at Seaton Burn was off; yes, the weather was rough, but surely not bad enough to result in a raft of postponements? This was a desperate and unexpected piece of bad news, but symptomatic of how the opening weeks would turn out as things were to get even worse in the early part of the season, as the statistics relating to the games that were actually played tell their own story.

By October 21st, Percy Main had played the grand total of two league games. Admittedly there had been four cup games, as well as the phantom match with Westerhope, who'd subsequently resigned from the Alliance. While it was great that maximum points had been accrued from a 4-0 win at Red Row and a 2-0 victory over visitors Berwick United, the lack of matches played meant the new team was not really gelling. Defeats at home to Cramlington and away to Stocksfield in the League Cup and divisional Combination Cup respectively were no hardships; the crucial thing was to gain league points.

While home form was good from the off, with the three league fixtures played at Purvis Park before Christmas ending in victories, on the road the picture was bleak. Three successive defeats at Rutherford, Chopwell and Cullercoats (by the seemingly emphatic margin of 4-0 in a bizarre, lopsided game the Villagers dominated) were compounded by a desperate 3-1 loss at Hebburn Reyrolle on the Saturday before Christmas, when injuries, illness and other cry-offs left only 11 players available, one of whom, Lindsay Collinson, had crawled from his flu-ridden sick bed to play. Things had to get better and, post Christmas, they did; five successive home games accrued 11 points, which would have been 13 if Jason Ritchie hadn't missed a penalty in the 0-0 with Seaton Burn. Not only was this his first ever penalty miss, but it also prevented him from being top scorer in his debut season.

The last of these home games had seen a resounding 6-0 win over Red Row, which helped build confidence as the Main went to face Premier Division Cramlington Town in the Northumberland FA Senior Benevolent Bowl. Having already won away to Seaton Delaval in the first round of this competition, another victory on the road against higher division opponents seemed unlikely when going in a goal down, but the Villagers rallied to win 2-1 and advance to another top flight side, Ashington Colliers, in the semi finals, where yet another fabulous performance saw a further 2-1 win. Despite losing the Bowl final 2-0 to Blyth Town, the team had gained immeasurable confidence from the cup run.

The final was a scrappy game, Percy Main's young side putting up a gallant performance, but despite their best efforts were unable to lift the prestigious trophy last won by The Villagers in 2004. The Main had defeated higher ranked teams in all of the previous rounds en route to the final, with all victories coming on opposition soil, but failed to perform to their high standards of late as Blyth, perhaps deservedly, went on to lift the silverware.

The game drew a large crowd to Blue Flames, home of Northern League side West Allotment Celtic and HQ of the Northumberland FA, and those supporting Percy Main had hoped to see the continuation of the team's recent run of form, during which The Villagers propelled themselves into second place in the table, playing a brand of exciting football which had resulted in the team being beaten only once in 2009 prior to this game, during a kicking frenzy at home to Stocksfield that was more redolent of Greek political protests against their country's economic meltdown than a football match.

Blyth created the bulk of the goalscoring opportunities but had to wait until 15 minutes from time to break the deadlock. Percy Main had threatened throughout with the wing play and throw ins of Pierre-luc Coiffait, while forwards Jon McEnaney and Joe Betts regularly troubled the Blyth rearguard without being able to repeat their recent scoring feats.

Blyth went ahead on 75 minutes following an infringement by Dean Morgan on the edge of the area, and after teeing up his shot, substitute Joe Race fired home the resultant kick in some style. At the other end The Main pressed and hoped to restore parity as Earle saved bravely from the feet of Betts after Ritchie's flag kick, but Blyth responded in deadly fashion as Beresford ran unchallenged to the edge of the area before firing an unstoppable shot past Rodgerson.

Rather than folding in the league, the Main were spurred on by their Cup adventures and managed seven successive league wins between 21st March and 25th April, which saw Percy Main take a place in the promotion frame after a 2-1 win at Newcastle East End. If only the League could have ended that day. Sadly, three successive defeats, with home and away losses to Whitley Bay Reserves being the most damaging, in a run in that saw four reverses in five games, made promotion impossible. At the start of May, five teams had been in with a shout of promotion: Stocksfield, Killingworth, Whitley Bay A, Cullercoats and Percy Main, but our lot were the only ones who definitely couldn't go up as the final set of fixtures approached.

Perhaps the most dramatic thing about the final day of the Premiership season is its staged uniformity; games kick off simultaneously, with cameras at each ground enabling TV producers to cut from game to game, allowing the subscribing viewers to see the action as it unfolds. The presumably unscripted tension surrounding the denouement of nine months football is no longer the preserve of the top flight; as low as the Blue Square Premier, English football's fifth tier, the regular season ends at the same time. It isn't like that at Percy Main's level.

The final games in the Northern Alliance Division 1 took place on Saturday May 23rd, though Percy Main had completed their fixtures a week previously with a storming comeback from 2-0 down against a very handy Cullercoats side, to win 3-2 with an 88th minute header from Liam Knox. Despite this win, which cost Cullercoats a chance of promotion, we finished fifth as Killingworth were Champions and Stocksfield accompanied them in moving to the Premier Division. Of course, when comparing it to the previous season, it was a source of pride for the club to have progressed so markedly.

In 2007/08, Percy Main, in finishing 12th in Northern Alliance Division 1, had used 45 players, including seven different goalkeepers, two of whom were outfield players press-ganged into taking a turn between the posts. With 28 of the 45 players appearing in less than half a dozen games, it is no surprise that the utter lack of continuity meant that no two starting line-ups were the same throughout the season. Having to continually scrabble around on a Friday night or a Saturday morning to find players prepared to show up was a less than acceptable state of affairs, especially when several of the ephemeral shadow squad would clearly struggle not to be last one picked behind Billy Casper in a ***Kes*** inspired kickaround on a mud heap.

While 2008/09 eventually resulted in the club just falling short of actually winning something, there was a tangible sense of progress on the playing side. The number of players used fell to 35, with 18 of those forming the nucleus of the side from Christmas onwards. The spirit within the camp was evident to see, both on the pitch, in the stirring fightbacks against Newcastle East End or Cullercoats, as well as off it, during their post Benevolent Bowl Final bonding and booze session, and at the end of season awards night on June 5th.

In the Northern League, all clubs have an adjacent social club. While some are dusty, damp-ridden middens that you'd not wish to spend any time in other than enforced calls of nature, others, such as Ashington's impressive new facility, are local landmarks, opening seven nights a week for parties and live entertainment, providing a lucrative source of income for clubs able to offset the inevitable debts caused by running a non-league football team. Such premises are not common in the Northern Alliance. Heaton Stannington's legendary array of hand-pulled Real Ales is something of an exception to the rule.

Percy Main doesn't have a bar; the only alcohol consumed on site tends to be at the end of season Sunday Cup Finals by the spectators with their big bags of cans. For post match hospitality for the first team, the only option is a trip next door to the Cricket Club. It's a mutually beneficial arrangement as the cricket club is desperately short of punters outside of their season. Hence, as a way of saying thank you for giving the football team somewhere to go post match, all official club functions take place at the Cricket Club.

The official end of the 2008/09 season was marked by the Presentation Night. It wasn't the most glamorous or glitzy of gatherings, but what was particularly encouraging, and marked Percy Main Amateurs out as such a special club, was the incredible warmth and sense of community evident on the night in question. The whole committee and all bar two of the regular players, both of whom were on holiday, turned out. Admittedly the players were probably primarily in attendance in preparation for a debauched evening amongst the fleshpots of the Quayside and Bigg Market. To be frank, it is probably the case that the majority of supporters would normally be in watching the telly on a Friday, so the Presentation Night was a marriage of social convenience in some ways, though to be fair there was genuine appreciation of the efforts on both sides for what the others had achieved in the season just ended. When it came down to the awards, the lucky recipients were...

Pierre-Luc Coiffait (an early season signing from Red Row, who despite his Gallic name actually hails from Ashington) was the unanimous decision for the Young Player of the Year award. Coiffait, a skilful left-sided midfielder, tormented defences throughout the campaign and his ability to pitch Rory Delap throw-ins from the touchline to deep into the opponent's penalty area had created many goals for The Villagers. Memorably, he caused the Stocksfield keeper to punch the ball in to his own net in the opening seconds, and similarly against Killingworth, where barely a minute had gone before his exocet to the back post was touched in by Graeme Cole while the opposition stood in stunned immobility.

A closer run vote was the Players' Player of the Year, which was just shaded by club stalwart Tony Browell. An influential member of the squad who had figured all season in the heart of the team's defence, Browell added the accolade to last season's Player of the Year award. Tony is, in many ways, the absolute core of the club on the pitch. An experienced, combative player, he has spent almost a decade in total at Purvis Park. Certainly his heart and spirit make him a definite first choice starter in any game.

The Player of the Year, another close run affair, was won by club captain Chris Locke. Another player in his first season following last summer's switch from Bedlington Terriers, Locke, an energetic box to box midfielder, had racked up six man of the match awards during last season and won many admirers with his leadership qualities on the field. In addition, he's an absolutely smashing young man who is a credit to the club. We'll forgive his red card at Seaton Burn for stamping on an opponent's chest as an aberrant rush of blood that was totally out of character, which it was to be fair.

The Clubman of the Year trophy was shared by Pat and Carole McHugh, a husband and wife team, for their vital, unstinting and often unseen sterling efforts behind the scenes throughout the course of the season. They performed the roles of groundsman and canteen manageress respectively, not to mention a vast array of other duties, including washing the strips and general maintenance of the clubhouse, which had contributed greatly to the cause. Sadly, they decided to call time on their involvement after the Presentation Evening and retired from taking any further part in the club's renaissance.

Hence, as the last taxi full of hair-gelled footballers in cashmere v necks and expensively distressed denim sped away from the cricket club towards Linekers, or another noisy bar that charges £4 for a bottle of Smirnoff Ice or some other vile alcopop, the final death knell for 2008/09 was sounded as the McHughs bade their farewells to us.

While the Northern Alliance had announced that the season would kick off on August 15th, the close season at Percy Main was appreciably shorter than that. The Players reconvened for pre season training on the beach at Tynemouth on Saturday June 20th and the committee met at the ground on the same date. As the playing side had started to fall into place during the second half of the 2008/09 season, moves to reinvigorate the club off the pitch began to take place as well.

It is no secret that football clubs at this level are run as a labour of love by a small, dedicated band of workaholic supporters who act as the committee. At Percy Main, the one person who is the total embodiment of such devotion to duty is Treasurer Bob Rodgerson. In his accumulated three decades of involvement Bob, despite working away for the past five years in Dublin initially and then Peterborough, has both played for and, between 1993 and 2008, managed the club with distinction. Having recently taken a sideways step from being involved in the running of the playing side, Bob now keeps the club financially stable, while seeing his son Rob play in goal and his son-in-law Andy produce the programme. Other club officials include Norman de Bruin as Secretary, a person who devotes about 10 hours a day on top of his work and family commitments to the running of the club. Former player George Mooney, who still plays in the Over 40s top division for Marden Bridge and has been involved with Percy Main in some capacity since the early 1980s, is Chairman, with Gary Reid acting as ex officio post match buffet chef and volunteer without portfolio.

Those four, with the help of Pat McHugh, have run the club almost by themselves for years, but the magnitude of the task required in moving the club forward needed more willing helpers, both in administrative and hands-on roles. The US Cavalry, in the shape of former Gosforth Bohemians manager and one-man administrative whirlwind Phil Kyle, arrived on the scene at just the right time to accept the role of Football Development Officer. With the aid of Norman and Bob, he helped complete the paperwork required to allow us to be granted FA Community Charter Club standard, as well as bringing on board Aidan Regan and Rob Meldrum to run a Women's team from the start of 2009/10. The final pieces of the jigsaw involved me being appointed Assistant Secretary and Laura taking over the running of the canteen.

While the apportioning of roles is an important task, it is all talk and of no material benefit when it came to preparing the club for the forthcoming season. As the summer went on, the date we needed to keep in mind was Saturday August 1st, as that was fixed as the date for the Gary Hull Memorial Trophy game versus North Shields. Everything needed to be ready by that time. In a sense, the traditional July monsoons that caused the cancellation of friendlies away to Wideopen and Seaton Delaval on the 18th and 25th of July were of great benefit, as it bought us more time to give the ground a bit of a makeover.

Obviously, with Pat having retired, there was a real and desperate need to sort the pitch out, in terms of marking it and cutting the grass and Phil Kyle was the person best placed to do that. While he busied himself with the white line machine and the petrol driven mower, Norman and Bob replaced the roof of the clubhouse and Geordie and Gary painted the changing rooms and doors. Laura and I scrubbed and cleaned every inch of the kitchen, aided by Norman's wife Ann, taking four successive Saturdays to make the place presentable. In total, our accumulated labours would have amounted to approximately 200 hours of physical graft, all given willingly and without charge. However, the feeling of accomplishment and pride at seeing the ground spruced up and ready to accept visitors for the Gary Hull Memorial Trophy against North Shields on August 1st was reward enough. In the meantime, the players had been alternatively running up and down the sand dunes at Longsands in Tynemouth or doing shuttle runs round cones on High Flatworth Rec at the top end of Percy Main in preparation for the big kick off.

All that was left to do was for Phil to trim the pitch and Laura to purchase the hot dogs, rolls and confectionary for the Gary Hull game, while I confirmed arrangements with the officials and opposition as Norman lay sunning himself in Majorca. Was I jealous? Not a bit!

August:
Balls Kicked in Anger

UNLIKE THE RAIN ravaged early weeks of the 2008/09 season, there wasn't the same sense of a phoney war going on as the clock ticked down towards the start of the 2009/10 campaign proper. While the lack of pre-season semi-competitive kickarounds in advance of the Gary Hull game was an unfortunate happenstance, it wasn't a massive problem; with so many of the squad, including Jason the manager, away on holiday at various times during July, we'd have struggled to put out a coherent team, even if it hadn't rained for a month.

At the pre-season meeting of all Northern Alliance clubs at Whitley Park (aka the former British Gas Sports and Recreation Ground, popularly known as Blue Flames, where Northern League side West Allotment Celtic play their games), the administrative if not spiritual home of the Northumberland FA, Percy Main were represented by Norman and I. Amidst all the pettifogging procedural details and arcane administrative regulations and refinements, there was time to firm up two friendly games against Shankhouse from Cramlington and Harraby Catholic Club from

Carlisle, both of whom were from the Premier Division and had been Champions in recent times; Shankhouse in 2005 and Harraby in 2008. These games were expected to be stiff tests for the Main, but the hope was that they would give a good indication of just how far the team had progressed, or indeed a guide as to the distance still to be travelled. However, exactly who was in our team and who would be training them had yet to be fully explored, despite the submission of a retained list to the League in mid July.

Two days before the Gary Hull game, Laura and I engaged in a local, low-key spying mission by taking in North Shields at home to FA Vase holders Whitley Bay at the bucolic majesty of Ralph Gardener Park. I was completely neutral at this game, as I don't have much real affection for either side; to be frank, the idea of Bay putting half a dozen past Shields was the more appealing outcome as it would have hinted at Percy Main being in with a realistic shout of a positive result on the Saturday. In the end, Shields held Bay to a 2-2 draw, which slightly flattered Whitley in all honesty. While that was worrying enough, even more bad news appeared in the shape of Main assistant boss Phil Hogg turning up at the game in a Whitley Bay tracksuit, as he'd decided to leave the Villagers and return to the club where he'd been reserve team keeper to resume his playing career.

The timing of this departure was unhelpful, but at this level of football, players are not bound to stay anywhere very long. If a Club X puts in seven days notice of wishing to sign Player Y from Club Z, there is nothing Club Z can do. Strangely enough, the transfer window applies at this level. Main squad midfielder Graeme Smith had decided to leave for Heaton Stannington, the only trouble being he'd also signed a registration form, meaning he'd been included in the Percy Main retained list submitted by us to the league in mid July. Consequently, he was a Main player until September 1st regardless of the wishes of any party involved in this. To complicate matters further, Percy Main signed another Graeme Smith (no relation!) to play at left back while Jason was out injured with broken toes. The Phil Hogg situation was made easier for him, but worse for us, by the fact that he hadn't registered as a player with Percy Main, so he could go off in an instant, which he did. Hence we needed a proper back up keeper, even if right-side midfielder Lindsay Collinson was a dab hand with the gloves in 5-a-side, and Jason was left to run the team with his dad and physio cum glorified kit man Geordie Crooks.

Of course, such news was put into perspective by two tragic, if expected, deaths that were announced on July 31st and August 1st. Firstly, Sir Bobby Robson passed away at his home, surrounded by his family, finally succumbing to the cancer he'd been battling for 15 years. While many other people will write Sir Bobby's obituary for what he achieved as a player with Fulham and West Brom and as a manager with Ipswich, England, PSV Eindhoven, Sporting Lisbon, Porto and Newcastle United, it is not my duty to do so; instead, I will pay tribute to my own father, Eddy Cusack, who died just after midnight on Saturday 1st August at the Freeman Hospital. Another fine Geordie gentleman succumbed to cancer after a proud and honourable life. I respected Bobby, but I loved Eddy. As the notice of his death in the ***Evening Chronicle*** said, Eddy was the *most beloved husband of Kathleen, dear dad of Ian and Elaine, a treasured father-in-law of Sara and David, adoring and adored grandad of Ben and a much loved brother and uncle, who will be greatly missed by all his family and friends.*

Though this book is about Percy Main Amateurs, I crave your indulgence for just a few short moments. One of the absolute keynote qualities of my dad was a humble selflessness that I've never quite seen to such an extent in any other human being, though I suppose I could be a little biased. In my eyes, he simply couldn't help but put other people's needs ahead of his own. I know for a fact he would have been proud but slightly embarrassed at the enormous turnout at his funeral, wondering why people had gone to all that bother for him. Also, there is no question that he would have hoped people would go about their normal business on the day he passed away, which is why I firstly went to play football for my Heaton Winstons Over 40s team before heading to Percy Main.

I arrived around 1pm, in plenty of time to ensure that all final preparations were in place for the game. With Norman on holiday, it was particularly essential we all pulled together. Bob and Geordie put the goals up, then sorted the strips out, while Gary and Andy, who had done the programmes, were on the gate, leaving Laura and I to man (person?) the canteen. In the wider world there had been two very recent deaths to mourn, but they would not be mourned here. There was no mention of Sir Bobby or my dad, much less a minute's silence; this game was all about keeping the memory of Gary Hull alive, so any personal grief had to be kept private. Anyway, once the game kicked off, there was plenty of action on the pitch to think about, for in a highly entertaining game that finished 2-2, North Shields claimed the trophy 5-3 on penalties. The game was described as follows on the Percy Main website by an ace local reporter (me):

Followers of Percy Main Amateurs could well have been forgiven for viewing the prospect of the seventh annual Gary Hull Memorial Trophy game between the Villagers and North Shields with something approaching trepidation. Not only do the Robins operate two divisions higher in the non-league pyramid than their hosts, but had held FA Vase winners Whitley Bay to a 2-2 draw on the Thursday preceding this match, a game which they could well have won, while in contrast this game was Percy Main's first outing of the season, following the calling off of friendlies against Wideopen and Seaton Delaval.

In the end, it was only the brilliance of Shields' keeper Michael Robinson, who palmed away Main centre half Graeme Cole's well-struck spot kick, that decided the tie in favour of the side from Ralph Gardener Park by the narrow margin of 5-3 on penalties after a pulsating 2-2 draw. To be fair, the beautiful game was the real winner on the day, with Shields' sizeable contingent of former Percy Main players enjoying their return to Purvis Park by participating in an excellent advert for the game at this level.

Resplendent in pre-match white shirts and pink ties, the Main cut quite a dash on the pitch as well, taking the lead in the 19th minute when centre forward Joe Betts angled a firm shot across keeper Robinson, after great work by Callum Colback, following a firm nod across the box by the ever dependable Tony Browell. In all honesty, this was harsh on Shields, who continued to demonstrate an insatiable appetite for fast flowing attractive football, especially with the outstanding Lee Gray, whose performance on the left was a constant threat to his former club, stinging keeper Rob Rodgerson's fingers on several occasions, while home right back Steven Shadforth had a sterling game and was rightly judged the outstanding home performer.

However, it was another old boy, in the shape of Robbie Livermore, who drove the Robins on to equalise with a storming 60 yard run that ended with a neat pass to John Amos, who finished cheekily by slotting the ball through the advancing Rodgerson's legs on the half hour. Two minutes later, Amos was on the spot to give Shields the lead, tapping in a loose ball after Rodgerson had parried Lee Gray's thunderbolt.

In the second half, Shields rode their luck at times but seemed content to hang on for a single goal victory, though new striker, former Cullercoats and Whitley Bay Town target man Femi Akinbolu, was a constant danger. Indeed, when Percy Main did equalise after 85 minutes, it was something of a surprise, as the home threat appeared to have dissipated. Grant Patterson, looking suspiciously offside in front of goal, collected an astute through ball from combative substitute Liam Knox and finished at the second attempt after hitting the post, with the bemused Shields keeper a confused onlooker.

With the clock running down, the Main could have snatched victory, with Liam Knox having a clear run on goal cynically halted with a trip by Marty Graham and the ever-dependable Dean Clay seeing a last gasp effort shave the post.

And so to penalties; with Percy Main's custodian Rob Rodgerson firing home an unstoppable effort, followed by equally excellent strikes by Lindsay Collinson and Liam Knox. Sadly Shields proved even more successful, scoring all 5 of their kicks, resulting in heartbreak for Graeme Cole.

However, the Main could take many positives from this game, not least the fact that Dean Morgan went through a whole game without seeing yellow, in to the coming season.

Reading it back, it seems as if I was insistent on using every sports reporting cliché available. Well, it was enough to get it published in the ***Whitley Bay Guardian*** so I must have ticked the right boxes on some level. To be frank, this article wasn't strictly true in parts; Rob Rodgerson's penalty was so badly struck it bounced three times before apologetically plopping over the Shields keeper's outstretched palm. The team, it has to be said, put in a good shift, with new strikers Callum Colback (ex Whitley Bay and Killingworth) and Craig "Ziggy" Ewart, from Bohemians, really looking the part.

Even more importantly, the day went off well. All the programmes were sold, over a hundred quid was taken in the canteen and the visitors were as gracious in victory post match as we'd been dignified in defeat. Perhaps the only down side had been the length of the pitch as Phil hadn't had time to cut the grass, though he promised to have that sorted out before the Shankhouse game on the Wednesday.

Wearily crawling home on the day my father had died, it seemed almost sacrilegious to be contemplating not his passing, nor my mother's needs, but the situation at Purvis Park for Wednesday coming. I'm sure if he'd known Norman was away, Bob was at work and Geordie on nightshift, my old fella would have helped us if he could have, as that's the type of bloke he was. But the question remained; just how would Phil, Gary, Laura and I cope?

While the Gary Hull game is a major date in the calendar of both clubs, other pre season friendlies between Alliance clubs tend to be more no-key than low-key. As I've said before, in many instances this league is more about playing than spectating, so the number of interested onlookers at such games can be in the low teens. Certainly it isn't unusual for the players to easily outnumber the supporters. Perhaps for that reason, there is an assumption that what happens in these outings doesn't really matter, which is generally the case if your side has had a crap warm-up going in to a new season.

Percy Main, on the other hand, had two magnificent results, beating both Shankhouse and Harraby 2-1 after going a goal down in each game. However, there are lowlights as well as highlights to deal with; in winning the first of these two matches, a series of ludicrous events took place that resulted in Phil Kyle leaving his post as Community Development Officer, either on a point of principle or flouncing off in a fit of pique, depending on your point of view.

Having spent Wednesday afternoon picking up essential bits and pieces for the canteen, Laura and I arrived at Purvis Park at 5pm, just as Gary was being dropped off. While the pitch had been mowed and marked, the grass cuttings had been left on the pitch. It was playable, but it looked unsightly and there was no sign of Phil to discuss how this situation had arisen, so the rest of us simply got on with things and made sure everything was in place as best we could. There wasn't going to be a post match buffet, so that was one less job to do, but the 7pm kick off meant we'd be struggling to get all the stuff put away before it got dark, especially being shorthanded. At Percy Main, the goals and nets are portable and can be quickly dismantled. In addition, the advertising hoardings are taken inside post match.

Sadly, this is a sensible precaution to stop vandalism occurring. The sponsorship money from the perimeter boards is essential to keep the club running and the sponsors wouldn't be best pleased if their products don't get match day publicity because some teenagers have stolen, defaced or burnt the advert. While Purvis Park is a beautiful little ground, it is in a fairly exposed location and very close to the less than salubrious Meadowell Estate, scene of the 1991 riots, though to be fair, the ground has suffered no vandalism other than the odd spot of ungrammatical graffiti on the clubhouse walls.

The game with Shankhouse was being refereed by my favourite official in the North East, Keith Scoffham, a fella from the old school. Last year I'd seen him take charge of Newcastle East End versus Cullercoats and not give a free kick in the first half an hour despite a dozen or more robust challenges that erred on the side of rough-housing. Keith thinks football is a man's game and likes to play things on whenever possible. While this is a laudable philosophical and sporting standpoint, you have to remember that Percy Main had an appalling disciplinary record in 2008/09, not helped by three major incidents of histrionics by Jason's dad on the touchline I have to add. When Percy Main lose it, they really lose it and, unfortunately, a bit of that happened in this game, in the first half at least.

Phil eventually arrived just before kick off and everything seemed in place for a good game. From the very start new signing Dean Ellis on the left wing looked a lively performer, with his first minute run almost creating an immediate opportunity for Joe Betts. However, Ellis was considerably relieved to see referee Keith Scoffham brush away appeals for a penalty after the Main man appeared to sweep the legs from under a visiting attacker after ten minutes, which was perhaps the cause of all the subsequent unpleasantness, with loud Shankhouse complaints seeming to be utterly out of proportion with the importance of the game.

Saturday's Man of the Match, Steven Shadforth, was not so lucky in similar circumstances after 19 minutes. Fired up by the protein rush of one of the new 8½ inch Wikinger Bockwurst hot dogs available for only a quid in the canteen as his pre match meal, Shaddy was adjudged by the vegetarian ref to have bitten off more than he could chew when tangling for the ball with a Shankhouse player and pointed to the spot. Thankfully, the opposition striker charged with the responsibility of putting his side ahead made a dog's breakfast of the kick, firing it clear over the privet hedge and on to the adjoining cricket pitch.

Five minutes later the competitive edge to the game spilled over into a bout of nonsense that required the calm, authoritative manner of referee Scoffham to restore order when some scuffling for the ball in midfield resulted in the Shankhouse number 14 losing his head completely and launching an elbow into the face of Main central midfielder Dean Morgan. Morgs is not known as one to shirk a scrap, as his 15 yellow cards in 2008/09 indicated. However, he was utterly blameless in this incident and did not react in the slightest. This can only be a good thing, though perhaps he was simply stunned.

Thankfully things on the pitch didn't escalate to a full-scale scrap, courtesy of the referee's insistence on some judicious substitutions, which resulted in both sides continuing to play out the game with a full set of participants. Three cheers for common sense! Now, the Main's management weren't too happy about this, with Jason and his dad Mick berating the referee, saying that Shankhouse should be down to 10 after such an awful challenge, but Scoff stood strong and gave us the benefit of such a tolerant approach when Jonathon McAneany announced his arrival for the season with a fairly robust ankle tap that saw him removed from the action for a few minutes to consider his ways.

The game reached the interval scoreless, with first Craig Ewart and then the Shankhouse centre half both hitting the outside of a post with efforts from the edge of the area. It had been a good opening half and it would be unfair to pick the better eleven. However, the second period belonged to the home side in what could only be described as an excellent game of football and a superb endorsement of Keith Scoffham's approach to refereeing the game.

From the start of the second half, Betts and Ewart were a constant worry to the visitors, with Main's dominance being absolute when a suitably chastened McEnaney re-entered the fray. Thus it was a major surprise when Shankhouse took the lead following a speedy break down the left, an excellent low cross and an unerring finish into the bottom corner. The Villagers were not fazed by this setback, and with new signing Wayne Stobbs proving to be a regular danger to the away team, it was no surprise when he fastened on to an accurate and incisive Ewart pass to fire in a deserved equaliser.

It got even better for Percy Main in the 82nd minute when McEnaney notched what turned out to be the winner with a cultured rising lob that defeated the despairing leaps of the defender and keeper, who had gifted him the ball in the first place by comically running in to each other. From this moment the visitors were beaten and the Main could well have scored further goals if they had demonstrated attacking composure and the ability to pick out the best ball. However, let's take nothing away from this result; a friendly it may well have been, but Percy Main thoroughly merited their win against a team from a higher division.

The game ended in gathering gloom, and while Gary and I took the goals down and Laura closed up the canteen, we assumed Phil was cleaning out the changing rooms. Sadly, we were mistaken. Having arrived just before kick off, it actually transpired he'd done a disappearing act just before half time following the on pitch clash between the elbowing Shankhouse player and Dean Morgan. Ignoring the fact that he wasn't the manager and Jason was, he'd intervened in this disagreement, telling Jason to take two of our players off, a suggestion Jason had rejected in somewhat industrial terms. As a result, Phil had stormed off, pausing only to text Norman (in Majorca) and Bob (in Peterborough) to announce his resignation.

When analysing this incident and Phil's response to it dispassionately, it is crystal clear that Phil made two massive errors of judgement in reacting the way he did, one on a philosophical basis and one on a more practical level.

The philosophical point is that he was not the team manager; that is Jason's role. Therefore everything that goes on once the players enter the field of play is entirely the responsibility of the team management and nobody else connected with the club. If any of us on the committee have a problem with any aspect of the club, we have the ideal opportunity to raise it at our monthly meetings, one of which was scheduled for the Sunday following this game. None of us like to see disorder on the pitch, but a couple of players letting the club down is a preferable state of affairs than the dreadful sight of a launderette full of dirty washing being done in public, which was the ultimate result of Phil's behaviour, serving to escalate events to the level of a major crisis. Not least because he was the one who was supposed to be washing the strips after this game!

On the practical side, it left three of us to sort the whole club out in semi-darkness. Fortunately, Lindsay Collinson's dad gave us a hand with the posts and Mick Ritchie swept out the dressing rooms. Thanks to both of them and thanks also to the referee, who was great company and in good form in the Cricket Club post match, which was good news as he was in charge of the Harraby game on the Saturday.

As I arrived on the Saturday, having conceded four (the last one was my fault) in a five-goal thriller for Winstons away to Southwick Club in scenic Downhill, Scoff was having a quiet word in Jason's ear in advance of the game. It must have worked because the game passed off completely without incident, though with a decidedly firmer refereeing hand on the tiller.

In our final warm-up game before the real action began, Percy Main produced another thoroughly excellent, disciplined performance to come from behind to beat Harraby Catholic Club 2-1.

While the real stuff didn't kick off until the next Saturday, it has to be said that much heart was taken from a superb shift by the Villagers. Despite going a goal down on the hour when a speculative cross from the touchline deceived the otherwise faultless Rob Rodgerson, who pulled off a series of superb stops throughout the game, the Villagers stormed back in the manner they had done against Shankhouse in the previous home friendly to win the match with a quick double by Joe Betts and Liam Knox, both of whom tapped in from almost on the line, each at the second attempt.

While the nature of Main's goals was not particularly eye-catching, the rest of their performance was, with the quality of the football the team played, the strength in depth from the bench and the obvious team spirit displayed by the whole squad clearly in evidence. Perhaps some teams think their responsibilities end when they leave the pitch; not these lads. Having secured a fully merited and highly credible victory against top division opponents (who were Champions in 2007/08 to boot, let's not forget), the team rolled up their sleeves and helped to put the goals away at full time, showing a clear bond between the club on and off the pitch. Clearly the squad knew that we'd been short-handed off the pitch on Wednesday, and with Norman still away and Phil having spat the dummy, they wanted to muck in. To say it was much appreciated would be an understatement, even if it wasn't necessary with Geordie, Gary, Bob, Laura and me there.

The performances in pre-season seemed to hint that Percy Main could look forward to the coming campaign with confidence, providing that temperament, form, fitness and luck all went the Villagers' way. In addition, I'd never seen Scoff referee a game quite as tightly as this one; perhaps we all learned something from the Wednesday.

Post match, with the bait in the Cricket Club to be sorted, the ground to be secured and the strips to be washed, the fact that Newcastle kicked off their Championship season away to West Brom barely registered; indeed, by the time we got to sit down in front of the telly the game was 1-1, which was the final score. In a way, that pleased me, as not even having to make a conscious attempt to ignore this game showed just how much Percy Main meant to me.

At the committee meeting on Sunday 9th in the clubhouse, I said just that. Despite the off-field dramatics and on-field wrestling, I had loved every second of it so far. At the meeting there was a real sense of common purpose, shared passion and a desire to drive the club forward. However, it has to be said, all of us were united in telling Jason we were 100% behind him when it came to the argument with Phil at the Shankhouse game. On the eve of the season, it was an undisputed fact that everyone concerned with Percy Main Amateurs was on the same wavelength; we love our club and we want it to succeed.

And so to the real thing... Percy Main kicked off their 2009/10 Northern Alliance Division 1 campaign with a home game against Hebburn Reyrolle on Saturday 15th August. Pre-match, the signs that the club was moving forward were very positive; the whole committee were in attendance and a presentable crowd of over 50 had gathered, who were to spend an average of over a quid per head in the canteen, but perhaps the most encouraging news came from within the dressing room. Considering that for our last meeting with these in December 2008 we'd only assembled a bare 11, with one player signed on the morning of the game and another dragged from his sickbed to play, it was an almost unprecedented state of affairs to see a squad of 20 turn up for this game, including Phil Hogg, who had apparently had another change of mind and wanted to be a coach not a player after all. Very smart they all looked too; with a new match day Metrosexual dress code of suits, white shirts and pink ties, in complete contrast to the tracksuits and beach wear of the visitors. Norman seized the opportunity and took a couple of photos of the squad for the website; one with and one without Phil Hogg, just to be on the safe side. When Jason announced the starting eleven and bench, there was genuine disappointment on the part of those not selected. Obviously it's about quality and not just quantity of player, but there were no actual or metaphysical dummies being spat here that day.

When the game got underway, Jason's choices were almost immediately vindicated as things looked equally impressive on the pitch as the Main strolled to an easy 2-0 victory, seeing an incredible number of chances squandered late in the game, which would have given the scoreline a more comprehensive gloss. The defence was untroubled, the centre midfield of Chris Locke and Dean Morgan were in sublime form and the front three, including significant new signing Callum Colback, ex of Whitley Bay and Killingworth, who grabbed the opening goal, looked almost unplayable, especially considering that Hebburn had, in Tony Robinson, a player who will be 50 next birthday, in central defence.

Of course, there is always a down side with Percy Main, and this one was provided by the number of bookings; four to be precise, with three of them awarded for deliberate handballs. Never mind the fact there's a women's football team starting at Purvis Park, with cautions like that it would seem more appropriate to try and start a blokes' netball side! However, such minor quibbles were forgotten post match in the Cricket Club as the opposition's gracious manager, Mark Collingwood, tipped us for promotion, not knowing just how crucial games between the two sides would be in the shake up for honours at the back end of the season. That kind of public endorsement of the team felt good, as did Newcastle's 3-0 win over Reading, with Shola Ameobi amazingly getting a hat trick in the late kick off game. I'd been offered free tickets for this one, but I had turned them down as Newcastle didn't mean that much to me any more, or so I was pretending.

By the following Wednesday, as Norman drove Gary, Laura and I home from Amble, this pretence had well and truly been dropped while we sat nervously listening to the local radio commentary, willing the referee to blow for full time as Newcastle just about managed to hang on for a 1-0 win over Sheffield Wednesday at St. James Park. The audible gasps of relief at the final whistle showed that it's hard to get Newcastle United out of your system (even if you're half Canadian, half Mackem like Laura). Although it could have been something to do with still being in denial about the game we'd just witnessed at the pleasant natural amphitheatre that is Coquet Welfare.

Amble United 5 Percy Main Amateurs 0. None of us had seen that one coming! The form team of the division, on the back of an excellent pre season and a stroll to victory in the opening game, were pounded from start to finish by a side who'd just been promoted from the bottom tier, but who were to dog our footsteps for the entire season. There was no way this result was either a fluke or a harsh reflection on the performance of the visitors. While there had been a couple of enforced changes up front, with Colback and Betts unavailable through work (the curse of all Alliance teams with midweek games kicking off at 6.30) and Craig Ewart and Shaun Wilkinson slotting in for them, the spine of the team that had performed so well thus far was unchanged. Basically though, the performance wasn't good enough from the first whistle and we were righteously battered.

After a fairly even opening 17 minutes, Amble United took the lead with something of a fluke. With the benefit of a strong tail wind, a cross was fired in at pace from the right wing by Ian Common that caused Rob Rodgerson in the Percy Main goal a deal of trouble. However, a crucial fingertip on to the post appeared to have averted the danger, until the ball cannoned off the shin of the hapless Steven Shadforth for a truly unfortunate own goal.

Fired on by the promptings of the tireless Chris Locke in midfield, the Villagers tried to get back into it, but were again undone by cruel luck. When Ian Common took advantage of space on the edge of the Main area to fire in a shot, Rob Rodgerson seemed to have things under control, that is until a wicked deflection off the back of Main's bemused captain Chris Locke took the ball away from its initial trajectory and into the goal just after the half hour.

At the break, manager Jason Ritchie attempted to regroup by bringing himself on for the unlucky Dean Ellis on the left side of midfield, with Mick Haley coming on in midfield to allow Dean Morgan to drop back to centre half to replace the injured Graeme Cole. For twenty minutes, with the wind at their backs, Main attempted to up the tempo but were making little headway against a resolute home defence and tireless midfield. When the Villagers stood statuesque at an Amble corner halfway through the second period, allowing centre back Martin Humble to lash home a loose ball, then it was clear it was not to be the visitors' night. At 3-0 down you just want the ref to bring things to a premature close and let you get home in one piece.

Things, sadly, got far worse when Dean Morgan mistimed a tackle on Amble United's Ross Gair in the area and an inevitable penalty ensued.

Chris Moffit took the spot kick and managed to evade the despairing dive of Rodgerson to make it 4-0. The Main's keeper, despite the scoreline, put in an excellent shift, making a superb save from Martin Humble immediately from the restart. However, there was still time for the home side to turn a comfortable win into a rout when centre half Ross Young jumped unchallenged at the back post to head home a corner.

This game took place on Dean Morgan's 21st birthday, and to be perfectly honest, there was absolutely nothing for him or any of those travelling to Amble to celebrate as Percy Main were outplayed in every single department, going down to a heavy defeat about which there can be no complaints whatsoever. Frankly, everything that could go wrong did so, as was exemplified by Jason, on his return from injury as a half time substitute, crumpling in agony when attempting to close down a clearance by home keeper Ross Stewart, with a seemingly serious knee injury which necessitated the summoning of an ambulance and left him on crutches for a week afterwards.

Ruefully sipping on soft drinks and munching coronation chicken sandwiches at the post match buffet in the endearingly shabby pretend wine bar, ***Pier 81***, the four of us all admitted to travelling with a hankering belief that we would win the game with something to spare. So much for optimism; sometimes you've just got to accept that things can go disastrously wrong, which is where narrow home wins by Newcastle come in handy as a source of secondary succour.

Presumably having had their fingers burned by last season's early downpours, the Alliance management committee had left nothing to chance as regards inclement weather by scheduling seven games in the first three weeks of the season, meaning a quarter of the whole programme would be completed by the time the schools went back, though obviously they weren't to know of the arctic winter we had in store. Anyway, the next challenge for Percy Main on August 22nd was another away game, this time against the newly named Morpeth Sporting Club, who had been known as Red Row Welfare. Last season they'd been the division's whipping boys, finishing bottom of the table and enduring 4-0 (H) and 6-0 (A) defeats to the Main. They'd only avoided relegation because of the resignations from the league of Westerhope and Penrith United. In a spirit of defiance and regeneration, they'd moved grounds from the spartan playing field at the pleasingly euphonious Red Row Rec, to the crumbling wreck of Craik Park. Built only 15 years ago, Northern League side Morpeth Town had vacated the place after it failed a rigorous ground inspection on numerous issues relating to changing facilities and the acute lack of showers. However, Alliance teams are made of sturdier stuff and Red Row's decampment has saved the ground from falling in to disuse, if not disrepair.

Having had not only to play on the left wing but also to stand in as secretary for Heaton Winstons, as the two normal incumbents were on holiday (not together I must add), in our narrow 8-1 victory over Billingham Vets in the Billy Lorraine Cup, I was unable to take in this game, settling instead for Benfield's tame 2-0 home defeat to Norton and Stockton Ancients and text updates from Norman, while Laura was winning first prize in the cake-making category at the North Tyneside Allotment Show.

Despite severe injury problems, which saw Tony Browell miss out, Graeme Cole able to only hobble through the 90, out of necessity rather than design, as well as Jonathon McEnaneay, Liam Knox and the returning Joe Betts, who scored the opening goal, all come off injured in the opening half an hour, the team dug deep to win 3-2. Callum Colback was back and he and Chris Locke grabbed a goal each to help the Main to a narrow but decisive and welcome victory.

After three games Percy Main were in mid table, in 8th place, but with two home games to come, which provided an opportunity to kick on up the table. Hopefully there would be more players available, as off the pitch the committee would be in short supply. With Gary on holiday and Geordie and Bob at work, it was left to Norman, Laura and I to run things on the Wednesday against Wallington. Thankfully, Pat had agreed to come out of retirement and cut the grass, which was one less job to do.

My normal working week is a contractual 37 hours that in reality tends to weigh in somewhere around 45 hours, with the bulk of those hours on Tuesdays, Wednesdays and Thursdays. It isn't physically arduous, but it's highly mentally taxing and it often leaves me with a wearying headache by the time I make it home. The shift we put in for the Wallington game, which effectively lasted from 2 until 11, was tough in both senses, but enormously rewarding as I undertook a baffling array of tasks, none of which I would previously have considered myself qualified for.

First up, I was a kitchen porter and sous chef, as Laura and I did the shopping for both the canteen for spectators and the players' post match buffet, which is normally Gary's baby. Of course, bearing in mind her employment background in catering and hospitality, not to mention the Best Cake in North Tyneside Award, Laura put her own stamp on this; the bait would not simply be sausage and chips, but quality chicken breast and sweet corn sandwiches, with a touch of parsley, as well as organic allotment-grown salad and off the bone ham rolls. Indeed, it was easy to mistake the battered onion rings for Mediterranean calamari as we spent a good three hours shopping and then preparing the majority of this less-than meagre repast.

At quarter past four, Norman arrived to ferry us down to the ground and I had one of those moments where I truly felt as if I belonged, when I was handed my ceremonial match day attire of blue Percy Main polo shirt and claret Percy Main sweatshirt, which committee members are supposed to wear to identify them from the general public, though this evening as we were about the only two blokes there not playing or managing, it was perhaps superfluous. Slipping in to that ceremonial polo shirt made me feel I belonged to the club and that the club was part of me.

Arriving at the ground, Norman and I left Laura to sort out the kitchen while we put the goals up and corner flags in place, attached the hoardings to the perimeter pitch rail, unlocked the dressing rooms, switched the heater for the showers on and inflated the match balls, all before any of the players arrived.

At about 5.30 the players started to arrive; while Joe Betts and Liam Knox were out through injury, Tony Browell and Graeme Cole were fit to play (even if Jason wasn't, still being on crutches). Crucially, Callum Colback was available and he was to have a telling role this evening.

Wallington play their home games in the back of beyond at Oakford Park in Scots Gap, which is about a dozen miles out in the wilds, North West of Morpeth. Public transport and mobile phone reception are as alien to them as licensing hours in the pubs in those parts. They had always been a handy side as well; we beat them 3-2 at home and lost 1-0 away last year, when Joe Betts was sent off and Mick Ritchie had a hissy fit at full time, demanding that the referee was breathalysed. Consequently, we needed a good performance to win and a professional one to show we weren't bad losers. Luckily enough, we proved we could be good winners on the night.

Following an early scare for Wallington, when the tireless and predictably excellent Chris Locke just failed to intercept a weak back pass when keeper Chris Straker touched the ball clear, the first twenty five minutes saw a relentless series of attacks on the Percy Main goal, with Nathan Williamson and Sam Walton particularly dangerous. After only five minutes, Walton fastened on to a long kick from the keeper and lobbed Rob Rodgerson, only to see the ball strike the angle of bar and post before bouncing safely away. Soon after, Shaun Wilkinson was forced to hack a teasing cross from Walton almost from on the line. Perhaps the biggest let-off was after 12 minutes, when Williamson tapped Kyle Reardon's cross in, only for an offside flag to be raised. It seemed as if an impressive away win was set in stone when Walton's long range shot was deflected an inch wide after the quarter hour.

We could easily have found ourselves four goals down in the opening 15 minutes before we attempted to get to grips with the game, mainly through the excellent work of Callum Colback, who was tireless in his probing of the opposition defence all night. Despite not really creating anything of note, the Villagers surprisingly took the lead after 25 minutes when excellent work by Chris Locke in the penalty area gave Jon McEnaney the opportunity to open the scoring with a precise drive from eight yards out following a measured cut back by the Percy Main captain.

Even though Nick McLoughlin was unlucky to see his effort deflected wide of Rodgerson's goal after 38 minutes, Percy Main appeared in control and were confidently looking to half time when Graeme Smith was dismissed for retaliation following a nasty foul in the centre circle by

Paul Crate. The second half saw Percy Main regroup and stand firm, though we were indebted to the combative Dean Morgan, who chested a goal bound effort by the excellent Walton away for a corner with Rodgerson beaten. While the visitors appealed for a penalty, the referee was well placed to rule Morgan's intervention legitimate.

Callum Colback was leading the away defence a merry dance, but with a man short, the Main were tiring and Wallington were pushing the home side back. Steven Shadforth came on for McEnaney and did a good job of holding the ball up, but Rodgerson's goal continued to lead a charmed life. An unbelievable scramble in injury time saw four Wallington shots cleared off the line before the ball deflected wide. From the following corner, Chris Locke took the ball upfield on a strong break, only to be fouled on the edge of the box. Callum Colback took the subsequent free kick and gloriously sealed the win with a sparkling finish into the top corner that rendered Straker a spectator. It was a scorching strike and would be voted our goal of the season.

On the long journey back to Scots Gap, Wallington would be forgiven for repeatedly asking themselves just how on earth they lost a game that they dominated for large swathes against a home side who were forced to play the entire second period a man short. It would eventually get even worse for Wallington, who were docked three points by the league for fielding an unregistered player.

The game ended in near darkness just after 8.15, so we had no time to bask in the glory of this win as Norman and I took the goals down, put the corner flags away, collected the advertising hoardings, swept out the dressing rooms and locked up the clubhouse, while Laura and Norman's wife Ann made the buffet, then took it through to the players, who devoured it all with the exception of the organic allotment-grown salad products of course ("Ah! Cucumber!" "Urgh! I hate tomato" etc etc). When they'd eaten, we feasted on the scraps, sold domino cards and cleared up. Arriving home at 10pm, Laura went for a bath while I wrote up the match report for the website, finishing just in time to see the highlights of Newcastle beating Huddersfield in the League Cup at quarter past eleven.

So, nine hours of hard work later and three points in the bag, we reflected on an excellent job both on and off the pitch, with everyone pulling together. Sadly, we'd had the grand total of just four paying spectators who'd bought only three programmes, although they had spent £20 at the canteen. Was the effort worth it? Of course it was! Roll on Saturday and the visit of Rutherford.

Founded in 1878 as Science and Art FC by pupils and masters of Rutherford's College, the club, which is the longest continuously existing football club in the region (Wallington claim to have been formed in 1877 but have disbanded and reformed at least twice in the intervening period), changed its name to that of the College's founder and first headmaster, Dr John Rutherford, in the 1890s. They have played their home games at Farnacres, near Lobley Hill in Gateshead on the other side of the river to where they were founded, since the 1980s.

Similar to Percy Main and Gosforth Bohemians, Rutherford are a venerable old club with a proud and lengthy history who are still operating on strict amateur principles, though it has to be said that Percy Main don't quite have the same academic antecedents as the other two clubs. However, it is encouraging to see the three elderly clubs doing well at the top end of the table. Indeed, after four straight wins, Rutherford were joint top with Amble United going in to this game.

As if to emphasise the gap between lofty academic principles and Percy Main, Jason, Steven Shadforth and Jon McAneaney were missing from this game as they were attending a weekend dance festival by the name of ***Creamfields***. I don't know what it was, I don't know where it was, but it sounded terrible. The responsibility for running the team was jointly shared by Mick Ritchie and Phil Hogg, who had to deal with Callum Colback limping out of the warm up and both Chris Locke and Joe Betts playing with heavy strapping on their left and right ankles respectively. This had all the hallmarks of a tough game, but that is just the way our lads like their contests.

Hard work from all sections of the team was the key as we won our fourth of five league games with a brace of goals from Craig "Ziggy" Ewart, the first from the spot after 35 minutes and the second from the six yard line with ten minutes remaining. The value of this second goal was underlined when Rutherford's Michael Jeffares pulled one back in the fourth of seven minutes of second half injury time. While this game was nowhere near as beguiling as Wednesday's 2-0 win over Wallington, this reshaped and reorganised Main side deserve enormous credit for grinding out the win.

Rutherford started like an express train, and when Rob Rodgerson juggled a backpass after 20 seconds, with opposition number 9 Daniel Robinson bearing down on him, it looked like it was going to be a hard 90 minutes for the home side. It got no easier after two minutes when Robbie Frame was clean through, only to be superbly tackled by Dean Morgan. However, after Jeffares headed a Loughlin corner just wide after 10 minutes, the Rutherford threat began to dissipate as Main pushed them back, but without creating a significant chance until the half hour, when Dean Morgan sent Ziggy away and his shot across the face of goal rolled agonisingly wide.

Minutes later Ewart was upended in the area and picked himself up to send the keeper the wrong way, ensuring Main went in to the break with a slender but crucial lead. On the hour Joe Betts almost doubled the lead, but his shot went just wide, while at the other end Rob Rodgerson distinguished himself with a great reaction save from Jeffares. Ewart nearly made the points safe when breaking the offside trap, but the keeper did well. Ziggy was not to be denied though and minutes later Dean Morgan sent him away with a great ball, allowing him to finish with ease. It seemed as if Percy Main were home and dry until Rutherford's late nerve-shredder. Ultimately though, a third successive home win was achieved.

While the Villagers never had it easy, it has to be said the Main deserved their win and Ziggy Ewart deserved a medal as big as a dinner plate for his graft. However, the impressive midfield, especially Chris Locke and Dean Morgan, outdid him in terms of the Man of the Match Award level of performance.

This time, instead of simply sitting in the Cricket Club enjoy a glass of pop and quietly mulling over the joy of victory, the Committee went out for a decent drink in The Alex in North Shields. Ostensibly, we were watching Manchester United versus Arsenal, but Norman and Ann, Bob and Michelle, Andy and Joanne, as well as Laura and me, were just out to enjoy ourselves. While the players might be standing in the middle of a field waving glowsticks in the air, the middle aged supporters would be having just as much fun with a few pints. Percy Main; the club that parties hard and plays just as hard.

And, to round August off properly, we all ended up at the club on the Sunday, glugging pop to assuage our hangovers for the inaugural competitive match of Percy Main Ladies team in Northumberland FA Womens' League Premier Division against Newcastle Medicals. For a while, we thought we were still plastered as Percy Main squeaked home by the margin of 19-0. A second companion volume to this book is being prepared, which will include descriptions of each of the goals scored!

September:
Hello Goodbye

I'VE ALWAYS WANTED to be able to make people laugh, intentionally I mean. In an attempt to follow this dream, I made a few abortive attempts to be a stand up comedian at open mic events when I was a postgrad student at Leeds Uni in the late 80s. I was so successful at being a funny man that I've been an English teacher for over 20 years. So it goes.

One example of my brilliant sense of humour is a gag I crack every June 22nd at around 10 o'clock in the evening, when I gesture at the imperceptibly darkening sky and state, "mind the nights are fair drawing in, aren't they?" No-one ever laughs; they never have, they never will, but on Tuesday September 1st when I had cause to utter this remark to Laura a propos the thick gloaming that was massing before 8pm, it gained a stately nod of approval. As Percy Main were due to play Cullercoats on Wednesday 2nd September, with a 6.30 kick off at a pitch without floodlights, my concern with the quality of natural illumination at that time in the evening was a pertinent one.

While the fact that the Alliance had kicked off a week later than most other leagues (bar The Premiership, ironically) hadn't been a great problem for Percy Main as a club, especially as Norman was on holiday on August 8th and any secretarial duties would have been devolved to me for that date and presumably the midweek following on Wednesday 12th, the two games that could have been played on those dates would clearly not have been as adversely affected by the earth's diurnal course as this final, scheduled midweek contest would be. Obviously an earlier start to the season would have meant teams would have played a startling seven league games in the first month, but such fixture congestion was only partially delayed by starting the fixtures week later; it's still seven games by the first weekend in September and the attendant inconvenience of one midweek game that will almost certainly be concluded in semi-darkness, whichever way you look, or try to look at it.

The Cullercoats game was going to be a stringent test of the Main's mettle; at the end of last season, we'd beaten them 3-2 at home after being two down, which had infuriated them to the extent that one of their number had kicked a hole in the dressing room door at full time. It wasn't just the result that had hurt their pride; it was the significance of it. The unpalatable fact for them was that they'd comprehensively blown promotion after leading the table at Christmas, having won all their games before the turn of the year; losing at Purvis Park mathematically meant they couldn't go up. Perhaps last season's disappointments had resulted in a hangover for the start of this one, as Cullercoats had surprisingly lost their opening four games, before winning 3-0 at Newcastle East End while Percy Main were defeating Rutherford. If this latest result meant that a quality team was belatedly starting to find their form, it was an ominous sign for us, as we were missing Joe Betts, Jon McEnaney and Dean Morgan, all through suspension, while Callum Colback was injured and Mickey Haley at work. It looked a big ask.

On 22nd November 2008, Percy Main suffered a thoroughly depressing 4-0 defeat against Cullercoats on a bitterly cold afternoon, when the Villagers' trip to Links Avenue was one of only two games to beat the freeze on Tyneside that afternoon. Even then, this was only possible after the match started half an hour early as the pitch was hardening by the minute. Perhaps a similar decision as regards this evening's kick off would have allowed players and spectators to have a better view of the crepuscular proceedings on an Autumnal evening by the sea than was afforded by the gathering gloom and persistent drizzle, when only the lights of the 76 bus going down Broadway (the Tynemouth one, not the New York one) every ten minutes allowed the pitch to be intermittently visible.

In what was the last midweek fixture this side of Easter for Percy Main, we rode our luck at times to come away with a point. Cullercoats, boasting no less than seven former Percy Main players in their squad, displayed a fluid, high-tempo passing game from the off that had the Main rocking back on their heels.

It was no surprise when Robert Watson fired Cullercoats into a thirteenth minute lead, seizeing upon a loose ball in the box and firing home from just beyond the six yard line. Within five minutes, the lead could have been doubled as Craig Deighton was denied by a goal line clearance by returning Main player manager Jason Ritchie. Rob Rodgerson excelled with a superb block from Deighton's follow up effort.

At the other end, Tony Browell headed a Chris Locke corner just over the angle of post and bar, while Graeme Cole, enjoying this game far more than his inglorious debut for Percy Main in last year's encounter, saw a goal-bound header deflected away. These efforts were isolated examples of the Villagers as an attacking force, as the defensive qualities of Ritchie's side were far more prominent, with Rodgerson saving well from Deighton. In the last significant action of the opening period, the same player was denied yet again by a goal line clearance from Ritchie, which saw the clearing header hit the underside of the bar before being shepherded away from danger by Chris Locke, who released a quick-breaking Ewart whose cross was almost deflected in for an equaliser.

After a lengthy half time break, the game continued in the same fashion as before, with Deighton hitting the bar with a header from a corner before Rodgerson smothered the rebound. However, a Main renaissance was imminent; Jason scampered away down the left, cutting into the box and firing in a cross cum shot that Locke was inches away from tapping in. If the away side felt frustrated by that, they did not have time to dwell on their ill-fortune as within a minute they were level.

While Cullercoats may have justifiable cause for claiming that their luck was out all evening, especially as Rob Rodgerson was three times indebted to his defenders for hacking the ball off the line with the Main keeper beaten, it is an undeniable fact that Percy Main came back into the game with a spirited second half performance that was rewarded with Ziggy Ewart's emphatic finish from a David Tapsfield pass.

The fact this marked the end of the scoring was as much to do with worsening conditions as it was with good defending, though Rob Rodgerson proved his handling to be faultless on several occasions as Cullercoats attempted to once more seize the initiative. Despite several half chances and the occasional bout of mayhem in the box, Percy Main did not allow their goal to be breached and could have snatched it when Ewart headed a Shaun Wilkinson cross just wide.

My worry that Percy Main and Cullercoats would conclude their game in semi-darkness proved to be unfounded; it finished in complete darkness. And it was pissing down. And Norman had a flat tyre from a slow puncture that would cost him sixty quid to get repaired. Still, after a bowl of homemade curry and a welcome pint of blackcurrant and soda in Cullercoats's home pub, *The Magpie* in Marden Estate, afterwards, we were refreshed, full up and all dried out. Sadly, the incessant rain that had started in the second half and continued all through the night and on through Thursday, and until Friday morning, meant that the pitch at Purvis Park was very far from being the latter.

Around noon on Friday, Pat cut the grass and marked the lines, more out of a sense of duty than expectation, but to confound the weather forecast, the rain stopped around 2pm and the sun was out soon after. With the aid of a stiff breeze and clear skies, the pitch looked utterly immaculate on the Saturday for the visit of the magnificently named Chopwell Officials Club.

The last game between the two sides at Purvis Park on January 17th was, by common consent, the best home game of the 2008/09 season. Today's encounter did not aspire to the same high quality or fast tempo as that meeting, but the result in the end was the same; the Villagers claimed a vital three points after going a goal behind, this time by 2-1 as opposed to last year's 3-2 final score.

As the league took a back seat for a short while, with the following week seeing the visit of Amble United to Purvis Park for a Kicks Leisure, Stan Seymour League Cup first round tie, it was worth reflecting on the perfect home record that we were able to boast after the first three weeks of the season; four home games, four home wins. While the last two fixtures against Rutherford and Chopwell had been more prosaic in terms of the football on display, compared to the expansive, attacking tactics of the Hebburn and Wallington games, the crucial fact was that all of these encounters have ended with the home side claiming maximum points. Interestingly, the Main's haul of 16 points by 5th September is in marked contrast to last season, when the same total was reached on January 17th, after a home win over Chopwell ironically enough.

Still shorn of suspended trio Joe Betts, Jon McEnaney and Dean Morgan, as well as being forced to keep injury-restricted Callum Colback on the bench, it was a tribute to the developing tactical acumen of Jason and his assistants Mick and Phil, not to mention the quality of a rapidly maturing side, that they were able to select one formation for a first half that required the stifling of the visitors and another for the second, when it was time to go for the victory.

In truth, the 4-5-1 formation that saw Ziggy Ewart ploughing a lone furrow in the first half made for a desperately congested midfield, resulting in chances being at a premium after David Tapsfield shot over from Jason's quick free kick in the tenth minute. Chopwell's livewire striker Lee Best did hit the bar with a header, but the whistle had gone long before following a clear push in the back on Tony Browell.

Certainly that push was far more easily discerned than the supposed barge the referee detected by Graeme Cole on Chopwell's Best after a corner. However, the man in the middle was convinced of what he had seen and the visitors' centre half Gareth Powell powered in a spot kick beyond Rob's despairing leap.

An aggrieved home side took the game immediately to the visitors and within two minutes were level, also from the spot. Good work by Ziggy had seen him round the keeper and prepare to fire home between the two defenders on the line when opposition custodian Lee Rowland took

Ewart's legs away. The referee gave the spot kick but did not deem it to be the denial of a goalscoring opportunity. The home number 9 shrugged off such concerns to confidently send the keeper the wrong way with an accurate side-foot finish.

Parity at the interval was only maintained after a superb one-handed flying save from Rob Rodgerson denied Lee Best's measured curling effort from distance. Strangely, this was Chopwell's last meaningful attempt of the game as the home side took up the cudgels in a more positive style in the second period. The main reason for this shift in emphasis was the introduction of striker Callum Colback; his never-say-die attitude, intuitive flicks and tireless running, in harness with the excellent Ewart, wrested the initiative away from Chopwell.

The winner came with ten minutes remaining, when Ewart's superbly cushioned header fell straight into the path on the onrushing Colback. His first time strike was low, fast and accurate, and in a flash it was clean through keeper Rowland, who may feel disappointed to be beaten from such distance. However, it was reward for a vastly improved second half performance by the Main.

Unfortunately, the win did little for the Main's position in the table, as Bohemians emphasised their superior goal difference by trouncing Seaton Burn 6-0. Rutherford stayed on track with a 3-2 win at South Shields United, though Amble United came unstuck, losing 5-1 at home to Cullercoats, meaning the top of the table looked like this :

	P	W	D	L	F	A	+/-	Pts
Amble United	7	6	0	1	26	6	+20	18
Rutherford	7	6	0	1	21	12	+9	18
Gosforth Bohemians	7	5	1	1	21	8	+13	16
Percy Main	7	5	1	1	12	10	+2	16

The table would remain looking like that for another fortnight as the League Cup took centre stage on Saturday 12th.

Meanwhile, on Sunday 6th, the women's team continued their impressive start to the season with a 6-1 away win against Forest Hall, played on one of the community pitches adjacent to Newcastle United's training ground. With Norman's daughter Rachel making her debut and Jason coming along to lend support, it was a fine way to spend a Sunday afternoon and far preferable to sitting in the pub watching Fulham against Wigan or some other Premiership delight.

While the start of this chapter alluded to the playing conditions at the Cullercoats game, it seemed as if the Northern Alliance had taken the threat of games being ruined by darkness a little too seriously, with the Amble United game being scheduled to kick off at 2pm. Of course, with it being a cup tie, it had to be decided on the day, but still it seemed unlikely that a penalty shoot-out would manage to prolong the game much beyond 4.30, never mind 7.30 when daylight would fail.

On a gloriously sunny and decidedly warm afternoon that seemed far more suited to cricket than football, on the day Durham CCC retained the County Championship, a sizeable crowd, who had not been caught out by the earlier kick off time, made their way to Purvis Park to see a Percy Main side somewhat limited in the striking department. With Jon McEnaney completing his suspension, Joe Betts still out injured and Callum Colback unavailable due to personal commitments that involved watching his brother turn out for Roy Keane's Ipswich in their 3-1 defeat on Teesside, it was left to Steven Shadforth (pre match meal: two Wikinger $8\frac{1}{2}$ inch hot dogs with plenty of ketchup, plenty of mustard) to play the role of target man in trying to hold the ball up for the dangerous Ziggy Ewart. In midfield, Dean Morgan's unfortunate absence on a stag weekend (as I'd written an acrostic in the programme where his name was the answer) gave Lindsay Collinson the chance to step up to the plate to partner Chris Locke in the centre of the park.

There were 18 Kicks Leisure Stan Seymour League Cup first round ties taking place, meaning that the winners would be rewarded with a place in the last 32, alongside the 14 teams who had been granted a bye. Such mathematical and procedural complexities held no fears for the Main, who had been forced to defeat Gosforth Bohemians in the sole Preliminary Round tie the previous season in order to reach the first round proper, when Cramlington Town had arrived at Purvis Park and ended our interest in the competition with a 2-1 win.

Thankfully, today saw a win for Percy Main, which while nowhere near as emphatic as the mauling at Amble in August, did go some way towards exorcising the demons of that evening's display, though it was probably of more significance in the fact that it was the last game of Ziggy Ewart's season.

During the opening ten minutes, the away side sought to lay down a marker for their attacking intent; Ross Gair's gentle header was deflected behind for a corner by Graeme Cole, who also nipped the ball off Greg Dance's toes at the edge of the area, while the Amble number 9 dallied with a shooting opportunity.

Tony Browell had cause to feel aggrieved at the non-award of a penalty in the eleventh minute when he seemed ready to nod home a Jason Ritchie corner at the back post, only to be unceremoniously barged out of the way. However, this was the only possible point of complaint in yet another almost faultless refereeing display by the consistently excellent Keith Scoffham.

Perhaps such a valedictory judgement of the man in the middle would not have been forthcoming if Rob Rodgerson had not smartly saved with his feet from Christopher Moffit when play swung to the other end immediately after the penalty claim. Moffit was again denied when his shot was deflected wide minutes later, with Amble's Lee Harker putting an effort from the resulting corner over the bar.

At the other end, Steven Shadforth collected a loose ball at the edge of the box and fired narrowly over the angle, while Graeme Cole failed to direct a free header on target. The closest Main came to taking the lead was when a gloriously flighted Jason Ritchie cross was intercepted by Tony Browell's magnificently timed run, only for the ball to end up in the side netting.

Perhaps buoyed up by this narrow escape, Amble United took the game to the hosts in the closing seconds of the half, with Brent Aisbitt collecting a Greg Dance knockdown and hitting the outside of the post with a fine effort from distance.

The exertions of the opening period appeared to have sapped the energy levels of the players as much of the opening action of the second period, after Ziggy Ewart had hooked over in the first twenty seconds, was poor, dull fare. For over 20 minutes, the game had little to commend it to the large, shirt-sleeved crowd basking in late summer warmth. The action, such as it was, involved little to concern either Rob Rodgerson in the home goal or Ross Stewart, the visiting gloveman, as the half reached its midpoint with only one effort on goal to speak of.

With the dreaded spectacle of extra time and penalties already beginning to loom, the Main bench made a decisive move with a brave triple substitution. Off came Chris Locke, Steven Shadforth and Lindsay Collinson; on came Dean Ellis, Kriss Carr and David Tapsfield, with the latter two providing the vital difference between the two teams in the final analysis. This was Carr's first competitive appearance of the season and he proved himself to be an effective and efficient target man, able to hold the ball up well and act as a constant nuisance to the Amble defence.

Immediately before the only goal, Rob did well to tip over a high hanging cross from Moffit, with Ross Gair in close attendance. From the corner, the attack broke down and Main went away, with David Tapsfield and Ziggy Ewart combining superbly to switch play to the other end of the pitch. Once in the box, Ziggy rolled the perfect ball into the path of Tapsfield, who coolly slotted the ball under the advancing keeper to give Percy Main a lead that would prove decisive.

Amble were stirred by this and Rob was twice called to make smart saves from Dance and Martin Humble, allowing himself to display faultless handling while under pressure on both occasions. These saves were enough to snuff out the Amble threat and the game ended with the final notable chance seeing Kriss Carr just head over at the back post.

Frankly, while it was nice to win the game, promotion was the be all and end all of this campaign. We knew we would not win the League Cup, despite the fact that we'd drawn Premier Division bottom side Heddon at home in the next round. However, the best thing about getting through the first round is that it scotched the awful spectre of having to participate in the Alliance's *repechage* for losers known as the Charity Cup, which is the one trophy nobody wants to win as participation is confirmed by losing in the opening rounds of the League Cup.

The worst thing about the day was the ankle injury sustained by Ziggy deep into injury time in an accidental collision with an Amble defender. He was carried from the pitch and lay prone in the clubhouse for an hour with a pack of frozen onion rings pressed on the injured spot in an attempt to restrict the swelling, while Norman seized the initiative and completed the signing of Ian Lee and Malcolm Morien, a striker and an attacking midfielder respectively, from Whitley Bay A. The two of them were to have markedly contrasting influences on the rest of our season. Both players had been at the Main previously, with Morien's main claim to fame being his pre-match arrest in the changing rooms by Military Police following his desertion from the Army! Hopefully his return to Civvy Street would result in a decrease in such potential selection headaches.

His debut came on Saturday 19th away to Seaton Burn. In April 2009, I'd had my first experience of stand-in secretarial duties for this fixture as Norman had been unavailable, agedly skanking to the sounds of the reformed Specials! In all honesty, I'd coped fairly well with the requirements of the task as we'd run out 2-1 winners, despite having Chris Locke sent off for a stamp on one of their players, an action so out of character that the mortified midfielder spent the rest of the evening expressing his profuse apologies to the victim and the ref. Such a display of conscience is not shared by the notoriously chippy, moustachioed Seaton Burn manager, who had shown himself to be a mouthy, vindictive and poor loser. Post match last year he had rounded on Pat and Bob's 78-year-old dad, shouting and bawling about how Percy Main bullied and intimidated his team. Percy Main prefer to do our talking on the pitch, apart from Dean Morgan that is, who'd responded with characteristic diplomacy: "Shut your hole you stupid tachey mong."

Dean was absent from this game, apparently romancing a young lady in Glasgow, which firstly marked the imminent end of his time as a Percy Main player, though we weren't to know it, and allowed Malky, who was able to provide as many goals as Dean had yellow cards, to make his debut alongside Ian Lee. There were neither Military Police nor childish histrionics from Northumbria Constabulary at the game, though another three valuable points made their way back to Purvis Park.

Seaton Burn is effectively a single street of houses past Wideopen, on the utmost northwestern edge of North Tyneside. Bounded by the A1 to the left, with the A19's starting point two fields further away, it is a venue as much for trunk road spotters as for football fans, though wildlife enthusiasts such as Laura are well catered for by the smallholding next door that boasts lambs, geese and turkeys on public display. There's a hell of a lot of rabbits in these parts as well, but nothing to eat or drink at the ground, nor any shelter. While it was cool, with a breeze, at least it stayed dry for the duration.

Coming in to this fixture we were able to boast a near perfect record against today's opponents, with the only game not to end in a victory for the Villagers since Seaton Burn's promotion to Division 1 being a 0-0 draw at Purvis Park last season, when Jason's missed penalty proved crucial. This encounter saw the Main continue the excellent run of form against Seaton Burn, but a 3-1 away win does not tell the full story of a match where we enjoyed utter domination for the entire first period, hitting the frame of the goal on no less than six occasions.

In going for an adventurous 4-3-3 formation, the two new players both made their mark with eye-catching performances and a goal apiece, with Morien's tireless, all-action game, not to mention his superb two-footed artistry in the middle of the park, allowing the midfielder to collect a richly deserved Man of the Match Award. However, it also has to be said that Callum Colback was also a constant threat in attack and Mickey Haley had a tremendously effective 90 minutes, in what was probably his most accomplished game since signing for Percy Main.

As early as the fourth minute, the Villagers could have been ahead when a robust challenge on Ian Lee saw the combative striker felled in the box, but with no spot kick ensuing, Callum Colback drove the ball goalwards, only to see home keeper Chris Carr smother the ball. Seaton Burn briefly threatened in the tenth minute with a sharp break down the left, but Graeme Smith moved smartly across to snuff out any danger by clearing the ball for a corner that came to nothing.

By the quarter hour, Main were well on top, with both Morien and Lee showing a good range of skills and giving the Villagers possession in dangerous areas. On 17 minutes, a Colback shot hit the angle of bar and post, with Lee's follow up effort being deflected wide. The pressure soon became relentless on the Seaton Burn goal; Lee shot just over following a sparking run and cut back from Colback, then Betts lobbed the advancing Carr, only to see his effort drop an agonising foot wide of the far post.

Whenever Seaton Burn got the ball out of the area and away from the front three, the Main midfield, spurred on as ever by the tireless Chris Locke, brought it back again. So it was with the opening goal, when Malcolm Morien collected a loose ball at the left edge of the penalty area, shook off two defenders and drove in a tremendous low shot, which beat the surprised keeper at his near post.

It was the minimum the visitors deserved for their attractive, attacking play and seconds later it ought to have been added to. A brilliant run and cross by Chris Locke saw Ian Lee hit the bar with a header and Callum Colback strike the post with the rebound. The final seconds of the first half saw more of the same, with first Joe Betts and then Ian Lee hitting the same post during the same attack.

At half time, when a more realistic score could have been 5-0 to the Main, there was no sense that these missed chances could come back to haunt us. However, it seemed as if they might when, minutes into the second period, Nicky Hara scored with Seaton Burn's first credible effort of the game. It was a wonder strike as well; picking up a loose ball in midfield, he crashed it first time into the roof of the net from almost 40 yards with Rob Rodgerson motionless.

For ten minutes, the Main seemed stunned by this unbelievable turn of events, but they soon got back in their stride. Joe Betts hit the post again with a header from a corner, and then Callum Colback shot into a grateful keeper's arms, before Ian Lee marked his debut with the winner. Fastening on to a David Tapsfield through ball, he cleverly flicked it over the keeper, chested down the loose ball and calmly drove it between the two defenders on the line to restore the lead.

Jason took advantage of the breathing space afforded by this goal to make three substitutions, with Betts, Tapsfield and Lee making way for Shaun Wilkinson, Lindsay Collinson and Steven Shadforth. It did not materially affect Main's play as Colback and then Morien were denied by smart saves by Carr in the space of a minute.

With four minutes remaining, Shadforth made sure of the win. Picking up a loose ball after Colback's effort had been blocked, the substitute fired home a smart low drive right into the bottom corner to ensure Main would move into third place following Bohemians' loss away to Morpeth SC.

Job done, Laura and I made a sharp exit, taking the bus back into town, with our arrival coinciding with the final whistle at St. James' Park, where Newcastle had beaten Plymouth 3-1. While being glad at the result, I didn't feel a pang of jealousy or guilt for not being one of the so-called Toon Army any more. My team are Percy Main.

My other team are Percy Main Women, and it was sad to see them lose their 100% record with a 3-2 defeat at home to Tynedale on the Sunday, but they are a new team and a young team, so there's plenty of time for them to gel and kick on.

Home defeats were not on the agenda for the men's team. Last year only Stocksfield and Whitley Bay 'A' emerged from Purvis Park as victorious visitors in the league. This season all six home games before the end of September resulted in home wins; the sixth taking place on the 26th, when Northbank travelled across the A69 from Carlisle, leaving a couple of hours later on the back of a 2-0 defeat.

On the surface, this game was as near to a home banker as one could imagine. The Villagers, in possession of the best home record in the Alliance, were sat in third place in the table, with Northbank sitting at the very bottom of the table, without a point after seven games. As the game ended in a 2-0 home win, the casual observer could be forgiven for imagining that it was a routine victory, though that does not tell the whole story of a game whose result was in doubt until Jason confidently struck home a late penalty.

A first half desperately short on quality saw Main, forced to choose a front pairing of Betts and McEnaney, with strikers Colback (in Ipswich watching his brother Jack play for the Tractor Boys against Newcastle), Ewart (still injured, but at the game with three of his mates, who drank the bar dry of Stella Artois 4%) and Lee (allegedly at work) all unavailable. Consequently, Jason's side were unable to create the sort of openings that the predatory striking pair normally feasts upon. In fact, indomitable away defending was the order of the day, with resolute clearances and strong tackling keeping a wall of bodies between impressive Northbank keeper Jack Twentyman and frustrated home attackers.

That said, Malcolm Morien, on his home debut, provided key passes that almost led to openings for Betts, who shot over in the 16th minute, and McEnaney, who headed wide from a corner when well placed and free of markers. Twentyman excelled himself with a magnificent tip over from a Morien blockbuster on the half hour, with Tony Browell firing in to the side netting from the resultant corner.

Northbank's first effort on goal was in the 59th minute when Steven Brown curled a long distance effort a yard or so wide. By then the deadlock had finally been broken, when Shaun Wilkinson's measured cross from the right wing was nodded powerfully and accurately home by McEnaney beyond the despairing leap of Twentyman. Frankly, the lack of pace on the ball deceived the keeper, who had finished his dive before the ball actually reached him.

The goal was undeniably deserved and it was definitely the best thing for the game, as the brilliant late summer, early autumn sunshine was complemented by a subsequent half an hour of dazzling attacking play from both sides that saw the correct outcome in the final analysis, but could have seen a considerably higher number of goals scored at either end. Jason twice saw Twentyman hold accurate free kicks, while Rob was called on to make his first save after 70 minutes. The home custodian blocked a stinging Rhys Walker effort, which fell to Luke Barwick, who unbelievably headed wide of a gaping net from barely two yards out.

Northbank threatened again after 84 minutes when Brown's speculative overhead kick from a corner dropped wide. Main then went up the field in a superb passing move from Haley to Wilkinson, whose cross was nearly turned in by McEnaney. A half clearance fell to Morien, whose goal-bound effort was blocked at some personal cost to a Northbank defender. From the corner Morien was again inches wide with a powerfully struck half volley.

The final action of the game saw Shaun Wilkinson cut in to the box and attempt to go round Twentyman, whose despairing lunge caught the attacker's trailing leg. Ritchie, befitting his role of both player and manager, confidently scored from the spot.

Post match, watching Newcastle effortlessly dismantle Ipswich by the frankly unflattering margin of 4-0, news came in of Rutherford's 4-1 victory over Amble United in the clash of the titans at Beggarswood. As a result, the Northern Alliance Division 1 table looked like this as September drew to a close:

	P	W	D	L	F	A	+/-	Pts
Rutherford	9	8	0	1	32	12	+19	24
Percy Main	9	7	1	1	17	11	+6	22
Amble United	9	7	0	2	28	10	+18	21

Things were looking pretty good; we'd taken a total £100 on the door and in the canteen for the first time this season, no doubt as a result of the innovative catering products Laura had debuted, including chocolate chip muffins decorated with sugar letters spelling either Percy Main or, more popularly among our players, swear words. Even more importantly, we had moved into a promotion spot, however temporarily that may be with so many games still to be played. In addition, Hibs won 3-1 at St Mirren, Winstons won through to the Billy Lorraine Cup semi-final after beating Mill View WMC 4-2 on penalties after a 2-2 draw (I was an unused sub) and Ben's rugby league side, Wallsend Eagles, had won 46-4 to make it through to their cup final at Gateshead Stadium.

Even better, Royston Maurice Keane had been humiliated live on television. Yes, Saturday September 26th 2009 was a good day at the end of a good month. Percy Main were looking at the coming autumn with confidence.

October: *Minor Threat*

WITHOUT QUESTION, THE most compelling aspect of the 2008/09 season for Percy Main was our run to the Northumberland FA Senior Benevolent Bowl Final, even if the deciding match itself was a disappointment. In the local football authority's second most prestigious competition, lagging slightly behind the Northumberland Senior Cup in terms of sporting kudos, the Villagers won three away games against Alliance Premier Division opponents (3-2 versus Seaton Delaval after being 2-0 down with 15 minutes to go, 2-1 against Cramlington Town and 2-1 versus Ashington Colliers, having turned round a goal behind in the latter two games), before coming up short in the final at Whitley Park, when Blyth Town beat us fair and square by 2-0.

In recognition of our achievements in the previous year, Percy Main were unceremoniously relegated in 2009/10 to the local FA's third competition, the Northumberland Minor Cup. Apparently it's so called because there are that many Colliery Welfare teams in it.

Previously, the Senior Cup has been contested by, in order of seniority, Newcastle United Reserves, Blyth Spartans, Blue Star, the Northern

League clubs in Northumberland FA territory: namely Ashington, Bedlington Terriers, Benfield, Morpeth, North Shields, Prudhoe Town, Team Northumbria, West Allotment Celtic and Whitley Bay, as well as the top four sides in the Alliance, which is why Percy Main were invited to participate in the competition in 2004/05, losing away to Ashington in the first round. However, a policy decision was made for the 2009/10 season by the Brass Hats and Blue Blazers to exclude Alliance clubs, which, in conjunction with the disappearance of Blue Star and Prudhoe, left the competition running with a mere 10 teams.

There was no such problem in the Benevolent Bowl, which ran with 16 teams as ever. In the past, the competing teams were drawn from Alliance Premier and First Division sides from within the Northumberland FA boundaries, which pre-date the 1974 Local Government Act by a considerable distance. A common myth is that the River Tyne is the boundary between Northumberland and Durham, but this is not always so. Why else would Prudhoe be in the Northumberland FA?

2009/10's Alliance Premier Division consisted of 17 teams, of whom Carlisle City and Harraby are in Cumberland FA territory, while Murton are under Durham FA jurisdiction. Consequently, to make it up to an easily divisible number of teams for the Benevolent Bowl (an idea not seen to be a requirement in the Senior Cup interestingly), Whitley Bay A and Cullercoats, who finished third and fourth in the 2008/09 Alliance First Division, were afforded places at the middle table.

Thus, every team from fifth in the Alliance First Division, which is where Percy Main finished as a matter of fact, to the bottom of Division 2, providing they play in Northumberland FA territory (bye bye Rutherford, South Shields United, Peterlee Town, Hebburn Reyrolle, Chopwell and Northbank from the First Division as well as Swalwell from the Second) were given a place in the Minor Cup. However, the Northumberland FA didn't just want the remaining 25 Alliance teams in this competition; they invited teams from the Tyneside Amateur League, the North Northumberland League and the Newcastle Corinthian League, then decreed there would be an open draw involving all those who sent in the £20 entry fee by the closing date. This resulted in a grand total of 78 entrants, of whom Percy Main were the highest ranked. This logistical and numerical nightmare meant 50 teams had a bye into round 2, while 28 teams had to slug it out at the preliminary stage.

Now I've nothing against the Northumberland Minor Cup; in 2007 I watched Amble beat Willington Quay Saints in the final, attending the game to support a student of mine who played for Willington. I was also there in 2009 to see Tyneside Amateur League outfit Blakelaw Crofters Lodge deservedly lift the Cup after beating Alliance Second Division side Wallsend Town 2-0. I also recognise that the Minor Cup has a proud and glorious history, having first been won by Heaton Wanderers in 1889, while Percy Main ourselves claimed it in 1920, a mere year after the club's reformation, but where is the logic in a competition whereby teams of the calibre of Jesmond Mysterons, Newcastle Philosophers, Red Star Benwell, Diggers United and Heaton Rifles, not to mention Newcastle Chemfica Independent, Newcastle Chemfica Independent Reserves, Newcastle Chemfica Independent A and Newcastle Chemfica Independent Development all get a bye into Round 2, while Percy Main, who were sat in second place in the Alliance First Division, as well as being the highest placed team from 2008/09 required to contest the Cup and, let us not forget, the beaten finalists in the Minor Cup's more prestigious cousin the Benevolent Bowl, were drawn away to play the singularly named Ashington Booze Brothers Athletic on a public park on the windiest day of the year?

At least the referee deemed the conditions playable. Even more thankfully, we won 4-3 when Malcolm Morien's last minute corner was blown straight into the net. It was a huge relief, especially as we had been 3-0 up at half time, meaning we were through to the last 64 of the competition, allegedly drawn away to North Sunderland (it's a fishing village south of Bamburgh, not the red and white striped Albania on Wear of course, as that godforsaken hole is within the Durham FA's bailiwick) and in with a shout of emulating such famous previous winners as Science and Art (1890), Prudhoe Woodbine (1909), East Chevington Black Watch (1912), Lemington Glass Works (1925), Walker Temperance (1936), Walker Naval Yard (1956), White Horse Unique (1971), DHSS (1972) and Hirst Progressive (1982).

However, as with so many matters pertaining to amateur football in the North East, things are often not what they seem. In 2008/09, North Sunderland finished 6th in Division 1 of the North Northumberland League, but a cursory glance at the 2009/10 league table included no such team. A quick phone call to their secretary told us more; having seen most of their players leave for pastures new and unknown, North Sunderland called it a day in July 2009. This fact had seemingly escaped the attention of the Northumberland FA, who allowed a non-existent team a bye into the second round of the competition when 14 real sides were knocked out at the first hurdle. As a result of there being no opponents to play, Percy Main were belatedly given a bye into round 3. It is clearly no coincidence that the Northumberland FA's Chief Executive, Roland Maughan, is a celebrated writer of Christmas pantomimes for local Am Dram societies.

Hark now hear, the Villagers sing;
North Sunderland ran away
And we're in Round 3 without playing
Because of the NFA!

I am proud to say I wasn't at the Ashington Booze Brothers Athletic game; not out of any misguided boycott of Northumberland FA policies, but because I was watching with immense pride as my son Ben helped Wallsend Eagles beat Durham Tigers 44-14 in the final of the North East U14 Rugby League Cup at a blustery Gateshead Stadium. At least the weather conditions allowed me and his mam to claim it was the wind that was making our eyes water. I have no excuses other than a free ticket to explain my subsequent presence at Newcastle United's entertaining 0-0 draw with Bristol City in the afternoon, rather than at the evocatively named People's Park in Ashington.

However, another person also not at People's Park was Ian Lee, who, after a Percy Main career lasting all of one game, had gone back to Whitley Bay A. Though proving that transfers after a single game are also the preserve of players Percy Main sign rather than sell, Graeme Smith has returned from Heaton Stannington, meaning we now have two

Graeme Smiths at the club, though only the full back who'd arrived from Shankhouse played this season. No chance of any mix-ups for referees or club secretaries there then!

The importance of officials getting things right was brought home to me somewhat forcibly on the Sunday when, following a nasty wrist injury sustained by one of the players of Lowick United Ladies, necessitating their manager taking the distressed young woman to North Tyneside Hospital A & E to have a cast put on it, I stepped in as emergency assistant referee in a match officiated by one of my students. Thankfully, I had a trouble free game as the Villagers' distaff side prevailed 11-1 in a sparkling encounter on a glorious afternoon with smashing company.

Post match, a dozen of us sat shooting the breeze and drinking cans in the clubhouse; good times with good people. Who the hell cared Chelsea were playing Liverpool in the Premiership? Thoughts of an away trip to Gosforth Bohemians on the Saturday for the blokes and another home game against Blyth Town on Sunday for the lasses were more than enough to keep us going through the dying embers of Sunday afternoon and the jugular torment of the working week.

Six days later, on another warm Saturday afternoon, I arrived at Benson Park at the far end of Gosforth in a chipper mood. Work had gone well, I'd seen a nostalgic gig by three ex Fall members under the guise of Factory Star on the Friday night in the company of two similarly ageing punk rocked orientated mates, then played well in Winstons' 7-1 thumping of Mill View WMC in the morning, and now had the prospect of an eminently winnable Percy Main away game to round the day off in perfect style.

If I'd turned up in a bleak mood, then the semi-rural charm of Benson Park would have soon put paid to any gloom. Set back from a row of detached retirement bungalows in the exclusive Brunton Park estate, it is a charming oasis and a fitting home for this venerable club, run on even more strictly amateur principles than Percy Main, as these lads are stung for a hefty annual membership fee as well as paying to train and play. Their official club history tells their story in this fashion:

During the season 1894-95, a meeting was held in the house of a Mrs Hope in Leazes Terrace, Newcastle, where the Bohemian Club was formed. It was by an amazing coincidence that in another house in Leazes Terrace, about eighty years later, Newcastle Garnett FC were also formed.

The first fixture was played on the Bull Park Recreation Ground (now Exhibition Park) and thereafter the club played successively at South Northumberland Cricket Club 1897-99, the North Road 1900-04, Newton Road 1904-22, the Forest Hall Cricket Ground 1923-26, Lloyds' Bank Sports Ground 1926-39 and after the war on the Thermal Sports Ground. So it was with deep satisfaction that in 1951 the Club entered into a 99-year lease and secured a more or less permanent domicile at Polwarth Drive in Brunton Park. When the present pavilion was erected, in the mid 1960's, the ground was renamed Benson Park in memory of the late Secretary, Rex Benson, whose generosity made the building of the pavilion possible.

In 2000, due to a gradual decline in player involvement off the pitch the Bohemian club stopped fielding a team but help was on hand from Garnett FC, who were looking for a ground. Bohemians were reborn in 2001 under the name Garnett Bohemian FC. Garnett were originally a struggling University Intra-Mural team but by the time of the rebirth had established themselves as the largest club in the North East of England. Five Saturday and three Wednesday teams are fielded with a paid up playing membership of 81. All players from the 1st team, who play in the Northern Alliance Division 1, down to the 5th, pay an annual subscription and match fees. The universal pay to play philosophy and willingness to work hard off the pitch remain central to the success of the Bohemian Football Club.

It will be generally conceded, however, that the greatest honour won, and for which no medals are struck, is the proud name and tradition of the "Bohs" throughout Northumbrian football circles. In the building of this tradition there have been no star players but just those members who, loving the game, and the Club, have carried on where their predecessors left off.

Football and football conditions have changed a great deal over one hundred years and the fortunes of the Club have varied considerably since the first match in the Bull Park in 1894 but we are confident that the Bohemian Football Club can still give much to football and it must be our continued aim to make that contribution worthy of the Club.

Lofty and perhaps unattainably ambitious sentiments indeed, but ones whose provenance stretches back to the late Victorian era of public school and lecture theatre Varsity sportsmanship, meaning Bohemians come from a very different social and philosophical mindset than those returning veterans of the Great War, who, to take their mind off the carnage they'd witnessed, the economic privations they now faced and the raging Spanish flu epidemic that was to kill more than the conflict between 1914 and 1918 had, began kicking a ball around on what was then Middle Row Park in Percy Main. If ever there was a town versus gown fixture in the Northern Alliance, this was it.

One man who had attempted to straddle the gulf between the two clubs was Phil Kyle; even then, he'd walked out of Bohs when manager and Percy Main when Community Development Officer, but he was here today, affecting a studied neutrality Eamon de Valera would have envied. Like a zealous Junior Cabinet Minister pressed in to service at the hustings for a marginal by-election in mid-term, he earnestly pressed flesh and mouthed neutral platitudes to bemused passers-by in a remarkably healthy crowd notable for its lack of floating voters.

On a ground where I'd fetched my mates from County Kildare, John and Ciaran McQuaid, to cheer on Percy Main in a 2-0 defeat in the semi final of the Northern Alliance Combination Cup in February 2008, in advance of seeing Newcastle banjoed 5-1 by Man United at SJP, I'd brought along my pal Rod, the left back from Winstons. Well, he does live on Polwarth Drive so it was a short walk home for him. I think he would have enjoyed the game far more than Phil Kyle did, as the saintly Bohemians belied their straw boater, punting and comic operetta image by having two players sent off for professional fouls, which isn't bad going for a totally amateur team. Stood with his Labrador, Poppy, on the opposite touchline to the rest of the crowd, Phil had the perfect view of proceedings. I wonder what he made of them. Sadly, I had to push off at full time to babysit my mam, so I didn't get a chance to shoot the breeze post match.

The previous occasion on which likeable, communicative referee Andy Gray had officiated a Percy Main away game was at Seaton Burn in April

2009, when the popular Bedlington whistler had cause to show Main's captain Chris Locke the first and hopefully only red card of his football career for a stamping offence. Today the Villagers were able to keep a full complement of players on the pitch, while it was the hosts, supposed upholders of the spirit of Corinthians Casuals on Tyneside, who were depleted by dismissals as referee Gray twice brandished red for mirror image offences by their players.

A mere 66 seconds had been played when Jon McEnaney burst through the Bohemians defence following an astute through ball from Malky Morien. Just as the Main front man appeared ready to shoot, the magnificently named Steven Slaughter hauled McEnaney back and, as last defender, his (blood) red card was inevitable. After debutant home keeper David Herrington made a sound stop from Jason Ritchie's scorching free kick, the Main were unable to capitalise on this numerical advantage and indeed it was the home side who drove Main back, mainly through the promptings of long-serving centre forward Harry Tulip. Despite having a name seemingly more suited to a Noel Coward comedy than a football team, the gangly striker was a constant menace.

On nine minutes, Tony Browell saved Rob Rodgerson's blushes when Tulip fastened on to a loose clearance from the keeper and lofted the ball towards an empty net, only for the stalwart centre back to rescue his team with a solid header from the line. Minutes later, Rodgerson excelled himself with a flying, one-handed stop from the dangerous Paul Menton.

Certainly as the game progressed, a common feeling among the Main faithful was that it would have been preferable for McEnaney to have scored and Bohemians to have stayed with the full eleven for the sake of the game. However, the visitors' unease began to lessen as the half drew on and Morien almost snapped the bar with a stupendous drive from the edge of the box that bounced high and over following the initial contact with the frame of the goal. It was a clear indication that Main meant business and weren't prepared to mess around waiting for a fortuitous, though seemingly inevitable, opening goal.

Early in the second half a frustrated McEnaney saw yellow following a tussle in the box, then Colback shot narrowly wide, before Bohemians were further reduced to nine men in what was the pivotal moment of the game. In an almost carbon copy of Slaughter's early departure, Danny Sherwood was dismissed for dragging down Callum Colback, who was clear in on goal after another excellent Morien pass. The foul certainly ended in the box, though the initial contact was deemed to have started outside and so only a free kick resulted, which sailed over the bar from Morien.

With still 40 minutes to go, Rob Rodgerson in the Main goal may well have gone off himself as Bohemians crossed out of their half only sporadically after that and failed to have a single effort on goal in the remainder of the game. That said, it seemed as if the Bohemians defence would never be breached, especially when substitute Dean Morgan, on for McEnaney, headed against the underside of the bar on the hour from a Jason Ritchie cross.

In the next 10 minutes, Dean Ellis fired inches wide before keeper Herrington palmed away a Colback effort, and impressive left back Ben Edusi, who used to be a barman in my old local The Newton, threw himself in front of a goal-bound Chris Locke effort. It seemed as if the game would finish scoreless, until Dean Morgan calmly slotted home a loose ball with a precise, powerful finish from 12 yards, for his first Main goal, after an almighty scramble in the box. We weren't to know it, but this was Dean's last goal in his last game for The Main as he simply disappeared from the scene, preferring to concentrate on Caledonian courting. Putting women before football? Well, he'll learn.

Freed from the shackles of searching for the elusive opening goal, the Villagers threatened repeatedly from then on but were unable to grab a second. Somehow, a 35-yard snorter from Chris Locke pinged off the bar instead of dipping in, while Herrington denied Malky Morien with a brave diving save.

Sadly, the normally sporting Bohemians side appeared to have taken on more of the spirit of the snooker hall than the Junior Common Room, as their powerfully built, shaven-headed management duo enthusiastically produced volleys of industrial language aimed at the referee, as well as visiting players and officials, which the Main contingent on the sidelines purposefully rose above. Amazingly.

There was a thoroughly unpleasant incident near the end of the game that did Bohemians FC no good whatsoever. In the last minute, Dean Morgan took a quick throw-in to Callum Colback 20 yards from goal on the left. As Callum swivelled and shot over in a split second, the referee, seemingly simultaneously, blew the whistle to indicate a home substitution.

Immediately, the home side's assistant petulantly called over the referee and interpreted Callum's shot as kicking the ball away, resulting in a nonsensical booking, ostensibly for time-wasting. While these may be the rules, I would have more sympathy with the assistant attempting to rigorously uphold them if he hadn't been the same Danny Sherwood who'd been red carded in the second half. The regulations state any player who has been dismissed from the field of play should move back behind the rail at the side of the pitch, so he shouldn't have been running the line in the first place. This kerfuffle resulted in another bout of hot air and invective, until the full time whistle blew and the relief of the three points kicked in.

Second place had been maintained, but with Amble United at home to Seaton Burn on Saturday 17th, while we entertained Heddon in a League Cup tie, we would be faced with playing catch-up after that.

Exactly a year since Premier Division outfit Cramlington Town came to Purvis Park to knock Percy Main out of the Kicks Leisure Northern Alliance League Cup by 2-1 at the second round stage, Heddon did exactly the same, dismissing the Villagers from the competition at the same stage and by the same score. In the process, the top-flight side were the first opposition to leave Fortress Purvis Park with anything after six successive home wins in all competitions had made Percy Main an intimidating place for sides to visit, which in the wider scheme of things is probably the most, and possibly only, galling thing about this loss.

In truth, Heddon were good value for their win, achieved courtesy of a goal in each half by the excellent John Dunn, whose pace, vision and mesmerising footwork made for a very uncomfortable afternoon for a rearranged Villagers defence, featuring stand-in stopper Steven Shadforth, deputising for the unavailable Tony Browell. Shaddy was lucky to stay on the pitch following his unsuccessful attempt to wrestle Dunn to the floor late in the second half. Luckily for Shaddy, the referee played an excellent advantage and Dunn went on to score, despite some less than charitable shadow squad team mates of the Main defender demanding the chunky utility player should see red, presumably as a suspension for him would improve their chances of some first team action.

Despite a clear gulf in class between the two sides in the first half, Percy Main made a real fight of it in the second, acquitting themselves admirably, with Heddon forced to rely on the acrobatics of keeper Alex Curran to maintain their advantage. One save in particular from Callum Colback, tipping over a piledriver of an effort after the striker had fastened on to a Liam Knox flick, was worth the admission fee alone.

The game began with Main on top for the opening 15 minutes, with Colback and McEnaney both just failing to find the net with early efforts that drifted just wide. However, slightly against the run of play, Heddon took the lead when Dunn cleverly picked his way through a series of challenges before stroking the ball past Rodgerson in the home goal for the opener. This goal signalled a change in the balance of play and Heddon were all over Percy Main for much of the rest of the half.

Tall striker Daniel Robinson saw his low effort kicked on to the post by home custodian Rob Rodgerson just before the half hour. The unrelenting pressure was admirably dealt with by a home defence, who restricted Heddon to speculative efforts from distance that failed to find the target. However, Main almost equalised with the last kick of the half when Colback headed a Jason Ritchie free kick wide, with an unmarked and better-placed Graeme Cole seemingly ready to nod the ball home at the back post.

Perhaps this near miss gave the Main some hope, as in the second period they were clearly the better side, with substitutes Liam Knox on for McEnaney and the returning Pierre Luc Coiffait replacing Dean Ellis, giving the home outfit a cutting edge and much more of a goalmouth threat, though Darol Lucas almost doubled Heddon's lead, slicing a pass from Dunn into the side netting.

Apart from this isolated effort, it was all Main for half an hour: Wilkinson was dispossessed when ready to shoot in a good position, Cole headed a Ritchie corner just over and a Morien effort from distance was deflected, fortuitously, into keeper Curran's arms. Out of nowhere, Dunn fastened on to an Edwardson through ball and shrugged off the desperate attentions of Shadforth, before going round Rodgerson and tapping in to an empty net for 2-0 with 12 minutes to go.

Hope flickered when Colback was fouled in the area, with Ritchie scoring from the spot in emphatic fashion, but time was against a valiant Main, who were forced to bow out battling, rather like Newcastle, who then went down 1-0 away at Forest, which we all watched in The Alex in a slightly subdued mood.

The weekend got worse when the ladies' team lost 3-1 at home to a Forest Hall side they'd crushed 6-1 away six weeks earlier in the Northumberland Women's Cup. Dark rumours of threatening behaviour on facebook and MSN by the away side were muttered as excuses, somewhat incredibly. Sadly, for whatever reason, both Percy Main sides had come up short this weekend. However, the games had gone. We had to move on and a good way to focus the mind was to flog Christmas Bottle Draw tickets.

We'd had 2000 printed, which cost us £38 up front. They were selling for 50p each and we were hoping to receive the prizes as donations to maximise our profit. Already there were seven bottles of wine and spirits left over from the Gary Hull game and Laura's mam had promised a bottle of whiskey she'd won at a tombola somewhere. Bearing in mind that only about five of the players ever bother to sell them, it is really up to the committee to do the donkey work. The thought of making almost a grand clear profit is a real spur to us all, as money to a club like ours is a precious commodity so often in short supply. I did my best, flogging £85 worth in a week.

Presumably the news of my prowess as a salesman resulted in a tolerant Bob waiting around at the club to give a tardy Ian a lift down to Peterlee on Saturday. To be fair, it wasn't my fault I missed the 12.30 departure time. Admittedly, I'd taken advantage of the lack of a Winstons fixture to have a lie-in, but I was on the Metro by 11.45. The thing that slowed me down was the train being so full at Whitley Bay that the doors wouldn't close. The cause of such a delay was the huge number of Doncaster Rovers fans, uniformly attired in bobble hats, scarves and replica kits so shiny as to appear they'd been purchased from the club shop the day before (which no doubt they had, judging by the conversation of a couple of them who admitted they were actually Manchester United fans who "liked to see the local team do well" and "just fancied a weekend away") who were trying to get on.

Doncaster Rovers eh? How the mighty have fallen. As a Newcastle season ticket holder from 1989 to 2009, I never once had a freebie ticket. However, since I chucked my membership, I've been inundated with spare tickets; I'd already been to three games and knocked back offers for two others. For this one, I got two spares from our secretary at work, so I passed them on to Ben, who'd been in Doncaster the night before to watch a rugby league international between England and France, and Sara's dad, who as a Sheffield United fan from Barnsley always likes a bargain. What he didn't like was leaving early and missing Kevin Nolan's winner, as 10-man Newcastle turned it around to come from a goal down and win against a Doncaster side that had also missed a penalty. Victories where you come back from the dead are always the sweetest I always find.

Meanwhile, back in the Alliance, we were headed for Peterlee, a hideous concrete 60s new town in east Durham, which is our furthest trip south by a considerable distance. Goodness knows why this former Northern League side don't play in the Wearside League, which affords closer opposition for them and is only one division in size, so theoretically providing an easier route back to the Northern League. Mind, having come down three divisions in five years, including being bottom of the Alliance Premier last year, promotion is a long way off for today's hosts. Frankly, despite the glittering, restored Victor Passmore Pavilion, a monument more to bad planning than civic pride, there's neither hope nor comfort to be found anywhere in Peterlee, or the economically blighted and socially blasted environs of Horden and Easington, where *'Billy Elliott'* was filmed. When the mines went, so did the spirit and soul of these communities.

We arrived in sheeting rain and a howling gale to see the social club packed with all day problem boozers, already half cut by early afternoon.

Consequently we decamped to the snug and inviting clubhouse that adjoined the bar, for hot drinks and to warm our ample arses on the fiery radiators in the centrally-heated changers. After 15 minutes, with the Villagers 2-0 down and playing quite appallingly, we all wished we'd stayed there. In fact, other than Mick Ritchie barking out his mantra of "good lad" in his broad Ashington brogue (*Gud laird*, approximately) ten times in the opening dozen minutes, there was nothing remotely of interest in a shocking, shoddy performance.

At half time, as the icy rain lashed down on Percy Main's shell-shocked side, who sheepishly made for the safety of the dressing room still 2-0 down to a spirited but desperately limited Peterlee Town side, who had made more than a little use of the gusting wind behind their backs in the opening period, only those of us among the regular half dozen away fans (Bob and his dad, Gary, Geordie, Norman and me), who teeter on the brink of delusional optimism (me), could see anything other than a heavy defeat for a side who were unbeaten in the league since mid August. However, a speculative wind-assisted header from Jason early in the second half utterly changed the complexion of a game that was in serious danger of derailing the Villagers' promotion drive. The final half hour of the game saw a superb, disciplined performance that caused the Main contingent to leave Peterlee on cloud nine.

Despite the dismally inclement conditions, the expansive Eden Lane pitch was in immaculate condition. In front of a modest crowd of about 15, that more than trebled as the game progressed (in other words when the bloke collecting the quid admission money buggered off for a well-deserved cuppa after half an hour), Percy Main kicked off attacking the graveyard end of this superbly-maintained former Northern League ground into the teeth of a stiff breeze that gusted aggressively, directly assisting both Peterlee goals. In the sixth minute, a lively run forward by Shaun Wilkinson, as was to be the pattern for most of the day for the luckless right-winger, resulted in play breaking down with no cross or other end product. From the clearance, the ball fell to midfielder Stephen Newham, who hit a speculative 40-yard effort that deceived Rob, flying in from the underside of the bar, literally out of nowhere.

If the half a dozen of us stood in the lovingly maintained, covered stand had imagined this would be a wake-up call for the Villagers, they were mistaken. Joe Betts chased a loose backpass, but Peterlee keeper Russell Blenkinsopp got there first to hit a huge clearance that Graeme Cole misjudged the flight of. It fell to Brad Smith, who hit the byline on the left side of the area and crossed for Chris Howe to score at the second time of asking. His initial effort hit Tony Browell, but fell kindly to allow him to stroke it in the corner past a despairing Rodgerson. It could have been worse soon after when Rodgerson needed to athletically smother a Smith snapshot.

Frankly, Peterlee deserved their lead and Main were only able to offer inaccurate long-range efforts from Morien, Locke and Ritchie; all of whom have proved in the past they are far better strikers of both stationary and moving balls from distance. However, Joe Betts can count himself unlucky when his deft header was smothered by Blenkinsopp an inch from Chris Locke's toe in the six-yard box.

The last action of a frustrating half saw Peterlee squander a chance to make it 3-0 when Paul Callan dragged his shot woefully wide after Damien Gee had set him free with a nicely judged pass. Thankfully, it was to be almost the last we saw of Peterlee as an attacking force.

However, the seismic change in fortunes that lay ahead was not apparent in a sluggish opening to the second period, when Tony Browell headed a Ritchie free kick just wide and a Wilkinson shot hit the keeper's legs. Then, completely contrary to all that had gone before, Ritchie's excellent, if unexpected, header changed the game, as it deceived Blenkinsopp to drop over his head and across the line. Almost immediately, the rain stopped, the wind strengthened and a blinding sun came out, shining right into the Peterlee keeper's eyes, which no doubt caused him to miss Main's equalising effort.

Jason Ritchie's headers are like London buses; you wait nearly two years for one then a couple pop along in five minutes. His first got Main back in the game; his second set up Callum Colback to equalise, as he ghosted in at the near post to force the ball home from barely two yards out.

After being in complete control, Peterlee were now reeling and within five minutes had gone behind when Ritchie's superb close control and swivel in the box game him the chance to finish in a cultured fashion to score what was, in the final analysis, the winner. Ten glorious minutes of graft, guts and guile had caused a complete turnaround, meaning the Main were back on course for a spot in the promotion places of Alliance Division 1. Suddenly, it was all smiles and short passing to feet as everything came good at last. Mick Ritchie was in "good lad" overdrive, using it three times in five seconds as Callum Colback went on a run late in the game. Even Shields natives like Rob and Tony were saying it as well. Seemingly, team spirit can be measured by the players adopting the manager's idiolect.

However, Peterlee still had their chances, but when an unmarked Callan put his free header following a Howe free kick weakly over the bar, it seemed clear Main had weathered the metaphorical as well as literal storm. The final action saw an emphatic gloss put on the scoreline, when final sub Steven Shadforth's impudent flick over the Peterlee defence was finished unerringly by the lethal Morien.

Post match, as we collected the muddy and soaking kit, the dressing room was like a party. Cola, who an hour earlier had contemplated retirement, was wreathed in smiles and the rest were dancing and punching the air. It was only three points, but it felt like so much more, considering where we'd been an hour earlier. The post match hospitality was sausage, boiled spuds and mixed veg; it may have been as tasteless and stodgy as any school dinner, but it was Michelin guide material for us. The fact only four home players came back showed the depth of despair they were feeling. News of Nolan's late winner at St James' that filtered through as we ate made our victory even sweeter. The food was still tasteless, but you can't have everything.

One thing I didn't get was a megaphone. Ever since I saw Mark E Smith of The Fall use one on stage in June 1980, I've coveted one. The week before Laura and I had seen one in Tynemouth station flea market, but the stallholder wasn't selling it just yet as it needed cleaning up. We went back on the Sunday, but he'd flogged it. Imagine the looks I'd get from the opposition if I had a megaphone to use on the touchline at Northern Alliance games! Our depression was lifted by news of the ladies drawing 4-4 away to Prudhoe after having been behind four times. They've got some *cojones* those lasses.

In the wider world of football, Blackburn boss Sam Allardyce was blaming his side's 5-0 thrashing at Chelsea on a swine flu outbreak that had lain low several of his squad, while the FA were warning players that spitting on the pitch could spread the disease. Even at our level, the dreaded virus could have a deleterious effect, as was demonstrated by Andy's email on Tuesday saying he'd be unable to knock up a match programme for the visit of South Shields United on Halloween as he had succumbed to the disease. Norman and I thought about sympathising, but instead we just got on with doing the programme ourselves. This was my first effort at doing it, and while it may have lacked a little in visuals, the word count was impressively high! Using the goodwill of the lads in repro at work, we knocked out 30 copies, resplendent in blue card covers, for the Halloween visit of South Shields United to Purvis Park.

This was a big game and one I'd developed a growing sense of unease over as the week progressed. Despite lying in second place in the table, our squad was looking decidedly thin in certain areas. Clearly I'm not talking about Shaddy, but chances were he'd need to play up front to try and improve on his record of one goal in 40 appearances as the Main were suffering something of a striker shortage. Ziggy's ankle had kept him out of the frame since September 12th, while Callum's rib injury, sustained by colliding with the post at Peterlee the week before, made him a no show; added to this, both Joe Betts and Macca were away for the weekend, on some stag do piss up in Blackpool. Could you credit it: four top quality strikers and none available? Not only that, Laura wasn't around to do the catering as she was accompanying her mam to a rug making demonstration in Tynemouth Station.

South Shields United were no mugs either; formed in only 2007 as the brainchild and obsession of their chairman and manager Gareth Allen, they'd been granted immediate admission to Alliance Division 2 and had been promoted at the second time of asking. While their ground is a humble one, this is a club that is going places. They have reserves and junior teams, with a women's section in the pipeline. Before this game, they stood in 5th place, having already won five away games. Clearly, this wasn't a game you'd want to go into with no proven firepower.

In addition, they'd beaten us once before; 6-2 in a friendly at Purvis Park in April 2008. That day we'd been awful, as we almost always were that season when finishing 11th, but it wasn't the game that stood out, it was the appalling conduct of their manager, Gareth Allen, or Beanie as he likes to be known. His nickname is no doubt from his ginger crop and ovoid cranium, which gives him the look of a human baked bean. Attired in a grey leisure suit several sizes too small, his repeated volleys of industrial language and confrontational style gave him the appearance of Humpty Dumpty with Tourette's, or George Daws from ***Shooting Stars*** with severe anger management issues. Percy Main Amateurs are never knowingly outsworn, but today we met our match in the potty mouth stakes as Beanie was left with plenty to curse about, loudly.

We deservedly won 2-0, and it was one hell of a good game. Being honest, both Percy Main Amateurs and South Shields United can take great satisfaction from producing as high quality a game as the spectators at Purvis Park would have witnessed in a long time. While the Main got the season off to a cracking start with a superb 2-0 victory over Hebburn Reyrolle back in mid August, their performance in this game, ironically also against opponents from South Tyneside, was even better. Certainly the high tempo first half showing by the Villagers was outstanding in every single department and enabled them to outclass a shell-shocked opposition all over the pitch.

Due to injuries and unavailability, Jason found it necessary to select two substitute keepers, in the shape of Phil Hogg and Sam Dodds, to fill the bench. Consequently, the emphatic win over a side that had won their only other meeting against the Main was all the more praiseworthy.

From the first whistle, Percy Main started in the determined and ruthless fashion that had been the key to the second half fightback against Peterlee the week before. In the second minute Chris Locke forced a corner on the right, which was beautifully floated over by Jason, allowing Graeme Cole to rise powerfully at the back post and send a dangerous header across goal, which was smartly claimed by keeper Gavin Newbrook. Moments later Malky tried his luck from well outside the area on the left hand side, seeing his trademark powerful effort fly just over the angle of post and bar.

In their next attack, Percy Main went ahead. A strong piece of running down the right by Shaun Wilkinson resulted in him pulling a good ball across the box, which caused a calamitous mix up by visiting keeper Newbrook and otherwise impressive defender Assan Jallow. Their collision resulted in the ball running free to onrushing Main captain Chris Locke, who put in yet another sterling, tireless performance in the game. Locke's finish was unerring as he crashed the loose ball home from around the penalty spot. From the restart, a dominant Main almost doubled their lead when another poorly cleared Wilka shot was returned with some venom by Jason; his effort drifting wide of the left hand upright.

Jason distinguished himself at the other end with an assured piece of defending when intercepting a dangerous Liam Robertson cross and calmly running the ball out of defence. Indeed, the whole home defence were in sparkling, indomitable form all game, with Graeme Smith deservedly winning the man of the match award for an excellent performance that nullified the opposition as an attacking force all afternoon. The midfield also took their share of the workload in Main's half, with David Tapsfield superbly dispossessing the dangerous Aaron Kah when the latter was well placed to shoot at the midpoint of the half.

In their other rare forays forward, South Shields United were repelled when Rob distinguished himself with a magnificent block from an unmarked Michael Alexander shot at the back post and Ryan Shave headed wide when unmarked following a corner. The last attack of the half saw visiting custodian Newbrook hold a dangerous Wilkinson cross, with Ritchie pressurising him.

The second half began in explosive fashion, with Malky hitting the bar from inside the centre circle straight from the kick off, Newbrook a bemused onlooker. Seconds later Shaddy bravely headed home a Wilka cross, but saw his effort ruled out by an earlier offside flag.

Soon after Shaddy was replaced by Liam Knox, who distinguished himself in the lone striker role, chasing tirelessly every lost cause and upsetting the rhythm of the visiting defenders by his physical, all-action style.

Apart from a powerful, long-range effort by Kah, Shields United offered nothing going forwards in the opening 25 minutes of the second half. Instead, the home side were almost entirely encamped in the visitors' half. Firstly, a heavy touch by Jason robbed him of the chance of putting Main 2-0 up following an astute ball by Locke. A Ritchie corner caused pandemonium in the six yard box, with several home players having swipes at the ball, but none being able to force it in, before the Main player manager made the game safe with either a deliciously floated effort or a sliced cross that deceived the keeper. Whichever it was, the end result was the same; a cross from almost on the touchline deceiving a flat-footed keeper Newbrook, who could only watch in horror as Ritchie's effort slowly arced over him and struck the inside of the post before falling almost apologetically behind the line. The vociferous cheers that greeted this goal paid tribute to the sense of value placed on it. We knew, at that point, that we'd won another game by digging in and grafting all over the pitch.

Fittingly perhaps, this was Jason's last touch as Dean Ellis replaced him, with the game going into a lull as the visitors sensed their luck was out. If they had doubted this, then they were given confirmation on 70 minutes when Robertson's goal-bound effort was hacked away by Graeme Smith with Rob beaten. Smithy again foiled the same player with an excellent clearing header moments later.

Shields United then retreated in to their shell as the Main toyed with the visitors for the remaining period of the game, with Morien almost adding a third with a curling effort that Newbrook did well to hold, before the referee brought the game to a close with Shields United failing to lay a glove on the Villagers all game. Beanie saw things a little differently, publishing this semi-literate match report on his club's website, reproduced in its original form:

Frustrating afternoon from Shields Uniteds point of view. Assan Jallow (LB) and Shaun Newbrook (GK) who have been our two most consistent players in the last two years made a double mistake after 5 minutes to give percy the lead. in fairness we seemed to have a bit of the ball but first half we were poor in the final third. Half time percy hit the bar from the kick off, then there winger (ritchie i think) crossed the ball and it hit the back peg and went in. United should have pulled one back when scott graham was 8 yards out but couldnt get the ball out under his feet.

We host them next week so will hopefully decide to shoot next week, but overall we discussed after the game if we can leanrn to be hard to beat like percy are shown at the moment, then we will do all right.

Things seem to be going well for percy which in fairness there lads really wanted it today, you could see by their passion it meant something today. cheers to norman and richie, while the touchline was hot the last ten minutes it was all good banter and everyone shook hands afterwards and shared a pint, thats what its all about.

We will beat you next week though lads......

So, Main start November in a promotion position, having won the last six league games and being unbeaten in 10. Instead of a free weekend, courtesy of the North Sunderland fiasco, Shields United were offered an opportunity for revenge, as the two sides meet again in a rearranged league game.

In the cricket club post match, Andy's wife Jo, who is Bob's daughter and Rob's sister (Percy Main Amateurs; a real family club) gave us an update on his condition. Having been rushed to hospital and kept in the High Dependency Unit for three days, he was now about to be released. He apologised for not doing the programme, but promised there would be one for the next home game, versus East End on November 21st. However, doing the programme for this game had whetted the appetites of Norman and I, so we decided to knock a debut issue out for the women's match at home to North Shields on November 15th. Who knows, perhaps it would attract the groundhoppers? There'd been one who'd travelled up from

Stoke for the Shields United game, taking more photos than a tabloid snapper and gorging himself in the snack bar like a non-league Mr Creosote.

October had been another good month. Putting the League Cup defeat to one side, we'd seen maximum league points secured and had advanced two rounds of the Minor Cup, while the Ladies team continued to develop. Crowds were up, as were sales of programmes and food, with Laura planning on introducing broth and gravy and chips on to the menu for the next fixture as winter began to set in. Not only that, we awaited a delivery of claret and blue woollen hats from Canada, knitted by her Auntie Linda. Yes, things were looking good for the Villagers and the Village People.

November:
Mickey Haley Super Goalie La La La La La La!!

OCTOBER WAS A success; maximum league points and untroubled progress to the last 32 of the Northumberland Minor Cup, courtesy of the win over Ashington Booze Brothers in Round 1 and the disappearance of North Sunderland rendering the need for a game in Round 2 obsolete, meant that the relatively unimportant departure from the League Cup could be easily and quickly forgotten about. We'd gone 10 league matches unbeaten, having won 6 in a row, which left us lying second with games in hand on the leaders Rutherford :

Rutherford	P14	W11	D2	GD +24	Pts 35
Percy Main	P12	W10	D1	GD +11	Pts 31
Amble United	P12	W10	D0	GD +28	Pts 30
Whitley Bay A	P13	W7	D3	GD +16	Pts 24

If we could keep the run going away to Shields United, then against Rutherford the week after in the Combination Cup, a competition purely for teams in Alliance Division 1, they would start feeling the pressure, but with only two sides to be promoted, there was no way we could afford any slip-ups.

With the Ladies being afforded a free weekend, on account of the odd number of teams in their division, I spent the first Sunday of the month, which was also the first day of the month, designing a programme for their local derby on November 15th at home to North Shields Women, which would be the first meeting between the two clubs. Putting false modesty and self-doubt to one side, I know I managed a better effort with this programme than the Shields United emergency one I'd produced. However, I was glad to hand back editorial responsibility to Andy; contributing to a programme is one thing, designing it is quite another, and personally I'm happier with words than images. Apparently this means I'm a verbal rather than a visual or kinaesthetic learner.

I also used this spare Sunday afternoon to compose a couple of articles that I sent to Shields United for their programme, for our rapid return match. Arriving at Quarry Lane in time for kick off on Saturday 7th, I wasn't best pleased to find that the illustrious Beanie hadn't used my work as the promised programme hadn't materialised as he'd been "*owwer busy at graft*". As their Quarry Lane ground was a park pitch, where I'd played Over 40s game at the start of the season (won 5-1 as well), it clearly wasn't as if he'd been busy on stadium improvements.

Ground grading requirements in the Alliance Division 1 are pretty basic; a rope around the pitch and changing rooms being the extent of them. A kid's chalkboard with 'Shields United v Percy Main' at the entrance to the car park indicated the game was on, but there were no hot drinks or refreshments of any kind, nor facilities for spectators, though Beanie had raided the garden furniture section at B&Q for half a dozen white plastic chairs for their subs to recline on. We at Percy Main are made of sterner stuff and stood at the pitch side in the punishing wind. I made a mental note to myself that it was now time to start wearing two pairs of socks on Saturday afternoons.

Their ground may have been a shambles, but it was also an educational experience for the Percy Main squad, as we could use these modest surroundings to point out to our lot how lucky they are to have fortress Purvis Park and its many architectural features and comforting benefits to call home. Within the first two minutes, the penny appeared to have dropped when Malky put us ahead. Similar to his goal at Peterlee a fortnight previous, Morien ran through a static home defence to collect a pinpoint pass, before steadying himself and finishing in emphatic fashion under the body of advancing home custodian Newhouse.

The game was a straightforward 2-0 victory over a tenacious if uninspired Shields United. Admittedly, the football on the pitch did not reach the same impressive heights as the previous week's contest, though that was of little real concern as we finished the game only a point behind leaders Rutherford, but with a crucial game in hand.

Our second was a picture book effort; Joe Betts produced perhaps the pass of the season, bisecting Shields United's two towering centre halves with a glorious push that left them utterly flat-footed, allowing Shaddy the opportunity to elegantly lift the ball past Newbrook for a well deserved second.

Credit to Shields United for stepping up to the plate and attempting to get back into the game, but against the mean Main rearguard, they must have realised this would not be their day. While Rob Rodgerson had cause to palm a low Jack Lawton cross shot out for a corner, the Main were relatively untroubled for the rest of the game. Indeed, it could have been more as Shaun Wilkinson seemed to have a good shout for a penalty turned down by the ever excellent referee Mr Forshaw.

Post match, as we basked in the glow of victory, I actually felt a twinge of sympathy for the previously offensive Beanie. Almost single-handedly he has formed the team out of nowhere, and continues to manage, train and chair the club. Not only that, he collected the rope from round the pitch by himself and sorted the dirty strips out, meaning that we were already halfway through our blackcurrant and sodas, with the sausage and chip buffet a fond memory, by the time he arrived in their home bar, a depressing estate pub called the New Mill. As a Mackem, he'll have been delighted his arrival coincided with Spurs going 2-0 up on the Wearsiders and Newcastle scoring a third at home to Peterborough. I'd turned a ticket down for that one and felt pleased I had after the Main had marched on.

Of course, Saturday 7th November should have seen us in North Sunderland, which I suppose is a reasonable name for parts of South Shields, in the Minor Cup. In contrast to the vacillation by the NFA regarding our second round game, they were quick off the blocks to give us the third round tie, away to Wallsend Boys Club Seniors (their women's team is called Wallsend Boys Club Girls) on December 5th. They play at the unromantic location of St. Peter's Fields, a public pitch at the side of the A1058 Coast Road, directly opposite Tyne Metropolitan College where I work. This game would slip in, weather permitting, between a run of four straight home league games: Newcastle East End November 21st, Berwick United November 28th, Whitley Bay A December 12th and Cullercoats December 19th. Tough times lay ahead, but before then there was Rutherford away in the Combination Cup.

Northern Alliance football is eminently susceptible to bad weather. With so many teams playing on hired council pitches, a policy decision by a town hall jobsworth on an unpromising Friday morning to call games off on all pitches under their control can ruin many a sporting weekend. The weather may pick up dramatically after the fateful verdict has been handed down by email to club secretaries everywhere, but that is of no consequence as the council's decision is final, especially as any team choosing to play in those circumstances is invalidating their pitch hire agreement as well as rendering accident liability insurance null and void. With constant rain from Wednesday to Friday afternoon, the sporting outlook, if not the weather forecast, was bleak. Thankfully, Rutherford own their ground and are not so hasty to declare their pitch unplayable. Hence an early morning inspection, on the back of a Friday tea-time cessation of the deluge, allowed our game to go ahead, even if the going was decidedly soft.

As I mentioned when we played them at home in August, Rutherford are the oldest continuously existing team in the north east. Their dressing room has graffiti of a similarly venerable vintage, with **HELLS ANGELS RULE OK** painted on the side of the pavilion. This quaint throwback to the carefree days of ***Straw Dogs*** and Altamont Speedway still remains, but will soon be a distant memory as Rutherford are building a new clubhouse and changing rooms. Considering the current hospitality and changing facilities consist of a pair of WWII prefabricated Nissen huts, and that they've got at least four Saturday teams as well as numerous junior sides to consider and cater for, they really do deserve the lottery funding to build a new facility. Good luck to them; I hope they finish runners-up in the league and that they appreciate how good a game they were part of today, even if they contrived to lose.

Percy Main Amateurs showed yet again that we are a side who simply refuse to accept defeat by turning round a seemingly impossible half time position at a damp but perfectly playable Farnacres. The latest in a series of semi-mythical comebacks by the Villagers saw us overpower the home side in the second period to turn a 2-0 deficit into a 3-2 victory, in an eagerly awaited top versus second cup clash that I'd like to pretend more than lived up to its billing as the top game of the day in the region. Well, I'd billed it as such on my ***facebook*** status.

Following last week's successful trip to Shields United, where the Main's first league double of the season was comfortably recorded, Jason kept faith with the same ten outfield players, resulting in captain Chris Locke filling in again with admirable composure at right back in the place of chickenpox victim Mickey Haley. The only change was in goal, where Phil Hogg came in for his second appearance of the campaign. The fact that Phil is an excellent keeper in his own right was demonstrated as early as the seventh minute when he was forced into an acrobatic tip over from the home side's David Laughlin that drew gasps of admiration and a warm round of applause.

Rutherford opened the scoring on the half hour mark when Andrew Reay beat the offside trap and collected a pass from Kevin Urwin, before lofting the ball over the advancing Hogg. It was a quality goal and no blame could be attached to any Percy Main player. This goal seemed to lift the hosts and they looked to press home their advantage, as Urwin drifted through a static Main defence right on half time. His first shot was beaten away by Hogg, but his second was powerful and true, leaving the unlucky Hogg a spectator as Rutherford went into the break two goals ahead.

Three weeks previous a similar situation at Peterlee had been rescued, which perhaps accounted for the lack of panic in the Villagers ranks. Certainly Norman and I weren't worried; it was only a Combination Cup game after all. Taking time away from the game to grab a ***Bovril*** from the ***NAAFI***-style catering outlet, we both agreed that, at the end of the season, we'd not regret losing this one. Foresight 0 Hindsight 6.

Arriving back at the pitch five minutes after the restart, we were just in time to see the Villagers start their fightback, when Shaddy's excellent flick left Joe Betts through on goal. His finish was powerful and true into the bottom corner. Five further minutes and the team from Purvis Park were level; Jay's excellent free kick was bulleted home by Malky, who seemed keen on tormenting the Rutherford defence. Moments later, he hit the top of the bar from thirty yards with a shot of power and accuracy. From ten yards further out, he saw the keeper off his line and chipped him, only for the ball to drop an agonising fraction wide.

Rutherford, from being in total control, were now barely hanging on and the Main were not to be denied. The winner showcased the talents of the two star performers on the pitch. Bettsy fed Malky and the result was the inevitable completion of another excellent comeback from the Lazarus-like Villagers. If only it had been a league game, we'd be top of the table!

On the Sunday, we assembled at Purvis Park for the clash of the titanesses, as the Main Ladies took on the North Shields women. Ordinarily, crowds for the women's games have been limited to friends and family only, but Norman and I had done our bit to publicise this game in the local press and on the Internet. Laura was working the canteen and I'd got 50 programmes and a dozen metal lapel badges to sell to the gangs of marauding groundhoppers we were expecting. Sadly, they must have got lost on the way as the crowd was possibly only marginally larger than usual, with few neutrals or disinterested, in the original sense, observers. At least all the players bought programmes so we managed to shift a load of them. Also Jason and Shaddy turned up to watch, the former in a terrible state of intoxication and the latter in the throes of a desperate hangover fear. A couple of hot dogs each sorted them out and kept the till ticking over.

The game itself was a 3-3 draw, which was disappointing as Percy Main had been 2-0 and 3-2 to the good, but the more experienced North Shields side did more late running on the heavy pitch than our ladies could manage. Good game mind.

I had hoped for a few days away from club responsibilities as work was entering a busy stretch, but unfortunately Andy's return to rude health coincided with him going on a course for two weeks. Hence he could assemble the programme for the visit of Newcastle East End, with the aid of Microsoft Publisher, and then email it to me, but he couldn't print it. Cap in hand, I beseeched the lads in repro and they came up with the goods, sensibly waiting until late Friday afternoon when 60 straight dry hours seemed to suggest the game being on was a safe bet.

Simultaneously, Laura was preparing a pan of traditional homemade broth, unwrapping a parcel of a dozen knitted hats in Percy Main claret and blue from her Aunty Linda in Canada and purchasing items for the post match buffet as Gary was away for the weekend. Busy times, but rewarding all the same.

We've had some good results against Newcastle East End over the past few years; I've seen 2-1, 3-1 and 4-1 victories over them in the last couple of seasons, so this 5-1 success was a fitting, if flattering, scoreline. On a dismal afternoon, with the pitch cloyingly heavy, we stormed to the top of the Pin Point Recruitment Northern Alliance Division 1 with a stunning second half performance of sunshine football that simply blew away East End. The four-goal salvo in just over 20 minutes saw The Villagers at the summit of any league for the first time since 2003, when we went top of the Premier Division after thumping West Allotment 5-2.

However, any spectator who had slipped away from Purvis Park on pressing business at half time, with the game delicately poised at 1-1, and returned an hour later to find out that the game had ended up 5-1, may well have been entitled to assume that the victors had been the side from Millers Dene on the Fossway, such was the poor standard of Main's performance before the break. To be fair to the visitors, Newcastle East End were worthy opponents for the Main and played a full and praiseworthy part in a contest that was nip and tuck for the first hour.

Jason dropped himself for flying winger Chris Doig and made several other changes following last week's 3-2 win away to Rutherford. Rob Rodgerson assumed his position back between the sticks, while up front the returning Callum Colback replaced Joe Betts, who took a place on the bench alongside the fit again Mickey Haley and the ever combative Jonathon McEnaney, meaning Shaddy retained his place up front and Chris Locke continued in an unfamiliar right back role. This line up drew a couple of murmurs of discontent, as it had a kind of Coca Cola Cup ring to it, almost as if Jason had assumed we'd easily do the business and so he could afford to have a strong bench and still coast to victory. That looked a bit presumptuous during the opening period, though we eventually took the lead on the half hour.

Shaddy, having earlier had a clinical finish from a Tony Browell knockback ruled out for the ball having gone out of play, produced another cameo finish for his burgeoning portfolio of stylishly taken goals, finishing David Tapsfield's measured through ball with aplomb. It was a truly lovely goal. In truth, East End could have been well in control of the game by this point and they did roar back with a quality equaliser, as Studholme turned in Bright's astute cross at the near post to take the wind out of the Main's sails five minutes before half time.

Jason must have produced a pertinent and articulate half time talk as after the break we moved up through the gears, to simply blow East End away. First Wilka buried a headed pass from Tony Browell with an emphatic rising drive, and then Colback pounced on a loose ball in the box. Only with a two-goal lead could the lads relax and start to enjoy themselves. As a result, two further goals arrived to give the score an emphatic, if undeserved, gloss.

Firstly, Malky and Maccas broke the East End offside trap; Malky's shot was saved, only for Maccas to stroke the loose ball home. Graeme Smith then completed the scoring with over 20 minutes remaining by forcing home a loose ball from a corner. Credit to East End for preventing any further scoring, but Percy Main deservedly moved to the top of the table after this result.

While elated with our good fortune and deserved place at the top of the table, I felt sorry for East End boss Anth Doyle; not only had we hit his side for five, but also as a player for Newcastle BT in the Over 40s league, Winstons had recently defeated his side on their own turf 3-2. He's a smashing fella, as is his dad, who lives near me and drinks in my local, and his brother, who used to be my son's football coach before Ben took up the oval ball game.

To be frank, I didn't allow these mild feelings of guilt to cloud my week. There were always enough Percy Main related events to keep me busy. Firstly, Wallsend Boys Club had successfully convinced the Northumberland FA that Purvis Park rather than St. Peter's Fields would be a good venue for a Minor Cup 3rd round tie. Hence, the first weekend in December would see our turf churned up even more than we'd expected.

One surprising event was the disappearance of midfielder David Tapsfield. Having arrived in August, fresh off the plane from six months in the States, and making his debut in the 5-0 crushing at Amble United, the Whitley Bay born graduate of Lafayette College, Pennsylvania had decided to go off travelling again after making 14 appearances and scoring one goal, which defeated Amble in the League Cup. This time he'd packed snowshoes and salopettes rather than sunscreen and sandals, as he was off skiing in Chamonix until "I run out of cash". Who says football is a working class game? Some of our lot act as if they're chief executives on a hundred grand a year!

At least they know how to play the game, which gains them many indulgences as far as I'm concerned. Thankfully, their ability kept us top of the table with three more points after Berwick United were beaten 4-1. Rather like when Northbank came over from Carlisle for a bit of a laugh and a few pints, the raucous guffawing from the away dressing room of the basement travellers suggested they were here more for the beer than three points.

Suprisingly, the first significant action of the match, when Simon Hargraves nodded home Sandro De Oliveira's precise cross at the back post with only five minutes on the clock to give the visitors a shock early lead, was accompanied the whistling sound of a flying form book being hurled out the window. Ten minutes in and the chances of a ninth straight league win for the Villagers, or even the preservation of 13-game unbeaten record, seemed two remote prospects.

However, Percy Main have made the remarkable recovery their stock in trade this season and, in the final analysis, this is precisely what happened at Purvis Park again in this game, but until Callum Colback equalised after 20 minutes, fastening on to Rob's goal kick and beautifully timing his run to evade the Berwick offside trap before strolling round keeper Stewart Thompson and rolling the ball into the empty net, it had seemed likely that it was going to be just one of these days when the ball simply wouldn't go in the net.

Things became less frenetic after the equaliser, but for the second week running, Main went in at the break level against a lower-ranked side, having played distinctly below par. But, thankfully, and for the second week running, home fans were treated to an outstanding second half display. Jason helped to establish the lead with an astute piece of play five minutes after the break. A quickly taken short free kick invited Malky to advance and finish with trademark authority as a somnolent Berwick back line stood staring in mute disbelief.

Malky almost made it 3-1 in unlikely circumstances when his hanging cross from the left landed on the roof of the net with keeper Thompson beaten. A third goal did come moments later though, when Cal collected an unavailing opposition goal kick in his stride and went straight for goal, beating Thompson with a low shot across him into the far corner. Despite not playing to the top of their game, the Main had seemingly secured a win with this goal. One further goal did eventually come, but not before a late scare.

In a rare foray upfield, Berwick won a corner and the home side were forced to stare down the barrel of an uncomfortable closing period when, with Rob on the floor after a heavy Berwick challenge, Darren Cromarty's effort on goal was palmed instinctively over the bar by Mickey Haley. Referee Forshaw was left with no choice but to show red to Haley, no doubt arousing a Kingston Park-based regular observer of Percy Main's disciplinary record.

What a November Mickey Haley had; laid up for a fortnight with chickenpox, left on the bench when fit again as Chris Locke played out of his skin in the number 2 shirt, then brought back in only to be sent from the field of play. Luckily for Main, Cromarty shanked the spot kick well wide of the right hand post. By this time a bemused and showered Haley was stood at the top of the pavilion steps quizzically shaking his head and informing all and sundry, "I dunno why I did it. I just did." It's an instinctive rather than a cerebral game I always find.

The Main took heart from Cromarty's pitifully weak penalty and Malky gratefully accepted a quality cushioned through ball from Wilka to add a fourth almost on time as the Main completed our second consecutive perfect month. November's nine league points and Combination Cup success meant we'd won nine league games in a row, won all eight home league games and gone undefeated for 13 league games, a run stretching back to August. We'd collected 40 points before the Advent calendars have been hung up and the table made comforting viewing:

Percy Main	P15	W13	D1	GD +20	Pts 40
Rutherford	P15	W12	D2	GD +27	Pts 38
Amble United	P12	W10	D0	GD +28	Pts 30

Amble United remained a threat, but they hadn't kicked a ball in the league since Halloween and points in the bank are better than games in hand, or so we reflected as we celebrated the end of another successful month in the Cricket Club. And then the Tynemouth Lodge. And then the Maggie Bank. And then the Bell & Bucket. And then the Oddies. At closing time of another month, there was one, joyous, irrefutable truth to celebrate; we are top of the league!

December:
Christmas High Spirits

WHEN THE NORTHERN Alliance management committee emailed out the fixtures for this month, it seemed as if they had come over all Festive. With both Christmas Day and New Year's Day falling on Fridays, clubs could legitimately have expected games to be scheduled for Boxing Day, Bank Holiday Monday December 28th and Saturday January 2nd, as that was the case not just in the Premier League and Championship, but in the Northern League as well. Instead, the blue blazers and brass hats in charge decreed that the Alliance would be having a little mid-season break on those dates, although I'm not sure they realised just how long the break would be.

Advance information relating to January fixtures told us the Minor Cup round 4 was scheduled to take place on Saturday 9th and the Northern Alliance Pin Point Recruitment Combination Cup quarter finals, in which we had been drawn at home to Wallington, were scheduled for the 16th. Consequently, were we to progress past Wallsend Boys Club Seniors in the Minor Cup third round on December 5th, we'd be looking at a break from all league games between December 19th and January 23rd. If only we'd known what the weather had in store for us, we'd not have given these complexities a second thought.

However, all we at Percy Main could do was keep our side of the bargain by beating the snappily abbreviated WBCS on the first Saturday of the month, which we duly did 3-0. The good fortune we'd endured with the weather seemed to be running out when a heavy downpour from early evening Friday until mid Saturday morning made a pitch inspection necessary As we were in the midst of a run of five successive home games, not to mention the chance of two ladies matches also taking place on the 6th and 13th, it was unavoidable that the pitch was about to get more than a little churned up. Of course, a lousy surface and an unplayable one are two different things and a dry late morning meant that referee Ray Cushing was happy for the game to go ahead, which meant that the seventh and final freebie for Newcastle v Watford that I'd held on to for insurance purposes became surplus to requirements, thankfully.

As an aside, I have to say that the standard of refereeing in the Alliance this season was absolutely first class; in the shape of blokes like Ray Cushing, George Forshaw and the legendary Keith Scoffham, we had seen superbly consistent decision making, a desire to let the game flow and a sensible approach to discipline. At Percy Main, we had had two red cards by this point, for Graeme Smith versus Wallington and Mickey Haley versus Berwick United, but both of them were justified. The 22 yellow cards we'd collected were a worrying figure, but as two of them went to Dean Morgan, we weren't worried about him replicating 2008/09's impressive personal total of 15 bookings. Jon McEnaney is another serial caution collector, having accrued five so far, which was enough for him to miss a game through suspension. Presumably that's why he and his family had booked an executive box at St. James' Park for the Watford game.

Another player missing was Lindsay Collinson, who, after being unavailable through work commitments for most of the autumn, had slipped down the rankings in team selection to the extent he decided to try his luck at Division 2 Cramlington Blue Star. Good luck to the lad; he gave his best and never let us down, especially when crawling off his sick bed to help give us the bare eleven away at Hebburn Reyrolle in December 2008.

With the WBCS match being a cup game, kick off was at the earlier time of 1.30, so I arrived at the ground in expensive style, by taxi. My profligacy was in stark contrast to the frugal economics practised by the Main. As the tie had originally been scheduled to take place at St. Peter's Fields, it was still theoretically a Wallsend home game. Consequently, we provided neither programme nor post match buffet, or paid for the ref. We did charge a gate and open the canteen, which gave us a presentable income of £80 for zero outlay, so in combination with the events on the pitch, it was a decent day all round.

As so often this season, the lads showed in quite emphatic terms that they are a late-flowering team, with three unanswered goals in the second period as we made steady, untroubled progress into the last 16. While the margin of victory was an accurate, if perhaps slightly conservative, reflection of the balance of play, Wallsend Boys Club proved to be worthy, organised opponents, who acquitted themselves with credit by turning in a disciplined display. On this evidence, the Northern Alliance Division 2 must be a competitive league if they are not challenging for promotion. Mind, their keeper was hopeless like!

Jason gave Phil Hogg a start in our goal today, as has happened in other cup games this season, and Shaddy came in for the corporate hospitality abusing Jon McEnaney up front in the only changes from the side that had beaten Berwick United. It was perhaps a surprise that Shaddy was given the nod to partner Callum Colback up front ahead of the ever dangerous Joe Betts, but the powerful striker showed his mettle with some delightful flicks and lay offs, not to mention a slightly fortuitous goal, and was a worthy winner of the Man of the Match accolade.

Despite the authority over their opponents, Main were unable to find a breakthrough in the opening period. However, after 52 minutes the deadlock was broken with a simple goal. Jason's well-delivered corner was despatched by a textbook Colback header, which I didn't see as I was returning a collection of dirty soup mugs to the kitchen. I'm sure it was goal of the season.

With the wind in their sails, the Main built up a clear momentum. Wilka saw his close range effort flicked wide by keeper Holgate, who had earlier dropped a Jason cross almost on the line, but somehow recovered. The Boys' Club custodian saw things get appreciably worse for him when he fumbled a low cross cum shot from Shaddy, who had been almost on the dead ball line, into his net.

After this, the opposition's heads dropped and Main were able to close the game out, mainly through the vice-like grip exercised on the centre of midfield by Malky and especially the tireless, superb Chris Locke. Substitutes Chris Doig, Joe Betts and Liam Knox came on to press home Percy Main's advantage. Betts shot just wide, then Doig's speculative lob was a foot over the bar, before Liam Knox's brave stooping header from an excellent Betts cross put a comprehensive win to bed and provided a more realistic scoreline, though Chris Doig almost made it four in the last of seven minutes of stoppage time.

A good day at the office was made even better as we arrived back at Laura's to the news that Fabrice Pancrate had assured Newcastle's eighth home win with a late second that was apparently a Goal of the Season contender. Ben's subsequent text of 'Mint seats. Mint finish' put me in good fettle as we prepared to head out for Winstons' Christmas do. I love it when a plan comes together.

The pounding of my head on the Sunday morning after an evening of carousing reflected the pounding Purvis Park's pitch had taken the day before, so the ladies match was postponed. I used the free time to visit my mam so we could see my dad's headstone for the first time; a very fitting monument to the old fella it is too.

Thursday 10th saw a full meeting of all Alliance clubs at Blue Flames. As I was at work, I could not attend, but Norman was there and he came back with the fixtures and latest administrative edicts, including the fact that we had been drawn away for the fourth successive round in the Minor Cup. Our last 16 opponents were Shilbottle Colliery Welfare, currently lying third in the North Northumberland League. All I know of Shilbottle is that the sign at the entrance to the village is repeatedly defaced to read 'Shitbottle', which is probably all I need to know. The other alleged fixtures for the far distant future were our furthest distant trips to Berwick United on January 23rd and Northbank in Carlisle the following week (both of which ended up being played in May), but the only game we were worrying about was the imminent visit of Whitley Bay A on December 12th.

Almost unavoidably, the weather had been rough early in the week, but it dried out on a foggy Thursday and warmed up on a cloudy Friday. Unbelievably, Newcastle City Council called off all games on their pitches for that weekend. Hence Winstons' home cup game versus Steels SC was out the window. Ironically, at 10.30 Saturday, which should have been kick off time, it was an almost balmy eight degrees as a pale sun shone in a cloudless sky on a still morning; perfect football weather. Instead of moping, I used the time wisely by getting down to Purvis Park and preparing for what was a big, crunch game, which thankfully went our way, with almost ridiculous ease.

In front of the season's best crowd, who played their full part in creating a tinderbox atmosphere on a surprisingly mild day at Purvis Park, the lads, with their ninth straight home league victory, stretched their winning run to ten games in the Northern Alliance Division 1. As a result, we extended our lead at the top of the table to five points over an inactive Rutherford side that have a game in hand.

Whitley Bay A, who comprehensively defeated the Main 6-1 at Hillheads and 3-0 at Purvis Park within five days at the tail end of the 2008/2009 season, had two former Villagers players in Dean Porter and Ian Lee, a Main scorer at Seaton Burn back in September, in their ranks, though there was no sign of their other former Villager, Ian Graham. Similarly, Percy Main included former Seahorse Callum Colback, and it was the nippy, cultured Main striker who had cause to take much more satisfaction from today's game, scoring the second goal in his side's comprehensive 4-2 win, than the combative Lee, who saw red for an unnecessary and petulant elbow on Main left back Graeme Smith midway through the second period.

For so much of this season, Percy Main have been the comeback kings, building their impressive run on a series of fine second half fightbacks.

Today, for a change, the Villagers were quick out of the blocks, roaring into a two-goal lead in the opening fifteen minutes. After a tremendously feisty opening on a soft pitch, that had seen Maccas yellow carded after being forced to use all his guile and wits to evade the unwelcome attentions of several muscular challenges launched on him by Bay defenders, the Main striker gave the home side the lead by bundling home a flighted Jason Ritchie free kick from the six yard line. Seconds later Bay were almost level, but Rob produced a tremendous block from Dean Porter, who had streaked through the home defence.

The importance of this save was reinforced within moments when Callum Colback's beautifully judged back header looped over an out of position Chris Compson to give Main a 2-0 lead. Maccas nearly made it three after 15 minutes, but a desperate last-ditch challenge kept the game alive as a contest. Ian Lee almost got his side back into it, but his well judged lob dropped inches wide of the far post, much to Rob's relief. He was unable to stop Dean Porter halving the deficit with a low, stooping header that went in off the post.

A setback such as this could have put a lesser team off their guard, but not Percy Main. Jason grabbed his third assist of the half, when his excellent corner was headed home by Maccas through the keeper's hands, giving the home side a comfortable 3-1 half time lead, which was an adequate reflection of the balance of play.

In the second half, Bay briefly threatened when Porter's first time effort from the edge of the box hit the outside of the post and bounced to safety.

Main almost went 4-1 ahead on the hour when Jason's dipping 25-yard effort from the angle just cleared the bar. Five minutes later, the game was seemingly sealed for the home side when Lee's momentary indiscretion saw him sent from the field of play. The sending off caused raised hackles on the sidelines as things turned decidedly ugly. A furious Lee kicked out at the dressing room door, bringing Bob Rodgerson in to the action as he went to unlock the changing room. A snarling confrontation saw Lee seemingly attempt to headbutt Bob, until Norman stepped in to calm the situation down before the referee belatedly got involved, doling out a sombre and shallow lecture to all in earshot. Having previously praised the standard of Alliance referees, it was sad to see a weak and arrogant official, who, despite being assessed during this match, doing very little right all game. Indeed, you could tell it was nearly Christmas the way he kept handing cards out to everyone. Ian Lee's belligerent mother threatened to have Bob done for assault, the disgraced Bay striker told her to fuck off and so she clouted her 6ft 13 stone bairn across the lug before the game started again.

A glorious finish sealed things in the Main's favour, Shaddy stroking home a loose ball from well outside the box to maintain his record of spectacular finishes. In injury time, Whitley Bay's Joe Riley stabbed home a loose ball in controversial circumstances, with the home defence standing still after the ball appeared to have been pulled back from approximately two feet over the dead ball line. Obviously referee Whitfield was so sure of himself he found no need to consult with Geordie, who had raised his flag when the ball went out. Frankly, the 4-2 score line did not do justice to the home side's utter dominance for most of the game. What a fabulous result!

An even better one was the ladies beating Prudhoe 7-1 the next day, when the Alliance informed us, for no apparently discernible reason, the next weekend's fixtures had been changed, giving us not Cullercoats but Peterlee at home. Of course, a deluge of snow on the Thursday 17th, which settled, froze and remained until the middle of January, meant there was absolutely no chance of any games being played for the foreseeable future.

However, never let it be said that Percy Main Amateurs do not know how to let off steam occasioned by the frustration of a postponed match. On Saturday 19th, both teams and the committee assembled in the Cricket Club for the Christmas Bash; the blokes all drinking ***WKD*** and ***Smirnoff Ice***, while the lasses ploughed through pints of lager. It was a genuinely affectionate and uplifting evening. Neither team had won anything yet, but the half-term report card showed straight As for effort and achievement right across the board. At ten o'clock a series of taxis took them up to town; men first, naturally enough. The team spirit was demonstrated as the final carload of ladies arrived at some Quayside taverna to see half the blokes being slung out for fighting. That's my boys! Of course, Bob, Norman and I stayed in the Cricket club until closing time; we're far too old for such high jinks. Also, none of us own an expensive enough piece of cashmere knitwear to fit in with the lads.

The next day, I grabbed my weekend football fix with a freebie at St. James' Park to see Newcastle sleepwalk past an abject, terrible Middlesbrough by 2-0. I thoroughly enjoyed this, not just because Newcastle won, but also because I have a dislike for Boro that has nothing to do with their supposed geographical proximity. I'm not one of those traditionalists who calls for a return to the early 80s bear pit atmosphere and squalid conditions of English football grounds, but neither am I tolerant of the foam-handed, face-painted, replica-shirted, deliberately wacky Sky Sports influenced, post 1992 approach to our national game. Middlesbrough, having provided some of my most terrifying experiences as an away fan in the 80s when trying to get out of Ayresome Park alive, have now embraced the fancy dress approach to fandom and I loathe them for it. I also hate Everton (aka the Scouse Mackems) because I got kneed in the bollocks by a copper outside the Park End in February 85 before we lost 4-0, but I don't know any Toffees fans, whereas Andy is a lifelong Smogs supporter.

My motto is always 'gracious in victory; dignified in defeat', which is why I didn't say anything about the game when we all met at the football club on Sunday 20th evening to make the Christmas bottle draw. However, I did engineer things when I made everyone a hot drink, which went with the tremendous chocolate cake Laura had made Norman for his birthday, to serve Andy his coffee in a *Newcastle United's Number 1 Supporter* mug. It got a laugh, but I also got a round of applause for selling £170 worth of tickets. I didn't win a drop, but I felt a sense of real achievement when we totalled up to discover we'd made £600 profit for the club, which was more than double the year before. Successful players and a hard-working committee; Percy Main Amateurs ended 2009 in fine style on the pitch and in good shape off it.

January:
The Bleak Midwinter

ANY PERCY MAIN supporters waking up late on New Year's Morning with a thick head and a furry tongue would have had their hangovers quickly cured by a glimpse at the Northern Alliance Division 1 league table. It certainly made for enjoyable reading :

Percy Main	P16	W14	D1	GD +22	Pts 43
Rutherford	P15	W12	D2	GD +27	Pts 38
Amble United	P13	W10	D1	GD +28	Pts 31
Morpeth SC	P13	W8	D1	GD +1	Pts 25

Even better, the table didn't change all month. The snow and ice that came in on December 15th to decimate the pre-Christmas programme stayed to ruin the New Year's card, then got progressively worse until January 15th, when it rapidly melted and waterlogged the pitches that had first been frozen and subsequently snowbound, before making an unpleasant return at the end of the month, causing us to wake on Saturday 30th to yet another blanket of snow across the region.

In every section of the media, breathless, hysterical references were made to the winters of 47/48 and 62/63; I wasn't alive for either of those, but it certainly had an element of 78/79 or 86/87 about it. However, my experiences of those years paled in to insignificance when compared to the two punishing winters I spent in Bratislava; the difference being that in Eastern Europe, people are geared up for the predictable cold spell in January. Society doesn't grind to a halt, sleet doesn't make the front pages, schools and offices don't close (unlike the two day jolly I had on January 7th and 8th) and football has a defined winter break from the end of November to the start of March, which may be terrible but at least it's timetabled.

The Shilbottle game didn't go ahead on January 9th, so it was put back until January 16th, as county football association competitions always take precedence in the FA's eyes over league commitments, meaning the Wallington divisional cup tie was postponed (though the draw was still made for the next round, presenting the eventual victors with a home semi-final tie with Berwick or Shields United). Of course, the rearranged Shilbottle fixture didn't go ahead on the 16th either.

While the football came to a halt, the bureaucracy rumbled on. All disciplinary matters, in terms of suspensions and fines, are handled not by the Northern Alliance, but by the Northumberland FA, who post regular bulletins naming and shaming miscreants. The missive that arrived in the first week of January indicated that Ian Lee of Whitley Bay had received a seven-day ban for his dismissal at Purvis Park. Unfortunately, arriving simultaneously under separate cover was another letter, charging Bob with bringing the game in to disrepute during the same bare-knuckle encounter.

In many ways, the football disciplinary process is contrary to the principles of English Common Law and an embodiment of the concept of presumed guilt, whereby appeals procedures cost money, take time and are almost always fruitless. The underlying philosophy behind this, which is one I have to say I subscribe to, is that referees should have the final say and their word is consequently law. Winstons had two bookings in a game away in Sunderland in November, one of which was a case of mistaken identity, but we accepted the £8 fine for it rather than shelling out £30 for an appeal hearing, as the cost outweighed the principle. However, the charge against Bob, when it was all Ian Lee's fault, stuck in the craw. Norman penned a poignant and pertinent letter of explanatory mitigation and we crossed our fingers in hope.

While we waited for a reply to his heartfelt missive, the situation on the pitch was affected by the competition rules of the Northumberland Minor Cup, which state that after two postponements, home advantage in any tie should be ceded, meaning that we were facing the prospect of hosting Shilbottle on January 23rd rather than making a long trip to Berwick. As it was now our home game, unlike the Wallsend game, according to some procedural nuance whose explanation eluded me, we had to pay the referee, put on the bait, prepare the programme, open the canteen, then hope enough punters showed up to help us break even.

During our enforced inactivity, some games did get the nod, so I took the opportunity to watch a bit football: Newcastle 3 Plymouth Argyle 0 in an FA Cup replay, the frankly awful North Shields 1 Washington 0, Whitley Bay 3 Poole Town 1 in a barnstorming FA Vase tie and Team Northumbria 1 North Shields 2, simply because it was almost on my doorstep. None of them stirred the blood in quite the way the Villagers do, although it might have been something to do with temperatures barely rising above freezing at each game. Perhaps the most enjoyable moment in all those games was hearing North Shields supporters at Team Northumbria being a tad harshly described as "stupid, pathetic, thick tramps" for singing songs in praise of their Chairman.

Norman came to the Whitley Bay game, but used the rest of his snowbound spare time to get some reading done. Newcastle United club historian Paul Joannou, in collaboration with Alan Candlish, a regular contributor to Newcastle fanzine ***The Mag***, had co-authored a fascinating history of Victorian and Edwardian football in the region entitled ***Pioneers of the North***, which mentioned in an aside that Percy Main Cricket Club had been formed in 1860 and that many local cricket clubs were keen to take up football to give them something to do in the winter.

As time has gone on, the official 1919 formation date of Percy Main Amateurs has been proved anecdotally, not least by the photo of the 1913 squad in the Clubhouse, to be wrong. Hence, the current semi-official position is that we were reformed in 1919. Norman contacted Alan Candlish to see if he could help shed any light on the Villagers' dream time, but the only information he had for us was that one of Newcastle's most celebrated pre-WWI players, Jock Rutherford, had played for the Main between 1897 and 1900.

Born in Percy Main on October 12th 1884, John "Jock" Rutherford played for the Percy Main club, perhaps as a junior, until signing for what was then one of the football forces in the area, Willington Athletic. From there, Rutherford transferred to St James' Park for the huge sum of £75 in 1902. He went on to represent The Magpies for the next 11 years, winning Football League Division 1 Championship medals in 1905, 1907 and 1909, as well an FA Cup winner's medal in 1910. He also collected FA Cup runners up medals in 1905, 1906, 1908 and 1911, as Newcastle suffered what was known in Edwardian times as their 'Crystal Palace hoodoo', failing to win in any of their five final appearances at that venue.

As an outside right, known as *the Newcastle flyer* and one of only three Englishmen in the side, he scored the crucial equalising goal with a header eight minutes from time in the 1910 Cup Final against Barnsley in the only match at Crystal Palace where the team in black and white avoided defeat. Newcastle went on to win the replay 2-0 at Goodison Park to claim the FA Cup for the first time.

Rutherford signed for Woolwich Arsenal for £800 in 1913 after a fall out at St James' over wages, proving that there's nothing new under the sun on Barrack Road. Jock fought in the First World War for four years, returning home thankfully unscathed to resume his football career, and played his last game for The Gunners on March 20th 1926 at the age of 42. To this day, he remains the oldest player to have ever represented Arsenal. Incredibly, Rutherford played another nine games for Clapton Orient the following season

In total Jock, or Jackie as he was sometimes known, played a total of 600 top flight games, despite the intervention of hostilities, and represented England 11 times, scoring three.goals. He died on April 21st 1963 aged 78.

Will the current squad ever achieve such greatness or longevity? Considering they opted not to train on the beach on any of the spare Saturdays as it was, in Jason's words, "too cold" that seems unlikely. However, the return to the fold of Lee Gray from North Shields and last season's Young Player of the Year, Pierre Luc Coiffait, following a spell working in London, could only be good news, which was only minimally offset by the departure of Kriss Carr to Newcastle East End. All we needed was the chance to get out on the pitch and play some football.

Finally, the weather relented and, despite a few misgivings about soft patches that would cut up badly, the Shilbottle game got the go ahead for Saturday 23rd. Having played three games to reach the fourth round, while being drawn away on all four occasions, this was our second home game in this competition, following two postponements and three pre-match inspections. The game itself was considerably less complex than our route to this stage and our 3-0 winning margin could easily have been doubled, if not trebled.

Despite the all too apparent gulf in class between the teams, it should be noted that Shilbottle put in a tremendously praiseworthy performance, especially keeper Chris Murray, who excelled himself with a number of superbly agile diving stops, spirited, tenacious defender Alex Markin and tireless, effective front man David Hubbard, who all put in displays of which they can be justifiably proud.

That said, the Main were always in control in this game; in the 28 minutes leading up to Jason's opener, the Shilbottle goal lead a charmed life as wave after wave of Main attacks came down the left hand side, mainly prompted by Ritchie. The Villagers' outside left delivered innumerable quality deliveries from the left flank, only for a succession of brave Shilbottle interventions to stop Cal, Malky and Shaddy (on for early injury victim Jon McEnaney) from opening the scoring. Colback's ability to dive underneath one low cross when faced with an open goal inside the six-yard box showed a level of agility that suggested limbo dancing could be a sport of choice for him if he ever tires of football.

The deadlock was broken just shy of the half hour when Jason stroked home a penalty with consummate ease following a handling offence in the Shilbottle back line. The penalty was well taken, but the header that followed it to make the half time score 2-0 was a work of sublime football artistry. Shaddy's measured cross from the right was delightfully powered home by Jason from the edge of the box for one of the best goals seen all season at Purvis Park.

The second period saw the Main in utter control, with the only surprise being that Shaddy's tap-in, following keeper Murray's parry from a Colback effort, was the only reward the home side had for absolute domination. In the opening period the Villagers exploited the left flank to good effect, but after the break attacks came from all parts of the pitch, with midfield duo Morien and Chris Locke relishing the chance to roll their sleeves up and graft for their team. Out wide, substitute Chris Doig produced a superb cameo of beguiling artistry as the Main displayed enough quality to leave visitors Shilbottle on the ropes, and it was great to see Lee Gray back in Percy Main colours following his period with North Shields.

To be fair, the visitors were a credit to their league and Rob had twice to be alert to handle speculative efforts of pace and power from the impressive Hubbard. However, the undoubted class of the home side told in the final analysis as Percy Main progressed to the quarter finals. Even more importantly, I won the post match raffle of a case of ***Stella***, which tasted very good but had a pronounced affect on my balance.

In need of fresh air to blow the cobwebs away on the Sunday, I took in the Ladies' friendly with Newcastle United Women's Reserves. Following the resignation of the hapless Medicals side that we'd battered 19-0 from the Northumberland Premier Division, the Magpies second string have picked up the slack by entertaining the resulting 'spare' team each weekend. The game was played on the 4G astroturf at the Coach Lane Campus of Northumbria University, which was good in one way as it meant the match definitely could go ahead, but bad in another as we could have made a quite few quid at the snack bar out of the crowd of about 50.

On the day, Percy Main Women learned a tough lesson in finishing, but acquitted themselves nobly in going down to a 9-0 defeat. Sadly, it coincided with Rob Meldrum's return to joint managerial duties after his period travelling round New Zealand, which may have persuaded him to return to Christchurch post haste. I left on the hour at 8-0 as we had a committee meeting down at the Club and knew my bike wasn't as fast as other people's cars. I still made it back before Norman, Rob and Aidan, who were probably scared to show their faces in case they received a vote of confidence over that day's result!

This was the first meeting we'd had of the full committee since August, but there wasn't a huge amount to talk about. Matters on the pitch were easy to deal with; top of the league in both divisions meant that there was little to discuss. Off the pitch, the increased crowds and superb catering products on offer meant that we were actually making money at each home game rather than losing it; demonstrable progress indeed. Obviously there were a number of administrative matters to deal with: Bob's appeal hearing had been scheduled for February 9th, when Norman would be pleading in mitigation and the future fixtures were discussed. The complexities of these equations kept us sat shivering round a table until nigh on 8pm, proving yet again that Northern Alliance football is full of glamour.

The lousy weather meant that not only had there not been an Alliance Division 1 game since December 12th, but that any planning of future fixtures was fraught with difficulty. Initially, we believed we'd be travelling to Northbank for a league game on the last Saturday of the month, but Carlisle City Council had nixed this option by declaring the Sheepmount pitch out of bounds until mid February because of the harm the snow had caused. We then thought we'd be hosting Amble United on that date in a league game, but their Minor Cup tie at Berwick took precedence, so we were then presented with an away game at Chopwell Officials Club. Of course, that didn't happen because of the overnight snow that did for all the fixtures that day, as well as the women's game at Tynedale on the Sunday.

Instead, we had another Percy Main Amateurs committee pub trip to see Leicester v Newcastle live on Sky on the Saturday night. It was a 0-0 draw and the commentary was drowned out by a Ska cover versions band soundchecking in the lounge. Still, it was nice to see everyone.

February:
Missing (In)Action

FOOTBALL ADMINISTRATION AT Step 7 of the non-league pyramid is a thankless task, but one that often attracts a certain kind of volunteer, pettifogging egomaniacs whose personality appears to be an unhappy collision of George C. Scott in ***Patton: Lust For Glory*** and Dustin Hoffman in ***Rain Man***. Happily, the Northern Alliance's fixture secretary, George Davision from Shankhouse, is not one of those sorts; he's a genuinely warm and witty bloke who is engaging company and loves his football. However, even he must have been starting to reach saturation point with both the relentless, harsh weather and the arcane deliberations of the Northumberland FA when attempting to compile the card for Saturday 6th February. No sooner had he sent out a tentative fixture list that gave us a home game with Bohemians than the NFA announced the Minor Cup draw. Predictably, we were presented with our fifth successive away tie, this time to Division 2 side Amble on the same date.

With two inches of snow on the ground on Tuesday, freezing temperatures forecast for Wednesday and Thursday and rain scheduled Friday, it seemed unlikely the game would take place. Sure enough, an early afternoon text from Norman on Friday 5th told of its postponement and rearrangement for the following weekend, meaning the Peterlee home game timetabled for February 13th was a non-starter.

Amble informed us that they'd moved pitches from Coquet High School, scene of our 5-0 trouncing by their neighbours Amble United back in August, to the ground formally home to Red Row Welfare (where we won 4-0 last season), who have changed their name to Morpeth Sporting Club and are playing at Morpeth Town's former Northern League home, Craik Park, while the owners groundshare with Bedlington Terriers. All well and good: Alliance teams, many of whom have little or no history to compromise and are solely concerned with players and not supporters, often swap home grounds if they can get better facilities cheaper elsewhere. South Shields United, formed in 2007, went from Chuter Ede to Quarry Lane and in August 2010 will be at the former home of the now defunct Harton and Westoe, while Chemfica, dating all the way back to 2005, seem to oscillate between Heaton Sports Ground and Benfield School, depending on competition or climactic conditions. The only trouble with Amble's arrangement is that they, as the newcomers, have to play second fiddle to the real leaseholders, Red Row Brick Club Sunday team, who get the final say so as to whether anyone else plays on their pitch. The rain forecast for Friday 5th February forced their hand.

Left at a loose end, Laura, Norman and I took in parts of Chemfica Independent Development's Newcastle Corinthian League mud wrestling bout with Philosophers' United that ended 5-1, before stepping in to Sam Smith's Park for an altogether more satisfying encounter as Benfield thumped Horden 3-0 in the Northern League, joined by three generations of Rodgerson, in the shape of Rob the keeper, Bob the treasurer and Norman the patriarch. While the game was a good one, conversation repeatedly turned to Bob's imminent disciplinary hearing in front of the Northumberland FA on the Tuesday to discuss the Ian Lee confrontation during the Whitley Bay A game.

We were pessimistic as to his chances, but Norman must have an element of the Perry Mason about him, as the letter he'd written that acted as Bob's plea for mitigation worked like a charm. Bob was found guilty, but other than a mild admonishment, no punishment was levied. Effectively this was an absolute discharge and a vindication of Bob's conduct, not to mention saving him from paying the standard hundred quid fine. Quite what the supercilious referee made of the verdict is a matter for speculation. With a bit of luck he'll have looked upon this as a chance to learn from his mistakes and apply common sense to his refereeing skills in future.

Unfortunately, he wasn't able to use them when determining the playability of Amble's pitch on Friday 12th February, as it was, unbelievably, called off again. When it is a home game that suffers a postponement, at least you have the consolation of first-hand knowledge of just how bad the pitch is. If it is an away game, then such epistemological evidence is often lacking. Obviously, when there's eight inches of snow on the ground or a frost so thick that you'd be better off ice skating on it than trying to play football, there is no doubt as to the legitimacy of the call-off. Problems rear their heads when the actual day of the game is bright and sunny and games are taking place elsewhere. Natural cynicism and a finely-honed bullshit detector go into overdrive and you start to suspect that we've been left kicking our heels because half the opposition are at a stag do in Manchester, or because their star striker has to work a double shift that day. Sometimes the problems aren't as fundamental as those two scenarios, but often just as intractable. There were last minute hopes of a potential switch to Warkworth, but nothing came of it and the tie transferred to Percy Main for February 20th, meaning the Wallington Combination Cup quarter final was required to sit out this number.

At that point, there was still a minimum of 16 games to go until the end of the season, with a maximum of 15 Saturdays until the last possible date of the season, so the loss of a fixture on February 13th was paradoxically seen at the time as something of a relief. For a start, neither Norman (accompanying his daughter to Nottingham University Open Day) nor I (conceding half a dozen in the Over 40s League at Esh Winning) could have been there, meaning that admin tasks would have to have been shared round. At least we'd found a stand in match report writer, as Cola's brother Jon had volunteered to step up to the plate; his time will surely come.

To keep our legions of fans up to date with all the exciting postponements, I mean events, emanating from Purvis Park, I opened a Percy Main Twitter account, whereby news from the club could be relayed in the 140-character microblogging format so beloved of the young and tragically trendy. Within days, Norman, Laura, Cola and his brother signed up and comprised our entire total of followers. It's still in use. Get yourself to http://twitter.com/PercyMainFC and sign up, though the entries for February 2010 had a mild air of repetition to them:

> Amble v Percy Main Saturday 6th February POSTPONED 11:33 PM Feb 5th via web

> Amble v Percy match off 2morro, try again nxt Sat at our place 2:28 AM Feb 12th via txt

Now, we've already alluded to those two call-offs, and the Shilbottle experience had previously told us the game now had to be switched to Purvis Park, but things just didn't get any better.

On Friday 19th, Laura and I went to see Billy Bragg at the Tyneside Cinema in Newcastle. While the week leading up to this could not have been described as temperate, the weather had been nothing out of the ordinary, so a confident Norman had assured us the NFA Minor Cup game would finally be taking place the next day. Andy had printed the programmes and we'd got the bits of shopping required for the canteen in. It was thus a shock to find a thick carpet of snow, similar to that which had fallen while we'd slept on Friday 30th January, had returned while we had been watching the former bard of Barking, whose defection to the Liberal Democrats makes him Baron Bridport in my eyes. Repeated snow flurries overnight meant we woke up to brilliant sunshine, white pavements and gardens, as well as an inevitable text from Bob to say the game was off, resulting in a predictable Tweet:

Percy Main v Amble NFA Minor Cup POSTPONED for third time. We try again next week at Purvis Park Sat 27/02/10 with 1.30pm kick off 1:16 AM Feb 20th via web

In point of fact, almost every Northern League game and a good few Alliance fixtures took place on Tyneside that day (including Rutherford chipping away at our lead by besting Peterlee 3-2), as the clear sunshine and relatively warm temperatures melted the snow. Our particular problem had been the competition rule that stated we had to kick off at 1.30; if it had been a 2.30 start, as all Alliance league games had reverted to as the days lengthen, there was a good chance we could have played. On the Sunday, the women did play, drawing 2-2 away to Durham City on a pitch right next door to the Riverside in Chester Le Street.

As regards our Amble game, all we could do was hope for decent weather and that no one noticed the wrong date on the programme cover. Unfortunately, the lousy weather wasn't just playing havoc with our fixtures; the incessant wet weather was making the pavilion roof even more porous as new leaks sprung up on a daily basis. We obviously didn't have the resources to replace it, so Norman had gone cap in hand to the ***cash4clubs*** scheme administered by ***Betfair*** in the vain hope of a handout. Typically enough, on the day the snow disappeared and temperatures rose, two unpleasant arrivals made their presence known. Firstly, torrential rain became constant across the north east and, secondly, Dame Kelly Holmes, Tim Lawler CEO of Sports Aid, Ben Clissitt, sports journalist, and James Radford, Head of Growth at Sport England, regretfully informed us that in this instance our club had not been successful, but they did wish us every success for the future. Thanks, it really meant a lot to us.

In a way, I saw their point. After all, we were a football club that didn't seem to play any football. With three quarters of the pitch covered by standing water and the rest a bog, Friday's postponement that meant we had gone through the whole of February without kicking a ball was a polite rubber-stamping of all we knew was inevitable.

The NFA now insisted the game moved back to Amble. With no end in sight to the punishing winter, the only viable solution was to book an astroturf pitch and share the costs, so we did :

> Percy v Amble OFF, game will now be played next Sat, March 6th 1pm at Hirst Welfare, Ashington on 3G about 8 hours ago via txt

Obviously, this meant our squad have been denied the chance to play football for a whole month, meaning their fitness levels were in danger of dropping. At least some of them tried to keep on top of this by involving themselves in other sports; for example Maccas, nicknamed "the cage fighter", had a Mixed Martial Arts K1 contest at Newbiggin Leisure Centre on Thursday 25th February. He'd taken his preparations seriously for this, getting in plenty of practice both on the football pitch and in Lineker's Bar during the Christmas night out. Sadly, his Facebook status told us he'd come up short in this bizarre interpretation of the noble art; *Thanx 2 every 1 4 there support 2 nite, soz 4 the let dwn.*

On a more serious note, Craig "Ziggy" Ewart, who'd not played since injuring his knee against Amble United in a League Cup game on September 12th, went into hospital for an operation the day Macca was showcasing his pugilistic skills. The hope that he would one day play for Percy Main Amateurs again was also extended to the rest of the squad.

March:
In our Cups

THE MONTH BEGAN on a Monday, which is always an unpromising day on which to start for those of us still insistent on Hunter S Thompson style weekends in our mid 40s. However, the booking of the astroturf pitch at Hirst Welfare in Ashington for the Amble cup tie at least assured us of a game to look forward to at the weekend. In some kind of cosmic, karmic coincidence, this reservation also assured us of enough favourable weather to suggest Winter was finally ending; there were still overnight frosts, but the snow and rain abated, leaving glorious sunshine and a stiff breeze that started to repair the ravages of three months of climactic torture. If the Amble game had been scheduled for Purvis Park, there's no doubting it would have been on.

Typically enough, the 1pm kick off time meant I was unable to get up there and see our first game in five weeks, as I had to play in the morning and stand in as secretary for Winstons. While that was great fun, as we won 7-2, I did feel slight pangs of guilt when Geordie, who was fresh off the pitch for his Over 40s side, phoned to ask if I wanted a lift up to Hirst so we could see the second half. Unfortunately, I was knee deep in paperwork and a high trans fat buffet in ***The Corner House***, so I was unable to avail myself of this kind offer and instead relied on Norman's text updates to keep me appraised. If only there had been a Percy Main ***Twitter*** feed to rely on.

The first message came within five minutes of kick off and told of us taking the lead through Malky. This solid opening perked me up and I slipped off home to wash my kit and decide on what game to attend. Newcastle were at home to Barnsley, but I didn't have a free ticket and wasn't minded towards lashing out £20 on that lot, so Benfield hosting South Shields seemed the favourite, until a scan of the Northern Alliance fixtures revealed Newcastle Chemfica Independent were at home to Ponteland United in the Stan Seymour League Cup.

At that point, second division Chemfica were the only side through to the NFA Minor Cup semi finals and so I could combine a visit to a new ground almost on my doorstep (Chemfica play at Cartington Terrace in Heaton) with potential scouting for the Main, which would assuage my conscience for knocking back a lift to see the lads in action. I hopped on the bike and whizzed down, stopping near the entrance to the Newcastle University Medicals Sports Ground to check a text that had just been delivered. It was semi-bad news; we were still a goal up, but Callum Colback had been sent off for what the referee claimed was a two-footed tackle, though Norman, a scrupulously fair observer regardless of his affiliations, felt it was a harsh punishment. Simultaneously, Chemfica took the lead with a goal in what must have been the first 30 seconds of play. Oh dear, it seemed as if my plan to spy on potential opponents may have been an overly ambitious one, and not because I'd missed the kick off at Chemfica. Despite being a goal up, a second half against a useful Amble side, including tricky former Main striker Wyn Fremlin, would be a stiff test.

Luckily, class won out everywhere that day; Ponteland came from behind to win 3-1 and put Chemfica out, meaning I was able to cycle down to Benfield and catch the second half of a comfortable 2-0 win, while being regularly updated on Newcastle's 6-1 crushing of Barnsley. Most importantly, texts from Norman telling me *2-0 Maccas 69* and *3-0*

Malky 82 allowed me to breathe easily and subsequently drink deeply all around Shields.

Sunday was glorious: the best weather of the year so far. While FA Cup Sixth Round games dominated the television schedules and football supplements, there was the important matter of the Women's team versus Forest Hall, who had knocked us out of the County Cup at home before Christmas, in the League Cup to consider. Thankfully, there were no such slip ups today and, despite the worst machinations of an appallingly corrupt Forest Hall linesman, we cantered home 5-1, putting in the best performance of the season so far.

The weekend got even better late Sunday night when I checked the various websites relating to the Alliance; not only had Rutherford lost 4-2 at home to Reyrolle, meaning we were still top now with a game in hand on them, but the NFA had been quick out the blocks with the Minor Cup draw. The two quarter finals still to be resolved pitted Morpeth SC with Blyth Town Reserves and Gosforth Bohemians Garnett Reserves with Stobswood, with the two winners playing each other. This meant Percy Main had drawn Chemfica, at Purvis Park on March 20th, so my pretend scouting mission had not been in vain.

Following months of impotently cursing the weather, it was borderline surreal to spend a week almost bathing in the pale sunlight and warm days that indicated the arrival of spring. Acres of newsprint and hours of inane talk show psychobabble were devoted to the absence of daffodils, but the regular occurrence of football games acted as my personal phenomenological signifier that the seasons had turned even before the vernal equinox. It was still a little disconcerting when it pissed down on the Friday before the Wallington Combination Cup quarter final. However, dry conditions prevailed from early evening and the game was never in doubt.

Laura had decided upon thematic catering for this one; as it was a cup game, she baked some cup cakes, in male and female varieties. The male ones featured an iced approximation of the Percy Main lion in claret and blue; while the female ones were fancified with cherries and chocolate, as a Mothers' Day treat. All well and good, until culinary gender lines were blurred by Norman piling in to the female cakes and demolishing a couple in five seconds flat. Personally, I made short work of the lentil and bacon soup with complementary sunflower seed wholemeal bread. You don't get that sort of quality for 80p anywhere else in the non-league world. Those of you paying over three quid for a mass-produced pie at Premiership grounds don't know what you're missing, you really don't.

What we were missing, in the first half at least, was coherent play and fluent passing as a woeful opening period saw us going in a goal down to a sprightly Wallington side belying their lowly league position, and looking very unlikely to turn things round. Thankfully, the ability to find victory in unlikely circumstances had not deserted us as we eventually prevailed by the unlikely and enormously flattering margin of 4-1, after extra time. Make no mistake, we endured a thorough examination of our mettle by a plucky Wallington team, who pushed us almost the entire way, before running out of steam as months of inaction finally took their toll on heavy legs.

Whilst the previous week's performance against Amble had apparently shown no signs of ring rustiness after the lengthy weather influenced winter break, there was a certain lack of sharpness and cutting edge in this contest, despite an early flurry of action in the Wallington box.

However, this encouraging start counted for nothing when Chris Locke was adjudged to have brought down Wallington's Josh Gilmartin in the box. It seemed a clear-cut decision from the sidelines, but the player, normally so respectful and accepting of referees' decisions, was adamant he hadn't touched the man, but to no consequence. The kick was given and Nathan Williamson sent Rob the wrong way to give the visitors a lead they held until half time as Percy Main's game fell apart amid predictable, rancorous acrimony and dissent, with only Malky's late strike that the Wallington keeper Chris Straker desperately just shovelled round the post, at the end where a personal nightmare lay in store for the tall stopper only an hour hence, to show we were still in the contest.

It was a very different, more determined, Main who emerged for the second half. Within three minutes Lee Gray had pulled the Villagers level with a smart shot following a great pull-back from Cal Colback. However, things were still nip and tuck and a mix-up in the home area gave lanky Wallington striker Dave Featherstone a chance to restore the visitors' advantage, but he could only shoot weakly into Rob Rodgerson's arms.

The tie began to inexorably swing in the home side's favour with the introduction of the pugilistic McEnaney on the hour mark. Same as against Amble last week, he came off the bench to score a goal and shove the opposition defenders all around the place. However, these strikes (goals I mean!) would not come until extra time as the Wallington goal led something of a charmed life, with chances being squandered by Maccas, Shaddy and Cal as we started to dominate.

In extra time, Wallington keeper Straker distinguished himself with three stunning blocks from Maccas and a good save from Mickey Haley. Sadly, the game turned away from Wallington when Straker fumbled a trundling long-distance effort from McEnaney into the net and with this, Wallington heads went down. It was a terrible mistake; awful, horrific, humiliating. The slow, bobbling ball barely appeared to have the strength to reach the keeper, who unaccountably dived over and across the shot that crept timidly across the line. Immediately it did so, five or six Wallington players hit the turf and the rest gazed heavenwards in anguished despair. One simple error had lost them the game, and they knew it.

In the academic second half of extra time, Wallington failed to get hold of the ball for more than ten seconds at a time. Subsequent headers from Maccas and Malky made for an emphatic scoreline that was unfair on a battling Wallington, who had matched the Main. If it had been a league game, they would have been worthy of a point. As it wasn't, the Main advanced to the semi finals to host Berwick United.

Sadly, there had been an ominous shadow cast over the game. Long-serving Northern Alliance Chairman George Dobbins passed away on the Friday evening after a heart attack. The League Management Committee asked his family if they'd like all games postponed as a mark of respect, but they felt that George would have wanted the matches played, which they were, prefaced by an immaculately observed minute's silence.

Following our victory over Wallington, the Combination Cup semi final was scheduled for March 27th, which meant there would be a gap of 112 days between our last league game at home to Whitley Bay A on December 12th and the next one on April 3rd, with the result that we would have 14 league games to fit in after the clocks had gone forward. Ouch! No such problems for the women, who drew 0-0 away to Tynedale on Sunday 14th, meaning they had only two league games remaining.

Despite the death of George Dobbins, the Alliance's administrative machinery ground on and Monday saw us presented with nine league fixtures for April, five at home and four away, meaning we would be occupied every Saturday and Wednesday and a Monday on top of that. As well as that, notice came through that the East Northumberland Youth League wanted to book Purvis Park for all their finals, from Under 11 to Under 17, between April15th and May 13th on Tuesday and Thursday nights. The money generated from pitch hire, at the snack bar and on the gate from these games was simply too good to turn down, but an extra seven games, not to mention the four finals for the Newcastle Central Sunday Afternoon League that were yet to be confirmed, left us looking at a potential 21 more games in all competitions at Purvis Park. No wonder Norman called a committee meeting for Sunday March 21st to discuss this. However, before then there were the minor matters of the NFA Minor Cup semi final at home to Chemfica on the Saturday and the women away to North Shields on the Sunday afternoon.

This is not the place for lame attempts at creating suspense; we won them both! I'd not expected Chemfica to trouble us on the evidence of my low-key secret scouting mission when they'd played Ponteland. Decent outfit, plucky and well organised, but utterly lacking in the striking department. All we had to do, on a heavy pitch that cut up badly as a result of prolonged rain on the Friday night, was score and we'd almost certainly win. We managed to do just that.

In front of a healthy, enthusiastic crowd at Purvis Park, we booked our place in the NFA Minor Cup final by defeating Newcastle Chemfica Independent 2-0. While the second division side gave a good account of themselves and played some attractive, eye-catching football, their horizons were limited by a game plan seemingly devoted to containment, valuing possession and ball retention over attacking flair, leaving Rob

Rodgerson somewhat underemployed with most of his touches coming with his feet, fielding backpasses from team mates. Indeed, it was not until the 83rd minute before Chemfica tested him with their only effort on target, when Mick Crozier's shot was easily parried. However, by then game had long got away from the spirited visitors.

To be brutally honest, the result was never in doubt after Joe Betts had fired us into the lead in the 19th minute with a glorious individual goal of real quality and class. Picking the ball up about thirty yards from goal on the left hand side of the pitch, Joe advanced a couple of paces before unleashing a vicious, low swerving shot that was destined for the bottom corner from the second he connected. It was a goal worthy of winning any game and part of the reason why he was deservedly selected as Man of the Match.

With Chemfica content to soak up pressure and unwilling to advance on the Main goal, the match lacked the tension one may have expected of the occasion and much of the game slipped by without undue incident. That said, a serious foul on Tony Browell that went unpunished as it occurred while the ball was out of play led to a dramatic increase in the levels of competitiveness displayed by the home side as they sought to turn their superiority into further goals. In other words, Malky's mam began to unleash a relentless tirade of foul and abusive language directed at the opposition team and officials that was remarkable for both it's length and content.

Despite good efforts from Lee Gray, Malky and Bettsy that were all deflected wide, it took the Main until the 66th minute to finally put the game to bed. Malky 's free kick from the left touchline was astutely headed in by Cal, who had intelligently drifted away from his marker and was then able to deftly angle a header past a static keeper. It was no more than the Main deserved and a clear sign that Chemfica's vain hope of grabbing a breakaway goal would not bear fruition. Hence, after a campaign that started with a first round tie away to Ashington Booze Brothers Athletic on October 3rd, we had reached the final following six rounds and five games that had also seen Wallsend Boys Club, Shilbottle and Amble defeated. It is a tribute to Jason and the squad that our progress had been so untroubled.

I felt sorry for Norman, who missed today's game taking his daughter to Northumbria University Open Day, but as I was standing in for him as secretary, I didn't have too much time to ponder his ill fortune. We caught up later on in The Alex as we had a Percy Main informal evening, watching Newcastle come back from the dead to draw 2-2 away at Bristol City. For obvious reasons, nothing much of note was spoken about the club, in contrast to Sunday's meeting.

At six o'clock the next day, we all assembled in the pavilion; Norman, Rob and Aiden fresh from a crucial 1-0 win at Gardener Park against North Shields, Bob (who has an Amy Winehouse song as his ring tone, curiously enough), Gary, Geordie, Laura, me and, finally, Jason, who'd just crawled out of bed. The main item to discuss was the forthcoming Junior Cup Finals and the need for us all to pitch in with putting the goals up and working in the snack bar. A kind of rota was worked out, but the reality of the situation would no doubt be slightly different when the games came around.

While everything on the pitch was running smoothly, there were a couple of worries. Firstly, Wallington had complained we'd played an ineligible player in the Combination Cup quarter final the week before, namely Jason. Obviously he was eligible, so there was no way we'd be slung out of the competition, but he was a late addition to the squad after Chris Doig had been injured in the warm-up. We consequently altered the team sheet the referee had been given and the one we later sent to the Alliance, but not the copy we'd given to Wallington, and it was on that basis they'd made a complaint, which cost us a £10 fine. Perhaps the reason for Wallington's administrative zeal was the six points they'd been docked for playing wrong 'uns earlier in the season, including three of them following the league game at Purvis Park in August.

Other things we discussed included the vast volume of games and the need for extra bodies to be registered to be on the safe side before the 31st March deadline, which was presumably why Jason had signed six new players who'd be able to help us out in league games but were ineligible for the cup ties. We looked at the viability of the Women's team taking a voluntary promotion that would include travel as far as Scarborough next season and, ominously, the state of the pavilion roof. Winter had ravaged this ageing structure and it seemed pointless to even contemplate tidying up the rest of the place without sorting that out. The first proper estimate we'd had put the cost of a new roof at £25,000. We'd get it done cheaper elsewhere, but it would still be a lot of money for Percy Main Amateurs. Basically, a new roof was essential not just desirable and we'd have to look everywhere to find money to go towards paying for it, which is another reason to humbly thank you for purchasing this book.

The last game of the month saw us playing our fourth cup-tie in successive weeks, which was actually our fifth one in a row and our third consecutive home match. This time it was Berwick United in the Pin Point Northern Alliance Combination Cup semi final.

As Tony Browell (work), Johnathon McEnaney (wedding), Liam Knox (bereavement), Chris Doig (injured), Lee Gray and Phil Hogg (both ineligible) were all unavailable, the Main entered this game with only the bare bones of a squad and only Steven Shadforth to call on from the bench. However, the Villagers had relentlessly proved themselves to be both indefatigable and resourceful, not to mention combative and tenacious, in a season that continued to provide followers of the Purvis Park outfit with the promise of both silverware and promotion. Consequently, there seemed little doubt that Percy Main would come out on top in this encounter, which the boys did by winning 3-1 with a minimum of fuss and only a token effort at the kind of exhilarating play we had become accustomed to.

The stiff breeze that blew across the ground, while not ruining the contest, did hamper the desire of both sides to play a close passing game. Too often balls in the air held up, while balls on the ground seemed to pick up pace, frustrating both sides. There was no-one more frustrated than Malky Morien, who had seen a sublime chip from thirty yards kiss the top of the bar and go out of play in the fifth minute, with Berwick keeper Stewart Thompson a bemused observer.

Youthful winger Dean Ellis, making the most of a rare starting place, almost gave the Villagers the lead, but his snapshot drifted just wide, with Cal Colback unable to get on the end of the ball as it zipped across goal.

Rob was called into action after twenty minutes to deal with a presentable volley from Berwick centre half Paul Wood, but this represented their only threat in the first period.

Dean was again denied the opening goal when his header from a Malky corner was adeptly tipped over by Thompson. Perhaps frustrated by this, Ellis soon saw yellow for a silly trip on half way. This booking was perhaps a sign of burgeoning frustration by the home side. However, any such feelings were extinguished by Jason's emphatic penalty, given following a crude body check on the ever-dangerous Colback. Almost immediately from the restart, Percy Main doubled their advantage with a goal of stunning quality. Malky collected the ball on the edge of the home area and advanced a few yards before giving Chris Locke the chance to race through central midfield. The Main captain came almost to the edge of the area before feeding Betts, whose first time effort went under the body of the on-rushing Thompson.

Berwick showed little sign of getting back into the game after half time and Main were content to idly push the ball around, enjoying a vice-like grip on possession and unrelenting territorial advantage. Bettsy, Malky and Mickey Haley, from a Jason corner, all saw efforts shave the woodwork, before Cal put the game beyond the visitors with an excellent, first time half volley from Jason's cross. It is a measure of the quality of the earlier goal by Bettsy that Cal's goal wasn't the toast of the post-match celebrations.

The game Borderers grabbed a late consolation when Michael Robinson, who had previously hit the side netting with a speculative effort from distance, finished with aplomb into the bottom corner past the dive of Rob Rodgerson, but it was the Main who advanced to their second cup final of the season.

After the game, word came via the Northumberland FA that the Minor Cup Final would be at Blue Flames on Wednesday 19th May. They sent us their congratulations, then reminded us we'd be fined £50 if we didn't send in player pen portraits and a club history to go in the programme by early April. They're all heart those administrators and this was one job none of us minded doing. However, we had plenty of league games to think about before then.

April: *When he gets the ball he scores a goal, Graeme, Graeme Cole!*

ON DECEMBER 12th 2009, the day we beat Whitley Bay A 4-2, the top of Northern Alliance Division 1 looked like this :

Percy Main	P16	W14	D1	GD +22	Pts 43
Rutherford	P15	W12	D2	GD +27	Pts 38
Amble United	P13	W10	D1	GD +28	Pts 31

On April 3rd 2010, a mere 112 days later, during which intervening period Percy Main had played three Minor Cup and two Combination Cup ties, we finally managed to stage our next league game. Norman's Birthday, the Shortest Day, Christmas, Hogmanay, Epiphany, Burns' Night, Chinese New Year, Valentines' Day, Shrove Tuesday, St. David's and St. Patrick's Days, the Vernal Equinox, the Northern Alliance

Transfer Deadline and Good Friday had all been and gone during the time between the initial date for our home game with Peterlee (December 19th) and Easter Saturday when it finally took place. It has to be said that the game was worth waiting for, though perhaps not for such a long period of time. The two teams played out a 4-4 draw in probably the very worst conditions in which I've seen a game make it to a conclusion. The effect on the top of the Northern Alliance Division 1 was to make the table look like this :

Rutherford	P19	W14	D2	GD +25	Pts 44
Percy Main	P17	W14	D2	GD +22	Pts 44
Amble United	P16	W12	D2	GD +32	Pts 38

While the next day's north east football headlines were deservedly shared by Newcastle United, whose 3-2 away win at Peterborough (that Bob had chosen to forego the pleasure of watching in favour of supporting his beloved Main) all but mathematically guaranteed a return to the top flight and Whitley Bay, who reached Wembley to defend their FA Vase title after overcoming Barwell 3-2 in the semi final second leg, it is a fact that the events unfolding at both London Road and Hillheads simply could not have been any more exciting than the spectacle that I felt honoured to be watching at Purvis Park.

Because of the holiday season and the competing football attractions up the coast and on dodgy satellite TV, the game was played in front of a modest, yet rapt, crowd, several of whom commented that it was the best 90 minutes of action they'd witnessed all season. One groundhopper who'd come up from North Yorkshire, replete with camera, sketch pad and dictaphone, was in a frenzied state of hysteria by the start of the second half, and not just because we palmed a load of buckshee back issue progs off on him.

Regardless of the quality of performance put in by all of the players involved, and there were some sparkling cameos on both sides, a huge debt of gratitude must be paid to the referee, David Dowling, whose excellent handling of the often fiery contest, which was played in quite incredible weather, was absolutely faultless from start to finish. From a Villagers' perspective, the only down side was that Peterlee were the first away side to claim anything from a trip to Purvis Park in 2009/10, meaning that our fond hope of a perfect set of home league results was dashed.

The frustrations of three and a half months of league inaction were soon blown away when Wilka tore down the right wing in the second minute, before slipping over the perfect cross for who I believed to be Joe Betts. By the time the Peterlee keeper had returned the ball for the kick off, the heavens had dramatically opened. Bearing in mind that it was Easter, the spectacular hailstorm of Old Testament proportions seemed cataclysmically appropriate. I half expected a cloudburst of frogs to further drench the pitch.

A dazed Peterlee side were required to put everything they had into keeping themselves in the contest as shots rained in from all quarters, often with the same velocity, intensity and rapidity as the hail that began to pile up, inches thick, like a carpet of miniature golf balls. Joe Betts had one effort deflected wide, and from the resulting corner Malky's header was blocked on the line. It was only a temporary respite as Betts turned provider by racing down the wing and cutting the ball back for an unmarked Colback to bury the chance with some relish. Straight from the restart, Chris Locke almost made it three when picking up a loose ball in the box, but he was only able to steer his shot into the side netting.

With 20 minutes gone and Main 2-0 up, the only clouds on the horizon were the ominous, gargantuan black ones that continued to saturate the pitch, which by now had a good inch of standing water on the pavilion touch line. With the game in progress, players fell and slipped, coming up again caked in mud, their shirts indistinguishable beneath the slime, while Bob and Gary forked and sanded the touchlines and Norman and I placed buckets at strategic points by the edge of the pavilion roof in the vague hope of catching the torrents of water that cascaded down.

Amazingly, within half an hour, the rain and hail stopped and, seconds later, the sun came out, turning what had seemed to be a dress rehearsal for the Apocalypse in to a glorious spring day, just in time to save the game and allow Peterlee to get a grip on it, as any further rain would surely have led to an abandonment. Firstly, Scott Henderson rose unchallenged to nod in from a corner and seven minutes before half time, the visitors from East Durham were level when a hotly contested opposition corner was fired home by Adam Stanley, courtesy of a wicked deflection from a home defender, as Rob stood and berated Geordie for giving a flag kick when he felt sure he'd kept the ball alive. A bad goal in every sense.

The Main were not downhearted by this setback though as, straight from the restart, Malky drove forward and unleashed a rasping low shot that nestled in the bottom corner to give us a 3-2 lead we held until the second half, though Peter Crawford almost brought Peterlee level seconds before the interval when he struck a post when through one on one with Rob. It was Crawford who drew the two teams level on 55 minutes with a curling right foot effort, but our defence had to be disappointed with the amount of space the scorer was afforded.

The equaliser was definitely against the run of play, as Malky and Dean Ellis had both gone close in the minutes before the third Peterlee goal. Again we attacked and on 63 minutes, and Joe Betts was unlucky to be adjudged offside when slipping the ball home, but Main were not to be denied for long. Two minutes later, Malky's measured through ball put Cal away and he calmly slotted past an on-rushing Blenkinsopp, for what I was later to discover was his hat trick.

This was not to be the end of Peterlee, who duly battled back to level in the 76th minute when Crawford scored with a shot from distance that flicked off Cola's heel to ruin his birthday and totally wrongfoot Rob. That was to be the finish of the scoring, despite the best efforts of all the players. A special word must go to Peterlee's Sean English, who battled all game despite clearly being unwell. At one point his shirt was so caked in mud he appeared to be a second referee! At another, he threw up behind the goal having swallowed gobfulls of rainwater when his attempted slide tackle on Wilka had been sidestepped with ease.

At full time, the pitch looked like it was ready to be planted with potatoes and completely unsuited for the purpose for which it existed. It needed a rest and a good roll once the excess water had evaporated. The last thing it needed was another game on it the next day. Thankfully,

Whitley Bay Development had cried off from their League Cup tie with the Women scheduled for the Sunday on account of being unable to raise a team. Typically, being Whitley Bay, they were allowed to postpone rather than concede the game.

Whitley Bay were dominating the non-league scene in the north east, as ever. On Easter Monday, I watched them beat West Allotment 2-1 at Blue Flames, as the collection of geeks, oddballs, social inadequates and care in the community cases who made up their new fanbase, flushed with FA Vase success and entirely unaware of the travails that caused their club to plummet out of the Unibond League five years previously, sang "What's it like to see a crowd?" at a Northern League game. Clever lads.

From West Allotment I moved to St James' Park, rather like most of the new Bay fans will be doing next season I'd imagine, to see newly promoted Newcastle take on Sheffield United; there were 49,000 inside and the whole of the region's sports fans tuning in at home. Well, apart from Cal Colback that is, who appears to take more of an interest in cyberspace than the Championship. A week after informing me his name was Colback and not Colbeck, occasioning a deep-clean edit of the club website and the manuscript of this book, he texted me as the teams were shaking hands before kick off:

> *The website report for Saturday was wrong as I scored a hat trick and the first goal was given to bettsy when it was me who scored. Text jay and ask him. Wilka crossed it and I ran front post and tapped it in! Mick Ritchie knows cos he sed well done for running front post*

Unfortunately, as I tend not to take a laptop with me to the match, I was unable to input this information, though I did update Twitter. Just to show that I'm happy with new technology, I combined watching the game with a text conversation with Norman, who was away to Yorkshire for a Silver Wedding do. Percy Main's next game was at Hillheads against Whitley Bay A, with a scheduled kick off time of 6.15. As Bay's ground, once of the Unibond League, has floodlights, it seemed crazy not to use them, especially as players would be racing from work to get there in time.

However, kick offs are normally only moved with the consent of both teams, but not in this instance. Apparently the ref was struggling to get there for 6.15, so kick off was pushed back to 7.00, which would still be no good for Tony Browell, who had to work late.

I had told Norman to inform Bob about the Twitter service, so he could keep in touch with the game against Whitley when down in Peterborough, but it turned out he would be assuming his usual stance ranting and raving on the Hillheads terraces, having secured suitable employment in this area. At least Laura kept in touch with the Whitley Bay game on Twitter, even though it was nothing to microblog home about, as we went down 1-0 for our first league defeat in almost eight months.

After 15 games unbeaten, it was disappointing to see the record go in such a desperately poor game. As well as missing Tony Browell, we were severely lacking up front, having been denied the services of Cal, suspended following the Amble Minor cup red card, and Macca, injured sparring the week before, though whether it had been in the gym, a taxi rank or kebab shop was not clear. Whitley Bay were also short-handed as their first team were in action the same night, so several fringe players had been called in to the squad, including Ian Lee, denying us all the opportunity of seeing round two between Bob and Mrs Bugner.

Rather than attempting to get around the player shortage by promoting fringe members of the squad, Alliance clubs often exploit a registration loophole at this time of year. Players are eligible to play for both a Northern League and an Alliance club, as the two competitions are at different steps of the non-league pyramid. As the Northern League has to finish by the first weekend in May and the Alliance can continue until the end of that month, there is often a distorted set of results caused by this procedural anomaly. Certainly Ryton's elevation to the Northern League in 2005 was helped by Blyth Spartans striker Robbie Dale banging in a load of goals in the last half dozen games.

Whitley Bay A versus Percy Main Amateurs ended up as something more akin to a North Shields FC training exercise, with The Robins' manager Tony Woodhouse and coach Robbie Livermore, a previous Percy Main stalwart, lining up for the home side and two other Shields players, John Amos and the highly impressive centre half Chris Hunt, taking the field for the Villagers. Watching from the stands was the former Bay and Percy Main centre half Brian Smith, who is also the captain of North Shields. Incestuous, unpleasant times and one of the reasons why I didn't feel particularly disappointed by the result, just a little bit put out by the whole affair.

The last game staged at Hillheads had seen a crowd of almost 2,800 crammed in, but this evening only a fraction of that number were in attendance, with the majority of them being a healthy away following. Sadly, those who travelled in hope left disappointed as a drab encounter was settled by Chris Compson's close range finish after 73 minutes, when the Bay defender, whose brother had played in goal for Bay at Purvis Park in December, stabbed home a loose ball at the back post with the Villagers' rearguard guilty of a prolonged bout of ball watching.

This encounter was always going to be decided by a single goal and it went to the home side with what was effectively only their second shot on target, their first having seen the excellent Chris Hunt clear off the line from Josh Brooks after a goalmouth scramble. Despite the fact that Percy Main had enjoyed several periods of ascendancy during the game, the goal killed it stone dead, as the home side's prolonged bouts of gamesmanship and the kind of time-wasting associated with ***La Liga*** were indulged, if not encouraged, by a weak referee.

I gloomily cycled home, just in time to see Man United suffer a loss on away goals to Bayern Munich that was almost as crushing as the disappointment felt by Percy Main supporters half an hour previously. In fact, I probably had more grounds for despair as Rutherford and Amble had both won away from home as well. However, there was no time to dwell on the past; the weekend's game away to Chopwell Officials Club was now all that mattered.

In contrast to the previous week's hailstorm, Saturday 10th April seemed to mark the official start of the summer binge-drinking season. Cutting through town to catch a bus to Chopwell from outside the Central Station, it seemed as if sunglasses, vest tops, combat shants and flip flops were de rigeur (well they are for Chris Locke even when there's six inches of snow on the deck, but that's another matter). The Newcastle United promotion love-in was being added to by the visit of Blackpool, though from the colour of their shirts you'd have to take a second glance to make sure it wasn't Holland that were in town. The beer gardens and smoking areas were thronged with boozing football fans, while the aroma of barbecue, another indicator of hot weather and all day sessions, hung heavy in the air over Chopwell Town Park.

The bus journey to Chopwell took an age. From the Metro Centre to Swalwell and then on to Winlaton Mill, I knew where I was. After we hit Rowlands Gill, the next settlement in this odyssey through the Wild West of Gateshead, I was out of the known universe, never mind my comfort zone. Eventually we came across a blasted heath masquerading as Warsaw circa 1972; this was Chopwell. The walk down Karl Marx Street and Lenin Terrace to the ground reinforced the ideological provenance of the locale. This was the Stalinist land that time forgot; a no horse town existing on benefits and typical rural pleasures and pastimes. The pitch was scarred by the efforts of burrowing rodents, resulting in a home side substitute catching a somnolent rabbit, breaking its neck and throwing the corpse behind the goal for a pair of Jack Russell terriers to squabble over. We weren't among the Café Society here.

After two games without a victory, the team were desperate to get our promotion push back on track by taking all three points from the curiously named Chopwell Officials Club. Despite producing one of our trademark second half comebacks after going a goal down to Lee Best's confident spot kick when Tony Browell was harshly adjudged to have deliberately used a hand in the box, with firstly Malky Morien levelling things up with his own penalty after Chopwell keeper Ryan McVitic had cleaned out John Amos and then Man of the Match Mickey Haley putting us in the lead, when he perceptively headed home Lee Gray's shot, the visitors were forced to accept only a single point, when Lee Best grabbed his second with a cool finish into the bottom corner with twenty minutes remaining.

Tension from the touchline, in terms of anguished reactions to near misses, transmitted itself to the players, whose own anxiety levels began to grow exponentially with every strangled curse from the side. It reminded me of Newcastle in 1996; blowing the title by playing with fear rather than fluidity as Manchester United relentlessly ground down the 12-point lead Keegan's team had amassed.

Once they had got their noses in front, it seemed as if the Villagers would go on to win easily enough, but no more than 20 seconds after Lee Gray was withdrawn for Dean Ellis, Chopwell advanced down that side, taking advantage of the newly created gap to get behind the exposed Graeme Smith to set up the opportunity. It was a kick in the teeth, but a desperate Main poured forward; there were two good handball appeals in ten seconds as a procession of corners were won, with Chris Locke seeing his effort tipped on to the inside of the post by McVitie and Graeme Cole having a header blocked on the line, though it was not to be.

If the frustration levels were increased after this unfortunate draw by news of Rutherford and Amble United picking up maximum points, they reached critical mass during the next, midweek game against Gosforth Bohemians. Having checked the pitch was recovering well during a gentle friendly between Percy Main and North Shields Ladies on the Sunday, which we won 1-0, it was marvellous to see the ground looking so splendid on the Wednesday. If only we could have gained the result our superb performance merited.

An oft-repeated complaint of supporters, who feel their team has been hard done to by the final score, is that they have been robbed. This evening such an ungracious lament was the justifiable mantra of all Percy Main followers as, after 90 minutes of unremitting pressure, the Villagers could only manage to accrue a single point from a 1-1 draw with Gosforth Bohemians. To borrow another sporting cliché, it is an indisputable fact that were this to have been a boxing match, the referee would have stopped it, such was the overwhelming superiority of the home side in every department, other than the one that counts most of all; goals scored.

As a result of Paul Hodge's beautifully judged chip from the edge of the box, having turned Mickey Haley inside out and left Rob Rodgerson a helpless onlooker seconds before half time, Gosforth Bohemians' solitary effort on goal during the whole game was enough to prevent the Main from collecting their just rewards for their Herculean efforts. Spectators leaving Purvis Park, chastened by the knowledge that we had collected a mere three points from the last 12 available, could reflect on the fact that football may be a funny old game, but on instances such as this, it is a cruel and wicked one.

To be scrupulously fair, we did take the lead in decidedly fortuitous circumstances in the ninth minute when Saturday's goalscoring Man of the Match Mickey Haley was on the mark again with a looping speculative effort from almost on the touchline that utterly bamboozled Gosforth keeper Dave Herrington and flew in via the inside of the back post. At full time, Mickey did admit it was a complete fluke and, as he was shooting into the sun, he'd not even seen the ball cross the line.

Such was the complete Main dominance of the contest, it was a shock when Gosforth Bohemians, in a rare sortie, grabbed their goal with the ultimate sucker punch. An aimless long ball out of defence should have proved no threat, but we allowed it to bounce and that gave them a chance. In all honesty, Hodge did superbly well to deceive both Haley and Rodgerson. Despite this setback, it seemed unlikely that the home side would not go on to seal victory in the second period. Indeed, considering the way the game progressed, it was something of a miracle that Bohemians escaped with a point. The second half was a mixture of relentless waves of Percy Main attacks and dogged defence from Bohemians, resulting in utter frustration for the Purvis Park faithful. The whole game was summed up by Malky Morien's 93rd minute cross that rolled invitingly along the six-yard line, only to evade every Main effort at forcing it home. Thank goodness Phil Kyle wasn't there to see this result.

Make no mistake, this was an excellent performance and on another day, we could have won by four clear goals. However, as we glumly sipped our soft drinks in the cricket club, this was of no consolation, especially as news of Amble United's 2-0 win at Cullercoats and Whitley Bay's ominous 7-0 thrashing of Peterlee filtered through. We were no longer in a promotion spot, as only two would go up. Indeed, there was a sense that what we'd always believed to be a three horse race now had a fourth contender, as the top of the table now looked like this:

Rutherford	P21	W16	D2	GD +27	Pts 50
Amble United	P19	W15	D2	GD +42	Pts 47
Percy Main	P20	W14	D4	GD +21	Pts 46
Whitley Bay A	P21	W13	D3	GD +31	Pts 42

Obviously, when confidence is low within the squad, what is really needed is a potential morale-boosting, easy home game against the bottom side. Seaton Burn had managed to win one game all season and sat adrift in last place with three points to their name. Despite Bettsy being unavailable through work commitments, we were reasonably strong as John Amos had decided to choose Percy Main over North Shields, as had Chris Hunt and their mate Craig Culyer, another former Robins player.

When John Amos ran on to Chris Doig's well-judged through ball and finished in some style after five minutes to give us the lead, it seemed as if we would get our slightly derailed promotion bandwagon back on track by completing a routine victory. Indeed, at half time, with the score remaining 1-0, there was absolutely no sense that anything other than a home win would be the final outcome in front of an excellent crowd. Perhaps the only things home fans could have been worried about at the break were the injury that caused the early withdrawal of Mickey Haley and Craig Culyer's inexplicable miss from inside the six yard box after Seaton Burn keeper Chris Cuthbertson had produced a magnificent, one-handed diving save to deny John Amos his second goal of the game with a bullet header.

The latter incident was to prove crucial as we were forced to endure a potentially mortal blow to our promotion hopes when Seaton Burn notched a seven minute brace of goals that allowed them to complete their first ever victory over Percy Main and double their points tally for the season. The equaliser on 50 minutes saw Ian Armstrong unaccountably unmarked at the left edge of the area and able to finish with a stylish swing of the left boot that evaded Rob. The winner came courtesy of a free kick, conceded by Chris Locke for no apparent reason, which Matty Laing fired in and was lucky enough to see it take a couple of deflections that wrong-footed Rodgerson. From that moment on, the game was conducted almost entirely in the opposition penalty area.

Chances were created and spurned, sometimes through good defending, sometimes through good luck and sometimes through poor finishing. Graeme Cole had a shot headed off the line following a Malky Morien corner. Malky himself twice saw thunderbolt free kicks tipped round the post. Tony Browell had a magnificent, towering header superbly palmed away by the agile Cuthbertson, who was undoubtedly the away side's star performer. Worst of all, an unmarked Malky contrived to miss the ball completely when only six yards out.

In addition, the frankly shit referee appeared to have taken against us and gave them everything, including chalking off what seemed a perfectly good equalising goal for offside in the last minute. As a result, the final whistle saw some predictable unpleasantness that I had a good view of, being stood at the entrance to the dressing rooms, having unlocked them for the players. First in for us was Craig Culyer, who'd been booked and missed an open goal. No doubt frustrated, he kicked a hole in the plasterboard wall outside the home dressing room in an act of mindless petulance.

An unidentified player (cough!) then sprayed the referee with a drinks bottle to complain about the disallowed goal, causing the big man in black, clearly schooled in the need for officials to maintain professional dignity and composed aloofness at all times, regardless of the provocation, to confront him in our dressing room. For no apparent reason, Seaton Burn's moustachioed manager decided he wanted to see what happened next and barged into our changers, before he and the referee disappeared into the officials' boudoir for a cosy chat.

It was a devastating result on every level; we'd lost ground, points, discipline and face. Even worse than the result was the damage caused by Culyer, as actions like that are both mindless and an insult to all of us who put in hours of unpaid graft off the pitch. Some clown in Total 90s can lace a hole in a wall in about 10 seconds, but it can take weeks to sort out the damage, not to mention the costs involved. The news that Amble had lost and Rutherford had only drawn served simply to make things worse, though Hebburn's triumph over Whitley in the other Combination Cup semi final was viewed as a tiny bit of good news. However, the Combination Cup final was not until May 29th; living in the here and now meant it was Amble United who were up next in a crucial promotion clash on the Wednesday.

Having only collected three points from the last 15, things were starting to look bleak. With nine games remaining, nine wins were needed to ensure promotion, regardless of the stumbles made by both our rivals on Saturday 17th. Otherwise, we'd be left relying on the other teams to falter.

Wednesday 21st was another day; a gloriously sunny one with a slight breeze from the North West that assisted me as I cycled from work to the ground. I had to admit to feeling apprehensive about this one. Not only were we in a poor run of form, but also this lot had trounced us 5-0 up there back in August. The night before Whitley Bay Development had snatched a 3-2 win with a harsh 89th minute penalty in the rearranged cup game with the Ladies, so it seemed crap luck was not a gender specific problem at Percy Main.

And yet, the sound I heard as I arrived at the club was the encouraging noise of hearty laughter; the team were sat together in the pavilion, drinking tea, scoffing banana bread Laura had made for them and having a bit of craic with each other. Young lads, good lads, exchanging banter, with no sign of nerves whatsoever, looking forward to a good game later on, which made me feel a little less nervous about the evening ahead.

In the end, the boys made me look daft and neurotic as they put in the performance of the season, showing that rumours of the demise of Percy Main Amateurs as genuine promotion candidates from the Northern Alliance Division 1 may well have been greatly exaggerated.

A season's best crowd were treated to an enthralling, comprehensive win as we moved back into second place following a performance of genuine quality, class and determination, characterized by a tactical master class from Jason, who deserved enormous credit for marshalling the talent available to him so successfully. But it has to be said; every single player stepped up to the plate and turned in a praiseworthy shift after the crushing disappointment of the calamitous Seaton Burn game.

For a variety of reasons, Jason was forced to ring the changes. Mickey Haley, so reliable this season, was injured and so Cola shuffled to right back, with Chris Hunt coming in to partner Tony Browell. At left back Graeme Smith again put in a steady performance as the whole back four produced excellent games that almost nullified the Amble threat, which had been so potent back in August when Jason left the ground in an ambulance following a knee ligament injury. How much more satisfying was this evening, and not simply because he won the post match 16 bottles of Carlsberg on the domino card either! Thankfully, the boss's decision to restore himself to the side at the expense of Chris Doig was vindicated by the fact he set up all three goals with magnificent, pin point crosses, the second of which was converted with great gusto by the returning Joe Betts, replacing the suspended John Amos, for a goal as beautiful as a painting. I don't mean "Guernica" either.

From the very outset, Main pushed Amble on to the back foot. After four minutes a long throw by Chris Hunt caused pandemonium in the visitors' area, resulting in Jason volleying wildly over with his right foot. However, his left foot is the more cultured and an astute pass played in Malky to break the offside trap, only for his attempted chip to be easily gathered by Amble keeper Andrew Patterson. Jason's next touch set up the opening goal. A flying break down the right by Wilka was ended near the by-line by a crude trip. Jason's delivery was superb, the ball striking the inside of the post before being forced in from almost on the line by Tony Browell for the big defender's first goal of the season.

At half time, with a single goal lead, the same as against Seaton Burn, there were cautious grounds for optimism in the home ranks. However, two minutes into the second period, such caution was thrown to the wind as Bettsy powered in a magnificent, unstoppable header from a textbook corner. Moments later, Craig Culyer, who was tireless and tenacious all night, proving he can be as much of a creative asset as he had been a destructive liability with his dressing room demolition the Saturday before, sent in a thunderous dipping volley that Patterson held at his near post. It showed he could kick a ball almost as well as he can hoof a plasterboard wall partition.

The Amble keeper had made two great saves, but they were routine when compared to a breathtaking tip over by Rob Rodgerson from a Darren Riddell header. Unmarked between the penalty spot and six yard line, Riddell bulleted the ball towards the top corner, only for Rob's prodigious leap and superb handling to flick the ball away for a corner. This was certainly the finest save he'd made all season.

Amble were deflated by this as the Main roared back on to the offensive. Joe Betts sent an effort inches wide, before Shaun Kelly almost put through his own net. From the resulting corner, Cola joined Tony Browell in getting off the mark for the season by forcing in Jason's cross after an unholy scramble. Mindful of the 5-0 loss back in August, we hunted more goals. Patterson was again required to thwart Joe Betts by clinging on to a rasping low drive, but it was not to be. Finally, in injury time, there was cause again for Rob Rodgerson to draw gasps of approval and spontaneous applause when going full length to tip Ian Common's venomous low shot round the post. The applause just kept on coming at full time, mixed in with some cheers. This had been a great evening, even if Seaton Burn had reverted to type by losing against Rutherford.

In some ways, Thursday's Under 12 Cup Final was an even better one as we took £110 at the snack bar, compared to £90 from the food, gate and programmes the night before. As we were so busy knocking out hot dogs, teas and chocolate bars, I'm unable to comment on the quality of the game in which North Shields Boca Juniors beat North Shields Boys' Club 4-1 in what must have been a hell of a local derby.

The same could be said of the visit of Cullercoats to Purvis Park on Saturday 24th for our fourth consecutive home game. The journey from their exposed public playing field home of Links Road to Percy Main is 3.7 miles, meaning they are a tenth of a mile closer to us than Whitley Bay A are. It isn't Celtic v Rangers, but there was the element of needle hanging over from the previous season when our 3-2 victory in the final home game cost them promotion and resulted in one of their players "doing a Culyer" on the away dressing room door after being red carded for handball on the line. Added to that there appears to be a blood feud between the two managers going back in to the depths of local football in the dream time of the mid to late 1970s, and you've got all the elements required for an unseemly pitch-side brawl and a damning list of charges to be answered in front of the Northumberland FA's management committee.

In the end, it was a surprisingly comfortable 2-0 home win in a game utterly without needle, niggle or the need for restraining arms round the neck of excitable young men. Admittedly, the Cullercoats management team accepted the result with a degree of equanimity comparable to Macduff's on learning of the demise of his family in the Scottish Play, but that wasn't our concern. All we were bothered about was the fate of Percy Main Amateurs and this result was an important one.

If Wednesday's 3-0 demolition of Amble United had been all about attacking artistry and defensive tenacity, this routine win, over a Cullercoats side that lacked any discernible threat, was characterised by midfield solidity and the ability to keep possession of the ball for large periods of the game, which frustrated the hell out of our opponents, who were singularly unable to lay a glove on us all match.

Facing the usual striker crisis (Bettsy working, Ziggy and Maccer injured, Amos suspended and Cal watching his brother play for Ipswich at SJP), Jason was forced to select Shaddy in an advanced position and the big bugger acquitted himself well in a solo role, often proving a handful for the Cullercoats defence. That said, the prime movers in an attacking sense were Malky Morien and Craig Culyer, both of whom displayed a healthy ability to spray the ball around the pitch with great aplomb.

Culyer, who had impressed in the midweek victory, was again excellent and with a few more of these performances it may be time to cut the lad some slack, if he pays for the wall to be repaired of course. It was Culyer who was unceremoniously barged over in the area on the quarter hour to give Percy Main a penalty. While it may have been an unnecessary foul and a soft decision by the Belfast-born ref with the anachronistic tight, curly perm, Jason's conscience did not bother him unduly and he purposefully stroked the ball home.

Other than a Peter Bradley free kick that hit the wall and a rebound that sailed harmlessly over from the same player, little was seen of Cullercoats as an attacking force. In contrast, full back Graeme Smith, the pick of the home side, twice went close with a header from a Ritchie corner and a left foot effort from a Culyer pass. Apart from these clear-cut chances, there were few penalty box incidents as a controlled Main took the pace and sting out of the game.

In the second half, things continued in this subdued fashion, though Rob was called in to action with a magnificent spread and block to deny Stewart Wright, who had outpaced Chris Hunt. Rodgerson was a relieved man to see a Tony Browell back header drop wide after the keeper had raced out to collect the ball and misjudged its flight. On only one other occasion did Cullercoats trouble the home side, when a suspiciously offside looking Robert Watson collected the ball at the left side of the area and fired in a shot that Rob gathered at the base of the near post.

The Main were content to soak up impotent pressure and draw the sting from Cullercoats's attacks, which seemed to have worked as the 90 minutes ticked by without major incident. However, substitute Liam Knox brought the house down with a glorious, impudent cross with the outside of his right foot that fell perfectly for Malky to bury from twelve yards out with the deftest of downward headers to secure a thoroughly merited three points for Main. All there was time for was the obligatory bleating from the Cullercoats bench as we collected the points seconds later.

After winning our first nine home games of the season, we'd expected to carry on in that fashion after the winter interregnum, though it didn't work like that. The Peterlee draw could be discounted as a fluke because of the weather, but a mere seven points from four consecutive home games was a disappointment, even if we could make a persuasive argument that we'd deserved the maximum 12 from them. Sadly, there's nothing to be gained from anguished theorising; points are only available on the pitch and we needed to face up to the reality of five successive away games and the need to win them if we wanted to go up.

The first of this testing series was on Monday 26th away to Wallington. Oakford Park, their scenic little ground at Scots Gap, has been the home of a football team since 1877, but unfortunately I couldn't make it for this one. At the Cullercoats game I'd been genuinely flattered when Geoff Suniga, one of our best fans, said that he enjoyed being able to follow our progress in away games via the Twitter updates. Previously I'd thought only Norman, Laura, Cola's brother Jon and yours truly took an interest in this cyber whimsy, but it seemed as if there were others interested too. While I'd kept Geoff informed about goings on at Chopwell, I couldn't help him with the Wallington game. Not only wasn't I there, as work had the audacity to detain me until almost five o'clock, but Oakford Park's splendid isolation meant mobile phone reception was non-existent.

Last season, I did go to Wallington away. It was a dull end of season game. We lost 1-0 and Joe Betts was sent off for asking if the referee, who Mick Ritchie wanted breathalysed, enjoyed sex and travel. In other words, it had been a run-of-the-mill Percy Main away game. Sure, I'd been disappointed we lost, but it didn't ruin my week or anything. A year on and this club had got under my skin and in to my blood the way Newcastle United had once done, meaning that I couldn't possibly relax until I knew the result.

Unable to sit in the house, I took my first trip of the season to Heaton Stannington, less than ten minutes walk away, to see them take on Shankhouse. It was a good game, ending up a 3-3 draw with both benches and sets of fans up in arms with the referee and assistants from the first whistle to the last, but it didn't engage me in the way it should have. I'd only missed three Percy Main games before this one; 3-2 away to Morpeth Sporting Club while I was at Benfield v Norton and the two Minor Cup ties, 4-3 at Ashington Booze Brothers, as I failed to really take in Newcastle's 0-0 with Bristol City, and the 3-0 win over Amble, when I'd scouted Chemfica. The three games as second choice options just hadn't grabbed my attention as my thoughts had been constantly with Percy Main, and so it was during this six-goal thriller.

Walking home I intently gripped my phone waiting for the fateful vibration that would signal the information I desired yet feared to learn. Eventually, at almost 9pm, probably an hour after full time, a message came from Bob; ***drew 1-1. missed too many chances***

My immediate thoughts were it could have been worse, but within 10 minutes news of Amble's 1-0 win over Morpeth appearing on the Alliance website darkened my mood considerably. Against a team in 11th place in the table that we'd beaten twice already, this was a bad result and definitely two points dropped. We had needed to win this one and had seemingly let ourselves down by failing to do so, yet emotions swung again when the story of the game emerged the next day while talking to Bob at the Under 13s Cup Final at Purvis Park.

We'd gone with a threadbare squad; none of the five forwards could make it and so Knoxy, because of his extravagant assist against Cullercoats, came in for Shaddy, but he was rusty after a month out himself and missed a couple of presentable chances. Malky had also squandered a pair of opportunities, but he'd only been able to play after keeping his bruised foot in ice all weekend. Craig Culyer and Tony Browell were working, so Dean Ellis and Richie May deputised. Richie hadn't played for Percy Main since 2005, but was always a good player. Thankfully, he'd been available tonight as he grabbed our equaliser in the last minute of stoppage time. Two points dropped or one point gained? I suppose that all depends on the outcome of the promotion race.

The game that would no doubt have a major influence on that issue was the final game of the month. Wednesday 28th April, Beggars Wood, Lobley Hill, 6.30 kick off; the Clash of the Giants. Rutherford v Percy Main.

In the run-up to this game, I'd idled away a few hours running the phrase Percy Main Amateurs through a few search engines. To my surprise and delight, I came across a groundhopper's blog which detailed his trip to the Cullercoats home game. At http://thetravellingfan.blogspot.com/ I was delighted by this write up of our little club:

> *I know exactly what you are thinking when you first read this. Level 12? However, Percy Main was too good an opportunity to miss and my wallet loved me for it. Spending a weekend away in Newcastle with el missus, I look around straight away to see what games on Tyneside I could go to. Newcastle at home to Ipswich? Seeing the Magpies finally win a trophy (of some description) was tempting but paying £30 was not. There was then Gateshead vs AFC Wimbledon, a game I actually had planned to go and see – however we were up for the weekend to watch Kevin Bridges and so going*

over to Gateshead may be cutting it just fine. West Allotment Celtic and North Shields were also looked at before I stumbled across the little village club of Percy Main, a rare issuer in the Northern Alliance and with admission only £1 – I was right on it. A short Metro trip to Percy Main station and a 2 min walk saw me to Purvis Park.

The ground today seems to be pretty decent for this level (compared to Level 12 in Devon), although I have no idea what other Div 1 Northern Alliance grounds are like. A building, which included the changing rooms, tea bar and toilets, met you on site and a walk through the building brought you out onto viewing the pitch. The building has cover, which is great when it rains (every 2nd day in Tyneside) while the rest of the ground is hard standing with most of it railed off. Behind one goal is the Percy Main Cricket Club, which is separated by a strange hedge, which allows spectators to view both games at once.

A great (and sunny) day near the Tyneside coast as my first dabble with the Northern Alliance was an extremely successful one. While the quality was not always the best on show, this is proper grassroots where a lot of teams in this league don't even have an attendance price. PMA though produce a great programme and with admission only £1, you really can't complain. The bright summer weather also made this better as even the cricket teams were watching with can of lager in hand, taking a break from their pishy sport. If you're in the area and want some cheap entertainment on a Saturday afternoon, then Percy Main is really great fun – and they do cracking food too!

Publicity like that is absolutely invaluable among the groundhopping fraternity. Mention of programmes, badges and food (especially the programmes) will get them to travel the length of the country in order to see the Villagers outswear just about every other Alliance team, bar South Shields United. Articles like this do us the power of good; almost as much good as three points in the Rutherford game would do us. By 8.15 on Wednesday night, we'd had a lot of good done to our cause!

Tony Browell's unstoppable bullet header closed the gap at the top to a single point after our thoroughly merited 1-0 victory at a windswept Beggarswood, when, in truth, the margin of victory could and should have been far more emphatic. From the first whistle, we meant business. Malky's probing pass down the left hand channel almost set Cal away, but desperate defending by Rutherford's Graeme Jackson saw fussy referee Tom Davie give a free kick their way. Soon after, Colback tested home keeper Knox with a looping header from a Jason cross. On eight minutes Malky sent a shot just wide, which had Knox scrambling across his area as the Main enjoyed utter dominance in all areas of the pitch. This was rewarded when Tony Browell scored the decisive goal at the back post from a Jason flag kick.

Five minutes later it ought to have been two when Malky's deft lob from a headed Chris Hunt pass just went over. On 18, Jason saw his speculative header from a Wilka throw clutched under the bar by Knox. Craig Culyer was again dominant and eye catching and he almost profited from Malky's bravery in charging down a clearance, but Culyer's instinctive swivel and hit fell agonisingly wide of the gaping goal, with Knox stranded out of position.

Eventually Rutherford came in to the game, with Andy Reay out-running Tony Browell and toe-ending an effort a fraction wide of Rob's goal, to the surprise of the Main keeper. Steven Tumelty was the next Rutherford player to try his luck, but his speculative effort sailed high over the bar.

Referee Tom Davie showed himself a stickler for the application of the laws of the game, playing in excess of five minutes overtime in each half. The stoppage period at the end of the opening half saw three clear cut chances; two to Main, with shots from the edge from Cal and Chris Locke being just off target, and one to Rutherford, when Reay sliced a good opportunity wide.

To be fair, the hard, bumpy pitch and strong cross-field wind did not help players trying to control the ball. Perhaps this was why the last action of the half saw keeper Knox drop a Morien cross, with Cal's shot from the loose ball being stabbed behind by a stretched home defence.

In the second half, a strengthening wind became even more of a factor as the quality of football played took a distinct dip as play lurched from end to end, with Main again the side with the lion's share of possession and chances. Craig Culyer headed the first chance of the half wide from a Malky cross, before Malky himself failed to trouble the keeper from a Wilka pass.

Rutherford had the first of several amazing let offs when a Colback header from a Ritchie corner was scrambled off the line by keeper Knox and seemingly three other defenders. Robbie Frame had a decent opportunity for the home side but blazed the ball wide, before a contentious offside flag thwarted Malky's tap in to an empty net. This could have been costly as seconds later Frame spurned a chance at the back post, shooting into Rob's hands with the whole goal at his mercy.

Sub Joe Betts could identify with Frame as his first touch saw him roll the ball agonisingly wide of the upright after Malky's pass had set him in on goal with only the keeper to beat. The final act saw Chris Doig break the offside trap, home in on goal and gently tap the ball into the keeper's hands, but it was of no great consequence as referee Davie ended the titanic contest after a mind-boggling 52-minute second half.

The looks of elation on the faces of players and fans made the whole thing worthwhile. We were all in this together and, having gone our separate ways home, most of us for the first time since that morning, mobile phone technology brought us together again as Tony's goal assumed even more importance in the context of the promotion battle when news of Amble being held to a draw by Wallington filtered through. The league table showed how close things were :

Rutherford	P25	W18	D3	GD +29	Pts 57
Percy Main	P25	W17	D5	GD +26	Pts 56
Amble United	P24	W17	D3	GD +42	Pts 54

A month of intense activity had settled nothing; we'd played nine games, winning three, drawing four and losing two, and the top three remained almost inseparable, though we appeared to be the marginal outsiders. In addition, Whitley Bay were on 45 points with two games in hand and the darkest of stalking horses, Hebburn Reyrolle, were in 9th place but still had ten games left, not having lost since September.

May would be our destiny; five league games and two cup finals were taxing my brain far more than the imminent General Election. As I would be voting Communist, I knew Percy Main were my only realistic hopes for success.

May:
The Perfect Combination

AS WELL AS a willingness to completely immerse oneself in the oscillating fortunes of the first team and steady progress of the women's side, an essential personal requirement for all those who wish to become members of the committee at Percy Main Amateurs is an understanding and an agreement that the economic realities of keeping our club going require attendance at Purvis Park approximately every other day in early to mid May for one sort of cup final or another as the minimum acceptable level of commitment to our cause.

The last week of April had seen the first team at Wallington and Rutherford on the Monday and Wednesday, while the Tuesday and Thursday saw the ground host U13 and U14 cup finals, both contested by Wallsend and Whitley Bay Boys' Club, who claimed a victory each. Of rather more interest to us than the results of the games were the cheques handed over for hire of the pitch, not to mention the £200 quid we took at the canteen, which was increased to a very respectable £300 after our endeavours in flogging hot dogs to what seemed like every spectator at the first of the Newcastle Central Sunday Afternoon League Cup Finals.

Percy Main Amateurs; doing our bit to promote healthy eating on North Tyneside.

The last final of 2009 had seen Byker Key Club win 4-0 on the day Newcastle completed their 16-year stay in the Premiership by losing 1-0 at Villa. In a remarkable inversion of performances, the first one of 2010 coincided with Newcastle completing their Championship gap year when securing a 1-0 win at QPR, while Byker Key club lost 4-0 to a side hailing from The Turbinia (a rather awful pub on The Fossway, in Newcastle's bohemian easterly fringe of Walker), which is universally known to winos, radgies and hard-faced single mothers with extensive galleries of home-made tattoos as The Tub. It is precisely where I ought to have been the day before.

Newcastle East End hold their post match hospitality in The Tub, about 150 yards from their pitch at Miller's Dene. Last season we won there 2-1 in late April to move in to a promotion spot, albeit only temporarily, and the modest repast they offered us that day was a salver half full of cold roast potatoes. I didn't bother going back there after this year's game, not because I was worried about my carbohydrate intake, but because Laura and I had a very important evening engagement at The Oddfellows Arms Beer Festival in North Shields. However, having deputised as secretary for Norman, who was away running in Cumbria, I was able to cycle back from Millers Dene securely in possession of the completed team sheets, which showed we'd won 2-0 after doing the bare minimum needed to take all three points.

East End's boss Anth Doyle had, like me, played 80 minutes in the Over 40s league that morning. However, post meridian, my football responsibilities extended only as far as ensuring the ref and the opposition had a copy of our line-up half an hour before kick off and then completing the team sheet at full time, which I obviously had to hand on to Norman, our resident pathological perfectionist (not an obsessive anal retentive, honest) for intense scrutiny. Anth Doyle had a rather longer to do list that needed ticking off.

As I arrived, he was single-handedly and one-handedly putting the nets up, having already stuck the corner flags in place, while taking calls on his mobile from feckless young men explaining their unavailability because of drink-related injuries sustained on the Friday night. Of the 18 players he'd selected, only nine turned up, resulting in him drafting in one injured player and another one who'd finished work at 2pm, who arrived literally seconds before kick off.

Anth himself was the only sub and club linesman, poor bugger. No wonder he confided he was jacking it in at the end of the season. We may have a heavy workload at Percy Main, but at least there are a few of us to help out and share the duties around. On this day, even the City Council Parks and Recreation Department had conspired against East End; they'd cut the grass surrounding the pitch, but not the playing surface itself, which was above ankle height.

However, sentiment has to be forgotten about when the game kicks off. While Rutherford were losing 4-2 at Hillheads to Whitley Bay A and Amble United could only play out a stalemate at Benson Park against Gosforth Bohemians, we comfortably collected three points with a routine win. The result may well have been a predictable one if the league table and current form were taken into account, but the gallant home side, boasting former Main utility player Kriss Carr as their main attacking option, kept going all game.

With the grass reminiscent of Hampden Park in the 1970s, it was difficult for either side to pass the ball with pace, or for shots to be taken cleanly. The exception seemed to be Jason, whose crossing was superb, allowing him to present John Amos with three half chances that were dealt with by the admirable East End keeper Wayne Buglass.

Their goalie was a mere spectator when we took the lead though. Craig Culyer powered down the right wing and crossed deep for Jason to lay off a measured, cushioned pass for Malky that sat up invitingly, allowing the Main midfield maestro to bury the ball savagely in the left corner of the net. Ten minutes later the same combination almost gave us a second goal when Jason's cross was headed on by Malky, only for Buglass to make a superb tip-over. This was only a temporary respite as Jason's next pass, a long cross-field effort, picked out the on-rushing Amos who took a touch and then fired home to effectively seal the points after 37 minutes.

Despite the best efforts of Kriss Carr and Dieu Lomana for East End, it was a major surprise we did not add to our total in the second half. Jason hit a free kick that had Buglass at full stretch, a Chris Doig cross dropped just wide and Chris Hunt headed inches over the bar, which all contributed to the Main pushing East End further and further back, but fair play to them for standing firm. We did our bit by securing the points, and the bonus of other results going our way resulted in the League table looking like this :

Percy Main	P26	W18	D5	GD +28	Pts 59
Rutherford	P26	W18	D3	GD +27	Pts 57
Amble United	P25	W17	D4	GD +42	Pts 55

It was still tight, very tight, but the inescapable fact was that if we won our four remaining games, not only would we be promoted, we'd be Champions as well. However, even one draw could see us finish third, if results conspired against us. Our next game was away to Hebburn, who had won again. They were now in sixth with 40 points, having played a mere 21 games.

Hebburn's surge in form had also seen them reach two cup finals; the Combination Cup against us was still in the far distance (May 29th), but the Northern Alliance League Cup Final was played on the May Bank Holiday at Heaton Stann's ground. Rather like my trip to Chemfica in early March, I took the opportunity to do some scouting on my doorstep. Unlike the Chemfica experience, I came away impressed and worried as Hebburn strolled to a 3-1 victory over Heddon, who'd knocked us out of that same competition back in October. It meant our midweek trip to South Tyneside was a more daunting prospect than we would have expected after the opening day of the season, when we'd massacred Reyrolle, but only put the ball in the net twice in a 2-0 victory.

Instead of taking a bus to Hebburn, or scrounging a lift, I cycled there, going under the Tyne and through the foot tunnel, then wandered vaguely westwards. My insistence on pedal power meant that the eight-mile journey home from their ground would begin in gathering gloom and finish in complete darkness. Whether it was an ordeal or a pleasure would depend on the 90 minutes ahead.

Thankfully, it was an utter pleasure! In a warm dusk, I gleefully cycled west then north then east, reflecting in the unadulterated joy of our battling 3-2 win. This result was not as dramatic as the injury time leveller at Wallington, nor as emphatic as the four-goal salvo that won the points at Peterlee Town, but in terms of significance and quality of play, it was the equal of the previous two Wednesdays, when we'd beaten Amble United and then Rutherford. Being honest, it was not as comfortable as either of those games, but it was just as vital.

In the shape of elegant midfield artist Alan Pegram, Hebburn Reyrolle possessed the finest player on the pitch, as well as a dangerous attacking trio in Craig Watson, Ray Oshin and Channon North, who created problems for a rearguard denuded of Chris Hunt, but celebrating the return of Mickey Haley after almost a month on the sidelines, though at first it was not the Main defence but the attack that was seeing more of the ball.

Following several recent games where we had been decidedly short of striking options, this evening saw the Main with *un embarras des richesses* up top, resulting in a selection that saw John Amos partnered by Joe Betts and Maccas on the bench, alongside Pierre Luc Coiffait, another who had not featured recently, no doubt to do with his burgeoning career as a fashion photographer. It was encouraging to see such strength in depth. Despite additional absentees in the shape of Craig Culyer and Chris Doig, it showed that Jason had the necessary resources among a squad that on paper seemed larger than the one Fabio Capello selected for South Africa.

References to such tournaments may seem fanciful, but as this game took place not on Reyrolle's turf but on the adjoining, though appreciably larger and distinctly undulating pitch of Northern League Division 2 side Hebburn Town, and referee Ian Owens was accompanied by two young assistants, an unheard of luxury in Alliance D1, which was probably why there was the distinct feel of something special, something serious, something of greater moment than an amateur football promotion clash, in the South Tyneside air as the Main kicked off.

After six minutes those of us who had travelled from north of the Tyne were prematurely celebrating a certain goal when Joe Betts hit a thunderous, speculative effort a coat of paint wide of the far post with Hebburn keeper Rob McGregor flailing desperately at the ball. The keeper was more fully involved five minutes later with an acrobatic stop from a Betts header. Malky Morien, as so often this season, proved himself the consummate architect of chances galore; on 16 minutes an expertly weighted through ball saw John Amos running on, only to fire across and wide as McGregor sought to narrow the angle.

Hebburn came back into the game with the excellent Pegram breaking down the left and crossing exquisitely for Channon North, who turned the loose ball wide of the target. Moments later Hebburn full back Shotton put a perfect cross on North's head, but the big target man nodded it too high. The home side, playing with the advantage of the slope in the first half, had clearly gained the upper hand and their ascendancy was rewarded with the opening goal on 40 minutes when Pegram's cross was met with a firm downward header by North.

From then until the break, it was all Hebburn, but the Main stood firm and in the second half, with the introduction of Pierre Luc Coiffait, the visitors were a different prospect entirely. Coiffs's first touch was a trademark throw, which caused pandemonium in the Hebburn defence. Amid chaotic scenes in the box, Joe Betts was somehow denied, before Coiff returned the ball to an unmarked Jason who seemed certain to score, but ended up in the net himself, with the ball dribbling apologetically wide.

Hebburn sought to slow the game down, but their attempts at spoiling tactics meant the Main simply redoubled their efforts. An incredible Coiffait throw again resulted in bedlam in the area, with Jason once more heading over. He had more luck with his trusty left foot. On the hour an inswinging free kick from the right touchline was powerfully headed home by Joe Betts, before a cross from almost the same position minutes later was finished by Malky Morien's head, this time to seemingly turn the result round 180 degrees.

If the lads believed their hard work was over, they were in for a rude awakening as Hebburn put in an immensely testing ten-minute spell.

Substitute Maccas was lucky not to be penalised for handball in the box with what must have been his first touch. In the spirit of indecision that gripped the country in the run up to the General Election, the trainee assistant dithered and was seemingly unable to make the call. Thankfully for Main, referee Owens gave a corner. From this the ball broke to Michael Younger, whose piledriver was brilliantly blocked by Rob, only for the next Hebburn attack to provide an equaliser as Ray Oshin lashed in a loose ball.

The next goal was crucial and relief and celebration went hand in hand when it came our way. Malky's delightful close control on the edge of the area and sublime finish into the top corner gave the Main a lead that would not be relinquished. Indeed, it could have heralded more goals, as Tony Browell hit the frame from a corner and Maccas was flagged offside as he tapped the ball home.

Despite a couple of late flurries by Hebburn, the boys held out to maintain top spot in the league as the full time whistle was greeted with intense flurries of profane language from both benches while I rode sedately away, contemplating a potentially pivotal evening's set of results.

Our victory had almost certainly ended Hebburn's chances of promotion, while Rutherford's victory over Wallington by the surprisingly tight margin of 4-3, Amble United's shock 3-0 home loss to Morpeth SC and Shields United's plucky 1-0 home win over Whitley Bay A meant we now had a three horse race for the promotion slots, with the title being ours to lose:

Percy Main	P27	W19	D5	GD +29	Pts 62
Rutherford	P27	W18	D3	GD +28	Pts 60
Amble United	P26	W17	D4	GD +39	Pts 55
Whitley Bay A	P25	W15	D3	GD +31	Pts 48

The following Saturday, May 8th, saw Nick Clegg completing his personal odyssey from kingmaker to teamaker in accepting the role of Tom Brown to Eton Dave's Flashman, while the Main completed our five match series of away games with a trip to Northbank in Carlisle. As the other keeper for my Over 40s side was injured, I had no choice but to play, then take in Swalwell v Whitley Bay Town in Alliance Division 2, partly for groundhopping purposes and partly because it's right next to where my mam lives and I was off to see her after the game, rather than make the trip to Carlisle.

I was kept abreast of developments at the evocatively named Sheepmount Complex as Norman texted me updates, which I tweeted to twitter for a rapt watching audience of three:

Graeme Smith 1-0, 12 mins
Half Time 1-0
Macca 2-0, 51 mins
Malky 3-0, 60 mins
3-1, 62 mins
Chris Doig, 4-1, 70
Graeme Smith, 5-1 74
5-1 F/T

We were still top of the league, of course. Rutherford hadn't played and Whitley Bay A, no doubt turning out a side full of kids as their entire club was already on the pop in London in preparation for their second successive FA Vase Final at Wembley on the Sunday, led Amble 3-2 going into injury time. If it had stayed like that, we'd have been promoted there and then, but an Amble equaliser meant we now needed a single point to confirm our elevation. Consequently, I decided to make the 'Percy Main Potential Promotion Party' an event on Facebook and invited everyone I knew to Wednesday's final home game against Morpeth SC. Despite Laura's entreaty not to jinx things, I felt sure our success was almost guaranteed.

On the Sunday, while Whitley Bay retained the FA Vase with a 6-1 win over Wroxham and Chelsea became Premier League winners by squeezing past Wigan 8-0, the Main committee were at Purvis Park for The Wincomblee versus Bar Berlise in the Newcastle Central Sunday Afternoon League President's Trophy. Bar Berlise were 3-0 up in 10 minutes, but the second half saw a different story. The final score was The Wincomblee 7 Bar Berlise 4. Who needs the Premier League when you can get entertainment like that? We made £95 flogging hot dogs as well, which was thirty quid more than the U16s final on the Tuesday before the Morpeth game brought in, when a sunny evening made pop the refreshment of choice for most of the crowd.

The Wednesday of the Morpeth game wasn't sunny. We actually saw unseasonable hailstones bear down on an unsuspecting North Tyneside. I pondered whether they had any significance related to our potentially imminent elevation to Step 7 of the English football pyramid, but decided they probably hadn't.

I got to Purvis Park at 4.15, simultaneously rendezvousing with Laura, Jason and Norman; the cook, the chief, the middle distance runner and our blogger, as Peter Greenaway didn't quite say. Soon Gary, Bob and a succession of players arrived. The goals were put up, the strips set out and the food prepared, while I stuck up laminated posters of the review of the Cullercoats home game from http://thetravellingfan.blogspot.com/ . With the season ending in most other leagues, we were expecting a decent crowd, augmented by many groundhoppers who would be aware of our habit of 'issuing' for all home games; hence the posters of the Blog were intended to make them feel at home, while Andy did 30 programmes in anticipation of an influx of hoppers, which we sold, as well as knocking out several badges, contributing to a season's best total on the door. If only events on the pitch had reflected the positivism off it.

A week previous, Britain had gone to the polls in order to elect a new Government. The period of stasis and indecision that followed the inconclusive ballot and subsequent results left a void at the centre of society that was profoundly unsettling for the vast majority of the populace. That said, the emotions stirred by such a seemingly crucial series of events relating to democracy and the will of the people paled in to utter insignificance when contrasted with the dramatic and ultimately disappointing sporting theatre at Purvis Park. Michael Bowman's perfectly executed, unstoppable, 25-yard dipping volley left a stunned home fan base vacillating between pride at a magnificent, though ultimately futile, fightback and agonised despair at the devastating kick in the guts that his goal engendered, when giving Morpeth a 3-2 advantage as the game entered stoppage time.

It was a simply superb goal, worthy of winning any contest, and to claim that it was a slice of luck would be churlish in the extreme, though it has to be said that Bowman's effort represented the sum total of Morpeth's efforts in the second period as a rampant Villagers side pushed the visitors back deep in to their own territory as we sought to claim the single point needed to ensure promotion to the Northern Alliance Premier Division.

Last Saturday the Main had been four minutes from promotion; this evening, Johnathon McEnaney's uncompromising 85th minute equaliser, when turning home the rebound after Wilka's ferocious effort, following brilliant wing wizardry from Pierre-Luc Coiffait, had come back from the underside of the bar, again put the Main in the top flight for the length of time it takes to boil an egg. Sadly Bowman's stunner was a sledgehammer to crack us in the nuts.

However, it seemed initially that we'd surrender meekly rather than dying bravely. Having gone 2-0 down after 14 minutes, it appeared that the importance of the occasion had got to us. With two games remaining and a single point needed, the difficulty of facing a blazing sun in the first half should have been only a minor inconvenience. Morpeth's manager, Ritchie Latimer, a veteran of a single appearance for the Main (lost 4-0 at Cullercoats), had assembled a squad of such a weight of numbers that the job of selecting a starting line-up and bench must have seemed comparable to Eton Dave's task of fashioning the required set of spineless yes men to pursue his socially repressive programme from his 300 chinless wonders and Clegg's Vegan Wehrmacht. They (Morpeth Sporting Club not the ConDems) were able to utilise the dazzling properties of the sun to take the lead in the second minute.

Worse was to follow ten minutes later when more alarums in the Percy Main penalty box saw Scott Pocklington power home a low drive under Rob's despairing leap to put what appeared to be a Northern League All Star XI two up. Last week Morpeth had been the toast of Purvis Park when winning 3-0 at Amble United. However, the emphatic nature of that scoreline ought to have served as a warning to Percy Main that this evening's opposition were not to be taken lightly and the opening quarter of an hour proved the sagacity of such circumspection. Frankly, we were naïve in not realising that an experienced opposition campaigner such as Latimer would have called in a few favours from his lengthy list of "have boots, will travel and sod the lads who've grafted in the Alliance from August to April" avaricious journeymen contacts, who'd play for Al Qaeda Rovers if it got them £20.

Of course, the very touchstone of the Villagers in 2009/10 has been an astonishing resilience and mental fortitude. Yet again it came to the forefront this evening. Despite going in two goals adrift, the lads were resolute after the break. Chris Locke was a few inches over with a good shot from distance and Craig Culyer's first time effort from a beautiful Malky pass skimmed the post when perhaps he ought to have made sure by advancing closer in on goal. This was a minor setback, as substitute Joe Betts charged in on goal from the left on the hour, before feeding Maccas with a delicious pass that the powerful striker finished with a measured side foot. Main were now effectively one goal away from promotion and Coiffait almost scored it a minute later, but his impudent flick was inches wide.

Morpeth, despite their experience at their various Northern League clubs and a superb showing at the back by Ritchie Latimer, were hanging on grimly. Luck seemed to be on their side as all we threw at them was repulsed. When Maccas sidefooted a Malky freekick wide from six yards with 10 to go, it seemed the game was up. However, minutes later, the same player scored his second of the night following Wilka's ferocious drive. The celebrations following this goal were prolonged and heartfelt; sadly, they were premature.

Moments later the ball was half cleared to Bowman just outside the box and his instinctive swing of the foot flashed in to the top corner. It was a once a season goal; the kind you know is in even before he's connected. Despite the sheer power of the strike, events took place in agonised slow motion. It was unstoppable, it was shattering, it was heartbreaking. I felt sick and Laura was in tears, but you have to be as dignified in defeat as you are gracious in victory. We had corner flags to collect, goals to dismantle, dressing rooms to sweep out and a kitchen to clean. In the Northern Alliance, as everywhere else in life, self-pity is destructive and a waste of time.

In the cricket club post match, the atmosphere was a little reserved, but neither downbeat nor despairing. We still needed a point and had a trip to Berwick, a team we'd beaten twice already this season, to look forward to. I must admit though, the last thing I thought of before going to sleep and the first thing on my mind when I woke up was the image of the ball flashing past Rob for their winner.

The irony was, of course, that we had Morpeth to play in our next game; the Northumberland FA Minor Cup Final at Blue Flames on Wednesday 19th. We headed for the home of the county FA knowing that the title was probably out of our hands as we'd fallen to second place because Rutherford had won both their intervening games, away to Chopwell and Berwick, to guarantee their promotion. Amble United had kept up the pressure with a 1-0 win over Hebburn on Saturday 15th, in a rotten game that Phil Hogg and I took in as the Main had a free afternoon, desperately hoping for a Hebburn equaliser and trying to sheepishly blend in to the background among a crowd of about 20 on the day Chelsea won the FA Cup, which left the table looking like this:

Rutherford	P29	W21	D5	GD +32	Pts 66
Percy Main	P29	W20	D5	GD +32	Pts 65
Amble United	P28	W18	D5	GD +40	Pts 59

The day of the Minor Cup Final was glorious. Cycling home from work (I took the afternoon off to mentally prepare), I found myself covered in greenfly. The humid rush hour and early evening passed in a fug of worry as, now attired in regulation suit and tie (***sans*** extraneous aphids***)***, I nervously paced the car park of Blue Flames awaiting the arrival of our team. Resplendent in white shirts and pink ties, they showed up looking ready for some proper work. Even Chris Locke had ditched his beach shorts and flip-flops for formal threads.

Percy Main Amateurs may have looked professional, but that evening we were a shambles, a disgrace and an embarrassment to the good name of the club. This game, played in front of 292 spectators and which should have been a showpiece event and a chance to show how far the club has come, was a sickening, self-inflicted shambles. If I wanted to be disgusted by the side I watch, I could have stuck with Newcastle United.

On a night when calm heads and sober maturity were required above all else, the team were guilty of ragged, intemperate ill discipline as they failed to rise to the occasion. Having lost in the last few minutes to Morpeth the week before, it was essential that the players who were afforded the privilege of representing the club in this game did not allow any frustrations from that encounter to interfere with this occasion. Sadly, in too many instances, this was not the case. In particular the second half, which saw Maccas dismissed for an attempted head butt and half a dozen others yellow carded for a combination of vicious stamps, snide trips and studs up hacks, was a dismal excuse for a football match that saw the Villagers squad split themselves in to three distinct camps; those who tried, against overwhelming odds, to play football, those too timid to step up to the plate, who failed to produce the minimum level of performance their inclusion in the starting eleven should have merited, and those who were more concerned with kicking anyone in a yellow shirt and appeared to regard the outcome of the game as secondary to their ruthless pursuit of personal vendettas on all areas of the pitch. Frankly, once Morpeth, who adequately exploited their easily avoidable one-man advantage, had taken the lead, I stood in mute rage, willing the full time whistle to end this charade.

The contrast between this shambolic excuse for a football match and the sedate, untroubled progress of the Main to the final is as pronounced as it is galling. Perhaps the only crumb of comfort from this painful evening would be the knowledge that at some point, the realisation would dawn on certain of the squad that, having contributed to our defeat in this game, a further defeat at Berwick in the final league game would mean another season in the Northern Alliance First Division and, as a consequence, a season that promised so much would produce nothing tangible, unless they wised up.

Several of the players really needed to reflect that in this game, a cup final no less, they had let down the supporters, the club and most of all themselves; not Rob, not Chris Locke, not Tony Browell or Mickey Haley or Graeme Smith, and not Cola, who had to be carried from the pitch with a knee injury, but certain of the others, who may not be either as good or as hard as they think they are. The Percy Main Amateurs of 2009/10 were a squad of excellent footballers; they needed to concentrate on remembering that and showing it at Berwick to ensure that the campaign could be salvaged and did not unravel in bitter acrimony.

However, despite all this, within 30 minutes of the final whistle, the only people still in the bar at Blue Flames were the losing side. Morpeth picked up their trophy and buggered off, presumably on the lash in town. Over half our team stayed to drown their sorrows with us despondent, daft old sods who'd not kicked a ball, in some instances in their entire lives. News that Amble had beaten Shields United didn't darken our mood (well it couldn't really); it actually reinforced our determination. Percy Main Amateurs were going to Berwick to collect three points, to win promotion and to put things right.

The dehydration headache of Thursday morning made the booze bravado of Wednesday night seem a little excessive. We had beaten Berwick 4-1 and 3-1 at home this year, but our trips to the Borders had never been successful, with 1-4 in 2008 and 1-2 in 2009 as prime examples. The league table made for ominous but unambiguous reading:

Rutherford	P29	W21	D5	GD +32	Pts 66
Percy Main	P29	W20	D5	GD +32	Pts 65
Amble United	P29	W19	D5	GD +42	Pts 62

Saturday May 22nd 2010; Northern Alliance Division 1
(kick off 2.30pm)

Berwick United v Percy Main Amateurs
Gosforth Bohemians v Rutherford
Northbank Carlisle v Amble United

Neither Berwick nor Gosforth had anything to play for, but Northbank needed three points to avoid relegation; that hope was something positive to keep in mind anyway. For us, any chance of a treble had gone and the Combination Cup final the Saturday after versus Hebburn was of no meaningful consequence at this juncture. The whole season, all nine months of it, was coming down to this one game, which bearing in mind the amount of football played was almost unbelievable and vaguely insane. I suppose it was fitting that we shared the spotlight with the Champions' League final the same day, though I know which game interested me the most.

Saturday morning dawned dazzlingly bright and temperatures rose steadily. By the time we'd assembled at Purvis Park for the 41-seater coach that Norman had booked (£5 a head, no exceptions), it was an arid, airless morning in the high 20s. With the exception of the absent Chris Doig and Mickey Haley, Jason had a good squad to choose from and there was quality and depth off the pitch as well; Geordie Crooks in an 80s-style athletic vest that wouldn't have looked out of place in Sinitta's "So Macho" video, Mick Ritchie with a specially waxed and oiled bouffant hairdo, Gary Reid in touch with his feminine side with a pair of Armani shades that were more Milan than Main, and Bob with an all-important bin-liner full of out of date cans of lager for the lads, that would hopefully serve as a Champagne replacement to toast our elevation post match.

Despite Jason admitting to a dose of nerves that had seen him pacing Newbiggin beach at 5am, it was a confident and relaxed party that made funereal progress north on a traffic-choked A1. As we ground our way towards Berwick, it occurred to me that a decent result in this game would mean only a single journey up this road next season, to easily accessible Alnwick, which would be far preferable to returning here, to newcomers Stobswood and, worst of all, to Morpeth. Mathematics of course dictated that we'd not be visiting Amble, regardless of the day's results.

Having never experienced the discreet charms of the Ramparts Sports Ground before, I was unsure what to expect. I certainly hadn't bargained on a visiting London Routemaster number 38 bus, apparent destination

Piccadilly Circus, guiding us towards a pitch that was only separated from the North Sea by the East Coast main line. The sun was shining brightly and the distant sea was blue, which meant we had neither a cliff nor any shadows on our horizon, so God knows why the vehicular extra from 'Summer Holiday' was there.

Despite the glorious weather, the Ramparts Sports Ground was decidedly Spartan. While there may have been a rusty rail around the pitch, there was nothing else of note to indicate this was the intended location for a crucial promotion battle. As temperatures touched 30 degrees, the lack of liquid refreshment caused consternation. Thankfully, the advance party of Main fans, in the shape of the Cole family and Geoff Suniga, had done a good reconnaissance job. They pointed out Tweedside planners had thoughtfully erected a Morrisons superstore a short walk away, so the party split between shoppers and administrators as drinks and snacks were purchased and the team prepared themselves for this game by playing on the swings in the local kiddies' park, like Malky and Maccas!

The referee for this game was Michael Shearer, who had taken charge of the Peterlee away and Morpeth home fixtures, so each time he'd been involved, there had been an element of drama to the game. As we took the lead after 40 seconds in this one, you could say he kept up his record. Most importantly, the Percy Main players kept their side of the bargain.

Three days on from the disaster of the Northumberland FA Minor Cup Final, the boys put things right in triumphant, praiseworthy fashion with a rampant performance at the Ramparts. It was a day when the tone was set by Jason asking Graeme Smith to fill in at right back and, like the whole of the squad, Smithy acquitted himself superbly, doing more than was required and giving everything to the cause on a day when almost everything went well.

Kicking towards the inland goal, we were ahead almost immediately. John Amos ran at Berwick from the kick off, causing them to hastily concede a corner. Jason took it and Pierre Luc Coiffait headed home at the near post to provoke riotous celebrations on and off the pitch. Two minutes later Coiff's infamous long throw almost panicked Berwick keeper Thompson into handling the ball into his own net, but another corner was the result, from which John Amos saw Thompson save with his legs. The home keeper was again involved after six minutes when he desperately scrambled back to grab a Malky Morien lob almost on the line. Malky repeated this method after nine minutes, but saw his effort just drift wide.

After a period of relative calm, the Main had the chance to wrap up the game on 18 minutes when Shaun Wilkinson's explosive burst into the box was halted with a cynical trip. Perhaps it was the importance of the game, or perhaps it was the inordinate length of time that elapsed before he was able to take the kick following the protracted negotiations as to where the penalty spot actually was (the carpet of daisies on the pitch helped to obscure most of the markings), but Jason, who has proved so reliable from the spot in the past, lost his nerve and fired the ball straight at Thompson's legs, meaning the opportunity was lost.

Things got worse for a stunned Main when Berwick's Wood immediately charged down the left before pulling it back to an unmarked Leigh Walker, who confidently stroked the ball into the net. There were the usual recriminations and coarse invective among the Villagers side, but the fact was Walker ought to have been picked up by left-back Jason, who was still 60 yards up field after missing the spot kick. It was hard to keep perspective and remember a point was all that was needed to go up. When Rob made a magnificent block from Chris Falconer on the half hour, all of the Main's early pressure seemed a distant memory. News filtering through of two goal leads for Amble and Rutherford did nothing to ease the nerves either, nor did the spurning of two glorious chances to retake the lead, when Amos and then Malky were denied by the athletic Thompson in the moments leading up to half time.

Thankfully, both of them were vindicated in the second half. After good early pressure by Percy Main, when Joe Betts was twice denied by Thompson, Malky Morien scored the goal that sent the Main up. Coiffait's corner was perfectly delivered and Malky's firm nod was clearly over the line when desperately hacked away, though referee Mick Shearer was perfectly placed to give the goal. I was stood behind the goal with Graeme and Jon Cole and we saw it was in; or at least we claimed we did.

Soon after this Joe Betts was replaced by Maccas, who collected his usual booking about 50 seconds after taking the pitch. However, Maccas showed his good side with a deliciously judged chipped ball to the back post that John Amos headed home with the deftest of nods to spark pandemonium from the sun-drenched supporters. We knew we were up now; even the most pessimistic of spectators (or Bob as we know him) would have admitted there was no way we'd concede three goals in 15 minutes.

As the clock ran down, the party was in full sway; the team, the substitutes (not forgetting the injured but present Liam Knox), the management, the committee (including an emotional Bob, who I saw nipping away five minutes from the end, allegedly to put the beers in the dressing room for the lads, but more likely to try and compose himself) and the supporters (the Coles, the Sunigas, Latty, Peter and all) all joined together in glorious celebration. Rutherford had won, so we hadn't taken the title, but after all the swings of fortune and form in the last two months of the season, during which time we'd played half our league games, we didn't care!

The sumptuous post match buffet in the fabulous, atmospheric Thatch pub was memorable and appreciated, while the return coach journey was a delightful bonding exercise for all concerned, especially Graeme Smith, who'd managed a dozen cans by the time we reached Rothbury. Hell, he deserved it, they deserved it; we all deserved it. If you can't get plastered in 30 degree heat when your team's got promoted, when can you?

I would imagine Percy Main players and fans drank more than Internazionale did on winning the Champions League that same night, but probably not as much as the supporters of The Turbinia and The Wincomblee in the last of the Sunday afternoon finals. That lot cleaned us out of hot dogs and the cricket club of plastic pint glasses and bottles of cider.

The week between the Berwick game and the Hebburn Combination Cup tie was interspersed with a couple of hastily arranged Junior U19 finals between Cramlington and New Fordley. We didn't mind; it meant a few more quid in the club coffers. It also gave time for relaxed reflection on the league campaign that had just ended.

Obviously, the aim at the start of the season had been promotion and as such the season had been a success. However, as we'd beaten Rutherford three times, it seemed a mite galling we hadn't won the title, especially as we'd been in such a commanding position before the 112-day winter interregnum. If the start of the season had been characterised by easy wins when we'd spurned lots of chances (Hebburn at home and Bohemians away, for example) or had grittily fought back to grab vital wins (Peterlee away or Chopwell at home), then the second part had been all about the joys of superb, easy wins (Cullercoats and Amble at home or Berwick and Northbank away) contrasting with desperately frustrating games where we didn't get what we deserved (Bohemians, Seaton Burn and Morpeth at home in particular).

We'd played 14 league games in 49 days, winning seven, drawing four and losing three. During that period we'd experienced the elation of Hebburn and Rutherford, when our determination had seen us through, and we'd also suffered the agony of seeing the post come to Chopwell's rescue, or rogue offside flags denying us an equaliser against Seaton Burn. For the entire seven weeks I'd not been able, in all honesty, to state that I was convinced I knew where we'd finish up. Every game brought about a change of mind; after Seaton Burn, I thought we'd finish third, then after Wallington I felt we'd be runners-up, but after Rutherford I couldn't see anyone but us winning the thing, until Morpeth, when I feared once more that we'd be the also-rans in third place.

Second place didn't bring the plaudits associated with winning the title, nor did it have the despair of missing out in third place; it would have to do and it wasn't that bad after all, provided we could finally win a cup!

Back in May 1999, Ponteland United hosted West Allotment in the final Alliance game of the season, which, after some artful fixture manipulation turned it into a straight fight for the title between those two. Over 700 people saw WAC win 3-1 in a ground without cover, hard standing or toilets. Eleven years on, the facilities have not improved, but it's a great pitch they have up there and a large car park, so it was chosen as the venue for this final.

In contrast to our lot's week on the piss on the Quayside and in Whitley, Hebburn had been required to play two league games, drawing with Wallington and losing heavily to Whitley Bay. Jason, Malky and a few others had taken in the latter game, reporting that a leg-weary Hebburn didn't seem as intimidating as the side we travelled to face on May 5th. All well and good, but the Kafkaesque complexities relating to eligibility for the Combination Cup meant we were miles under strength.

The North Shields trio of Chris Hunt, John Amos and Craig Culyer were all ineligible, having signed too late to comply with the competition rules. Similarly, Pierre-Luc Coiffait and Chris Doig, who had both signed early enough, hadn't played enough league games for us before the semi-final, which was the cut-off point for eligibility; remember the semi final took place on March 27th and our last league game before that day was December 12th. Ziggy, Graeme Cole and Liam Knox were still injured, but Mickey Haley and Callum Colback, fresh off the plane from his second foreign holiday in a month, were there.

Consequently, the starting eleven picked itself; Rob, Mickey, Smithy, Tony, Jason (unfamiliar centre back role), Chris Locke, Malky, Wilka, Cal (out wide left and using his pace), Bettsy and Maccas. On the bench Dean Ellis and Shaddy were definites, but Cola and Knoxy were only named as subs to make up the numbers. Having conducted a team availability test by using **facebook**, Jay discovered Tapsy was back from skiing and so he ended up on the bench, not having kicked a ball for Main since late November, and by 4pm the jammy sod had a winner's medal in his mitt.

Hebburn, as I'd suspected, were running on empty. Their huge backlog of fixtures had been too much for them in the end. We won 1-0 when Chris Locke was tripped in the box and Jason, who never put a foot wrong all day and deservedly won the Man of the Match trophy, sent the keeper the wrong way from the spot. Considering his miss at Berwick the week before, this showed real guts on his part. I was delighted for the lad; obviously he's a complete crackerjack, but he's a good player, takes the game seriously and has achieved a hell of a lot to be proud of during his two seasons at the club.

In the end, the game was a slight anti-climax; it could have been more comfortable for us, as Malky hit the keeper's legs from six yards and Cal fired an inch over, but they hit the post and had one disallowed for offside as well. We should have had a second penalty in injury time when Bettsy's cross was punched away by a Hebburn defender, but it's of no matter; elation was general all around the squad and support when the final whistle went.

At least Hebburn had won a cup a few weeks earlier, so they had something to show for their efforts, meaning this result helped spread the trophies around, with Rutherford and also Morpeth, of course, getting hold of some silverware. The great thing for us, which occurred to me as Chris Locke was being sprayed with Cava by the rest of the squad, is that we won't get to defend the Combination Cup as it's for first division sides only. I like the irony of all the hard work we put in during the final and the Berwick game the week before to make sure we can't retain it. What I liked even more was that this final helped to expunge any memories of the Morpeth debacle.

Seeing a dressing room full of sweaty, semi-naked, beaming young(ish) men all drinking bottled lager and bouncing up and down told me this had been a successful season. I am almost inexplicably glad to have become involved with Percy Main Amateurs. We are a wonderful club; come and visit us some time. You'll be made very welcome.

Conclusion: *Sleep No More*

BY ALL ACCOUNTS, everyone had a decent night out after we'd beaten Hebburn in the Combination Cup Final, firstly at the Diamond in Ponteland and then out in Whitley. Not just the players, but Bob, Gary and Geordie all made it out for a few scoops. Sadly, I was unable to join them as I had to head off immediately after the presentation to Manchester for my Union's annual congress, which had started around the time Chris Locke was lifting the cup. Thankfully, I was able to toast the team's success with almost as much gusto as they did. In the process I learned that if you start a chorus of 'Jason Ritchie's Claret and Blue Army' on Deansgate at one in the morning, nobody joins in.

The club's official end of season do was at the cricket club on Saturday June 5th. In previous years it has sometimes been a fraught evening. Two years ago, former manager Colin Atchinson had decided to leave the club by mutual consent minutes before the do started, which gave the event a slightly sombre tone, while in 2009, the fallout from the retirement of Pat and Carol dominated proceedings. Thankfully, this year's bash went off without any unpleasantness or the hint of a bad atmosphere as both teams, the committee and plenty of supporters got stuck into the drink and had a bloody good night.

Norman started off the evening with a few well chosen words, and then I made a sombre and shallow contribution, which managed to be both brief and tedious in the manner of Quince from ***'A Midsummer Night's Dream'***, before Bob concluded the formal introductory speeches with a passionate and celebratory oration that was both inspiring and valedictory. The committee silenced, the event moved up a gear; first of all, the men's team were presented with their league runners-up medals by Geoff Mason from the Northern Alliance Management Committee, meaning that each of them had received three gongs for this year's efforts; even if two of them were for finishing second, it's a decent haul and further proof they'd done really well.

We then moved on to the rest of the men's team presentations, which was of great relief to Callum Colback, who, having recently discovered he was about to become a father, was also informed by his partner that the Presentation Evening coincided with his engagement party and that he had to be away from us sharpish.

Perhaps the most heart-warming aspect of the evening was club captain Chris Locke's speech. As the bloke is a secondary school teacher, he's used to keeping an unruly audience in their seats and silencing idle chit-chat; this he managed exquisitely, as well as name-checking every single player, committee member and supporter (we don't get huge crowds you know), thanking us all for our efforts in a humorous and genuinely touching contribution which brought forth a torrent of richly deserved applause and spontaneous laughter. To be fair the next act, Rob and Aiden, the managers of the women's team, gave as good a speech as Chris, being a highly effective and amusing double act.

In amongst this orgy of giggles, crude heckling and sarky in-jokes, we managed to see some gongs handed out. For the women's team, Vicky Freeman was Players' Player of the Year; Gemma Kerr was Most Improved Player; Kelly Rushworth was Top Goalscorer, and Managers' Awards went to Tina Oxman, Paula DiMarco, Amy Rostron and Cathy Foster. The men had far fewer awards to hand out than the women and the fact we didn't have either a top goalscorer or goal of the season award seemed to disappoint Malky and Cal, who'd have been the recipients in those categories, but they'd already got three medals from the season so there was no reason to be greedy. One of the Ultras (well Jason's former schoolmates and now drinking buddies who come along to the games), Peter, made a good point; we should have a Supporters' Player of the Season for next year. Until then, there were only three gongs to hand out.

In 2008/09, Pierre-Luc Coiffait won the Young Player of the Year trophy, which was this time awarded to Mickey Haley, who richly deserved it for an excellent campaign in which he has improved considerably. Mickey also won the Players' Player award, to pip Malky by a single vote, which had been won by Tony Browell last year. Tony won the overall Player of the Year award for a fabulous season in which he'd avoided being booked at all, which is incredible for a centre half. The luckless Malky was again in second place, poor bugger.

There was one final award to be given out, that of Clubman of the Year, for the person who has given the most unstinting service to Percy Main Amateurs during the season just ended. Frankly, there was only one candidate; the man who gives up more of his waking time to this football club than anyone else. He's secretary, website editor, motivating force behind the establishment of the women's team, general handyman and a million other things as well. He's also the reason why I got involved with Percy Main; Norman de Bruin. Well done mate!

Awards over, a fleet of taxis transported the players in their cashmere school jumpers, distressed denim, espadrilles and other quizzical fashion statements to the Quayside, while the Committee stayed in the cricket club and got gently hammered. It was a great night and a charming vindication of the validity of all we'd been engaged in over the past year.

Waking next morning, bleary-eyed and thick-headed, I glanced at my email inbox. The only new message was this one from Norman :

Good people of Percy,
The 2010 AGM of Percy Main Amateurs FC and a full committee meeting will take place at Purvis Park on Sunday June 20th at 6pm. As the Northern

Alliance AGM has officially ratified our promotion, there are several items to discuss for the coming season. I hope this is ok for all.

Also, the following pre season friendlies have been arranged;

Saturday July 17th - Newcastle East End (away)
Saturday July 24th - Annfield Plain (home)
Wednesday July 28th - West Allotment (home)
Saturday July 31st - North Shields ; Gary Hull Trophy (home)
Wednesday August 4th - Pelton (away)

There may be more to follow before the big kick off on august 14th, however there will be no home games before July 24th to give the pitch a chance to recover from the multitude of cup finals played on it during the last month and a half!

Finally, if anybody is feeling handy, there is a bit of work needs doing over the summer on the pitch and in the pavilion, starting from Saturday 12th at about 11ish. Why not come down, lend a hand and get a good thirst up for England's World cup game a bit later?

This will be the start of a rolling programme of works to bring the old place up to scratch, which should hopefully keep us busy over the next few Saturdays until the football starts again. All volunteers welcome!

Cheers, Norman

Here we go again! Percy Main Amateurs; the club that never sleeps.

Appendix 1

2009/2010 Pin Point Recruitment Northern Alliance First Division Final League Table

Team	P	W	D	GD	Pts
Rutherford (C)	**P30**	**W22**	**D3**	**GD +33**	**Pts 69**
Percy Main (P)	**P30**	**W21**	**D5**	**GD +34**	**Pts 68**
Amble United	P30	W20	D5	GD +43	Pts 65
Whitley Bay A	P30	W19	D4	GD +50	Pts 61
Morpeth SC	P30	W18	D1	GD +7	Pts 55
Hebburn Reyrolle	P30	W15	D6	GD +14	Pts 51
South Shields United	P30	W15	D3	GD +14	Pts 48
Cullercoats	P30	W14	D3	GD +20	Pts 45
Gosforth Bohemians	P30	W13	D4	GD +8	Pts 43
Peterlee Town	P30	W13	D4	GD +1	Pts 43
Chopwell Officials Club	P30	W10	D3	GD -20	Pts 33
Berwick United	P30	W8	D3	GD -51	Pts 27
Wallington **	P30	W7	D7	GD -19	Pts 22
Newcastle East End *	P30	W7	D3	GD -38	Pts 21
Northbank Carlisle (R)	**P30**	**W6**	**D1**	**GD –39**	**Pts 19**
Seaton Burn (R) *	**P30**	**W2**	**D5**	**GD –57**	**Pts 8**

** Deducted 6 points for fielding ineligible players

* Deducted 3 points for fielding ineligible players

Appendix 2

Percy Main Amateurs Results 2009/2010 (Home games in bold)

Date	Opposition	Score	**Competition**
01/08/09	**North Shields**	2-2 *	**Gary Hull Memorial Trophy**
05/08/09	**Shankhouse**	**2-1**	**Friendly**
08/08/09	Harraby CC	2-1	**Friendly**
15/08/09	**Hebburn Reyrolle**	**2-0**	**Northern Alliance D1**
19/08/09	Amble United	0-5	Northern Alliance D1
22/08/09	Morpeth SC	3-2	Northern Alliance D1
26/08/09	Wallington	**2-0**	**Northern Alliance D1**
29/08/09	Rutherford	**2-1**	**Northern Alliance D1**
02/09/09	Cullercoats	1-1	Northern Alliance D1
05/09/09	Chopwell	**2-1**	**Northern Alliance D1**
12/09/09	Amble United	**1-0**	**Kicks Leisure Stan Seymour League Cup Round 1**
19/09/09	Seaton Burn	3-1	Northern Alliance D1
26/09/09	**Northbank Carlisle**	**2-0**	**Northern Alliance D1**
03/10/09	Ashington Booze Brothers Athletic	4-3	Northumberland FA Minor Cup Round 1
10/10/09	Gosforth Bohemians	1-0	Northern Alliance D1
17/10/09	Heddon	**1-2**	**Kicks Leisure Stan Seymour League Cup Round 2**
24/10/09	**Peterlee Town**	4-2	Northern Alliance D1
31/10/09	South Shields United	2-0	**Northern Alliance D1**
07/11/09	**South Shields United**	**2-0**	Northern Alliance D1
14/11/09	***Rutherford***	*3-2*	Northern Alliance Combination Cup Round 1
21/11/09	Newcastle East End	5-1	**Northern Alliance D1**
28/11/09	**Berwick United**	4-1	**Northern Alliance D1**
05/12/09	**Wallsend Boys Club**	**3-0** **	**Northumberland FA Minor Cup Round 3**
12/12/09	**Whitley Bay A**	4-2	**Northern Alliance D1**
23/01/10	Shilbottle CW	**3-0** **	**Northumberland FA Minor Cup Round 4**
06/03/10	*Amble*	*3-0* ***	*Northumberland FA Minor Cup Quarter Final*
13/03/10	Wallington	**4-1 (AET)**	**Northern Alliance Combination Cup Round 2**
20/03/10	**Newcastle Chemfica**	**2-0**	**Northumberland FA Minor Cup Semi Final**

27/03/10	Berwick United	**3-1**	**Northern Alliance Combination Cup Semi Final**
03/04/10	Peterlee Town	**4-4**	**Northern Alliance D1**
07/04/10	**Whitley Bay A**	0-1	Northern Alliance D1
10/04/10	**Chopwell**	2-2	Northern Alliance D1
14/04/10	Gosforth Bohemians	**1-1**	**Northern Alliance D1**
17/04/10	Seaton Burn	**1-2**	**Northern Alliance D1**
21/04/10	Amble United	**3-0**	**Northern Alliance D1**
24/04/10	Cullercoats	**2-0**	**Northern Alliance D1**
26/04/10	**Wallington**	1-1	Northern Alliance D1
28/04/10	**Rutherford**	1-0	Northern Alliance D1
01/05/10	**Newcastle East End**	2-0	Northern Alliance D1
05/05/10	**Hebburn Reyrolle**	3-2	Northern Alliance D1
08/05/10	**Northbank Carlisle**	5-1	Northern Alliance D1
12/5/10	**Morpeth SC**	2-3	**Northern Alliance D1**
19/5/10	*Morpeth SC*	*0-1* ****	*Northumberland FA Minor Cup Final*
22/5/10	Berwick United	3-1	Northern Alliance D1
29/5/10	*Hebburn Reyrolle*	*1-0* *****	*Northern Alliance Combination Cup Final*

* Lost on penalties 5-3
** Tie switched to Purvis Park
*** Tie played on neutral ground; Hirst Welfare Ashington
**** Final played at West Allotment FC (aka Blue Flames, home of Northumberland FA)
****** Final played at Ponteland United FC

Appendix 3:

Percy Main Amateurs 2009/2010: pen portraits

GOALKEEPERS:

Rob Rodgerson: Now in his third spell at the club, having returned from Cramlington Town last season. Rob is reliable, agile and vastly experienced in playing at the Northern Alliance's top level. He is a vital asset to the team. His dad's the Treasurer as well.
Phil Hogg: Joined Percy Main last season from Whitley Bay. A former Darlington trainee, who has also appeared for Morpeth Town, Newcastle Blue Star and South Shields. Assistant to Jason Ritchie, apparently.
Sam Dodds: Young keeper, only 17, but with a bright future in the game.

DEFENDERS:

Tony Browell: Long serving, commanding centre half. He returned to the club in 2007 following a spell at North Shields and was voted this season's Player of the Year. Tony is an experienced player who is a great influence on the younger members of the squad.
Graeme Cole (Cola): Commanding, experienced centre half, who arrived from Shankhouse last season. Brother videos the games and puts highlights on YouTube and Facebook.
Mickey Haley: Converted from midfield to defence this season and has operated with distinction at right back, rarely putting a foot wrong all campaign. Voted Young Player and Players' Player of the Year. Sent off for a ridiculous handball against Berwick.
Graeme Smith: Vastly experienced, reliable, solid Alliance player in his second spell at the club after signing during the close season, also from Shankhouse.
Jason Ritchie: Player manager, left-sided defender who can also operate as a wide midfielder. A dead ball specialist and penalty taker, who is as good a swearer as he is penalty taker.
Steven Shadforth (Shaddy): An experienced defender who can also do a job up front. Strong and physical, Shaddy is a good motivator for those around him.

Liam Knox: A strong centre back who loves a tackle, is good in the air and reads the game well. He can be very effective up front as well. Death Metal fan.
Chris Hunt: Excellent centre half. Joined the club late in the season from North Shields.
Richie May: Played one game at Wallington and scored an injury time leveller. Never seen him personally.

MIDFIELDERS:

Dean Ellis: A close season signing. Young midfielder with bags of potential.
Chris Locke: Skilful midfielder and team captain. Chris likes to get forward and open up opposition defences. Last season's Player of the Year. Always attired in flip-flops and shorts, regardless of weather.
Malky Morien: Midfielder in his second spell at the club; transferred this season from Whitley Bay. He creates and scores goals, proving himself to be a vital addition to the squad.
Shaun Wilkinson (Wilka): Lightning fast winger and excellent crosser of the ball.
Chris Doig: Traditional, attacking right-winger with bags of pace and plenty of tricks. Returned to the club this season.
Lee Gray: Left-sided midfielder, former Percy Main Player of the Year, has returned to the club following spells at North Shields and Whitley Bay. A great crosser of the ball and strong tackler who shows his experience in games.
Pierre-Luc Coiffait (Coiff): Last season's Young Player of the Year. Skilful left-sided midfielder with a tremendous throw that would put Rory Delap to shame. Often away working in London and available only intermittently.
David Tapsfield (Tapsy): Laid-back, ball-playing midfielder who went on a six-month skiing holiday, returning in time to get his Combination Cup winners medal.
Craig Culyer: Tenacious and skilful. Arrived from North Shields.
Graeme Smith: The other Graeme Smith. Didn't kick a ball all season for us.

STRIKERS:

Joe Betts: A great young centre forward who arrived at Percy Main with a reputation for scoring goals that he lived up to. He finished season 2008/09 as joint top scorer with 13 strikes to his name.
Callum Colback (Cal): Former Whitley Bay and Killingworth striker who scored plenty against us in the past and is now, thankfully, doing the same for us, including the best strike of the season with a free kick against Wallington.
Craig Ewart (Ziggy): A close season capture from Gosforth Bohemians, "Ziggy", as he's known, proved himself a quick and tricky front runner and soon got among the goals before being injured against Amble United in mid September.
Johnathon McEnaney (Maccas): Hard, physical, old-style centre forward, whose work rate is first class. He has an eye for goal and is very good in the air. Has been known to have his name taken the odd time.
John Amos: Tough, quick forward who scored some important goals after arriving from North Shields.

NO LONGER AT THE CLUB:

Dean Clay: Great player but got sick of being on the bench all the time.
Ian Lee: One game for us when he scored a beauty and one against, when he was sent off.
Lindsay Collinson: Work got in the way of his football, so he dropped down a division to Cramlington Blue Star.
Kris Carr: At Newcastle East End.
Sean Potts: Went to Australia for a year.
Wayne Stobbs: Lost his wallet at Peterlee, then didn't come back. Has grown his hair very long.
Steven Pickering: One game as sub, then disappeared.
Dean Morgan: Disappeared after meeting a new woman from Scotland. Still owes us loads of money for his fines.

COACHING STAFF:

In addition to Jason Ritchie (player/manager) and Phil Hogg (player/assistant manager), there is:

Mick Ritchie (Assistant manager): Father of Jason. A well-respected and much admired figure in local football.
George Crooks (Physio/kit-man): Popular and hard-working member of the backroom staff.

COMMITTEE & HELPERS:

Norman de Bruin: Secretary. Tireless worker and compulsive anal retentive.
Bob Rodgerson: Treasurer. Superb ranter and raver at referees, players, opposition or anyone really.
Geordie Mooney: Club chairman. Leeds fan.
Gary Reid: Makes a superb post match buffet for a tenner.
Andy Johnson: Programme editor, Boro fan, allergic to Leicester.
Laura Huntley: Runs the best canteen in the Northern Alliance.
Rob Meldrum and **Aiden Regan**: Women's team managers.

NOT FORGETTING.....

Ann de Bruin, Michelle Hull, Joanne Johnson (and Olivia), Jon Cole (video and photographer supreme) and Family, Geoff Suniga (singlehandedly keeps the canteen operating at a profit) and family, Peter, Latty & the rest of the PMA Ultras.

Thanks for a brilliant season; you've all played your part!

MURDER?

A Swedish Crime Novel

Stockholm Sleuth Series
(Book 3)

Christer
Tholin

Stockholm, Sweden
contact@christertholin.one
www.christertholin.one

Translated by Maiwenn Kafka
Title of the original German edition:
MORD?
Published 2018
Editing: Charlotte Kliemann

Cover design by Anne Gebhardt

ISBN (ebook mobi): 978-91-985796-6-6
ISBN (paperback): 978-91-985795-6-7

For my son, Alexander

Content

PROLOGUE

JULY 2016

Her hand felt so good in his. He was always amazed how soft and delicate her hands were. He was entranced, watching her run along beside him. She was the very picture of loveliness, with her thick blond hair, green eyes and high cheekbones. But this morning he'd had the impression that something was bothering her. She'd disappeared into the bathroom right after breakfast and hadn't been the same since – somehow not as happy and lively as usual. He'd asked her what was going on, but she'd said, "No, nothing, I'm fine."

He was simply crazy about her. He'd never imagined that such a gorgeous young woman could ever be interested in him, much less fall for him. And now here they were beginning a new life together; sometimes he felt like he was dreaming. During the three days since they'd moved into the cabin, the harmony between them had been simply idyllic. And the sex was amazing too – just the love-making he'd been craving, a craving she knew exactly how to slake.

They were approaching the end of the forest path – and the highlight of the walk. The path led to the site of a landslide that had occurred a few years back. The landslide had created a long steep downhill slope that afforded a magnificent view of a large forest meadow dotted with rocks and bushes – and oftentimes animals, which took no notice if you stood there watching them. During a walk they'd taken here a couple of days ago they'd spotted reindeer, which she was very excited about as she'd never seen a reindeer in the wild.

At the end of the slope they stopped, and he turned toward her. She was staring over the edge of the steep cliff, but she wasn't as radiant today as she'd been during their previous walk.

"Is anything the matter? Did I say something wrong?"

"No, no, nothing like that...I really don't know." She let go of his hand, took a step away from him, and gazed at him. What did the look in her eyes mean? He couldn't tell for sure. He saw a lot of sadness there, but also anxiety. She averted her gaze. What was eating her?

As he was about to again ask her what the matter was, he became aware of a movement behind him. He figured it must be an animal and turned around. A huge muscular man was heading straight for him, was upon him in a flash, with a violent shock that shook him to the core. He staggered – and stepped sideways, into what he realized too late was an abyss. He lost his balance and the last thing he heard was Natalia screaming. His hands clawed the air, as he plummeted downward, almost head first. He managed to grab onto a bush whose thorns dug into his hands; but the bush was too small to break his fall. The branch he'd grabbed broke, and he continued falling.

His last thought before crashing into the ground below was of Natalia.

4

PART I

AUGUST 2016

1

Liv opened the large front door.

"Hi, Christina, great to see you. Come on in," she said.

"*Hej!* Nice to see you too. Your place is really awesome," Christina said, looking around in wonderment.

Liv gave her former coworker a furtive look. "Something's not right," she thought to herself. "Those rings under her eyes, she looks so tired, and kind of down." Liv couldn't remember Christina ever looking this way before.

But Liv kept all this to herself. "Yeah, well, I inherited all this from my folks," she said, laughing. Frankly, she felt embarrassed to be living in such resplendent surroundings. The house, which was located in a housing tract in the Stockholm archipelago, had its own beach and a long docking pier where a large motorboat was docked.

"It's really a shame that we spend so little time here; most of the time it just stands empty. But I must say it's great to have a vacation home near Stockholm." This was the first time Liv had spent time here since January, when she'd moved to Berlin with her kids.

"*Hej*, Christina. I'm Martin. Nice to meet you," Martin said as he emerged from the bedroom.

"Hi Martin. You speak really good Swedish."

"Yeah well, I'm getting there. Though I often have to ask if I'm using the right word." Martin was German, but he'd been attending Swedish classes ever since he and Liv had gotten together. Plus, they spoke Swedish at home more and more.

Suddenly three kids came barreling into the house from the back yard.

"Here come the offspring," Liv said. "How about giving Christina a nice hello? This here is my oldest, Saga, and her brother Hampus. Saga's 11 and Hampus is almost nine." The two children shook Christina's hand. Behind them was a little girl who was looking on anxiously.

"And that's Martin's daughter Lara. She's five and isn't fluent in Swedish yet, but she understands just about everything." Laughing shyly, Lara shook hands with Christina.

"Kids, do you want to have coffee with us, or would you rather have ice cream?" said Liv.

"Ice cream, ice cream!" the kids shouted in unison.

"Okay great, so go get yourselves an ice cream from the freezer, which we pretty much filled to the brim yesterday." The ice cream truck from Hemglass made its weekly rounds on the neighboring island, and yesterday they'd waited for it to come by. The kids ran into the kitchen, jostling each other.

"The veranda's the best place for quiet conversation, so let's go out there, shall we?" Liv led Christina through the large living room to the terrace door, which opened out onto a magnificent view. The property sloped down gently to the water, with expanses dotted with large rocks, and bordered by pine and oak trees – and as a backdrop to all this, an unimpeded and stunning view of the sea. The water glistened in the sun; the islands, with their trees and meadows, were bathed in a green, luminescent glow; and scattered around this idyllic scene were houses, most of which were painted red, and a few boats sailing past.

"What an awesome view. It doesn't get much better than this." For all Christina's apparent excitement at taking all this in, Liv couldn't help but notice, once again, the fatigue her friend exuded, and her drooping shoulders.

"Yeah, we never get tired of it," Martin said. "It's really great for me, as this is the first time I've been here. When I took a cruise through our archipelago last year, I couldn't have imagined that one day I'd be spending my vacation in a house like this one."

Liv recalled that back then, Martin had come to Stockholm in the hope of finding her. They'd originally met in southern Sweden, where Martin had rented a vacation home. They'd arranged to meet up again, but then Liv had been kidnapped – an event that had plunged Martin into a state of extreme distress. He'd found out that Liv was living in Stockholm with her family and had decided to go there to find her. Which he'd eventually managed to do, with the aid of two private detectives. But this was by no means the end of the story.

The three of them sat down on the veranda, where there was a large wooden table under a pergola, and around which comfortable, thickly upholstered lawn chairs were arrayed. Martin served the coffee, while Liv cut the cake that she'd baked in the morning with Saga and Lara. As they drank coffee and ate the delicious cake, they chatted about the weather and their vacation plans.

"Did you go on vacation?" Liv asked.

"No." Christina said, shaking her head sadly. "I'm not much in the mood for a vacation, to tell you the truth. Actually, my husband has gone missing. Which is why I wanted to see you."

She was fighting back tears, and Liv stroked her arm soothingly. "I was right," she thought to herself. "Something really is wrong."

She looked over at Martin, and their eyes met: yes, they were familiar with situations like this.

"So tell me," Liv said gently.

Christina cleared her throat. "Five weeks ago, he just vanished without warning. It was a Friday and he'd gone to work as usual, but he never came home. I called him a zillion times, but it just kept going to voicemail. The next day I filed a missing person's report with the police – who haven't done a damn thing about it. I'm at my wit's end, that's the long and the short of it."

"Did he show up at work that day?" Martin asked.

"Yes, though he left work pretty early, but there was nothing unusual about that, as it was a Friday."

"And why aren't the police trying to find him?" said Liv.

"They say there's no evidence of foul play or an accident. They think that Patrik just decided to disappear. They told me I need to just wait, and that in most cases people who've 'gone missing' eventually turn up safe and sound."

"What makes them think that?" Martin asked.

"Well, it's because Patrik took his passport and all his credit cards with him. Plus, his car hasn't been spotted anywhere."

"I see."

"So why did you want to see us?" Liv asked.

"Yes, well, maybe I'm wrong but rumors have been circulating at the company about what happened last year – I mean before you sold the construction business. 'Cause let's face it, your ex died under kind of mysterious circumstances and people have been saying that there was a kidnapping. There wasn't much about it in the papers – but wasn't some private detective or other involved who helped you?"

"Yes, that's true. It's a long story. We've been trying to keep a lid on all this as much as possible, and that's been going quite well."

"I see. Of course you're under no obligation to disclose any of this to me either. But please know that if you do take me into your confidence, your secrets will be safe with me."

"I have total faith in you on that score. After all, you handle confidential information at the company all the time." Christina was the human resources manager at Liv's property management company. And though Liv was no longer involved in the company's day to day operations – having hired a COO and resigned from the board – she'd been working alongside Liv until the end of last year and knew that she could always count on Christina to maintain confidentiality.

"The whole thing has since blown over, but as I'm sure you can understand we don't want the media, or anyone else for that matter, to get wind of this. So what you surmise is in fact true, but of course you need to keep it under your hat. Last year I was kidnapped, and then Saga was taken as well. Thank God for Martin, though, because if it hadn't been for him, I probably wouldn't have come through this ordeal safe and sound. He also hired the private detectives who ultimately got to the bottom of all this."

Christina gave Liv a look of consternation. "Wow, two kidnappings. That must have been horrible. Were you harmed or hurt in any way?"

"No, as I said, we both came through it in one piece. But Saga is still haunted by it. She has nightmares all the time and doesn't like being left alone. But I must say the move to Berlin has done her a world of good. Being in a new place, a new school, and so on is helping her to put the whole thing behind her. We were kind of concerned about how she'd react to coming back to Sweden for vacation, but she's been absolutely fine – at least thus far."

"I'm glad to hear that everything's worked out so well," Christina said.

"Yeah, we really love Berlin, the two little ones speak perfect German and Martin and I get along really well – like two peas in a pod, actually," Liv said, taking Martin's hand and gazing at him lovingly.

"Yes, all the upheaval was worth it in the end," he said with a sly smile.

Liv turned back towards Christina. "I cannot recommend those two detectives we used highly enough. They're really good. Trustworthy, easy to work with – and they really get things done."

"Wow, it would be awesome if they could help me out too," Christina said, once again fighting back tears.

"Really, you needn't worry. You'll see, everything will work out fine in the end."

"Could you give me their number?"

"I think it would be better if I called them and gave them your number instead," Martin said. "They work for an agency that employs a number of detectives, and you want to be sure that the two we worked with are assigned to your case. Besides, they'll already know what the case is all about, and that'll make it easier for me to introduce you to them. In any case I'd intended to contact Lars while we're here."

"Thanks, that's really nice of you. I wanted to avoid hiring just any old detective. It's much better when someone is recommended to you that others have had a positive experience with."

"Yes of course. And really, Lars and Elin are terrific. You can't go wrong with them," said Liv. "So tell me, Christina, do you have any idea what might have happened to your husband?"

"No," she said with a despairing look. "I just keep racking my brains, trying to fathom what might have happened. The whole thing makes no sense. Everything was peachy keen between us, I swear. We were planning to go to our summer home in Norrland in July. When he disappeared, and I was unable to reach him, I even went to Norrland to see if he might have gone there. But that was stupid of me, because of course he wasn't there. Though I had the impression that he might have been there for a little while."

"What makes you say that?" Martin asked.

"Well as you know, you have to pack everything away in the fall in order to close up a summer cabin for the winter. And some of the furnishings looked to me as though they'd been used recently. Or at least I had the impression that the cabin wasn't exactly as we'd left it."

"That's an important detail. The sort of thing you absolutely must tell the detectives."

"Yes, I will, of course. I'm sincerely grateful to both of you. Please tell them to contact me as soon as possible. But now I need to go, otherwise I'll miss the last ferry." All three rose, and Liv and Martin accompanied Christina to the door and said goodbye to her. They watched her as she got in her car and turned out of the driveway into the street.

"Poor Christina," sighed Liv, after Christina had left. "I really feel for her. It's a good thing I got Saga back after only a few days. I never would have been able to survive her being gone for five whole weeks."

"But look, Christina's husband is an adult – though the not knowing is a killer, that's for sure."

"Do you think he might simply have left her?"

"Hard to say. Though let's face it, she's no Miss Sweden."

"Really?" Liv shrieked, rolling her eyes, "You think he left her just 'cause she's a bit plump? But she always dresses really well, plus she's a super nice person."

"Yeah, but you only know her in her capacity as an HR manager, which perhaps isn't the most objective basis for judging someone."

"Yeah, maybe not. But by the same token, you can't just judge a book by its cover, you have to try to see what's inside."

"Yeah, and maybe she's a veritable tornado in bed," said Martin, laughing.

"Men," she snorted. "All you care about is physical appearance and sex."

"You know exactly what we're like. Fortunately enough, you have both – looks and sex."

"Thank God for that," she said, her voice dripping with sarcasm.

But then she put her arms around him and gave him a tender kiss.

"When are you going to call Lars?"

"In a minute. I hope he's not away on vacation. It's August and it's not back to school time yet."

"I'll keep my fingers crossed."

Liv went out on the terrace to clear the table. She was more upset by the conversation than she cared to admit. These things belonged, after all, to the recent past, and it didn't take much to revive the memories of events that had occurred only last year. She and Martin had often talked about whether it was advisable for them to return to Sweden this year, as they both feared that doing so would reopen old wounds, especially for Saga. But Hampus really wanted to go so that he could water-ski and swim every day. So they'd decided to take the risk and everything had been hunky dory, thus far. Liv had in fact gone to Stockholm a couple of times in recent months, as her presence was required at board meetings. But she was always happy to come back home to Berlin, and to Martin. And actually, here in the archipelago with her family, she'd hardly given last year's kidnappings a thought. That is, until the conversation with Christina a few moments ago. Now all of a sudden, the memories and emotions came flooding back, particularly her anxiety about Saga. She thought about how incredibly relieved she'd been to be able to hug Saga again. She was beginning to cry; she needed to pull herself together. She decided the best thing to do was to see how the kids were doing; she needed to feel their physical presence.

2

Lars was watching his two daughters sitting on the edge of the dolphin tank petting a dolphin. They were both in a state of utter fascination, especially his youngest, Olivia, who couldn't believe her luck. She was squatting right next to the dolphin, who was resting his elongated muzzle in her hand. She kissed the dolphin's muzzle again. The dolphin dived back into the water, only to reappear with a loud splash.

"Is he going to come back?" Stina asked

"Oh pretty please," Olivia begged. "I want to pet him again."

"No that's it for today. You both had an extra turn, and Luna needs to rest," said the keeper, who had reached the end of her shift as a tour guide.

Lars had booked a behind the scenes tour of the dolphin aquarium for the whole family and it had turned out to be the highlight of the day. After the keeper had taken them all over the facility, they donned wetsuits so that they could interact with the dolphins. Luna was especially trusting, and Lars was sure that Olivia would be talking about her experience with this dolphin for a long time to come.

His wife, Lisa, looked at him happily. "That was awesome. The kids are so excited. That was a terrific idea you had there."

The kids were hopping around the edge of the tank. They were still totally wound up and could hardly calm down. Lars had taken the day off, since there wasn't much going on at work and Stina's summer vacation wasn't over yet. They'd gone to *Kolmården*, the large zoo located a little over an hour's drive from Stockholm. The trip was meant to be a kind of closure event for the summer vacation.

Now that they'd taken off their wetsuits and had come back into the sunshine, they repaired to the ice cream stand.

Clinging to her dad, Olivia said: "Dad, can we come back again real soon? I want to pet Luna again."

"Oh pretty please, Dad," Stina chimed in.

"Well, we'll see," Lars said with a bitter laugh. The outing had set him back nearly 4,000 kronor – and that was just for the behind the scenes tour of the dolphin aquarium. Plus, he'd had to shell out for the zoo entry tickets, lunch and all the rest. He simply couldn't afford such extravagances very often.

Just as he was paying for the ice cream, his cell phone rang.

"Hello?"

"Hi Lars, it's Martin."

"Hi there, Martin. Hey, congratulations, you're speaking Swedish now!"

"Yeah, I've been making great strides. How are things with you?"

"Great, thanks. I spent the day with my family at the zoo. We just got done petting a dolphin and now we're eating ice cream."

"So maybe this isn't a good time? I can call back later if you want."

"No, now is fine. Lisa is looking after the kids," he said, giving her a questioning look. She nodded in assent, and Lars sat down on a nearby bench.

"We just got finished with the tour and will be heading home after we are done with our ice cream. How are you doing?"

"Very well, thanks. We're all here on vacation at Liv's summer estate in the Stockholm archipelago. Perhaps we could meet up while we're here. We'll be heading back to Berlin at the end of August."

"Sure, that would be great. I'd love to see all of you again. Have you acclimated to Berlin by now?"

"Yeah, Berlin wasn't new to me as you know, but living with Liv and the kids is going super well. And Liv and the kids like it there too. Plus, the kids are already fluent in German."

"Glad to hear it. Shall we set up a time to meet?"

"Sure, why don't you just e-mail or text me a couple of possible times. Do you think Elin might want to come along too?"

"For sure. I'll ask her and send you a couple of dates in August."

"Okay, let's do that. Say, Lars, there's something else I'd like to talk to you about. Something more urgent."

"Fire away."

Lars listened intently while Martin told him about Christina, and how her husband had gone missing. But this didn't prevent him from continuing to eat his ice cream, and when Martin was done telling the story, there wasn't much of it left.

"That sounds like a pretty interesting case, and we can of course take it on. Lots of people are still on vacation, so there's not much going on workwise. So taking this case should be no problem. Send me Christina's phone number and I'll give her a call."

"Will do. But it's really crucial that you and Elin are assigned to the case, because it's very important to Christina to have someone who comes recommended. But what about Elin? She isn't officially employed as a detective, if I'm not mistaken."

"Right, but all that's changed recently. A few months ago, Elin solved a really amazing case, and now she's a full-fledged private investigator with Secure Assist. I'll fill you in on the details when we meet."

So, Martin had a case for him once again, which brought Lars back to the time last year when Martin had a case for him on two different occasions. Lars had been injured during these investigations, and if it hadn't been for Elin, things would have been a lot worse for him. Which is why Lisa was not going to react well to the news that Martin wanted his assistance yet again; she'd probably be afraid that Lars would end up in the hospital like before. So he thought it was advisable not to tell her about this new case, at least not for the moment.

He went back to the kids, who'd finished their ice cream by now.

"Was that Martin?" Lisa asked.

"Yeah, he's on vacation with Liv and the kids in the Stockholm archipelago and he wants to meet up. I'll take Elin along and find out how they're doing."

Lisa seemed relieved to hear this.

3

Elin was intrigued at how smoothly the data record unspooled on the screen. Metasploit was a really nifty program that allowed you to hack into loads of servers.

"Won't be much longer now," said Carl as he shoveled pizza into his mouth.

Elin found Carl physically repellent. As if the dude wasn't already greasy enough, with his unwashed long hair and smelly T-shirt, now he was wolfing down greasy pizza. Carl had already offered to share the pizza with her, and though it came from a nearby pizza joint, she'd declined, as she'd rather not eat in this shithole. But this was part of the deal she'd struck with her boss, Tobias – namely that if she trained as a professional hacker with Carl, she'd have the opportunity to work under him as a full-fledged private eye. She'd jumped at this opportunity, as she didn't know then what Carl was like and how unpleasant it would be to have to sit right next to him for hours on end. But the good news was that she'd almost completed the training and there weren't too many sessions left. Plus, she had to admit that Carl was a master hacker – and not only knew the relevant software like the back of his hand but was a wizard when it came to modifying algorithms to make them do what you wanted them to in a given situation. This was the case too with Sweden's largest telecom company, Telia. For Elin's purposes, it was of particular interest that once you'd hacked into the company's servers, you could download all phone conversation and triangulation data for individual phone numbers. Which meant that you could determine the location of any given phone during any call – information that she needed quite often in her work as a private eye. Unlike the police, private detectives are not officially authorized to access such data, and so you have to find a workaround. Tobias's agency, Secure Assist, had availed itself of Carl's expertise in the past, but was no longer allowed to engage in these shady practices because his employer, IT Experts Support AB, had banned them. For Elin, this on the job training was the final concession they were making, out of goodwill for a good customer. And of course, this enabled Tobias to kill two birds with one stone, in that he obtained a private detective and hacker expertise in a single "package". And in the final analysis, this arrangement was perfectly okay with Elin, given her desire to work as a full-fledged private eye. It was this desire that had prompted her, over two years ago, to join Secure Assist as a secretary. Tobias had told her that by taking on this position, she'd be able to ease herself into detective work – though this rosy scenario turned out to be just a fairy tale. In fact, if her colleague Lars hadn't hired her twice over the past year, she would have spent the whole time chained to a desk. But thanks to Lars, she'd been involved in two kidnapping cases and had had a major part in solving them. But she'd still needed to go back to her job as a secretary, and Tobias hadn't lifted a finger to change the situation. So late last spring she'd founded her own detective agency and accepted a first case that she'd solved to such spectacular effect that Tobias decided to keep her on, so that the good media coverage the case had garnered could work to the advantage of the company's image. And given that taking the case had constituted a breach of her contract with Secure Assist, Tobias could have fired her on the spot. But Lars had helped her negotiate a deal with Tobias that stipulated as follows: First off – a condition that enabled her to keep her job – she was required to tell the media that she'd taken the case as part of her duties at Secure Assist and not on behalf of her own company. And secondly, she was granted the opportunity to be hired as a full-fledged private investigator, provided that she did the hacker training. So all things considered, it was a sweet deal for her, a real win-win situation.

The computer beeped, signaling that it had logged on to the Telia server. Carl wolfed down the last bite of pizza, causing a few crumbs to tumble onto the keyboard. But that didn't faze him, and he blithely began typing with his greasy fingers. God, he's disgusting, Elin thought. I sure hope I won't be using that keyboard.

Carl showed her how to navigate to various data sets in the server, a process that involved toggling between three different windows. Elin took a few pictures with her cell phone and made notes. Carl then asked her to do the whole process over again from the beginning.

"Experiential learning!" he said with a grin. Elin noticed that he had bits of pizza stuck between his teeth.

Using the other computer, which was connected to the second server, she launched Metasploit.

"What are you doing that for? My computer is already good to go."

"Because then I can look at your screen if I'm not sure what to do next. Also, I have no desire to type on pizza." Carl's jaw dropped in amazement, causing a large crumb of cheese to tumble out of his mouth – and of course right onto the keyboard.

"I rest my case," Elin said with disgust.

Carl wiped off the keyboard with his sleeve. "My apologies. Though aren't you perhaps a bit obsessive about cleanliness?"

Elin just shook her head in disbelief and began hacking into the Telia server.

A half hour later they'd finished the session, during which Elin had done everything perfectly save for a tiny slip and had been able to replicate Carl's hacking procedure. She emerged from the office building, which was located in a suburb of Stockholm known as

Kista. Now it was time to take the subway home – home being in central Stockholm on Kungsholmen, one of Stockholm's 16 islands. Kista was a kind of Swedish Silicon Valley that was home to virtually all information and communication technology companies in Sweden. As Elin was walking by the Siemens building, her phone rang. She could see on the screen that it was Lars calling.

"Hi Lars."

"*Hej* Elin, how's it going?"

"Well okay – now that I've left that shithole hacker locale. But I'd be a much happier bunny if I could get to a sink – or preferably a bathtub. I just hope that there won't be a hygiene check at the subway station, because if there is, they won't let me in due to the risk of infection."

"So was it really that bad?

"Well you've been to Carl's place a bunch of times, so you must know what it's like there. You could have given me a head's up before I agreed to this deal with Tobias."

"*Nej*, actually I've only been there a few times, and only very briefly. And when I was there, I just stood and watched Carl in action. But to tell you the truth, I didn't really notice how filthy the place was."

"Yeah, well, that's men for you – you also pee standing up," Elin said disdainfully.

After a brief silence, Lars said: "Look, do you want to keep talking about this or do you want me to tell you why I called?"

"Does Santa have a beard? Well of course I want you to tell me."

"Well, we've got a new case. The signed contract just arrived. We need to step on it, though, because the client wants to meet with us today if possible. Do you have time?"

"You mean right this minute? And does that mean I'll be working on the case?"

"Yes and yes. As I said, if at all possible, we need to see her today. I can pick you up in Kista in about half an hour. The client said she wanted us both for the job – on recommendation from Liv and Martin. I'll fill you in on the details later."

"I see. That's fine. I'll find somewhere to clean up around here, so I can be all spic and span for the meeting."

After walking a bit further Elin entered a large shopping mall, Kista Galleria, and found a restroom there. It wasn't the cleanest place in Stockholm, but it was a damn site cleaner than Carl's work space.

Lars arrived about ten minutes later and the two of them drove off to meet the new client. On the way there, Lars filled Elin in on the details of the case and what it had to do with Liv and Martin.

"Does that mean that I'm now officially a private eye?"

"Yes," said Tobias. "– provided that you complete your training with Carl."

“Awesome.” Elin was thrilled that she’d finally made the breakthrough she’d so longed for. Her girlfriend Maja would be proud of her, so they’d have to celebrate tonight.

“Yeah, but there’s one thing.” Lars gave her a piercing look.

Though she knew what was coming, she feigned innocence, and said, “What?”

“No going rogue! Whatever you might be thinking of doing, you need to clear it with me first. Got it?”

“Okay, okay.”

“Sorry ‘okay okay’ won’t cut it. I need to be able to trust you one hundred percent. I’m the person in charge of this case and Tobias will kill me if anything goes sideways. Also, given that this is your first case as a private eye, I assume you don’t want to get into yet another discussion with him.”

“Okay I get it. Tobias clued me in, too, so I get it, really.”

This was another precondition that Tobias had set when he offered Elin the opportunity to become a private investigator. Elin wasn’t totally sure that she’d always be able to do as Tobias asked, because sometimes, she felt, you really do have to forge ahead more rapidly and not wait for everyone to be on the same page. But she resolved to make every effort to do as she was told. And Lars was right. She certainly didn’t want to go rogue on this, her first case as a private eye.

"I promise, scout's honor, I'll clear everything with you first. But that applies in reverse too, doesn't it? You'll keep me up to speed on everything – every piece of information you get, every move you make. Right?"

"Absolutely. We're a team and we both need to have all the relevant information. Plus, we'll be comparing notes on a regular basis."

"Sounds good. So now, where are we headed? Where does the client live?"

"Her name's Christina Lindblom and she lives in Täby." Täby was an upscale bedroom suburb not far from Stockholm, with the sea on one side and forests and lakes on the other.

Lars followed the GPS's instructions. After exiting the highway and driving past the central- Täby exit, he arrived at a subdivision containing numerous townhouses.

"They look almost exactly like the houses where you live, only they're green instead of yellow," Elin said.

"Yeah, but they're probably twice as expensive."

"Really? Just because they're in Täby?" Elin knew that residential real estate was pricey in the Stockholm area and that prices kept going up. But she didn't know much more than that. She was paying Maja rent, so she'd never needed to concern herself with real estate prices. Perhaps someday they'd have a more spacious abode, but that wasn't a priority at present.

"Okay, here's where we're meant to park, I suppose," Lars said, as he drove the car into a visitors' parking space. They got out of the car and went over to the townhouses. Elin's right thigh was a bit sore from sitting in the car, causing her to limp for a bit. She had to smile. She and Lars must have looked like an odd pair, her with her limp and Lars dragging his left leg behind him. Two private eyes, one big and strong, the other petite, but both somewhat physically handicapped. But Elin's injuries from the case last June were almost healed. She'd suffered a torn ligament and a hematoma, while Lars would probably never get rid of his limp, the result of having been shot in the knee many years ago when he was a policeman.

Having quickly found the right house, they rang the bell. The door was opened by a small, somewhat plump woman in an elegant brown suit that was accessorized with an orange silk scarf. She gave them a friendly look and invited them in.

Having introduced themselves to each other, they sat down in Christina's well appointed living room. A few moments later, Christina appeared with coffee. Elin noticed that Christina was well dressed and made up, but not particularly attractive. It wasn't only that she was kind of overweight, but also that her face, though not downright ugly, wasn't particularly pretty either. She wore her expertly-cut hair short.

"So, we've heard that your husband Patrik has gone missing. When exactly did this happen?" Lars said, taking out a notepad.

"On Friday July 1st, Patrik drove to work as usual, but he never came home." Christina looked at the two sleuths despairingly. “I haven’t heard from him since.”

“Did he show up for work that day?”

“Yes, as always, though he left somewhat early, according to his colleagues.”

“Where does he work?”

“At the insurance company called If. He’s a nurse by trade, and at If he works in the health insurance division.”

Elin noticed that Lars was writing all this down on his pad.

“How long have you been married?” Elin asked.

“A little over eight years.”

“Any children?”

“No.”

“Didn’t you want any?”

“Yes, we’d originally intended to have kids, but then we got caught up in our careers – and so we decided we could be perfectly happy without children.” Elin could well understand this, although in Sweden this was rather unusual, particularly for a married couple. Many Swedish couples, including ones with kids, cohabitate without actually getting married.

This prompted Elin to ask: “Was that more your wish or his?”

“Yes, I... No actually we agreed not to have them. I could have imagined having children, but it wasn’t all that important to me.”

Lars chimed in: "Did anything unusual happen in the weeks leading up to his disappearance? Did he act strangely or get strange phone calls?"

"No, I've been racking my brains about this, but frankly I can't think of anything."

"But he did take his passport with him that day. Was that his usual practice? I mean, carrying his passport around with him?"

"No, I keep my passport in a bedroom drawer, and as far as I knew, Patrik's was in his closet. So I was totally shocked to find out he'd apparently taken it with him."

"Is anything missing? Clothing, laptop, credit cards?"

"No. We have a laptop that we both use, and it's still here. I've looked through his closet, but as far as I can tell nothing's missing. As for his credit cards, he always carries them with him."

"Do you have a joint bank account?"

"No, we have separate accounts. I don't have access to his, but the police checked it and no funds have been withdrawn since he disappeared; nor has he used the credit card attached to that account."

"Have any of his relatives heard from him?"

"Patrik's mother died a few years ago from breast cancer, and his father and brother live in Göteborg. His sister lives with her family here in Stockholm. None of them have heard from Patrik."

"How about his friends, or colleagues that he meets up with after work?"

"Yes, there are a few of those, and I've of course spoken with them. But none of them know anything."

"What does he do in his leisure time? Does he do any sports?"

"Yes, he plays golf at the local golf club. But he hasn't been seen there since he went missing."

"I see. Well, we'll need the names and numbers of all these people – his father, siblings, colleagues, friends, employer and so on. Could you compile a list of these numbers for us?"

"Sure."

"We'd also like to have a look at that laptop. Would it be okay with you if Elin checks it out?"

"Yes, by all means. But Patrik has his own user account and I don't know his password. I've tried various possibilities, but none of them worked."

"I'll figure it out, don't worry," Elin said. "But I'll need to borrow it for a few days. Is that okay with you?"

"Sure, no problem."

"Didn't the police do this?"

"No, they didn't ask me for anything."

"So are you saying that they haven't done anything at all?"

"They put Patrik on a list of missing persons, checked his bank account and talked to his employer. They also checked all the hospitals, but fortunately he wasn't in any of them. But I'm still very worried that something might have happened to him. And I thought that the police would have done a lot more."

"Well the problem is that there's absolutely no indication that he was kidnapped. No ransom demand, no violence. In such cases, the police don't do much."

"Didn't they check his phone data?" Elin asked.

"Oh yeah, right, they did, but not right away, only after a couple of weeks. It's a work-issued phone and apparently Patrik switched it off at work on the day he disappeared and hasn't used it since."

"Is it alright with you if we look through his closet?"

"Of course. His room's upstairs."

Elin and Lars followed Christina upstairs. She opened the door to Patrik's room, which contained a desk, a dresser, a clothes closet and a bed.

Noticing the bed, Elin asked: "So you have separate bedrooms?"

"Well yes and no. We also share a bedroom, but we also each have a room of our own. After all, there's plenty of space here. Patrik sometimes sits on the bed when he watches TV late at night."

Elin noticed a large flat-screen TV on the opposite wall – which prompted her to wonder whether Christina was telling the truth and whether Patrik didn't actually spend the whole night here from time to time.

"Elin, you have a good look around the room to see if there's anything out of the ordinary, and I'll go through the rest of the house with Christina." Lars left with Christina.

Elin started with the desk, which had nothing on it except for a couple of copies of a golf magazine and a few pens. She went through all the drawers, which contained nothing of interest – only office supplies.

The clothes closet seemed full to capacity, well stocked as it was with underwear, pants, shirts, T-shirts, sweaters, jackets and sportswear; nothing seemed to be missing.

She then turned her attention to the dresser, on top of which were a number of golf trophies, undoubtedly attesting to Patrik's golfing acumen. The topmost of the dresser's three large drawers contained numerous folders with documents in them about the house, insurance policies, product warranties, Patrik's golf club and his magazine subscriptions. It occurred to Elin that it might be a good idea to give these items a closer look later on, and she decided to ask Christina if she could take them with her.

The middle drawer contained various computer cables and an external hard drive, which she also intended to take with her. She wondered if it was really true that Patrik didn't have his own laptop, or if he'd been using all those cables solely for the couple's shared laptop.

The bottom drawer contained back issues of a golf magazine and other sports periodicals.

As Elin was peering under the bed to see if there might be something of interest there, Lars entered the room. "Found anything?"

"A bunch of folders containing all kinds of documents, plus an external drive. I'd like to take them home with me. How about you? Find anything?"

"No, not really. Though I did find out that they have a cabin in Norrland, near Östersund. Christina gave me the key to it and is going to give me the address."

"I see. So I guess it's time to scadoodle."

"Yup." They headed downstairs, where they asked Christina if they could take Patrik's documents and external drive with them. Elin also asked Christina again whether there was a second computer anywhere, but Christina insisted that they only had the one laptop.

"Patrik was of course issued a laptop at work," Christina said. "But his colleagues told me it's still at his office; plus he hardly ever brings it home."

"So what's your take on all this?" Lars asked Elin once they were headed back home with Patrik's laptop, external drive and folders stowed on the back seat.

"I really don't know. It sure is strange, though, that he seems to have vanished into thin air. But I have the feeling that their marriage isn't exactly ship-shape."

"What makes you say that? 'Cause they don't have kids?"

"Well that too. But there are some other things that bother me too. The fact that they each have their own room, that they don't sleep in the same bed, and don't have access to each other's bank accounts. Individually, these things aren't particularly significant, but taken together, for me they add up to spouses who are living very separate lives from each other. And I wasn't particularly taken with Christina either."

"Oh come on, she's a really nice person."

"Yeah but just being 'nice' doesn't cut it, not in my book anyway."

"Okay, but we've never met Patrik, maybe he's just the same."

"That's right, which is why we need to talk to his friends, relatives and colleagues. Either he and Christina get along well or their marriage is in trouble. In the latter case, hopefully someone will have noticed."

"Right. So we need to divvy up the people that we need to interrogate, once we've gotten the list that Christina said she's going to compile for us tonight. But then I think we should have a look at the cabin in Norrland too. Christina and Patrik had actually been planning to spend their vacation there in July. The Friday that Patrik went missing was his last day of work before Patrik's vacation leave, so his absence wouldn't have been noticed at work right away. Two weeks after that, Christina went to the cabin by herself, and had the impression that the furnishings weren't as they'd been left during their last stay there. So presumably Patrik had been there in the interim."

"That sounds promising. I didn't know that Patrik was scheduled to go on vacation the day after he went missing."

"Well I didn't either. Christina didn't tell me until we got around to talking about the cabin in Norrland."

"You're right, we really should go there – though it's pretty far away – a six hour drive, I reckon. And by the way, what kind of car does Patrik drive?"

"A Saab 93. Christina said she'll give us the license plate number."

"Has it been spotted anywhere?"

"Not as far as I know – which suggests that he has in fact gone missing of his own free will."

"Plus, he went to Norrland, of all places. You're from there, aren't you?"

"No, not really, though my dad is, but from a place further north. But when I was a kid, my parents often took me to our summer home there."

"So I guess you'll enjoy seeing it again."

"Well let's just say, I'm not opposed to the idea," Lars said slyly. Lars dropped Elin off at her house, and they arranged to rendezvous the next morning. Elin was very much looking forward to a quiet evening at home. She happened to have a bottle of champagne in the fridge, and this was the perfect occasion to open it. At long last she was a full fledged private eye.

4

Elin and Lars were in their office's small conference room going over the results of their initial investigations. Elin had spent the first hour of the workday going through Patrik's laptop and had found some promising elements there. But before discussing it with Lars, she wanted to hear what he had to say. She looked at him expectantly.

Placing his notes on the table, Lars reported the following: "First off, I talked to Patrik's father on the phone. He appears to be pretty old – at any rate his hearing isn't that good and so the communication wasn't optimal. He says he has no idea what's going on with his son. During a phone conversation he had with Patrik the weekend before he went missing, he told his dad how much he was looking forward to his upcoming vacation in Norrland. He also said that he was under a lot of pressure at work. He had nothing to say about any possible problems in Patrik's marriage – but in any case, he wasn't really sure that Patrik would have talked to him about this. He related that his late wife had always seemed saddened by the fact that Patrik was childless and often raised the subject with him. But Patrik had made up his mind that he simply didn't want children. Patrik's dad apparently accepted this and tried to console his wife by reminding her that Patrik wasn't their only child and that they already had a sufficient number of grandchildren. That's about all I was able to glean from Patrik's dad, who fully corroborated everything Christina has told us."

Lars looked through his notes. "Next, I called Patrik's brother, Ingmar, who lives in Göteborg, near their father and is married with three children. He told me he isn't very close to Patrik and that pretty much the only times they ever see each other is at family gatherings at their parents' house. He also said they never discuss their personal lives. The last time he saw Patrik was at their father's birthday party last April and he hasn't had any contact with him since then."

Lars glanced at his notes again. "Yesterday I paid a visit to Patrik's sister, Cecilia, who lives here in Stockholm. She's the youngest of the three siblings, and I suppose is in her early thirties. She lives with her husband in a small house in the Enskede neighborhood. She's on maternity leave, because she just gave birth to her second child. She's pretty close to Patrik, she says. They see each other regularly. Usually Christina and Patrik come over to her house, but from time to time she and her husband also go to visit Patrik in Täby. Also, every couple of months Patrik and Cecilia meet for lunch in Stockholm, usually at Gondolen, as it's located roughly equidistant from each of their homes."

"I can see why they'd want to eat there; it's got great food and an amazing view." Elin had eaten there a few times. You reach the restaurant via the Katarinahissen chairlift, after which you sit in an elongated dining room that extends out from the building. From there you have a view, from more than a hundred feet up, of the Baltic on one side and Lake Mälaren on the other; and between them there's Stockholm's Old Town, with Stockholm's other islands all around.

"So that's undoubtedly why they meet there. In any case, they talk about all kinds of things, although perhaps they tend to spend somewhat more time talking about Cecilia's kids, job and so forth. Cecilia said that Patrik talks about his work too, where there appears to be a major restructuring underway that has been having a major impact on him personally."

"Yeah, his boss and colleagues corroborated that."

"I see. However, Cecilia didn't say anything about any problems in Patrik's marriage. Though Patrik apparently isn't in the habit of talking about his – and Cecilia said she has the feeling that their marriage is pretty much at a dead end. But she finds it unthinkable that Patrik would suddenly abandon Christina, because in her view Patrik's far too honest and conscientious to do anything so extreme. I must say that Cecilia is the only person who seems to really care about Patrik – she said she's willing to do anything we feel might help us find him. She's of course quite worried that something might have happened to him. "

"Well I can understand that Patrik isn't very close to his older brother, but how about the father?"

"Yeah, over the phone he didn't give me the impression that he was overly concerned about his son's well-being. But maybe that was because the conversation was kind of stressful for him on account of his partial deafness." Lars glanced down at his notes again. "That's all I have. How about you?"

"Well, yesterday I went to Patrik's golf club, where I found out absolutely nothing of interest apart from the fact that Patrik used to play golf there at least once a week, but over the past six months has been playing less frequently. He's apparently quite a good golfer and has an 8 handicap. I myself don't play golf, but they told me that any handicap of 10 or less means you're a really good player."

"Did you find out who he plays golf with?"

"Yes, he plays with a colleague named Ivar Stenberg and with a friend of his called Mattias Liljequist. He's on Christina's list too. Patrik also plays with various groups from the club. I spoke to his colleague, Ivar, but I haven't been able to reach Mattias yet."

"What did Ivar have to say?"

"Nothing much. He said they talk about work, golf, politics and technical matters. The usual things men talk about. He has no knowledge of any problems with Patrik's marriage – though he has noticed that

Patrik's been having a lot of private phone conversations in recent weeks. But he thought that it was Christina on the other end, so we need to ask her about that."

Lars added this item to his to-do list.

"Anything else about his job?"

"Not really. As I said, they're all quite stressed out because the departments have been undergoing a major reshuffling since January, plus they have a new boss. So Patrik's boss doesn't really know him very well. All he's really concerned about is how long he has to wait to replace Patrik, should he fail to materialize. Given that Patrik's vacation leave is now over, they're considering sending him a work-absence dunning letter and then firing him."

"Nice people."

"Yeah, well, it's understandable from where they're sitting. The work needs to get done – all the more so since the restructuring got underway, because they eliminated some positions in order to ramp up efficiency."

"Good work, Elin," Lars said, with an approving nod.

"Hold on, that's not all!"

"Okay, go ahead."

"I managed to crack the password on Patrik's laptop."

"Cool. Did you find anything promising there?"

"I haven't gone through it yet. But the password itself was of interest."

Elin could see that Lars was really curious to know what the password was, but she waited a beat, flashing him an impish smile.

"Come on, tell me."

"It's Natalia15."

"Good lord, you're only telling me this now?"

"Yeah, I decided to leave the best for last," Elin said with a chuckle.

"Well *that's* interesting. So do you think that means he has a 15 year old girlfriend?"

"Well, I'm not ready to jump to any conclusions just yet. The number 15 could mean just about anything. But I do think this might be our first real lead."

"Well with all due reverence for your intuition, it might be a completely innocent choice for a password. Maybe he has a niece or something, or maybe it's his mother's first name. We need to ask Christina if the name rings any bells – or warnings." Lars made another note on his pad.

"Natalia ending in the letter 'a' isn't a common Swedish first name. So I doubt she's a family member."

"You might be right, but we need to check it out. Natalia might be merely a colleague who Patrik enjoys working with."

"Well I didn't come across any colleague by that name, but I'll ask his boss about it."

"Good idea. I'll talk to Christina. You should go through Patrik's laptop and talk to his boss again. But be discreet with the name. We don't want to start any rumors that Patrik is fucking a minor. Needless to say, if Christina got wind of that, she'd be extremely upset."

"Oh come on, I'm not an idiot. I'll of course handle the name with discretion." Elin was deeply upset. Did Lars really think she was capable of making such a dumb beginner's mistake?

"No need to get all worked up about it. I just wanted to remind you." Lars raised his hands apologetically. "I'm sure you'll be the very picture of discretion. So, what's with this Matthias, Patrik's buddy? Should I deal with him? Dealing with the laptop is probably going to take up quite a bit of your time."

"Yeah, that would be great. I'll send you his phone number. And don't forget about those files."

"So now let's get down to work."

Elin went into her office and turned her attention to Patrik and Christina's laptop. Given that, as far as she could tell, the name "Natalia" was her only real lead, before meeting with Lars she'd launched a search of the computer's hard drive for this name and figured it must be finished by now.

She moved the mouse and the screen lit up. The search was indeed finished – but to her surprise, there were no results. Was Natalia perhaps the name of a relative or colleague that had no particular significance beyond that? At any rate, she decided to have a look at the laptop's browser history and saved documents in the hope of finding something useful there.

But before doing that, she thought it might be a good idea to call Patrik's boss to find out if the name Natalia rang any bells for him. So she dialed his number, and fortunately he picked up right away.

"This is Oskar speaking."

"*Hej* Oskar, this is Elin. I'm calling in reference to our meeting yesterday about Patrik's disappearance."

"Right. It's good that you called, because I was about to call you in any case."

"How come? Have you found out anything?"

"Yes, we broke the locks on Patrik's desk drawers." Elin had totally forgotten to mention to Lars that Patrik's desk drawers were locked and that he must have taken the key with him. She and Oskar had discussed whether and how the drawers could be opened, and Elin had urged Oskar to get this done as soon as possible.

"So what did you find?"

"Nothing special, actually. Some confidential documents, but nothing of a personal nature. But we did find his cell phone, which was of course not working as the battery had died."

"That's really good news. Can I come pick it up? We'd very much like to go through the data in there." Elin found it odd that Patrik had left his phone at work.

"I'm not sure that we're allowed to give his phone to a third party, as this might constitute an invasion of privacy."

"But we talked about this yesterday. Patrik has gone missing and we need to follow up every possible lead that might help us find him. This is important not only for his wife, but also for you as his employer. His phone might have some important data in it that could provide us with a decisive lead."

"Well, okay. The phone is password protected. We charged it and switched it on, but we were unable to access the data."

"Leave that to us."

"Okay, I'll talk to human resources about it again. If they agree to release it, we'll give it to you within a few days."

"Okay, thanks. Let me know when I can come pick it up." Elin cleared her throat. "There's something else I'd like to ask you about, if you don't mind. Our investigation has turned up a first name and we'd like to find out if it has any relevance – and of course we'd also like to know the identity of the person in question. So to the best of your knowledge, does the name 'Natalia' have any significance? Do you happen to have an employee by that name?"

"No, I'm afraid not, at least not off the top of my head. Just a moment, I'll have a look at our list of employees." Elin could hear Oskar typing.

"No, there's no employee by that name. There's someone called Natali, but she works in our Malmö office, not here in Stockholm."

Elin was now becoming increasingly convinced that Natalia was the key to Patrik's disappearance. And the fact that Patrik had also left his phone at work made this scenario seem even more likely. Like most people nowadays, Patrik undoubtedly had a second cell phone.

She called Lars to tell him the news, and to ask him to talk to Christina about the phone, but his line was busy. So she texted him instead. She then went back to Patrik's laptop, in the hope of finding something about that second phone.

5

Lars had to use considerable force to open the Lebanese restaurant's door, as it was pretty hard to open. After entering the dining room through a small passageway, he looked around, but Christina was nowhere to be seen – though he was a few minutes early. To his right was a counter containing a large selection of dishes, in front of him about six tables, most of which were occupied; and to his left was the restaurant's cash register. Behind the counter there was a young Asian looking woman who gave him a friendly and expectant smile. Lars ordered the lunch buffet, which included everything arrayed on the counter, plus a beverage and coffee.

He took a tray, plate, cutlery and a glass and began serving himself appetizers. There was a dish called *meze*, which consisted of humus and myriad other items. He took a spoonful of each one and a slice of flatbread, and then some grilled vegetables. As his plate was now full, he'd need to come back for the main course. He sat down at a small table in a corner, poured himself some water, and waited for Christina to arrive. He'd called her after talking to Elin and had suggested that they meet up, because he wanted to see how she'd react to his questions. In the meantime he'd also received Elin's text message, and so he intended to confront Christina with the news that Patrik had left his phone at work.

Christina worked at Liv's company, which was headquartered in Solna, a Stockholm suburb that was home to numerous companies and that had a considerable amount of office space to lease. Christina had proposed that she and Lars meet in this restaurant, which was a short walk from her office.

Christina entered the restaurant, waved to Lars, and gestured to him that she was going to get some food before joining him at the table. A minute or two later, she sat down with him.

"*Hej*, Lars? I hope you like the food. I love this place."

"It all looks quite delicious and smells good too." He took a spoonful of the eggplant dip, which was very creamy and intense.

"I'm curious to see how you'll like the food. You said that you didn't want to say anything over the phone. Have you found any leads?"

"Well, unfortunately we haven't, at least not yet. But we have come across a few things that I wanted to ask you about."

"Okay, shoot." Christina dipped some bread into one of the dips and took a small bite.

"First, we wanted to know whether Patrik has a second cell phone apart from his work phone?"

Christina shook her head. “No, he doesn’t. If he had one, I would have of course given you the number. Why do you ask?”

“Well, we found his phone in one of the desk drawers at his office.”

She gave Lars an incredulous look. “Really? So I suppose that means it’s been sitting there for weeks. No wonder I couldn’t reach him. But why did they wait so long to search his desk drawers?”

“The drawers were locked, and the company was unwilling to open them – and only did so at our insistence.”

“I see. But why on earth did Patrik leave his phone at work? He’s never done that before, as far as I know.” Christina had stopped eating, and Lars feared that his next question wasn’t going to improve her appetite either.

“Yes, we wondered about this as well. Or maybe he simply didn’t want to take his phone with him on vacation, so as not to be disturbed by calls about work.”

“That’s highly unlikely. He always has his phone with him, and I can’t remember a single instance when he didn’t take it with him. Which is of course totally normal. It’s a Samsung, which he also uses for his private emails. He uses it as both a work and personal phone. He often says that he’s no longer able to remember phone numbers and that he’d be lost without his phone.”

"Hence my question about a possible second phone."

Christina shook her head pensively. "No, I've never ever seen him with a second phone. Nor do I have any other number for him. So what does all this mean? Did he simply forget to take his phone with him when he left work?"

"That's definitely a possibility – though that would be an unfortunate coincidence." But of course Lars was sure that Patrik had left his phone at work on purpose.

"But that also means that he can't call me if he's in trouble," she said despairingly.

There are other ways to contact a person, Lars thought to himself, but felt it was best not to mention this.

"Yes that would be a problem." He began eating again. These dips were heavenly, one better than the next. He'd now worked his way to the tzatziki. He looked over at Christina, who was staring into the middle distance, apparently pondering what all this meant. Lars wondered whether it would be advisable to ask Christina the other questions at this juncture but decided against doing so as he felt it might be counterproductive.

He waited a moment while he polished off the appetizers, and then asked: "Christina how often do you and Patrik talk on the phone? I mean, during the day, while Patrik's at work."

Christina appeared not to have heard him, but finally turned toward him. "Excuse me...what? You're asking me how often we talk on the phone? Not very often. We eat breakfast together every morning and spend almost every evening at home, so we have plenty of time to talk. But of course from time to time we call each other on the spur of the moment about who's going to go shopping for what, or an invitation to a dinner party or the like. But such calls are a rarity. Why do you ask?"

"So that means that normally you don't talk on the phone every day and only do so on the spur of the moment, right? And that didn't change during the weeks leading up to his disappearance?"

Christina nodded, but gave him a despairing look. "Right. Why do you want to know?"

Lars hesitated for a moment. "One of his colleagues told us that Patrik has been having relatively long private conversations of late. But of course this colleague may be mistaken, and maybe they were actually work related calls that Patrik wanted to keep secret."

"For sure. Or maybe he was just talking to his sister. Or the calls might have had to do with his golf club."

"Yes, that might well be the case. I hope that we'll be getting his phone soon so that we can find out who he's been talking to on the phone."

Christina nodded absently. Lars wondered whether he should get the main course now or should ask his remaining question first. He decided to do the latter, as he had the impression that Christina was finished eating.

"One more thing I'd like to ask you, Christina." She looked at him anxiously, apparently sensing that another blow was coming.

"Does the name 'Natalia' ring any bells?"

"Natalia? No, I'm afraid not. I have no idea who that might be, and I don't know anyone by that name. Is this the person Patrik's been talking to on the phone?"

"As I told you, we have yet to determine the identity of this person. So, are you sure that there's no one by this name in Patrik's family? A niece for example?"

"No way. What kind of a name is that anyway? Where did you come across it?"

"We found it on your laptop, where Patrik's password is Natalia15. So we thought she might be a niece of Patrik's who recently turned 15."

Christina looked at him incredulously. "Why on earth did he use this name as a password? It makes no sense. No, he hasn't got a 15 year old niece. His brother has three children. The eldest boy turned 13 this year, and the eldest girl just started grade school, so she's six."

Why, Lars thought to himself, were Elin's intuitions always right on the nose? For sure she was going to gloat when he told her about this. But on the other hand, the name was a good lead, even if it wasn't at all to Christina's liking. Which was all too evident from her next question.

"Lars, what the hell is this supposed to mean? Do you think Patrik might have run off with some girl called Natalia who's only 15? I find that very hard to believe." Christina was beside herself.

"Let's not get ahead of ourselves, Christina. Patrik might have simply read something about a certain Natalia and used the name as a password for that reason. Also, the number 15 can mean just about anything – for example the 15th of the month or a house number. We simply don't know at this point. We'd hoped that the name would ring a bell for you. So now we're going to ask other people who know Patrik and hopefully we'll be able to find out something from one of them."

Christina was sitting there, completely stunned, not eating, and kept shaking her head back and forth. Clearly, she needed time to process all this.

"I'm going to get the main course. Shall I bring something for you too?" This attempt to distract Christina failed utterly.

"No thanks, I've lost my appetite. Do you have anything else to report?"

"No, that's it."

"Sorry, but I really must be going. I'm in a state of shock, as I'm sure you can well imagine. It's really unpleasant to have to hear all this."

"I understand. But please, do me a favor, and don't overthink what I've told you. In my experience, there are all kinds of explanations for things like this."

Christina nodded, but didn't seem very convinced. She made her way out of the restaurant, head bowed, having eaten next to nothing. Lars went over to the counter and perused the main courses. There was fish with rice, chicken with bulgur and a kind of vegetable ragout. He decided to try all three and took a small amount of each.

As he ate, he reflected on the conversation with Christina. He hadn't expected her to react so violently to the findings of their investigation and the issues they raised – but he *had* expected her to express at least a little appreciation. That said, he had, after all, presented her with some promising findings. But he also realized that, given the circumstances, he couldn't really expect any kudos from Christina. Now that he knew that she and Patrik didn't talk on the phone all that often and that she had no idea who Natalia was, the pieces of the puzzle were beginning to come together. Patrik may have disappeared for the simple reason that he'd met someone else. This was an all too common occurrence, but for Christina it would of course be totally shattering. She appeared not to have noticed or suspected anything of this nature. He felt sorry for her, but that was no reason to ruin his lunch. The food was really good here, and he wanted to be sure to note down the restaurant's address, because this was a place he'd really like to eat at again.

6

Elin leaned back, shaking her head. She was at her wits' end. Patrik's laptop, phone and external drive contained nary a clue as to his whereabouts or why he'd seemingly vanished into thin air. She'd hoped that at least the name Natalia would crop up somewhere – but it was nowhere to be found in Patrik's address book, list of phone calls or e-mail program. There simply wasn't anything; nor was there any indication that Patrik might have a second phone.

But there was something else that struck her as odd as well. It seemed to her that data had been deleted from the laptop. The browser history was almost empty and only contained items from the week leading up to Patrik's disappearance. Plus, the history contained not a single usable piece of information. Only stuff about golf, cars, and insurance – nothing that Elin felt was relevant. For sure, she thought to herself, the older data would be of interest. And her search of the documents and photos saved on Patrik's laptop turned up nothing either. So either Patrik hadn't used the laptop very much, or he'd deleted files from it. To determine whether this was the case, Elin had connected the laptop to her PC and had run a data recovery program in order to restore the data that had been deleted from the hard drive. Though running this program had taken well over an hour, she was amazed to see that it hadn't found any deleted data to restore at all – not a single item. This could mean only one thing – that someone had used special software to wipe the laptop's hard drive, or at least the sector containing Patrik's account. And no one had accessed Patrik's account since. Someone must have really gone to a great deal of trouble to wipe the laptop clean, because a lot of freeware deletion programs aren't all that thorough and tend to leave at least some data intact enough to recover it – at any rate with the kind of good software Elin had. The fact that not a single piece of relevant data was to be found meant that an expert had run disc wiping software on Patrik's laptop.

Elin had obtained Patrik's phone from his boss that morning and had unlocked the four-digit password in a jiffy with her password unlocker software. The code consisted of the last four digits of Patrik's ID number. Swedish ID numbers consist of a birthdate followed by four digits. Patrik had used this number for his password but had reversed the order of the digits. Which is why the password provided no information about Patrik himself. The phone contained numerous addresses, none of which had anything to do with the name Natalia. Elin intended to ask Patrik's boss and Christina to go through the list again, but she suspected that it merely contained the numbers of business associates and people from Patrik's private life. The call list contained no indication that Patrik had been in constant touch with anyone else, and the text messages contained nothing of interest. There weren't many photos at all – a few from golfing and of his sister, plus nature snapshots.

Elin wondered whether data might have also been deleted from Patrik's phone. But at least it hadn't been completely wiped as the laptop had – though it was possible that data had been deleted selectively. But as she had no idea how to access such data, she gave Carl a call.

"Hello?"

"Carl, this is Elin. Do you have a moment? There's something I'd like to ask you." "Yeah sure, fire away!"

"Can data that's been deleted from a smartphone be recovered?"

"In principle, yes of course."

"So what does that entail?"

"Is it an iPhone or an Android?"

"It's a Samsung – so it's an Android."

"Then all you have to do is plug the phone into a USB port on your computer and run the relevant software. I'll send you a link to some freeware that does a good job."

"Oh that would be great, thanks. How much of the data is recoverable?"

"Well it depends on when the data was deleted and how much of it has been overwritten. Phone memories work exactly the same way as computer memories. When you delete a file, only the index entry is deleted so as to prevent the phone's software from locating the file. The file remains in the memory but can be overwritten by new data. In other words, if you don't use the phone after deleting data from it, you can recover the deleted data without any problem. But if you use the phone a lot after deleting data from it, then your chances of recovering the data are slim. Also, smartphone memories have much less capacity than computer memories, so you only have a short window."

"I see. Is it also possible to delete data from a phone in such a way that it can't possibly be recovered?"

"Yes, that works too, but you need special software that expunges all the data for good."

After installing the software for which Carl had sent her the link – the phone was still connected to her computer – Elin opened the data recovery program, clicked on "Settings" and then on "Run." The whole recovery process took under two minutes. It was odd, though, that the software found only one file – a video file consisting of more than 20 gigabytes. She opened Windows Media Player and played the video.

What she saw was a static shot of a desk with a wall behind it– no action at all, and no audio either. Fast forwarding through the video to the end revealed that it was the same thing throughout – just a shot of a desk and a wall. The video was more than two hours long and had been shot in HD. Perhaps it had been shot accidentally – which would explain why it had been deleted. What other explanation could there be for making such a stupid video?

Elin clicked on "Properties" to see when the file had been created and deleted. She contemplated the dates for a minute or two – and suddenly it dawned on her what was going on.

7

Martin served everyone coffee. Liv and he had prepared a three course meal that their guests had found absolutely scrumptious: toast skagenröra – prawns on toast – for a first course, grilled salmon with potatoes and dill sauce for the main course, followed by fruit sorbet for dessert.

Martin was glad that Lars and Elin had come over for dinner, as they had a lot to talk about. Lars and Elin were curious to know how Liv and her kids were doing in Berlin and how their all living together there was working out. Liv showed the others some photos of her apartment on Potsdamer Platz. Martin and Liv had begun living together only recently – a decision it had taken them six months to make. During this period,

Martin had in any case been staying at Liv's house, so it didn't really make sense for him to have his own apartment – which he'd only been going to in order to get a change of clothes. Liv had purchased the apartment, which had two levels: the bottom floor for her and Martin and the second floor for the kids. And as the apartment was quite spacious, Martin's daughter Lara also had a room of her own there. Lara lived with her mother and only spent every other weekend at Martin's place – though lately she'd been spending a lot of time there, as she got along really well with Liv's kids. And now her mother had even allowed Lara to spend this three week vacation in Sweden. Martin and his wife had divorced a year ago – an event that prompted Martin to take a trip to Sweden to get some perspective and figure out what he wanted to do with his life. But then the unexpected happened. He'd only met Liv briefly on two occasions, but they'd clicked immediately. And when she'd failed to show up at their first real date, he'd searched for her all over Sweden, never giving up until he found her. The search had been fraught with danger, and there had been deaths, but Martin never regretted what he'd done for a second. The search had been well worth it, for he was now living with the love of his life and had a new family. His life had changed completely. Plus, it now had a Swedish dimension – the magnificent scenery, the Swedish mentality – and the language itself, which Martin simply adored. Liv's children attended a Scandinavian school in Berlin and always spoke Swedish at home. And now here they all were on vacation together in the Stockholm archipelago – a vacation that was alas nearing its end. Martin had totally enjoyed this vacation: he loved the sea, cliffs, forests and wooden houses, a combination he found both stimulating and relaxing. He would have liked to make greater use of the 24 foot yacht that was moored at the pier down below, but he unfortunately had no idea how to operate such a vessel, and Liv didn't feel up to piloting the yacht on her own. But luckily, on two occasions, the couple next door had come with them on the yacht for day trips, and the husband had piloted it. Those two trips had been magical. They'd sailed between the archipelago's islands and had docked at marinas or restaurants, where they'd had superb meals before setting off again. On one of the outings they'd sailed to the outermost inhabited island of the Stockholm archipelago, called Sandhamn, where there's a village with hotels, restaurants and superb sandy beaches. The vegetation on the island, where they'd spent half a day, differed from that in the inner Stockholm archipelago, and there was a magnificent ocean view from the east side of the island. Martin fully intended to learn how to operate this type of yacht so that they could sail it on their own during their next vacation. Apparently, you didn't need so much as a drivers license for this.

He was also glad to see that Lara had enjoyed herself so much. She hadn't been the least bit homesick, which was great because this was the first time she'd been away from her mother for any length of time. The other two kids had helped her to feel at home and she seemed to be very happy here in the Stockholm archipelago.

Lars and Elin also had a lot to talk about, especially concerning Elin's most recent case – which had even made headlines in the local papers. They'd busted a pedophile ring, at great risk to life and limb. Elin had been injured a few times and on one occasion had nearly been killed.

"How's the little girl that you rescued doing?" Liv asked.

"Well she's finally begun to speak, but only to her mother and me thus far," Elin said. "But that's a giant step forward that her doctors regard as a real breakthrough."

"Do you think she'll make a full recovery?" Martin asked.

"I strongly doubt it. This experience will haunt her for the rest of her life – although hopefully she'll learn to live with the effects of such a traumatic experience. That one day she spent with those scumbags destroyed her whole life," Elin said with tears in her eyes. Clearly, she felt very deeply about this little girl.

Liv placed a hand on Elin's arm. "I imagine that this is a tough situation for you. You need to process your own experiences – but you're constantly reminded of them because you see the little girl regularly. Do you think this is advisable?"

Elin shook her head. "Actually, it's okay. I've put my part of the story behind me, and nothing really horrendous happened to me. But I feel so terribly sorry for Ebba. I've grown very fond of her, and we see each other twice a week – which her doctors recommended because she sees me as her rescuer and that's helping her to heal as well. Also, it was with me that she spoke for the first time. That was amazing, and I really had the feeling that I was helping her."

"What did she say, the first time she spoke, if you don't mind my asking," Martin said.

"Oh, nothing special. I'd been reading her a Pippi Longstocking story, and when I said it was time to stop, she suddenly came out with, 'Oh please, just one more chapter.' That she'd *finally* spoken touched me so deeply that I took her in my arms and shed tears of joy. It took me a full ten minutes to recover my composure enough to continue reading to her."

The others nodded understandingly. Martin noticed that Liv's eyes were also damp. Liv was easily moved to tears, and evidently felt tremendous empathy for Ebba and her plight. But Martin thought it best to change the subject, lest the mood turn unduly mushy.

"Seems to me things are moving in the right direction at least. We're keeping our fingers crossed that this continues. But tell me, how's Christina's case going? She told Liv that you've taken it. Have you found any trace of her husband yet?"

Lars and Elin exchanged glances, and Lars cleared his throat. "Well as you know, we really can't discuss our cases. But on the other hand, you wangled the case for us and we trust each other, so we'll make an exception for you. Also, it's very important to me that you not disclose anything I'm about to say to anyone else, and that you not tell Christina that we discussed the case. Is that okay with you?"

Martin nodded, whereupon Liv said: "Sure, I'll act like I don't know anything and let her talk about the case, in the event she calls."

"Okay, so here goes. We haven't found any trace of her husband. So it appears that he left of his own free will."

"Really? What makes you say that?" Martin asked.

"Well he went to considerable lengths to leave no trace of his whereabouts or his reason for leaving," Lars said. "We were unable to find a single clue on his phone or laptop. Elin's more familiar with the technical details and can explain them better than I can."

Elin leaned forward. "Yes, that's true. He apparently deleted a ton of data from both his phone and laptop, and the data that's left is utterly useless."

"But I thought there was special software that allows you to recover deleted data." Martin was no IT expert, but he'd heard about such things from watching crime shows on TV.

"That's right. But that's precisely what aroused our suspicions. On his laptop he clearly used software to completely delete everything he didn't want anyone to see, and in such a way that you can't recover the data, even with the best software in the world. And as for his phone, he was very crafty. He deleted everything that he wanted to keep secret. When you do that, the file names are deleted from the registry, but the data itself is still there. But this data can be overwritten, and that's exactly what he did. Crafty guy that he is, he shot a video of his desk that overwrote all the unused data on his phone. He then deleted this video – which turned out to be the only recoverable file on the phone: a two-hour-long static shot of a desk."

"So that's how you do it! Good to know," Martin said, laughing.

Liv flashed him a smile. "What's so good about it? Are you planning to abscond too?"

"God, no! No way! But I still find such technical maneuvers interesting."

"So if I understand you correctly, you have no clue as to this guy's whereabouts." Liv turned toward Elin.

"Well yes we do." Elin looked over at Lars, who nodded. "The password for his laptop account was 'Natalia' – a name that no one in his entourage could place. Which is why I believe that the reason he absconded is because there was another woman in his life."

"Really?" said Liv, arching her eyebrows. "What did Christina have to say about that?"

"She was devastated," Lars said. "There are so many indications that her husband carefully planned his disappearance that she simply can't ignore them any more. And of course this female first name casts a pall over the whole thing."

Martin found himself wondering about that password. "But isn't that kind of odd? If the guy went to all that trouble to delete his files, why didn't he simply change his password and replace it with something neutral?"

"I see what you mean. Yeah, I mean it doesn't really make sense, does it? So if he used this password on purpose, it can of course simply mean he wanted to send us on a wild goose chase."

Elin shook her head. "I doubt that. I think he simply forgot to change his password."

"Well hopefully that's the case, because otherwise that name is completely irrelevant."

"Have you found any traces of this Natalia person?" Martin asked.

"No, but it's still early days. That'll be our next step."

"Well then, good luck. Hopefully you'll make some headway soon."

After coffee, Lars and Elin took their leave, in order to catch the last ferry, and Martin cleared the table with Liv.

After stacking the dishes, Liv gave Martin a pensive look. "I really feel for Christina, the whole situation sounds terrible. Should I call her before we leave? What do you think?"

“I don’t know. Maybe not. After all, we promised not to tell her anything about this conversation. So it would probably be better to wait for her to call so that she can tell us the whole story herself.”

“Well, maybe. But I could call and simply ask how things are going with the private investigators.”

“Well then, you have to make sure not to let the cat out of the bag. I sympathize with Lars’ desire not to come across as someone who discloses confidential information.”

“Don’t worry, I’ll be super careful. I’d just like to say a few consoling words to her. I don’t know Christina’s husband, but I’m very fond of Christina.”

Martin nodded. As he’d only met Christina once he didn’t feel like he needed to console her – whereas Liv had been Christina’s colleague for a number of years. “Then by all means, give her a call... And hey, it was a really nice evening, wasn’t it?”

“Yeah, it was awesome. The two of them had a lot to tell us. I’m going to look at the articles about Elin’s case in the back issues of my daily paper, *Dagens Nyheter*. It’s sort of like a sensational robbery.” She picked up the stack of dishes and headed into the kitchen.

Martin remained behind. It had been a really great evening, and he definitely intended to keep in touch with Lars and Elin. Plus, he was curious as to what would come of their search for Natalia, and Christina’s husband.

8

Elin was in the *tunnelbana* – the Stockholm metro – on her way home from her latest session with Carl. Well I guess it wasn't as bad as the last time, she thought to herself. Though, like last time he'd been wearing a greasy T-shirt, thick glasses with smudged lenses, and a greasy ponytail – but at least his desk and especially his keyboard looked clean. She didn't know, however, whether this was just an accident or if perhaps his company had switched to a different cleaning service. But she did have the feeling that Carl had taken her complaints to heart and might have even done some of the cleaning himself. Anyway, as always, he'd been a great help to her. She'd set aside the afternoon to work with him on her current case, for which she needed the triangulation data from Patrik's phone – meaning not the current data, as the phone was back at Patrik's office, but the data indicating his whereabouts in the weeks leading up to his disappearance. Yesterday, Patrik's boss, who was being super cooperative, had given her the conversation data from Patrik's work phone. As far as she could tell, all of the calls were work related, and the nature of the lengthy conversations that his colleague had mentioned was indeterminable. Hence, she was now convinced – as was Lars – that Patrik was using a second phone.

Elin was sure that Patrik had taken this second phone with him when he left. He might have bought it in order to communicate with Natalia. This would keep his work phone free of any "incriminating" messages that Christina might discover if he happened to leave the phone lying around the house. But now the question was, did he always carry this second phone with him, or had he left it at work when he went home? And yet, Elin could well imagine that Patrik and Natalia might have wanted to send each other a text message in the evening – which meant that Patrik must have taken the phone home with him. Which in turn meant that he must have acted with utmost circumspection, given that Christina hadn't noticed anything suspicious.

This was why the phone triangulation data was so crucial. There were countless phones at Patrik's office, so nothing relevant was obtainable from there; but if he'd had the phone with him at home or at his golf club, it would surely be possible to determine whether two different phones were located there or had been moved to another location in tandem. And that's why she needed Carl's help. Elin could easily hack into the phone company's server and find conversation data there – but figuring out the triangulation data was more daunting. Carl had shown her where this data was stored and how to make sense of it. Using the data from three different cell phone towers, it was possible to determine a cell phone's exact location – that was triangulation in a nutshell. It had taken Elin nearly two hours to obtain the answer to her question. First, she'd hacked into the Telia server containing the account of Patrik's work-issued cell phone. The tower for this device was used for all phones that were located nearby, including phones that used other telephony networks. She then found a phone number that was almost always moving in tandem with Patrik's work phone, both at work and at home, and a few times at his golf club – and so more likely than not, this was Patrik's phone. She had then tried to find out more about this number, but needless to say it was a prepaid – and thus anonymous – SIM card. Also, the card hadn't been issued by the same provider that had issued Patrik's original card – which meant that the phone towers of that company TRE came into play. But she'd still managed to hack into this tower and call up the conversation and triangulation data. Though Elin hadn't analyzed all the data yet, it was immediately clear to her that there was no data at all after July 2nd, and that the phone hadn't been switched on since then – or else Patrik had installed a new SIM card. And so she'd called Lars to tell him that the localization data from the past few days was in fact of great interest.

Elin got off the subway at Stadshagen. As the platform was quite crowded with passengers waiting to board the train, Elin had to push her way through them to get to the escalator. When she arrived at street level, she noticed that it was raining – an event she hadn't reckoned with. And so she had neither a raincoat nor a hooded sweatshirt with her – plus the rain was really coming down and showed no sign of letting up. Pressing her body against the walls of buildings and with her head down, she made her way home – which was only a short walk. Maja, who was already home, heard the door open and came to greet Elin.

"Well, hello there, how's my favorite sleuth doing today? Give us a big hug! Wow, you're soaking wet. You need to dry your hair right away, otherwise you might catch cold."

"Okay, mom." Elin chuckled. "What are you doing here anyway? Aren't you supposed to be at work?" Maja normally taught judo and karate classes until 8 p.m. every day.

"We had a giant flood at the studio, so all classes were cancelled."

"Awesome," Elin said. "I mean it's awesome that you're here. The flood is of course shitty. How long will it be until they repair the water damage and you can go back to work?" Maja was self-employed and was paid an hourly rate for the classes she taught – and so being off work for a lengthy period was no joke.

"I hope we can reopen tomorrow. The reception area and one of the locker rooms got the brunt of it. We're probably going to have people change their clothes in one of the training studios so that we can get back to almost normal without delay. Luckily the flood didn't happen at night, because otherwise the water would have gone everywhere, and we would have been closed down for weeks."

"How did it happen?" Elin was drying her hair with a towel she'd gotten from the bathroom. As her hair was very short, it took her almost no time to dry it.

"Some contractor did some work on the building's heating system last week, and apparently he failed to tighten down a bolt on one of the new items he installed. At first the pipe was only dripping, but the drip soon turned into a steady stream of water. Luckily, there were enough of us there to contain the water in two rooms until help arrived."

"So does that mean that the contractor will have to pay for the damage?"

"Well either him or the insurance company. Luckily that's not my problem. I'm just glad that I'll be able to go back to work tomorrow." Maja sat down on the living room couch. "How are things with you?"

"Well we finally have a lead."

"You mean about the dude who disappeared?"

"Right. We're heading to Norrland tomorrow."

"How come?"

Elin told Maja about the upshot of the afternoon she'd spent with Carl. "And this second phone was taken northward on July 1st – the very day of Patrik disappearance. And the day after that the phone was in the vicinity of Patrik's and Christina's summer home."

"But didn't Christina search the house?"

"Sure, but not until two weeks later. Unfortunately, all data came to an abrupt halt on July 2nd, the day after Patrik left. He probably bought a new SIM card, and so after that he could have taken the phone just about anywhere and there'd be no way to track it."

"But you're going to the house anyway?"

"Yeah, because even if we don't find Patrik there, we'll hopefully find a lead or two that we can follow up."

Maja looked down at the table reflectively, then looked up again. She gave Elin a piercing look with her dark eyes. "So that means you're going to be away all weekend?"

Elin had to make a conscious effort not to blush; she knew where Maja was going with this. She nodded. "Yeah I guess so. Regretfully."

"I suppose that suits you just fine, doesn't it? 'Cause after all, endlessly putting things off is the perfect excuse, right?" Maja shook her head in frustration.

Much as Elin hated to admit it, Maja had a point. She'd actually planned to go see her parents over the weekend. And this wasn't going to be just an ordinary visit: she'd promised Maja to tell her parents she was gay. She'd been living with Maja for more than two years now, and they both considered the relationship to be serious. But unlike Maja – who was completely open about her sexual orientation and had been a confirmed lesbian even before she met Elin – Elin had tried sleeping with men and hadn't realized how much she was into women until she met Maja. Plus, she wasn't totally open about her sexuality: all her friends and acquaintances knew she was gay, but her colleagues at work didn't – except for Lars. As for private eyes, they were a pretty hard-boiled bunch and were leery of comments about their sexual orientation. Nor had her family been clued in either. She'd merely told them that Maja was a good friend who happened to be her roommate. So whenever she and Maja spent time with her parents, they had to control themselves – tender caresses and pet names, even reflexive ones, were strictly verboten.

Maja was finding this more and more irritating and tried to avoid spending time with Elin's parents as much as possible. And so when Elin had come home a week ago and had proudly announced that she was now a full fledged private eye, they'd celebrated this event in a manner befitting its importance and Maja had been truly happy for her. But after imbibing two glasses of champagne, Maja's facial expression abruptly changed, and she gave Elin a provocative look.

"So now that you're a big grown up woman, shouldn't you change the rest of your life so that it's in sync with your newfound 'adult' status?" Maja asked, drawing the words out.

Elin knew immediately what Maja was getting at. But she was feeling so upbeat that, on the spur of the moment, she promised to pay her parents the long overdue visit during which she'd at long last disclose to them the true nature of her relationship with Maja. Elin's parents lived in Uppsala, about 45 miles north of Stockholm, and she planned to go there on Saturday in order to accomplish the delicate task of coming out to them. Just the thought of doing this made her feel queasy, and she really had no idea how her parents would react. Though queerness was pretty well accepted in Sweden, her parents were quite conservative and would probably be none too pleased to learn that their beloved daughter was a dyke. Nonetheless, a promise was a promise and she intended to keep it. And yet, having an excuse to put off the visit suited her just fine.

"Look, this decision was completely out of my hands. Lars and Tobias decided that we urgently need to go there, because they're afraid the trail might grow even colder than it already is. I really had no say in this decision; nor did I insist that we make the trip on this particular weekend. Scout's honor."

Maja didn't look in the least convinced. "But you didn't object either, did you?"

"Not really. But, honestly Maja, what the fuck was I supposed to say? That I was planning to visit my folks? They would have just told me – and they would have been right – that such a visit could wait a week."

"Okay, okay, I get it," Maja said with resignation.

Elin set the towel aside and squatted down in front of Maja. "Sweetie, I'm going to call my parents right now and tell them I'll be coming to visit them next weekend. I know how important this is to you. I made you a promise and I fully intend to keep it." She kissed Maja on the mouth, but her lover was still upset.

"But isn't this important to you too?"

What's eating her? Elin thought to herself. Maybe the flood's got her all discombobulated. Or she's got her period.

"Sure it's important to me. But I can't say that I'm exactly looking forward to telling my folks I'm a dyke. It's kind of like a dentist appointment where you know beforehand that it's not some routine, painless checkup, but rather a root canal that's going to be a real ordeal."

Maja laughed, in spite of herself. "Well I hope it's not going to be as bad as all that."

Elin shook her head. "To tell you the truth, babe, I have no idea how it's going to be. Maybe they'll simply stop speaking to me. I wouldn't put it past my mother to cut off all contact with me. And that would be super painful."

"I don't think your mom would do that. At least not based on what I know about her from the time I've spent with her. I think you're exaggerating."

"Well let's hope so. We'll just have to wait and see. The most important thing is for us to be on the same page about this. So give me a hug now, please."

Maja laughed. "Sure thing. What is it you always say? 'Do bears shit in the forest?'"

Elin laughed and put her arms around her – and gave her a real kiss.

9

Lars was standing on the edge of the soccer field watching his daughter move the ball downfield. "Thatta girl, Stina!" he shouted, upon which the team's coach gave him a disapproving look. He of course knew that parents were not allowed to make comments and urge their progeny on from the sidelines; the coach had been very clear about this. And Lars also knew that it was problematic when people watching from the sidelines were constantly calling out to the girls. But, like the other parents, sometimes he just couldn't control himself.

In any case, Stina clearly needed no encouragement. She'd worked her way around the last remaining defenders and was now in front of the goal with the ball, all by herself. The goalie, who was none too skilled, was standing in the goal itself instead of narrowing the angle – thus making it easier for Stina to score a goal. Two defenders were in hot pursuit, but Stina was quick. She kicked the ball solidly with all her might, but missed the goal, and the goalie hardly reacted at all. If Stina had kicked the ball a yard more to the left, the goalie wouldn't have been able to block it. But unfortunately, she'd missed, and the score was still 0–0.

Lars was thinking about the trip to Norrland. He hadn't talked about it with Lisa yet, and was planning to do so after Stina's soccer practice. For sure she wouldn't be thrilled about it, but what was he supposed to do? He really enjoyed going there, and loved the region's landscape, with its massive forests and countless lakes. For the summer solstice they'd all gone to his father's cabin, which was right on the coast somewhat farther north than Östersund. But the landscape and people were very similar in the north, and a few hundred miles didn't make any difference.

The summer solstice festival had been very traditional. The residents of the small cluster of cabins had decorated and erected a maypole together – a new experience for their kids. In Stockholm, people tended to be mere onlookers of these things, as there were myriad small community associations whose representatives made all the necessary arrangements. But in the north, they'd danced around the maypole to the music from a CD. One of the residents had grabbed the microphone and acted as contra-dance caller. One of the cluster of calls involved a song about a piglet; then there was one about the various household chores for each day of the week; and finally a frog song that his daughter Olivia loved jumping around to, pretending she was a little frog. Lars had read somewhere that this song was derived from a French military march. As the French were known for eating frogs, someone had apparently composed a text about frogs and the sounds they make – and this eventually became a traditional Swedish summer solstice song. It was generally believed that the song had originally been written for the summer solstice and had been used accordingly for centuries; but this was in fact untrue.

The practice game was over and the girls went to the locker room to shower and change. Lars waited in the car for Stina, and they then made the ten minute drive home. He parked the car in front of the house. Their row house only had a one-car garage, and Lisa had parked her car there when she came home.

"Hi there," Lisa said as Lars and Stina stood at the front door taking off their shoes. "Come in, quick, dinner's almost ready."

The food smelled delicious. It must be spaghetti with meat sauce, Lars thought to himself. His mouth was watering already at the thought of this – the kids' favorite dish, though he liked it a lot too.

After taking off their coats, they went into the kitchen and sat down. The pasta was on the table, with steam rising from it and the sauce next to it. Olivia and Lisa had served themselves and Olivia was already eating. Stina and Lars each filled their plates with a generous amount of pasta and sauce, and then everyone dug in.

After dinner, the kids went up to their rooms, and Lars and Lisa had coffee.

"I'm going to Östersund tomorrow morning, about this guy called Patrik who's gone missing."

"Well thanks for finally letting me in on your little plan." Lisa was none too thrilled at the news, as Lars had expected. "How long do you think you'll be gone?"

"Sorry, the decision to go there was only made today. It'll probably take only a couple of days."

"Oh great, yet another weekend down the drain!"

"Oh come on, Lisa, it doesn't happen all that often. And compared to my schedule when I was working shifts at the police, it's really nothing at all."

"Yeah, well, I suppose," said Lisa. She looked furious. "Why Östersund of all places?"

"Patrik apparently went there after he absconded. He and his wife have a summer home there."

"Are you going by yourself?"

Lars had been dreading this question. What had been a merely tense atmosphere was now becoming downright explosive. "No, I'm not. Tobias doesn't want us to go on expeditions like this alone."

Lisa waited a beat, and as Lars didn't react, she said, "So judging from your hemming and hawing, I suppose that means you're going with Elin, is that it?"

Lars had no choice but to nod in assent.

"Oh terrific. Another exploit in the company of Madame Elin. And overnight into the bargain. Well I'm telling you, I have no intention of driving all the way to Östersund to visit you in the hospital, if you end up there from some injury or other. So please be advised that, in such a case, all of our communication will be by phone. You know Lars, I'm beginning to get really fed up."

Lars took a deep breath and counted to ten. He didn't want the situation to escalate.

"Well nothing bad happened to me last time," he finally said.

"You mean the time you rescued Elin when she was about to be hacked to smithereens by a child molester? Oh that's super reassuring!" Lisa said in a cuttingly sarcastic tone.

"And how about the time before that, when you came close to getting shot; and the time before that when you broke your collar bone. This sort of thing happens every time you're with Elin. She's a real Calamity Jane, that one."

Fuck, she'd reacted worse than he'd thought she would.

"Look, honestly there's nothing at all dangerous about this particular mission. We're simply trying to find a clue that'll lead us to her husband, who to all appearances has absconded with his new paramour. He's probably long since left Östersund in any case."

"Oh yeah? Well for all you know he's still there and won't be any too pleased to find out you're looking for him. And if he does, he'll for sure reach for his hunting rifle – and then, my friend, we've got a problem. Or even better, maybe he's left and you'll find a clue to his whereabouts. And of course you'll go wherever that clue leads you, and it'll end up taking much longer than three days, and you'll end up somewhere in the wilderness fending off an attack from some really pissed off bear. And I'll be left to bury whatever's left of you when the bear gets done masticating your body parts. Fuck it, Lars, I don't want to have to go through that," Lisa said, her face beet-red and her voice at peak volume.

Lars suddenly felt the urge to stand up; just sitting in a chair had become intolerable to him. He really hated the way women always made such a fuss about every little thing. The whole conversation was so ridiculous – he was at a loss as to what he should say or do. He went over to Lisa and tried to hug her, but she was having none of it.

"Lars I want to be neither consoled nor calmed right now, I mean it."

Lars squatted down in front of her. "Sure, okay, but then what would you have me do? Ask Tobias to send someone else there with Elin? And how, pray tell, would I explain why I'm making this request? Or do you want me to just quit?" He couldn't stay in this position for much longer, because his right knee, the one that had been shot, was starting to seriously hurt.

Lisa's face was turned away from him, trying to avoid eye contact. "I haven't got the slightest idea," she whispered. "But one thing I do know: I absolutely do not want you to make this trip with Elin along."

Lars put his hand on her arm, and this time she let him. "Lisa, babe, I'm telling you, nothing's going to happen. The most dangerous thing about the trip is the drive there and back. And I solemnly swear that I'll drive super carefully and that I'll always obey the speed limit. Really and truly."

Lisa stood up. "Oh, sure," she said. "You're going to do whatever the fuck you feel like, just as you always do. You don't give a shit about how I feel," she shouted angrily as she stormed out of the kitchen.

"That's not true!" Lars called after her, as, with some effort, he stood up.

Lars felt it was best to give Lisa some space to cool down, as it was clear that she was in no mood to listen to reason. While he was waiting for Lisa's anger to subside, he cleared the table, loaded the dishwasher and cleaned the stove. Maybe Lisa would give him credit, and even cut him a break, for cleaning up the kitchen and bringing her a glass of wine in the living room. These arguments with her, which were becoming stormier each time, set his nerves on edge. He desperately needed a couple of cases with Elin where nothing bad happened, because that's the only way he knew of to put Lisa's paranoid fears to rest. Lars was truly convinced that, when it came to risks and danger, Patrik's case was a cakewalk – and he hoped to god he was right about this.

TWO MONTHS BEFORE: JUNE 2016

10

She was watching Patrik walk down the path. He turned around again and blew her a kiss, before getting into his car – and she waved back. They'd spent two idyllic hours in her apartment – and the love-making had been really good for her too. As from the start with Patrik, she hadn't needed to do any dissembling or put on an act for him. But right now he needed to drive by the golf course in Täby: playing golf was also his alibi for today.

Yeah, she was really into him. He was a really nice guy, and honest into the bargain. So much nicer than the other guys she'd been involved with. Which was why over the past few days she'd begun having doubts as to whether she could really go through with the undertaking.

But Stanislov had reacted pretty violently when she merely mentioned this in passing. "You've spent more than six months on this, and now you want to bail out? Just at the point where he's gone so far, and everything's been planned? Are you insane?"

She knew that Stanislov would never accept this – particularly as it would be much more worthwhile this time than in the past.

But what were her options, after all? Leave Stanislov and begin a new life with Patrik? She could even imagine that Patrik would be attentive to her every need and that they'd be super compatible. But that wouldn't prevent Stanislov from looking all over for her – which he'd never, ever stop doing until he'd tracked her down. And then the shit would really hit the fan, that was for damned sure. She knew what Stanislov was capable of. How well she remembered the evening when he'd committed the first murder, by running over the victim in a stolen car. After plowing into him, he'd backed up and run over the guy, who was screaming in pain. Natalia had gotten a good look at Stanislov's face, and there wasn't an ounce of pity in it – to the contrary, he'd enjoyed making the guy suffer.

If she tried to bail out now, Stanislov would never forgive such a betrayal. He'd want one thing and one thing only: revenge. Plus, this wouldn't do Patrik any good either, he'd also be done for. So she was stuck between a rock and a hard place, and there was no way out.

She'd simply have to get a grip on herself, ignore her feelings for Patrik and act strictly according to plan. Being clear-headed, that was the only solution.

SEPTEMBER 2016

11

Lars pulled up to where Elin was standing on the sidewalk. She opened the rear door, tossed her bag on the back seat, and then opened the passenger door and got in.

"So how did it go?"

"Great, she's making real progress. Today she smiled at me when I arrived. That was the first time she'd ever done that."

"So it seems there's hope. I truly hope that everything works out for Ebba in the end. When's the trial?" Lars said, threading the car into the flow of traffic and heading for the E4.

"In two weeks, so I absolutely must be back by then at the latest."

"No worries," Lars said, smiling. "I don't think we'll need to spend more than three days there."

“What do you think might actually come of this? Do you think he really might still be in the place where his phone was last localized?”

“No idea. Probably not. After all, it’s been two months. But I’m hoping that we’ll at least find some proof that he was actually there. For the moment, it’s only a hunch that this is even his phone number. Someone might have spotted him. He would have had to go shopping at some point, and there aren’t that many grocery stores out in the boonies.”

“Unless of course he went to Östersund or Sundsvall to do his shopping.”

“Yeah, but you know how it is. You can do the bulk of your shopping there, but if you happen to run out of coffee or milk or the like, or if a light bulb burns out, then you’ll tend to go to a small local store. That’s what I’m hoping at any rate.”

“Yeah great, but then what? I mean, what happens if we find out he was in fact there, but has since left?”

“Then we’ll try to find a clue to his whereabouts. If we’re able to find out where he actually was, maybe you’ll be able to identify his new phone using the triangulation data – and then we can track it.”

“Yeah but guess what? I’ve already tried that. The last time his SIM card was activated, his phone was in the middle of a forest with no other phone nearby.”

“Which is why it’s so important to be where the action is – or more likely, was. We need to find out where that forest path goes. Maybe that’ll lead us to another place where you can check which phones were in the environs."

Elin nodded in agreement – though she had her doubts as to whether this would work. It had been hard enough identifying this phone in the first place, given that it had been carried around for a time in tandem with Patrik's work phone. So now, successfully analyzing a brief period in the absence of any direct physical proximity would be highly problematic. But on the other hand, Norrland was sparsely populated, which meant there wouldn't be an overwhelming number of phones in a given sector. She'd definitely give it the old college try, though.

Elin leaned back. She needed to chill out. Her session with Ebba had gone really well, but she always felt drained afterwards. She couldn't stop thinking about what those scumbags had done to them both in June. She'd be the main witness during the trial, and Ebba of course didn't need to testify; in any case she wouldn't be able to utter a word.

And anyway, the facts of the case were clear, because the photos and videos that those asswipes had taken proved their guilt. All four of them were in the pictures and videos, in unambiguous situations. The prosecutor was sure that they'd be found guilty, and he planned to ask for a life sentence for all four defendants. Elin planned to do everything she could to help him achieve this. Child abuse, kidnapping, assault, murder, and being an accessory to murder. The body of a child buried in the forest had been identified as being a missing girl who'd been clearly identified in the photos and videos. That should be more than enough to convince a panel of judges and lay assessors. Elin took a deep breath. She was looking forward to the trial being over – and to slowly but surely leaving all this behind her.

***

It took them six hours to get there. It was 8 p.m. and the sun was just going down. For the last two hours of the trip, all they'd seen were lakes and forests – and of course the ubiquitous trucks ferrying logs out of the forest in both directions, with their truck beds and trailers loaded to the hilt. You knew right away what the main industry was here. Because it was pouring, every single truck had splashed a massive wave of water on their front windshield, which made it difficult to drive at times.

They pulled up to Sörbygården B&B, a bed and breakfast in a suburb of Östersund called Brunflo, took their bags out of the car and checked in. They'd ordered dinner ahead of time and met in the dining room at 8:30. As Elin entered, a bunch of teenagers were getting up from a table. They were probably horseback riders, as she had realized that Sörbygården B&B also offered stalls for island ponies and horseback riding tours. Lars was at a small corner table, with a glass of beer in front of him, and was studying a map. Elin signaled to the hostess that she wanted something to drink and ordered a glass of white wine. Then she sat down opposite Lars.

"So are you planning our next moves?" She noticed that Lars had marked a number of places on the map with a red pencil.

Lars looked up from the map. "Yeah, I'm trying to get my bearings. You chose an opportune place to stay, by the way, because Christina's cabin isn't very far from here." He pointed to the location of Sörbygården B&B, then to a place to the east that was near a number of lakes. "It's only about seven miles as the crow flies – basically right around the corner."

Elin nodded – she'd of course verified this before making the booking at Sörbygården B&B.

"And here's more or less the place where Patrik last switched on his phone." Lars pointed to a marked point somewhat farther south, near a lake called Stor-Långtjärnen.

"It's about three and a half klicks south of the cabin." Lars drew a small circle around the cabin and the lake's location. "Here," he said, pointing to the area enclosed by the circle, "is where we're going to listen out and look for Patrik."

"Yeah, I also looked at that on my phone before we left. But unfortunately, there's nothing in this area but forests, lakes and a few houses. No gas stations or stores listed there."

"Yeah, unfortunately a lot of these country stores have closed because more and more people are moving to the city. And such stores can't survive from the tourist trade alone. So where's the nearest store?"

"There's an ICA supermarket here in Brunflo," Elin said giving Lars a gloating look, "as well as a Coop and two gas stations. We can go there on foot if necessary."

Lars shook his head, grinning. "Did you already know that? Or was it just a lucky guess?"

"That's what we call intuition," Elin chuckled.

"Good work, as always. We'll get started in the morning." Lars folded up the map to make room for their food, which the hostess had just brought to the table.

The food – roast venison with chanterelle mushrooms, root vegetables and boiled potatoes – smelled delicious. It wasn't until just then that Elin realized how famished she was.

12

Lars pulled up in front of the Coop Konsum store, where he'd dropped Elin off 20 minutes ago. While she was there, he'd paid a visit to the OKQ8 gas station located on the road to Östersund, but no one remembered seeing Patrik or his car there.

While he was watching the store entrance, the sun slipped behind the clouds and there was even a patch of blue showing through. It was surely going to be a beautiful day, after yesterday's heavy rain. Elin came out of the store and got in the car.

"Nothing to report – though both stores are far too large for anyone to remember a particular individual. Not exactly the mom and pop stores you'd been hoping for. And of course all the grocery clerks don't work the same shift. So if we want to talk to all of them, we'll need to come back in the evening or some other time. And you? How did you do?"

"Same here. Nada. Most people pay with their credit cards right at the pump. So at best you see the customers' cars on the security footage, but few customers actually enter the store." Lars sighed. "There's still one gas station that we haven't checked out. So let's head over there now."

Lars got back on the E14. After about a mile they passed the train station, and then came the Gulf gas station they were looking for. Lars drove in. All the pumps were free, except for one. At this place, too, customers had the option to use a credit card to pay right at the pump. He parked the car and looked over at Elin.

"I can go in, but I doubt we're going to find anything."

"I'll come with," Elin said. "At least this gas station is the one closest to the road leading to Christina's cabin."

Lars entered the store behind Elin, who made a beeline for the counter. Behind it was a young clerk dressed in a blue shirt and sporting a pierced eyebrow.

"Can I help you," he said with a friendly smile.

"*Hej!* You sure can," said Elin. "We're private investigators and are looking for someone who's gone missing. Have you by any chance seen this man?"

She laid the photo of Patrik on the counter. The young clerk smiled at Elin, nodded, and looked at the picture. I must admit, Lars thought to himself, Elin's a lot better at doing this than I am. He always acted as friendly as Elin did when he was seeking information from strangers, but even if Lars had possessed Elin's innate charm, the clerk surely wouldn't have been *this* forthcoming. And of course he had no way of knowing that Elin was gay.

"When is he supposed to have been here?" the clerk asked, furrowing his brow and continuing to examine the photo.

"About two months ago," Elin said.

The clerk looked up, nodded, and looked down at the picture again. "Well, it might have been a dude who came in here a while back who I think looked like the guy in this picture."

The clerk looked at Elin. "Why are you looking for him? Did he commit a crime?"

Elin smiled again. "No, nothing like that. He's gone missing and his wife has hired us to find him. Are you sure it was the man in this picture?"

The clerk picked up the picture again and scrutinized it. "Yeah, I'm pretty sure. I remember him because he paid in cash and not many people do that."

"Do you remember how much he paid?" Lars asked.

The clerk looked over at him. "I can't remember. But he did buy some items in the store and filled up his tank. So he must have spent more than a thousand kronor." The clerk looked back at Elin. "I asked him if he'd maybe robbed a bank," the clerk said, laughing.

Elin chuckled. "How did he react to that? Did he say anything?"

The clerk shook his head. "Nah, he just laughed."

"Did you get a look at his car? Was it a blue Saab 93?" Lars asked.

"Nope, no idea. And even if I noticed what kind of car he was driving, I've forgotten it since."

"Was he alone or with someone?"

"Well for sure he came into the store by himself. But I haven't got the faintest idea whether or not someone was with him in the car."

"Did he say anything else? Anything you can remember would be a great help to us."

The clerk seemed to be trying to rack his brains but ended up just shaking his head. "No, not that I can remember."

Lars thanked him and headed for the door.

"I'm going to look around for something yummy," Elin called after him. "I'll be right out."

Lars left the store and went back to the car. Well at least now they had something to go on: they knew Patrik had been here and that the second phone was in fact his. But it was a shame that they were still groping around in the dark about his actual whereabouts. Hopefully, Lars thought to himself, we'll find a clue at Christina's cabin that'll point us in the right direction.

Elin emerged from the store, plastic bag in hand, grinning from ear to ear.

"What's with the big grin?" Lars asked her as she got into the car.

"Well, I lingered in the store a little while to see if the clerk's memory might get jogged – and lo and behold it did," she said proudly. "So it turns out that Patrik asked the clerk if he knew of a cabin to rent in the area."

"No kidding! And what did the clerk tell him?" Lars was impressed – Elin's intuition to the rescue yet again.

“He gave Patrik the number of an uncle of his who evidently rents out cabins – though he didn’t know whether Patrik actually contacted the guy.”

“Yeah but I’m sure you got the uncle’s number, so what do you say we give him a call?”

“I do have it in fact. But Kent – the clerk – called his uncle while I was there, and the uncle said that he did in fact rent out a cabin to Patrik – who paid the uncle in cash. I made an appointment to meet up with the uncle for lunch at Restaurant Chili, which is just opposite the train station.”

Lars was amazed. “Way to go, Elin! I honestly hadn’t imagined that the clerk had any other relevant information.” It had been well worthwhile bringing Elin along. “So we still have enough time to go over to Christina’s cabin.”

Elin nodded, looking extremely pleased with herself. Which was totally justified, because if Patrik had indeed rented a cabin here, then they’d finally have a real lead.

***

Lars set his plate down, which was the size of a small food tray – square, with rounded corners and slightly curved. Large enough for a very sizeable portion at any rate. The restaurant had a large selection of Thai and Swedish dishes, which were arrayed on a buffet table.

Lars had opted for a number of different dishes. There was also seating on an outdoor terrace. But as it was a bit chilly today and the restaurant was within hailing distance of the highway, the terrace was going to be neither warm nor quiet. So Lars decided to sit inside. From the outside, the restaurant resembled a large wooden Swedish villa, painted light gray with white corners. The decor was bistro-like, and relatively simple.

Lars had told Klas, the gas station clerk's uncle, that he'd like to take him out to lunch. Klas was in his 50s, heavy-set, with sandy hair, an unkempt beard and brown glasses. He was out of breath by the time he reached the table with his plate, which was piled high with food. Elin, who'd chosen – albeit not as copiously as Klas – various Thai dishes, had already sat down at the table.

Having gotten beverages – water for Lars and Elin, beer for Klas – Lars got the ball rolling. "First of all, thanks so much for taking the time to meet with us."

After drinking some beer, Klas put his glass down. "No problem. I was planning to have lunch here today in any case. And the fact that it's your treat was an added incentive," he said with a grin that revealed yellowing teeth – and proceeded to devour the pile of food in front of him.

"Well then, bon appetit," Lars said, as he began eating.

He gave Klas a little time to eat – though in any case Klas clearly didn't want to be disturbed until he'd eaten almost everything on his plate. "So as I understand it, you rented a cabin to Patrik Lindblom, correct?"

Klas chewed for a moment or two before saying, "Yeah the dude's name was Patrik – though I don't recall his last name."

"When exactly did he rent out the cabin?"

"Well after Kent called, I rummaged through my files and fished out the receipt – I like to keep things organized, you know." He reached into his jacket pocket and pulled out a piece of paper, which he smoothed out on the table. "Have a look; hopefully you can decipher it."

Lars bent over the receipt, which said that Patrik had paid 3,000 kronor. His signature was illegible, but he'd printed his name just below it. The date was clearly July 2nd, the day Patrik went missing.

"What does it say here? 'Rent...'?"

"For one week, cabin 5," Klas said, still chewing.

"Did he pay in cash?"

"Yup."

Elin picked up the receipt and took a picture of it with her phone.

"Did you talk to him? Did he happen to say why he was here?" Lars asked.

"Yeah, well he said he was vacationing."

"Was he by himself?"

"Nah, there was a dame with him, pretty, blond."

"About how old would you say she was?"

"In her mid to late 20s, I'd guess."

Elin, who'd been listening attentively without saying anything, now asked, "Where did you meet up?"

"At the train station. Then we drove to the cabin, which was to his liking. He paid me a week's rent, and then I left."

"And what happened when the week was up? Did he extend his stay?"

"Nope."

Lars noticed that Elin was becoming increasingly annoyed with Klas, who like most northerners, was a man of few words. "Did they leave the area when the week was up? Did he return the key?"

"Nope, which pissed me off."

"What happened after that?"

"Not a thing. Didn't call, didn't bring the key back. I went over to the cabin the next day. No one was there. The cabin was unlocked, and the key was on the table. Uppity Stockholmers – can't even be bothered to bring a key back."

Lars swallowed; hopefully Elin wasn't going to choose this particular moment to jump in. "And you never heard from them again, right?" Lars added quickly.

"Nope, I just rented out the cabin to the next person."

Klas's phone rang. He wiped his hands on his napkin, picked up the phone and said, "Hello?"

Looking over at Elin, Lars could see that she no longer felt like continuing the conversation; and in any case doing so was unlikely to be very fruitful.

"Elin, would you mind getting us some more coffee?"

Elin at first looked as though she was going to object, but after glancing at Klas she realized it was best to just go get the coffee and keep her thoughts to herself. Klas was talking to someone on the phone about repairs for one of his cabins.

When Klas hung up, Lars asked him whether he'd been talking about the cabin that Patrik had rented.

"No, it was a different one, a cabin with a chronically leaky roof."

"Did they leave anything behind – I mean Patrik and his blond companion?"

"No, the place was completely cleared out."

"Can you describe the woman more concretely? Did you happen to find out what her name was?"

"No, I didn't. No idea what her name was." After a brief pause, Klas said, "She was one of these young chicks, I can tell you that. Dressed in pretty snazzy sportswear, shoulder-length blond hair. That's all I know about her. Except that she wasn't from Sweden."

"What makes you say that?"

"Well, she didn't say much, but from the little I heard it was clear she had a strong foreign accent."

"Any idea what kind of accent it was or where she was from?"

Klas rubbed his beard. "Not sure, maybe Poland."

“So she had an Eastern European accent, then?”

“Yup.”

That would fit with the name Natalia, Lars thought.

Elin came in carrying a tray with three pitchers of coffee on it, having taken her time in the kitchen.

“Thanks for the meal, folks. But I need to go meet the roofer at one of my cabins. So unfortunately, I won’t be able to stay for coffee.” Klas got up and took his rent receipt.

“One more thing: could we have the address of the cabin?”

“I thought you might want to go over there, so I brought the directions with me that I usually give to tenants. If you have trouble finding the place, give me a call. It’s vacant just now.” Klas placed a piece of paper on the table, turned around and made for the door.

Elin shook her head. “Jesus Christ, talking to him was like trying to get blood from a stone.”

“Yeah well just be thankful he was willing to tell us anything at all. That’s how people are here. They just don’t talk all that much.”

“But you on the other hand are quite talkative!”

“Yeah well, it’s all relative. And anyways I’m not from here, I was brought up in Stockholm, as you know.”

“Yeah but your dad’s from Norrland and you spent your summers here. Didn’t that have an effect?”

“Well as you can see, not much.”

Elin took a sip of her coffee and grimaced. "Yikes, it's strong! Needs more milk." She poured a splash of milk into her cup. "So what's our next move? Should we head for the cabin?"

"Well let's see," Lars said checking his watch. "It's only 1 now, so we've still got nine hours of daylight ahead of us. Which means we have time to examine the cabin and its surroundings. Hopefully more will come of this than what we did this morning."

But as it turned out, there was nothing to be found in Christina's cabin. The place had seemed completely uninhabited, and there'd been no sign of anyone having set foot there. They'd taken pictures of the cabin and sent them to Christina, who indicated that everything was exactly as she'd left it during her last visit.

"Weren't you going to ask Klas for the key? Because without it, we won't even be able to get inside."

"Well, I wanted to avoid being too insistent right off the bat. I think we should first have a good look around outside the cabin. We can always ask him for the key later. And anyway, he told us that there was nothing unusual inside and that he's rented the place out in the interim. So the likelihood of our coming upon anything unusual inside is pretty slim."

"Yeah, but then what makes you think we're going to find any clues outside the cabin? I mean after all, it's been almost two months now."

"Frankly, I have no idea. Let's just head over there and have a look around – maybe we'll think of something. That's my gut feeling in any case," he said, grinning at her.

"I see your point. So let's do that." Elin nodded and drank some coffee.

13

They were able to find the cabin without difficulty thanks to Klas's excellent directions. But getting there involved making their way through what seemed like endless tracts of forest. They'd now walked all the way around the cabin three times but had found nothing of interest – just as Elin had anticipated.

She looked over at Lars. "This is a waste of time, my friend. What do you think you're going to find here?

"Yeah, I guess you're right. Judging from what I can see through the window, we're not going to find any leads inside the cabin either."

"So what now?"

Lars let his gaze wander over the cabin. "Well, let's see, what do we know so far? Well, we know that Patrik left Stockholm on that fateful Friday, apparently in the company of a certain Natalia. They probably stopped for the night somewhere or other and then arrived in Östersund on Saturday, where they rented this cabin. On the way here, a mile or two before they arrived, the SIM card was removed from Patrik's phone. They rented the cabin for a week. And now they could be just about anywhere."

"But what I'd like to know is why they came here in the first place."

"Yeah, good question. Maybe Patrik wanted to show his new flame his ancestral vacation spot. Plus, the cabin's in an extremely isolated location – it's hardly noticeable."

"Could be. And of course he would have preferred not to use Christina's cabin in the first place."

"Exactly. So I'm hanging my hopes on the folks who live nearby – maybe they noticed something."

"Not much chance of that. We saw very few houses on our way here."

"Well let's drive slowly and keep a close lookout on our way out, since most of the houses aren't right on the road. If we come upon a row of mailboxes, we should stop and have a look around. Unfortunately, many of these cabins are used only in the summer and will be vacant now. But maybe we'll find someone who lives here year-round."

Shrugging her shoulders, Elin turned towards the car and thought, well maybe it's worth a try anyway.

But as it turned out, they didn't have much luck. They did come upon a row of mailboxes, but the houses, all of which were located back in the woods and far from the road, were vacant, every last one of them – or at least they looked that way.

So they drove a bit further until they came to an intersection, where they saw a house with a high wooden fence in front of it. Lars pulled into the driveway. Elin scrutinized the wooden fence, which was painted red. But the paint was peeling in many places and some of the boards were rotten and had fallen over. All they could see of the house was its roof, which was in pretty much the same dilapidated condition as the fence.

"Looks pretty desolate, Lars, don't you think? And with that high fence, I doubt they even notice when cars drive by."

"Yeah, but let's go ask some questions, shall we?" Lars opened the gate resolutely. "And anyway, we're sort of out of options here. Given that there are two directions you can go in from this intersection, our chances of finding someone who lives farther away and who noticed Patrik's car are going to get slimmer the farther away we get."

Elin nodded; Lars was right. From this house at the intersection, it would be very easy to see who turned into this street – and even easier to see who turned out of the street, because motorists had to stop at the intersection and yield to the cars on the other street. So there was a good chance that someone in this house had noticed *something*. That is, assuming someone who lived there was looking over the fence...

She hastened to catch up with Lars, who was already walking up the steps to the front door. What they observed in the front yard was of a piece with the fence – a pile of junk: rusty old bicycles, buckets, gardening implements. In the right corner there was a tractor, which judging from its age could have been a museum exhibit if it hadn't been half eaten away by rust. In the opposite corner there was a garden shed that looked to be in a hazardous state of disrepair. The house itself had definitely seen better days: it desperately needed to be repainted, and broken window panes had been replaced by plastic sheeting. Elin would have had serious doubts as to whether anyone even lived here, if it hadn't been for the kennel and the dog inside it. In the large steel cage, a large German shepherd dog was banging loudly against the bars and baring his teeth through them. I sure hope that cage is securely locked, Elin thought.

Lars stood in front of the door and banged on it with his fist. Elin, too, would have been surprised if this house had a functioning doorbell. It was not until Lars had banged on the door a second time that it opened, albeit slowly. A little old woman was standing there. She had long gray hair and a wrinkled face and was wearing a bluish gray apron over a brown sweater.

"Shut up, Sixten," she yelled in a hoarse voice. The dog fell quiet. She looked mistrustfully from Elin to Lars. "Whaddyah want? We're not interested in buying anything."

Well so much for Norrland hospitality.

"No worries, Ma'am, we're not salesmen. Sorry to bother you – we just wanted to ask you a question. If that's okay with you." Lars seemed to be trying to win the lady over by being friendly. But she was unimpressed.

"So what then?" she asked

Lars politely explained that he and Elin were private detectives who'd been hired by the wife of a man named Patrik to find her husband, who'd gone missing, and who'd rented a cabin at the end of the road.

"You from Stockholm?" she asked, glaring at Lars.

"Yeah, our office is in Stockholm, but my father's from Norrland and I spent all my summers here when I was growing up." Elin noticed that Lars was trying to speak with a Norrland accent. This seemed to be working, as the old lady was looking less mistrustful.

"Which cabin did the fellow rent?"

Lars began describing where the cabin was.

The lady nodded. "Doesn't it belong to that crafty devil Klas?"

"Right," Lars said, nodding.

"And what was it you were wanting to find out?" The old woman was no longer being so gruff. But she didn't seem about to invite Lars and Elin in either, as she was holding on to the door with one hand and to the doorframe with the other arm, thus effectively blocking the entrance.

"Patrik was here in the company of a young blond woman. We thought that they might have passed by your house and that perhaps you spoke to them. Anything you might be able to tell us would be helpful."

"No, we pay no mind to the tourists." The old lady shook her head and began turning away.

"Wait, please. Mightn't you have perhaps seen them driving by? Patrik drives a blue Saab 93."

Her gaze raking over him, she gave him a withering look and said, "Young man, do you honestly think I have nothing better to do than notice the cars that drive by here?" Whereupon she closed the door.

Lars turned toward Elin and shrugged. He went down the steps slowly. Together, they walked past the kennel, where Sixten was still baring his teeth but had stopped barking. Just as they'd passed by the kennel, they heard the elderly lady's front door open again.

"A blue Saab, you said?" she called after them. They both turned around and nodded.

"Right," Lars said.

"My husband spotted a car like that in the woods not long ago." Now things were getting interesting; Elin perked up her ears.

"Where was that?" asked Lars.

"You'd have to ask him, but he's not home right now. He'll be back tonight."

“Could I perhaps give him a call on his cellphone?”

“We’ve got no use for such newfangled gadgets.” She again made as if to close the door.

“When will he be back?”

“Some time after seven,” the lady answered, and shut the door.

Lars turned toward Elin. “So I guess we’ll have to come back later.”

Elin checked the time on her phone; it was just before three. “So what should we do in the meantime?”

Lars looked at her and said, “Well now that we know where the cabin is, you should be able to get the triangulation data again. For sure this Natalia person has a cellphone, and Patrik probably has a new SIM card by now.”

“Yeah, good idea. So what do you say we mosey on back to the hotel?”

Lars nodded, and they went back to the car.

***

There was the Saab. Elin had checked the license plate number: it was Patrik’s car for sure. This came as a complete surprise to both of them. The old man turned out to be far more cooperative than his wife and had even offered to drive them to the place where he’d seen the Saab two weeks ago. They had gratefully accepted his offer, as the directions to the place sounded complicated, involving as they did a number of forest roads to a clearing where the man had found the Saab. It was very odd that the car was still – or again – standing there. In exactly the same place, according to the old man. Lars had thanked him profusely and he'd left. Now they were peering at the car.

Elin looked at Lars and said, "Looks like the car's been here for a while. There are no tire tracks, even though the ground is soft." She looked around. "Is there a cabin nearby?"

"The husband said there aren't any which is why he found it so odd that the car was just 'hanging around'." Lars peered into the car and tried to open the door, but it was locked. He looked around the clearing. "It'll be light for about another hour. What do you say we split up and explore the area? I'll go this way and you go that way," he said pointing to a small path. "Give me a call if you find anything."

"Will do." Checking her phone, Elin saw that she had a signal, with two bars, even – which was a relief. She set off down the path, which, as it was a good three feet wide, afforded enough space for two people to walk next to each other. The path was muddy in places, but as Elin was wearing boots, she had no difficulty walking on it. Norrland was living up to its reputation, though: mosquitoes buzzed around her and she had to keep batting them away. The mosquito spray she'd brought along as a precaution seemed not to faze the insects in the least. How does the saying go? In Norrland mosquito spray only works from November to March. Luckily, she was wearing pants and she decided to keep her thin jacket on, even though she was starting to feel warm. As she moved pluckily down the path, she kept peering between the trees on either side to see if there might be something of interest there. She was hoping to spot a small cabin or some other sign of a human presence, but there was nothing of the kind in the forest. As the path was pretty straight and didn't branch off anywhere thus far, she kept following it. After about ten minutes, the path grew lighter up ahead, where there were apparently trees. A clearing perhaps? Curious to see what was there, she quickened her pace. Yes, in fact there were no trees here, just a few bushes. The path continued for a few yards and ended abruptly at a bluff with a steep downhill slope that was at least 30 feet deep. It was a good thing she'd arrived here while it was still daylight, because otherwise she might have noticed the bluff too late. She had absolutely no intention of clambering down there just now. But the view was magnificent. Below her a massive landscape of meadows was arrayed, dotted with rocks and bushes. Beyond, she saw what looked to be a small reservoir, with some deer – or were they perhaps reindeer? The birds were chirping in the trees behind her, and before her there was this breathtaking view. Elin took it all in for a while.

But no dwelling or other sign of human activity was to be seen. So exploring this path had been a waste of time – and she certainly wasn't here to take in the view. As she was about to turn around and head back, she noticed some movement down below. She paused and looked down. A raven was circling around something or other. What was it? Appeared to be a jacket. She looked closer. No, it couldn't really be a jacket.

She needed to find a way to get down there. To this end she surveyed the surroundings. Yes, if she went a few hundred feet to the right at the abyss, the wall seemed to be flatter, and she could use several large boulders as a kind of staircase.

About 15 minutes later, she'd clambered down to the bottom – a task that proved to be much harder than it had looked. She was already dreading having to climb back up to the top. Luckily her thigh was all better, so at least she wouldn't be in pain during the upward climb. She sniffed the air as she drew near the raven. What kind of a disgusting odor was that? Whatever it was, it was making her feel queasy. The raven flew away the second Elin came upon it perching on its prey. It was in fact a dark colored jacket, or rather part of one. It was part of a shoulder, with a sleeve. Elin froze. She gently nudged the sleeve with her foot, only to discover that there was a hand in there, or rather what was left of it. Practically all that remained were bones, and the odor was unbearable. With her gaze she followed the drag marks that the remnant of the jacket had left in the sand. Then she spotted something else back there, between two large rocks. She slowly drew nearer, until she was standing right at one of the rocks. What she saw there was truly horrific. A skull with hair on it – but the eyes and almost the entire face were missing. The body was partly clothed; a leg and half of the torso were missing. Bare bones were visible in many places, with worms and flies crawling all over them. The stink was so overwhelming, so nauseating, that Elin had to turn her face away.

She put some distance between herself and the corpse and took deep breaths. The nausea subsided. She pulled herself together and took out her phone – one bar. She pressed on Lars' name.

He picked up immediately "Did you find anything?"

Elin swallowed. "Yeah a corpse."

"Come again?"

"There's a body here, presumably a male – or rather what's left of him, thanks to all the damage the animals have done."

"Is it Patrik?"

"No idea. Judging from the clothes, it's a male. But beyond that, I can't really tell."

"I'll join you. How do I get there?"

After Elin told him how to get down there, she hung up and sat down on a rock, at a sufficient distance from the body. From here, she could neither see it, nor smell it very well, which was a good thing.

Is it Patrik? she wondered. His Saab was up at the top and the body of a male was down here. The condition the corpse was in suggested that it had been here for a while – but could it really have been two months? Elin had no way of knowing for sure.

But then what had become of Natalia? Had Patrik come here alone, maybe because they'd had an argument – and then hadn't noticed the precipice? This was unlikely, given that in the month of July the sun didn't really set, so it would be pretty hard to overlook the precipice, even at night. And why hadn't Natalia tried to find him? Had she perhaps thought that Patrik had gone back to his wife? The whole thing was bizarre; Elin couldn't make sense of it.

Well, be this as it may, they'd first have to determine whether or not the body down there was in fact Patrik. But she had no intention of going anywhere near that corpse again. Others would have to do that.

She waited a while, the dusk was deepening, and as she was wondering how Lars was going to make it down the slope with his lame knee, the raven reappeared. Or maybe it was a different raven, Elin wasn't sure – but in any case, it again tried to peck at the sleeve. Elin stood up and shooed it away. The raven flew up high and landed on a large rock that was overgrown with moss and lichen but was out of Elin's reach. The raven inclined its head and observed Elin from its perch on the rock. It was evident it was just waiting for Elin to move away from the sleeve. What should she do? She had no desire to stay here and keep watch over the sleeve. The odor was overpowering. Maybe, she thought, I should cover it up or weigh it down somehow. She looked around and found some rocks that were about the size of a head – though she had no idea why this macabre comparison had popped into her head – and dragged three of them over to the sleeve, in order to weigh it down. At least this would prevent the raven from making off with it. As she was doing this, she noticed a pocket – a sewn-on breast pocket that bulged as if something was in it. She hesitated for a moment, but upon hearing the raven's scornful cry, she took heart. She took a package of kleenex out of her jacket pocket, unfolded one, and placed it over her finger. She then opened the button on the breast pocket and carefully put her hand inside it. Yes, there was a hard, egg-shaped object in it, which she slowly removed. It was a car key with a Saab emblem on it. Now if that wasn't a good sign! She wrapped the tissue around the key, which she decided to take with her, as she was sure it would unlock Patrik's car. She took out another tissue and inserted a finger back into the pocket, as it had seemed to her that there was something else in there. And indeed there was – it felt like a credit card. When she pulled it out, it turned out to be a driver's license whose letters were very small; so she brought it closer to her eyes. And lo and behold, it belonged to Patrik Lindblom. So now there could no longer be any doubt.

She wrapped the license in a tissue as well and called Lars.

"I'm almost there," he said, "I can see you from where I'm standing."

"Stay there, I'm coming up."

"How come?"

"I found a driver's license and a Saab car key that prove beyond a doubt that it's Patrik's body."

"I see." Lars remained silent for a moment, she could hear him sighing. "I hope you haven't touched anything."

"Oh come on, I'm not an idiot. I wrapped both items in a kleenex. I'll bring them with me, before my buddy the raven gets hold of them."

"Okay, then I'll stay put."

Elin stowed the phone and the two wrapped pieces of evidence in her jacket pockets and began climbing up to where Lars was.

14

The door slammed; Stanislov was furious. But she was glad that he'd stormed out so that he could let off steam out of doors, instead of unleashing his anger on her. But this respite wasn't going to last long, that was for sure. Sooner or later he'd let fly at her and "teach her a lesson."

Natalia leaned on her elbows and covered her face with her hands. She hunched up her shoulders, she couldn't keep her composure any longer, and the tears just kept coming. It had been wrong of her to let Patrik die, she knew that now. She should have trusted her instincts and rescued him. He was a huge opportunity for her that she should have taken – and she should have left Stanislov. But now it was too late. Patrik was dead and Stanislov already had "deployed" her to the next guy, here in Jönköping. Except she knew she shouldn't be doing this. She kept seeing Patrik before her eyes. But of course, Stanislov found such "useless sentiments" utterly ridiculous. For him absolutely everything came down to business. Natalia had decided that she didn't want to do these "jobs" for Stanislov any more, but she knew he'd never accept that. What should she do?

She hadn't dared to leave Stanislov together with Patrik; but now she wondered, was she any better off trying this on her own? She had to think of something, because for sure she couldn't go on like this.

She had such fond, nostalgic memories for her home in Russia, for her Babushka. The years she'd spent with her had been the best years of her life. She hadn't had much in terms of material things, but her Babushka had truly loved her and had given her warmth and security. Natalia thought about the wood stove where there was always a pot of tea brewing. She thought about their two cats, who'd nestled down beside her so often. And she thought about her Babushka, who always smelled of apples and baked goodies. She'd taken Natalia in after her mother passed away. Natalia had been nine at the time, and actually things had improved once her mother was out of the picture. She'd spent a lot of time with Babushka – always during the holidays. While she was in grade school, she'd pretty much had to fend for herself, as her mother was either working or drunk. One night, after her mother had had too much to drink for the umpteenth time, she'd walked in front of a tram and had been killed instantly. So Natalia moved from her communist-era apartment in Moscow to Babushka's little oh so cozy hut out in the boonies. Getting to school had become something of an ordeal, but everything else was a vast improvement over life in Moscow. Oh, how she longed to return to the little hut, as she had so often done – but would never be able to do again. Babushka had passed away when Natalia was 16. She'd died of a heart attack, just like that. Natalia was placed in an orphanage and had been assigned a legal guardian; the government had confiscated the hut – and the best years of her life were over. There was no going back to any kind of security; she was left to fend for herself.

Stanislov had provided her with a livelihood and a certain amount of security – but was the price worth it? More and more these days, she felt it wasn't.

15

Lars drove them back to their hotel in Brunflo. They hadn't exchanged a word the whole trip. It hadn't been long before a patrol car arrived. Lars had called the police right after Elin told him about the body. He was glad he hadn't needed to clamber down that slope. When he'd arrived at the bluff, it was dusk; and by the time Elin climbed back up to the top, out of breath, it was nearly dark. Luckily Lars had a flashlight with him, which made it easy to avoid the muddiest parts of the path to the car. After they'd tried the Saab key – which of course worked – and given the car a quick once-over that unfortunately yielded nothing of interest – they went to Lars's Volvo and waited there for the police, who arrived about 30 minutes later. Lars had led them to the bluff and one of the policemen had clambered down the slope. The other cop had taken down Lars' and Elin's name and phone numbers, and then told them they could leave. Lars had handed over the key and license to the cop, who had chided them for fiddling around with the body; but Lars didn't think there'd be any hassles, as there wouldn't be any relevant clues left on a body that had been lying out in the open for two months and that had been exposed to the depredations of the local fauna.

He glanced over at Elin, who looked pretty done in, and he could well imagine that finding the body in this horrific condition had really taken a toll on her. Not that there was anything he could say that would make it easier for her to cope with all this. He had vivid memories of the bodies he'd encountered during his years on the police force. Sometimes the corpses were very bloody. Once he came to a crime scene where the victim had been stabbed with a knife. That was bad enough. But even more horrific were the bodies that had been dead for some time; the smell of putrid flesh was simply unbearable.

"Was that your first corpse?"

"Of course not, we had them lying around the house all the time," Elin said in a cutting tone; but then she looked at him remorsefully and said, "Sorry for that, I've been knocked around by life a bit. Actually, my grandmother died in our house when I was 15. But she passed away peacefully in her sleep. I'd never seen a corpse like the one I saw today, which was in pretty bad shape. And that horrific odor. I've had my fill for now."

"I believe you. Try to think about something else."

Elin nodded and stared into the darkness, where the first lights of Brunflo were beginning to come on. She scratched her neck.

"These damn mosquitoes have really done me in. I have bites all over my neck. Jesus Christ, do they ever itch! Did you get bitten too?"

"No, mosquitoes don't like me very much. I hardly ever get bitten."

"Really? How do you manage that? Is it your Norrland blood? It's so typical: the creatures leave the locals in peace and prey only on the tourists."

Lars laughed. "Yeah, they're particularly fond of 08 blood" – 08 being area code for Stockholm, and throughout Sweden a somewhat derogatory nickname for denizens of that city.

Elin snorted, and scratched her bites some more.

"Shall we give Christina a ring and tell her that we've found Patrik's body?" she asked.

"No, I think it's best if we impart this news in person. Telling her over the phone is something I definitely do not want to do."

"Yeah, but we need to make our statement down at the precinct tomorrow. And then, who knows when we'll be able to get out of this place. Do you think the police will beat us to the punch about notifying Christina?"

Lars thought it over. Would the Stockholm police go to Christina's house as early as tomorrow? Could be.

"Perhaps. When we get back to the hotel, I'll give Tobias a ring and ask him whether he can do it."

"Sounds good." Elin appeared to be very happy with this solution.

"How about dinner? I'm famished," Lars said.

Elin stared at him in horror. "No way. I wouldn't be able to eat. I'd be thinking the whole time of the pieces of flesh that the animals took from Patrik's body. Just mentioning it makes me feel sick to my stomach."

"Okay, then I'll drop you off at Sörbygården and eat by myself."

After dropping Elin off, Lars drove to a pizzeria he'd spotted in the morning, next to the train station. The place was about to close, but the manager said they'd make him a pizza anyway as the oven was still hot. While he was waiting, Lars phoned Tobias, who picked up right away.

"Hi Tobias. Seems like we've accomplished our mission."

"That's awesome. Did you find the guy?"

"Yes, but unfortunately he's dead – and apparently he's been in that state for quite a while." Lars then told Tobias about their investigation and how they'd found the body.

"Wow, that was quick! It's of course inconvenient that the guy has departed this life. But we can't do anything about that, can we?"

"Yeah well that's why I'm calling. I'd prefer if it was us, rather than the police, who informed the client of her husband's passing. But it looks as though we won't be able to get out of here before tomorrow afternoon at the earliest, because the police want us to give a statement. So I was hoping that perhaps you'd be willing to contact Christina early tomorrow morning."

Lars was waiting for a response from Tobias, who didn't say anything and appeared to be thinking the matter over.

"You still there, Tobias?"

"Yeah," Tobias answered hesitantly. "Sorry, but I don't think I'll be able to help you out here, my friend. We'll just have to take the risk. Let the police notify the lady, if they're really so quick. I don't know the lady from Adam, so I don't see any reason why it should be me who delivers such horrific news to her. You guys should go over there tomorrow and break the news to her. Either the police will have been there already, or they won't."

"Okay, then." Once Tobias has made up his mind about something, it was next to impossible to convince him of any other viewpoint. Plus, Lars was all out of arguments. "Well, I just thought I'd ask. At least now I know."

They said goodbye to each other. It sure would have been nice if Tobias had been willing to undertake this unpleasant task for me, Lars thought. He really had no desire to deliver this news to Christine, as he was certain that it would come as a shock to her – even though she would surely have realized by now that Patrik had left her. During his time as a police officer, he'd also noticed that none of his colleagues had ever volunteered to notify next of kin of the untimely death of a loved one. Such tasks were invariably unpleasant. Sometimes people got aggressive, while others simply fell apart before your eyes to the point that you had to call an ambulance – and some began emoting uncontrollably. You always felt horribly awkward and wished you were somewhere else. He didn't want to go through any of that ever again. He stared out the window, hoping his pizza would be ready soon.

***

Lars parked the car. He saw Elin and noticed that she was swallowing. She turned her eyes toward Christina's house. Lars had sent Christina a text message a few hours ago in which he asked if he and Elin could drop by her house at around 7 p.m. to tell her about what they'd found in Norrland. She said that was okay, and to Lars's relief hadn't asked for any details. They hadn't been able to leave the police station until noon. It was all routine, but everything had to be meticulously recorded and signed. They'd finally got underway, after a quick lunch at Restaurant Chili. The trip went smoothly, and they arrived at Christina's house 20 minutes before 7 p.m.

Lars opened his door, and noticing that Elin didn't open hers, said, "It's no use, let's just do it!"

"But how, Lars?" she said, with an imploring look.

"I'll do it, don't worry. You can help with the comforting part. You know, the way you women do it, you put your hand on the person's arm and maybe offer to make them a cup of tea."

“Okay.” Elin got out of the car. Lars had to smile. He would have expected her to take him to task for this comment about women. But she was evidently so pleased at this advantageous allocation of roles that she said nothing.

As they slowly made their way to Christina’s front door, Lars was planning what to say. When they got to the door, Lars rang the bell. They heard steps behind the door immediately, and then the door was opened cautiously. At first Lars couldn’t believe his eyes – could Christina really have aged so much in just a few weeks? But then he noticed the inquisitive look on the woman’s face and realized this must be Christina’s mother.

“ Lars and Elin, I presume” she said. She looked a lot like her daughter – and like her was on the plump side and wore her hair short. But she wasn’t as elegantly dressed as Christina usually was.

Lars nodded. “Yes, we’re here to see Christina. She’s expecting us.”

“I’m Christina’s mother, Agnes. Do come in. The police were here over an hour ago, so she’s already heard the news.”

“Ah, already?” Lars froze in his tracks. “How did she take it?”

“Well frankly she’s devastated. Although I imagine she’d guessed that something like this might have happened.”

Lars heard Elin breathe a sign of relief. His sentiments exactly. The police had beaten them to the punch – and in so doing had spared them the worst. But still, the conversation wasn't going to be a barrel of laughs.

They went into the living room, where Christina was sitting on a couch with a handkerchief in her hands. Her face was all red and her makeup was in disarray. She looked at them with moist eyes.

"Hi Christina," Lars said. "We're sorry for your loss. We sincerely regret that we failed to find Patrik alive."

Christina nodded resignedly. Lars and Elin sat down on the other couch, which was perpendicular to Christina's. Agnes sat down next to Christina and laid a hand on her arm. Lars saw that Elin was relieved that Agnes was here, as it meant that she didn't have to play the role of the consoler.

"I don't know what the police said," Lars said, looking over at Agnes.

Agnes shook her head. "I wasn't there. All I know is that they found a body that they presume is Patrik. They took his hairbrush with them to do a DNA test."

Lars looked over at Christina. She nodded.

"Yes," she said sniffling. "They found his drivers license on the body. And it wasn't very far from our cabin. Do you know anything else?"

Lars nodded. "Yes, we were the ones who found him. And Elin secured the drivers license."

"Is it really Patrik? The police said that the body was in horrible condition." She looked at Lars sadly.

"Well, the body had probably been there for two months or so, and with the heat it putrefied more rapidly," Lars said. He felt it was best to leave out the part about animals feeding on the body. "So I think it's safe to assume that it is in fact Patrik. His driver's license and the key to the Saab were on him, and the car was near to where we found him."

"But how did it happen?"

"Hard to say. What did the police tell you?"

"That they don't reach conclusions in the absence of hard evidence."

"Yeah, he tumbled down a really steep slope. Someone might have pushed him, of course – but it's more likely to have been an accident. Maybe he got too close to the edge and somehow lost his balance. We'll have to wait for the results of the police investigation. Hopefully they'll find something that will indicate exactly what happened." Lars highly doubted that they'd find anything of the sort, but one could always hope.

"Oh, poor Patrik." Christina put her face in her hands and burst out crying. Agnes stroked her shoulder. Christina calmed down after a time, blew her nose, and sat up.

"Did you find out more? Because the police didn't tell me anything else."

Lars nodded. "Yes, we know the approximate timeline leading up to the event. On July 2nd, Patrik was in Östersund, where he stopped at a gas station to fill up his car. The clerk there gave him the name of a person who rents out cabins in the area. Patrik then got in touch with the owner of the cabins and rented one from him that's about two miles from the place where we found the body. When the landlord showed Patrik the cabin, he had a young blond woman with him who had an Eastern European accent; and it's safe to assume that the two of them stayed in the cabin together." Lars looked at Christina to see how she'd react to this.

She nodded sadly. "Aha. Well, I suppose the woman was this Natalia person."

Lars shrugged. "We don't know for sure. We don't know her name, but it's of course a possibility."

"How old was she? Not a teenager, I hope."

Lars could well imagine why she said this – the Natalia15 password.

"No, apparently not. The landlord – who was the only person we spoke to who saw her – said that she was in her late twenties. And even if that's not accurate, for sure she wasn't a 15 year old. So the number 15 in the password must mean something else."

Christina signed resignedly.

"They rented the cabin for a week," Lars continued. "And then they just up and left, without notifying the landlord. We presume that the accident occurred at some point during the course of that week."

"And how about this Natalia person?"

"We haven't found any trace of her."

"But why didn't she report the accident? Perhaps someone could have helped him."

"I'm afraid, I have no answer for that."

Elin leaned forward. "It's possible that this woman wasn't even there when Patrik fell down the slope – because otherwise she might have used the Saab to get back to the cabin. Maybe she was waiting for Patrik back at the cabin, and when he didn't show, she left. Maybe they..."

"Yes, but this is pure speculation," Lars said, cutting her off. Lars didn't want Elin to engage in too much theorizing. "We simply have to hope that the police will be able to find out more."

Christina nodded. "Yes, I suppose that's how it was. I've had the feeling this whole time that something happened to him. I don't understand what this Natalia person has to do with it, but I'll try to forget that part, as it does me no good at all," she said, looking down at the floor.

Agnes cleared her throat. "Thanks for telling us all that. Hiring these detectives was a smart move, Christina. Who knows how long it would have been before Patrik was found?"

Christina looked up. "Yes, I really do appreciate your help," she said.

Lars got up; Elin did likewise. "We don't want to keep you any longer. Once again, we're sorry for your loss. We of course wish we'd had better news for you. We're sincerely sorry."

They took leave of Christina, who remained seated on the couch. Agnes saw them to the door and gave them a friendly wave goodbye.

It was dark outside as they slowly made their way to the car.

"Wow," Elin said, exhaling. "That went a whole lot better than I'd expected. Lucky for us that the police had already done the hardest part."

"You can say that again. And her mother being there made it much easier for us."

"Yeah, but it was still pretty awkward. I felt at such a loss. I didn't know what to say that might help her."

"Yeah, well, there really isn't anything that you could have said, unfortunately. She'll have to get through this on her own. But we need to focus on other things now; I'll drop you off at home. You should sit down with a nice glass of wine and settle in all cozy with Maja. All of us need to put this behind us and move forward."

"Okay I'll try," Elin stammered.

16

Elin's parents just stared at her. It was out in the open now – now that they knew her secret. She'd been skirting the issue for a while now, but she'd finally come out and said it. For sure, the way she'd told them had been somewhat clumsy – but she was so nervous that she hadn't been able to come up with anything better.

"But you used to have boyfriends?" her mother stammered. "That boy in high school – what was his name? Theodor? And then a few years ago there was that sweet blond guy who rode a motorbike. Why on earth would you want to have a romantic relationship with a woman all of a sudden?"

She'd known that this would happen. She simply had to forge ahead and fill her parents in on the details.

"Well I wasn't really sure back then and I wanted to see what being with men was like. But I never felt truly satisfied, I always felt like something was missing. The first time it felt totally right being with someone romantically was when I got together with Maja."

"Well maybe you just haven't met the right man yet."

Elin looked over at her father, who had apparently been struck dumb by this revelation. Looking distressed, his glance wandered from his wife to his daughter and back again.

"Trust me, Mom," she cried, "That's really not the problem. I'm blissfully happy with Maja."

Her mother shook her head. "Why commit yourself so hastily? Maybe this is just a passing phase, and in a few months you'll want to date men again."

"Mom, I've been with Maja for two years already, and we plan to grow old together."

Her mother shot her a scandalized look. "You mean it's been going on for *this* long? And you're only telling us now?"

Elin turned beet red. "Yes, I wanted to be totally sure before I told you... And frankly, I wasn't exactly looking forward to having this conversation with you. I'm so sorry."

Her mother turned toward her husband. "For god's sake, say something, Hans!"

Hans leaned back, swallowed twice, looked at Elin's mother, and then at Elin. "What am I supposed to say? This is a pretty big surprise. Though I must say I often find myself wondering why you haven't introduced us to a new boyfriend for quite some time. But I figured you were so busy with your work that you didn't have time to look for someone." He cleared his throat. "I'm quite fond of Maja, actually, but I need to get used to the fact that she's – how can I put it – so important to you. After all, it's your life, Elin, and only you can know what's best for you."

"I really appreciate that, Dad." Elin looked at him gratefully. She'd known that he'd be more accepting than her mother. "I do indeed know what's good for me. And that's Maja."

Her mother stood up. "I need time to get used to this. Believe me, it's not something that's easy to swallow. Not in the least. I'll clear the table now." She looked as though she were about to burst into tears as she went about stacking the plates and cups on a tray. It occurred to Elin that she should perhaps give her mother a big hug – but she decided against it. She watched her mother go into the kitchen with the tray. This hadn't gone at all well. She could only hope that her mother would eventually accept the situation.

An hour later her father pulled into the parking lot at the Uppsala train station.

Elin leaned over the handbrake and hugged him. "Thanks for being so understanding."

He pressed her to him and kissed her on the cheek. "You know, Elin, no matter what you do and no matter who you live with, you'll always be my daughter and I'll always love you and be there for you."

Elin was deeply moved. Her dad had never said anything like this to her, as he was someone who wasn't in the habit of expressing emotion. "I love you too, Dad."

He drew back from her a bit and looked her in the eyes. "Your mother needs to process all this, but I'm sure she'll come around eventually. She loves you every bit as much as I do and only wants what's best for you. She's just worried that things might be harder for you than if you were in a relationship with a man. You know, social acceptance and all that. And then there's the matter of grandchildren. Your mother was of course counting on you for that."

Elin shook her head; she hadn't seen this coming. She swallowed and said, "Well that's not an issue right now – but it's also well within the realm of possibility nowadays."

Her father nodded. "Yeah, with a sperm donor. I mentioned this to your mother too, but it doesn't jibe with her idea of what a traditional family should be like."

"How about you – what do you think it should be like?"

"Well for me, having grandkids maybe isn't quite as important as it is for your mother – though I must say I'd be more than happy to have some. But then again, it's kind of hard for me to wrap my mind around a kid having two mothers – but I'm sure I'll get used to it eventually." He gave her an encouraging nod.

"Thanks, Dad. I hope Mom will too. Though when we were saying goodbye, she acted like I wasn't even part of her life anymore."

"Don't worry, it'll work out. I'll help her to accept the situation, and for sure we're going to be discussing this at length."

Elin hugged him again, they said goodbye, and she got out of the car. She waved to him as he drove out of the parking lot. Then she went into the train station. Elin was relieved that this particular encounter with her parents was behind her now; but the fact that her mother had such difficulty accepting the situation made her sad too. She fervently hoped that her mother would come around eventually, because if her being a lesbian was going to permanently damage her relationship with her mother, that would make her very sad. This is precisely what she'd feared. But now there was no turning back either.

She'd wait to call Maja until she was on the train. She, at least, would be happy that Elin had come out to her parents.

***

Elin looked up when Lars came into the office.

"*God morgon,*" he said.

"A good morning to you too. So how's the Patrik investigation going?"

"Whatever are you talking about? The case is closed."

"Yeah, but there are still a bunch of unanswered questions. Actually, I thought I might try again to determine whether there was a second cell phone in that rented cabin." Elin had tried this once before, at Sörbygården B&B in Brunflo, the day before Patrik's body was found. But on that occasion, she hadn't wanted to use the hotel's network, and to avoid this had created a hotspot for her laptop using her smartphone. But unfortunately, the mobile network wasn't stable enough. After she had twice established a connection via multiple proxy servers in order to disguise her IP address, she'd had to abort her hacking attempt when the connections failed briefly. But given that this wouldn't happen with the office internet connection, she'd decided to take another stab at it today.

"Please let it go for now, okay? We don't need to take any further risks; this is a task for the police, not us."

"Do you really think they're going to delve into it that deeply? I had the distinct impression that they weren't the least bit interested in the phone data."

"Well, be that as it may, this is now a cold case that lies within the purview of the police. Our remit was to find Patrik, and we did that – so as far as we're concerned, the case is solved –over and done with."

Elin didn't like this a bit. She really wanted to know what had happened there. And she was particularly interested in talking to this Natalia person.

"What about Natalia? We could certainly try to track her down, don't you think?"

Lars sat down on a chair next to Elin's desk and gave her a serious look.

"Look here, Elin. The case is closed. We have not been asked to look for Natalia. The case was about Patrik, and Patrik alone. And we found him, he was dead – and sorry, that's it, end of story. Tobias is drawing up Christina's final invoice, and that'll be that. We shall be taking no further action of any kind on this case. That includes you. Got it?"

Elin nodded reluctantly. She'd never liked this aspect of detective work. In her last case, which she'd solved on her own, she hadn't been happy with the outcome either and had continued to investigate, even after the case was closed. She'd of course done this on her own dime – but she'd managed to solve the case, and hopefully the perpetrators were going to get a nice long prison sentence. Admittedly, the effort had nearly been a disaster because she'd done everything on her own. But nonetheless, she was really happy with the outcome, and didn't regret in the least the minor injuries she'd incurred during the investigation. But Patrik's case was different. There was no helping him now, and she could understand why Christina very likely didn't want to know more about this Natalia person. But she had the feeling that when it came to the events in Norrland, something was hinkey. She realized that the agency wouldn't generate any income by continuing with the investigation, but her own personal curiosity wasn't at all slaked.

"Look, Elin, I can see that you'd like to keep digging, but you really need to let this one go. We're going to be turning our attention to other cases now. Can I count on you to do as I ask?"

Elin nodded again – what else could she do? "Okay, fine. Message received. What new cases do we have?"

"We've been asked by a company to investigate a number of employees, one of whom the company suspects of embezzlement. I'll e-mail you the case documents."

"Okay, I'll have a look at them. Exactly what do you want me to do with them?"

"Check out the suspects. Whatever you can find about them online."

"You mean only the public parts of the internet, or the illicit ones as well?" she said with a mischievous smile.

"Just the public parts please, for now. Then we'll look over what you find and decide which people we need to take a closer look at."

Lars got up and left. Elin was glad to have a new case to sink her teeth into – particularly as she was now being treated like a full fledged detective. This was a new feeling for her, and a good one. And yet, something was playing havoc with her peace of mind – namely the whole thing with Patrik and Natalia. Oh well, she'd try to disregard this uneasy feeling and focus on the new case – the operant term here being "try."

17

Two parallel lines, no doubt about it. She stared at the stick's little window. This couldn't possibly be true. Though she'd kind of suspected it. The first time she missed her period she hadn't given it much thought – it can happen after all, and she'd been under a lot of stress lately. But when she'd missed a second period this week, despite her having stopped the pill, she had a bad feeling. And when she woke up this morning feeling nauseous, she'd decided to buy a pregnancy test.

Positive. When had this happened? It must have been the day they'd eaten at an Indian restaurant and she'd gotten the runs from it. But it hadn't been all that bad, had it? In any case, the next day, Patrik had come over and they'd had sex. That must have been when she got pregnant.

She looked at herself in the mirror. What should she do? Get an abortion? Would she able to keep the whole thing secret from Stanislov? Well, the good news was that she probably didn't have to start taking the pill again. Jesus Christ, couldn't life cut her a break for once? But right now, she needed to deep-six this pregnancy test. She absolutely did not want Stanislov to find it or know anything about her pregnancy – at least not for the moment. First, she needed to figure out what she planned to do. In a little while she'd take the pregnancy test with her and throw it away somewhere.

But what on earth was she going to do?

PART II

OCTOBER 2016

18

"But what do *you* think happened" Liv asked Christina.

"I think he was murdered," Liv said, furrowing her brow. "But I take it the police don't think so." "Right, they've closed the case. They concluded it was an accident or suicide."

"I see. Do you have any concrete reasons for your suspicion?" Liv asked, an excited look on her face. They were eating at Sturehof, at a table under an awning. This was probably going to be one of the last days when you could sit outside – and only thanks to the infrared heaters that were arrayed on the terrace. The hustle and bustle was hefty in Stureplan, the square in front of the restaurant. It was lunchtime and loads of people had left their workplaces in order to grab a quick lunch or do an errand. In the middle of the square there was a large mushroom-shaped concrete gazebo that people could stand under; currently a group of teenagers was occupying it. Liv was spending two days in Stockholm in order to attend her company's board meeting. Christina had asked Liv if they could meet up, but the only time slot Liv had available was during lunch. As the meeting was being held at the IVA Conference Center, which was right near Stureplan, they'd decided to have lunch at Sturehof.

Christina leaned forward. She was dressed all in green today, including a linen wrap, which she was rarely without; this one was in a soft shade of green, emblazoned with red branches. "It just doesn't make sense. Patrik clearly made elaborate preparations to build a new life for himself. I've now gotten access to his bank statements. Before he left, he transferred all of his savings, amounting to millions of kronor, to foreign accounts – so his bank can neither trace the funds nor retrieve them. Plus, he left his phone at work and evidently bought himself a new one. He also took his passport and ID card with him. And apparently, he'd been having an affair with a younger woman for quite some time and took her with him to this cabin in Norrland. People who do all this simply don't kill themselves – which is why I've ruled out suicide. And as for the accident scenario: why didn't the woman come to his aid if he had an accident? Or at least call an ambulance. No, I think she set him up. And now she's squandering all his money."

"So you think the gal pushed him off the cliff?"

"Either that, or she left him in the lurch when he slipped and went tumbling down. Whatever happened, one thing's for sure: it all worked out well for her."

"So now you want to try to get the money back?"

Christina shook her head. "No it's not about the money. I have enough for my needs. But I'd like to find out what happened. And I'd like to see this woman brought to justice. Despite the pain I feel at Patrik leaving me, I still think it was really naive of him to trust this woman. And just because he didn't want to live with me any longer – which, by the way, I regard as a spur of the moment thing, a passing phase that he would certainly have come to regret – doesn't change anything about my feelings towards him. I still love him, and I miss him. I want to know what led up to his death. I owe it to myself," Christina said, looking hard at Liv, almost defiantly.

Liv was impressed by Christina's determination. Most women in her situation would probably have just written Patrik off and felt sorry for themselves, rather than delving deeper into the circumstances surrounding their husband's demise.

Liv waved away the cigarette smoke that was coming from two men who were smoking at the table next to them – and of course the smoke wafted in their direction. Lots of people smoked in Berlin, but in Stockholm you rarely saw people puffing away. She looked over at the two men, who didn't look very

Swedish, so they were probably either tourists or naturalized foreigners.

She thought back to the situation she'd been in almost a year ago. Her husband had had her kidnapped and then died in a trap of his own making. She hadn't shed any tears over him and if it hadn't been for her daughter being kidnapped, wouldn't have wanted to find out more about what happened to him. This event had spurred her on much more than what had happened to her personally.

"So what's your next move? It's been quite a while hasn't it? How long has it been since he died? Three months?"

"Right," Christina said, nodding and taking a sip of her spring water. "Well I was thinking of enlisting the aid of Lars and Elin again. Do you think I should?"

Liv didn't need to reflect for very long. "I think it's an excellent idea. They're both really good, plus they already know the ins and outs of the case. If there's anything to be discovered, they'll find it. Elin especially is like a dog who gets hold of a bone and won't let go." It was Elin who'd identified the man who kidnapped Liv's daughter, without having been hired to do so. At first Liv was kind of miffed that Elin had decided to go it alone – but then she had to admit that Elin had done the right thing. And that she'd gone about it very intelligently.

"Okay then, I'll make an appointment to see them. Thanks for your advice."

Liv looked at her thoughtfully. "Yeah, but I wonder, what are you going to do if you find out that he was murdered, and you find his killers?"

Christina shrugged. "I have no idea. But anyway, we're not there yet, because nothing's been found thus far. And then you have to be really sure that what you've uncovered is true; plus, you need airtight evidence, in order to bring the matter to the police or the prosecutor. What matters most to me is getting a mental picture of what actually happened in Norrland. Living with this uncertainty is driving me nuts. All I can do is speculate. If it turns out that it was definitely an accident, then I'll accept that. Then at least I can put the whole thing behind me. See what I mean?"

"Absolutely. So I think you should go ahead and put Lars and Elin back on the case. And maybe you can keep me updated about what they find. I'm really interested."

"For sure, Liv. Talking with you always does me a world of good. Plus you're the only person who knows all the details. I'll give you a call as soon as I have anything of interest to report."

"Awesome. But I really need to fly now, otherwise I'll be late to the meeting." Liv reached into her purse for her wallet.

Christina made a dismissive gesture. "No, please, it's my treat."

"Really? Thanks." Liv stood up.

The two women said goodbye to each other and Liv left the restaurant. She hoped, for Christina's sake, that the investigation would turn up something useful – because for her friend, this was no laughing matter. She turned around and gave Christina an encouraging wave. She then walked quickly toward the IVA Conference Center.

19

Elin climbed the steps leading to the courthouse. She felt disenchanted with life – and particularly with *her* life, where nothing at all seemed to be going right. Why couldn't the judges and lay assessors have simply given all of the defendants life, as the prosecutor had requested? It was crystal clear to Elin that the four of them had killed the little girl together. And they would have done the same to Ebba if Elin hadn't intervened. This fucking lawyer was too smart for his own good. None of the four defendants had admitted anything, and each of them had claimed that one of the others must have murdered the little girl. They claimed that they hadn't discussed anything with each other and that the little girl simply vanished one day. One of the defendants had even said that he thought the little girl had been let go. Since there was no hard evidence that any of the defendants had participated in the killing – and because under Swedish law there's no such thing as collective guilt and thus only individuals can be convicted of committing a crime – the defendants were acquitted on the murder charge. And of course the bastards had also contested the allegation that they intended to murder Elin, and said that they were just trying to intimidate her. And so the judges and lay assessors had only found the defendants guilty of kidnapping, aggravated sexual assault and assaulting a minor – charges that no one could have contested, as there were countless videos, one of which had even been played in the courtroom. Three of the defendants had gotten 15 years, and the leader of the group had been sentenced to 18. But Elin wasn't at all happy with this outcome. Life sentences would have been far preferable – even though she knew that most life sentences are eventually commuted. What bothered her was the symbolism of it all: these defendants deserved the most severe penalty allowed by law. The prosecutor had mentioned that he might appeal the verdict, but Elin had the impression that he had just said this to assuage Ebba's parents, who were totally shattered.

Nor were there any other bright spots in her life at the moment. She'd gone to see her parents with Maja over the weekend, but the visit hadn't gone at all well. At first, she was glad that her parents had invited her and Maja over – particularly since her mother's phone call came from out of the blue after a week of radio silence.

Her mother had called to announce that she now wanted Maja to be part of the family and would like to invite the two of them over for dinner to celebrate this event. Upon hearing this news Maja had merely said, "See I told you so" – as if to imply that Elin's fears about coming out to her parents had been exaggerated.

The two women had been in high spirits during the drive to Uppsala, and everything had gone smoothly at first. Her parents had given Maja a big hug and had proposed a toast in which they welcomed Maja to their home as their daughter's partner. But Elin hadn't been totally convinced by all this, as she had the impression that her mother was just putting on an act. And unfortunately, this impression turned out to be all too accurate. When, after dinner, Elin put her arms around Maja and kissed her on the mouth, her mother was at first shocked, then burst into tears – and *then* began sobbing uncontrollably before retreating to the kitchen. All of her father's efforts to assuage her mother had been fruitless, and the evening was over. She and Maja were crestfallen on the drive home. Maja felt extremely insulted and took what had happened personally.

And now Elin not only had a problem with her mother, but also had to deal with Maja still being upset and not wanting to even discuss what had happened. But what could Elin have done? She'd known from the get-go that this wouldn't go down well with her mother. What could she do about that? The only person she could really talk to was her father. He seemed to totally accept the fact that Maja was Elin's partner – in fact it almost seemed that he was pleased to have acquired such a nice "daughter-in-law." He did his best to try to smooth things over and kept trying to get her mother to change her attitude. And the very next day he'd even called Elin and offered to come by her apartment by himself, but Maja wouldn't hear of it. The whole thing was a giant disaster and Elin was truly sorry that she'd ever come out to her parents.

Nor was there anything work-wise that could lift her spirits. Yes, she was a full-fledged private detective now, and she of course noticed the big jump in her salary at the end of the month; but currently there was nothing but monotonous surveillance tasks that she didn't find in the least satisfying. What she wanted most of all was a case that she could really sink her teeth into, a case that would challenge her, a case that would involve travel – anywhere, she didn't care where, as long as it took her away from the problems with her mother, away from the trial, which had stirred everything up again and whose verdict she'd found totally unsatisfactory. But unfortunately, no such case was currently on the horizon.

She thought about what she ought to do. It was just after three. They didn't need her any more today at the office, and Maja was at her studio, so she had the whole afternoon to herself. She needed to do something that would lighten her mood. Aha, she thought, I'll go shopping. I need some new clothes anyway, plus I've got money to spend, so why not? She could simply hop on the subway and go two stops to NK or Gallerian, where she was sure she'd find something great. Or maybe she could make a quick appointment at the beauty salon or the cosmetician's – that would be nice too. Something like this would in any case take her mind off her troubles, that was for sure. She turned right and headed toward the Rådhuset subway station.

***

Elin was having a manicure when suddenly her phone rang. The cosmetician was working on her right hand, so she grabbed her phone with her left hand, saw Lars's name on the display, and picked up.

"Hi Lars."

„*Hej,* Elin. Is court over with? Or maybe this isn't a good time."

"No, it's okay. No more court today."

"How'd it go?"

"Not as I'd hoped. None of those bastards got life. They were acquitted on the murder charge."

"But they did get jail time, didn't they?"

"Yeah, 15 years, and the leader got 18."

"Well, that's good."

"You think so? I think those sentences are too light."

"I've only been following the trial in the papers, but as I see it there was no hard evidence proving who actually killed the girl. Assuming of course it was in fact one of the four defendants."

"The judges saw it that way too. But the prosecutor had raised our hopes that his case was strong enough to send them away for life ."

"Yeah well, prosecutors always ask for the maximum sentence, but you can't really expect that they get it every time."

"That doesn't make me feel much better, to tell you the truth. The whole thing's unfair. Most of the time, convicted felons only serve two-thirds of their sentence – which means three of those guys will be released in ten years and can go right back to a life of crime if they feel like it."

"Yeah but actually, not everyone is released early – plus convicts have to meet certain requirements in order to be put on probation. I see your point, though. When it comes to such heinous crimes, it's pretty much impossible to be happy with the verdict. No punishment seems to fit the crime. How's Ebba doing, by the way?"

"Improving steadily. You can have an almost normal conversation with her now, and she even laughs once in a while. But of course she's nothing like the cheerful little girl that she was before the kidnapping. Plus she's only willing to leave the house with me or her parents. There's no question of her going to school on her own."

"Well that sounds pretty positive. She's making good progress and the rest will come in time."

"I sure hope so." Elin saw that the cosmetician was signaling to her.

"Was there anything else, Lars? I'm having a manicure and the manicurist needs my other hand."

"Oh I see. Yeah, I wanted to know if you've got some time today. Christina would like to meet with us to discuss giving us a follow-up assignment."

Suddenly, Elin was totally alert. This sounded really promising, since in any case she'd wanted to find out more about what had happened to Patrik. Plus this involved real sleuthing.

"Is the earth round? Of course I want to meet with her. What exactly does she want?"

"Curiosity killed the cat, you know. I'll fill you in on the details later. I'll pick you up at around 6, okay?"

"Great, see you then." Elin hung up, put the phone away, and extended her left hand to the cosmetician She felt energized again – the news about the new job from Christina had filled her with fresh enthusiasm.

20

So here they were, back on Christina's living room couch, with Patrik's bank statements spread out on the coffee table in front of them.

"Which is why I now seriously doubt whether Patrik's death was an accident," Christina said, giving them a challenging look. She appeared to be expecting them to contradict her.

However, Lars thought it best not to do so, because he really wanted Christina to hire them. "Well we had our doubts too, from the outset. Attributing his death to an accident seemed too pat to us." Lars saw that Elin nodded vehemently. "And the business with the disappearing money cast the whole thing in an even iffier light."

Christina seemed to be relieved. "So do you think you'll be able to shed some light on the circumstances surrounding his death?"

"Well we'll find something, that's for sure, but we can't of course guarantee you that we'll definitely be able to get to the bottom of this. Nor can we guarantee that whatever we do find will be to your liking. It might turn out that it was an accident after all and that the lady in question left for other reasons."

"I see. But, as I said, I'd in any case like to find out who this woman is – the one you believe is called Natalia.'

"We'll do our best," Elin said. "I'm positive that we'll be able to find her phone number, just as we did with Patrik's new number – and that number might lead us to her."

"But of course we can't be absolutely sure – but as I said, we'll do our best." Lars winked at Elin, who rolled her eyes.

"However, before proceeding, we will need to talk to our boss, as this is an unusual case. As far as I know, our agency has never investigated a murder before, so we need his go-ahead."

"Of course," Christina said understandingly. "When do you think I might be hearing from you?"

"Well," Lars said, "I plan to talk to him about the case the minute we get back to the office – assuming he's there. But I'm sure I'll be able to convince him to let us take the case. And then I'll send you the contract right away." Lars, however, wasn't so sure. Tobias tended to be quite cautious when it came to accepting exotic cases – but what else could Lars say to a client under the circumstances?

After Elin gathered up the bank statements, they stood up and bid Christina goodbye.

"At long last, an interesting case," Elin said gleefully. "You don't think Tobias is going to hit the ceiling?"

“Well, you never know with him. But I’ll do everything within my power to ensure that we get the case. I promise.”

They got into Lars’s Volvo and got on the highway heading south, which brought them to their office in the Södermalm neighborhood. As traffic was still pretty light, they’d arrive in about 40 minutes.

***

“A homicide?” Tobias said, looking at Lars incredulously.

Lars nodded.

“Surely you must be joking. You’d like to investigate a *homicide*?”

Lars held Tobias’s gaze. He had no intention of giving in. “Yeah that’s right – just like I did when I was a cop”.

“Oh is that a fact? I hadn’t known that you were a member of the homicide squad,” Tobias said sarcastically.

“Well, as you know, I wasn’t. But on a number of occasions I was part of the team that investigated homicides.”

Tobias shook his head. “But do the police think that Patrik’s death was a suicide?”

“Either that or an accident.”

Tobias gave him a penetrating look. "And you think you can prove the opposite?"

"Look, Tobias, I don't know what your problem is. But the fact is that the client asked us to find her husband. Which we did, but unfortunately, he had already kicked the bucket. There are plenty of indications that his death was in fact either an accident or suicide, but the client isn't buying it – and to tell you the truth Elin and I don't either. Which is why the client wants to dig around some more and see what we can come up with. If we can find evidence that it was a homicide and perhaps even find some clues that might help find the murderer, she'll be pleased as punch. If we don't succeed, we at least will have tried – and she's well aware that there's no guarantee that we will in fact succeed."

"Okay, okay," Tobias said combatively. "But face it, Lars, homicide really isn't in our wheelhouse. I simply don't understand why you and Elin always come to me with these exotic cases. Kidnapping, child abuse – and now homicide."

Lars leaned forward. "Look, Tobias. You really have no grounds for complaint. Each of those cases has earned us a pile of moolah – plus we got a lot of good media attention that attracted new clients. I realize that the agency is doing super well and that we're up to our ears in cases."

"That's true," Tobias admitted.

"And whenever problems have arisen, Elin and I have had to deal with the consequences. Or were you in the hospital or something? Or were you maybe testifying in court? It seems to me the time has come for us to discuss giving us a commission. Because after all, it's because of Elin and me that you got all these cases, and you've spent next to nothing on marketing."

Tobias put up his hands. "Give it a rest, Lars, okay? We'll discuss this some other time. And you can go ahead with Christina's case. Get to the bottom of this murder, for god's sake!"

Lars had to smile to himself. Tobias hadn't been at all pleased when he mentioned a commission – but he wasn't about to let Tobias off the hook that easily. "Okay, thanks. Once we've closed this case, we'll need to sit down and discuss the possibility of our getting commissions for future cases that I bring into the agency."

Tobias turned around in his chair. "We'll have to see about that."

"No, I'm sorry, that's unacceptable. We will definitely be having a discussion about commissions, or else this will be the last case I bring into the agency."

Tobias looked at him. Evidently, he had now understood that Lars was really serious about commissions. "Okay. But only for you, not Elin."

"And why not, may I ask?"

"Oh, come on, Lars. Elin hasn't been with us all that long, nor does she have nearly as much experience as you do. Plus, last summer she failed to prove her loyalty, in that she took on that child abuse case on her own instead of bringing it into the agency. She should be grateful that she's still even working here. And as a full-fledged private detective, no less."

Unfortunately, Tobias was in the right, and Lars couldn't really counter his arguments. He decided it would be best if he and Elin worked this out between them, however: if she had a new case, Lars could bring it into the agency, collect the commission and split it with her – and Tobias needn't be any the wiser.

He nodded. "Okay, I get it. So are we on the same page now? Though frankly I doubt that I'll accept a small commission."

"No worries, Lars. If we do this, we're going to do it right. It'll be ten percent or more. Let's shake on it."

Lars was quite pleased with himself, as he had just won two arguments with Tobias and left Tobias's office with a smile on his face. He hadn't thought he'd be able to make such good headway with Tobias. Now that he'd done so well for himself, he was looking forward to a calm evening and to celebrating his success with Lisa.

***

But as it turned out, the evening didn't go at all as Lars had planned. Lisa was in a foul mood when he came home. She kept bitching about everything, including to the kids, which wasn't something she normally did. Lars had helped make dinner and with the household chores and had pretty much ignored her biting commentary. He'd gingerly asked her what was the matter but she'd merely said that she had a headache.

Once the children had gone to bed, Lisa seemed somewhat less tense, and Lars thought that this was the right time to tell her the good news.

"Is your headache better? I was thinking about opening a bottle of champagne," he said. Lars had already seen to it that there was a bottle of bubbly in the fridge and that it was at the right temperature. "We have something to celebrate."

"How come? What exactly?" Lisa asked, giving him a questioning look.

"I made a deal with Tobias that whenever I bring cases into the agency, I'll get a commission." Lars squared his shoulders proudly, though Lisa didn't seem to be particularly impressed.

"What kind of cases would you be bringing into the agency?"

"Well you know how it's gone down with cases that have originated with Martin and Liv – and now from their friend. Elin and I brought those cases into the agency but were never compensated for doing so. It'll be different from now on, though."

Lisa nodded and stared straight ahead. Were her thoughts perhaps elsewhere?

"So what do you think? Want some champagne?"

Lisa said nothing and continued staring into space. Lars began feeling uneasy and was about to repeat his question, when she slowly turned toward him and looked at him with ice-cold eyes. "I see no reason to celebrate."

Lars was astounded. "How come? This means more money for us, and it's a first step toward my becoming a partner in the agency. That's good news, isn't it?"

"Lars, you know perfectly well that I hate these cases that you do with Elin. Every time, I sit here and tremble in fear for your safety. Not to mention the various times you've ended up in the hospital."

So *that* was the problem. Lars had hoped that Lisa would have calmed down somewhat after his trip to Norrland.

"But Lisa, everything went super smoothly during this last case. Elin and I spent two days in Östersund and nothing untoward happened, nothing at all."

"Well I wouldn't say that – after all you did find a *corpse*."

"Yeah, well, that was no fun, of course, but at no point were we in any danger. And we both came home safe and sound, no injuries at all, not so much as a scratch."

"Yes, but it might well have unfolded differently. If you'd gotten there sooner, it would have been dangerous for sure."

"Lisa, that's simply untrue. Christina's husband was clearly already dead long before Christina even hired us to investigate his disappearance."

"Well, now you're just splitting hairs. You know exactly what I mean."

Lars shook his head. "Well actually, to tell you the truth, I have no idea what you're talking about. You're simply inventing a dangerous situation out of whole cloth – a situation that couldn't possibly have occurred."

Lisa stood up and with her arms akimbo. "I'm inventing something, huh? Really? How about a fractured collarbone? Burns? Being shot at? Getting into fistfights with knife-wielding men? Did I by any chance invent all that too?"

"Yeah, well, that happened in past cases."

"Exactly, and now you expect me feel all merry about the fact that you're now going to be able to accept even more cases that are fraught with danger? And with Elin each time? Lars, I simply do not understand you. You resigned from the police force because you were shot in the knee. So why are you looking for danger all over again? Do you want to get injured again?"

"Lisa..."

"No, Lars, not with me. I'm sick and tired of having to worry about your safety all the time. If you want to live like this, be my guest. But you'll need to live this way without *me*."

She turned around and headed for the kitchen. Lars jumped off the couch. What the hell was going on with her? He hadn't seen this coming at all.

“What are you trying to say, Lisa – that you want to leave me?” he called after her.

“If need be, yes,” she said, as she began walking upstairs. Lars watched her, speechless, and heard the bedroom door slam. He simply couldn’t believe it. She couldn’t be serious about this, could she? In any case, this was clearly not the right time to thrash this out; it was best to give her a few days to calm down. Then over the weekend he’d sit down with her and discuss the matter calmly.

Lars sat back down on the couch. He was no longer in the mood for champagne, and his ebullience about his success at work had evaporated. Whisky – that’s what he needed instead. He got the bottle and a glass. Then he turned on the TV. He needed to distract himself.

21

Elin was staring at the computer screen; the volume of data displayed there was simply overwhelming. This was like looking for a needle in a haystack. She'd thought that finding Natalia's phone number would be a piece of cake. She'd presumed that Patrik had called Natalia frequently using his second phone. But this was not at all the case. Patrik had hardly used that phone at all and Elin could clearly identify the few numbers that he had dialed – including the phone number of Klas, the cabin's landlord. That was the last call he'd made with this phone. She surmised that Patrik and Natalia had communicated with each other using chat software, which was impossible to track. So the only remaining option was to use triangulation to identify the number. She'd assumed that it would be easy to find a second phone number that was simultaneously logged in at the cabin and that was also located in close proximity to Stockholm or Täby. But this surmise had turned out to be dead wrong. Unfortunately, triangulation wasn't an option, since for precise localization the number in question must be logged into three different cell phone towers – and only one was accessible near the cabin in Norrland. Plus, this tower had a range of about 13 miles, and so in early July a great many phones were logged onto this network. Which meant that Elin had hundreds of phone numbers in Norrland that she needed to check against an equally gargantuan list of numbers in Stockholm and Täby. Performing this task was strenuous and time consuming – and totally boring into the bargain.

So she decided to give Carl a call in the hope that he'd be able to suggest a workaround.

Carl picked up right away, and after they said hello to each other, Elin explained the situation to him.

"Do you think you might be able to suggest a solution?" she asked.

"Gosh, I don't know."

Carl wasn't being as helpful as he usually was. Was he having a bad day? Or was this problem really new to him?

"Well, look," Elin said. "You guys must have been confronted with this sort of thing before. How did you deal with it?"

Silence on the other end. Elin was just about to ask Carl if he was still there when he said, "Could be. Can I call you back in a few minutes?" And then the line went dead.

What the hell's wrong with him, Elin wondered to herself. Did I maybe call him at an inopportune moment? But if that were the case, he at least could have said so. So she had no choice but to wait for him to call back. She checked her Facebook Messenger, having already sent Maja a good-morning greeting with an emoji depicting a person basking in the sun. But apparently Maja hadn't seen this message yet. She'd still been asleep when Elin left the apartment for work this morning, but as it was already 11 a.m. she surely must be awake by know. Maja was still in a foul mood, and Elin had decided that she absolutely must talk to her over the weekend. At the very least, she wanted to talk to Maja about whatever it was that was bothering her. And if Elin could do anything to help, she would of course do so; but she couldn't do anything about her mother, if that was still the problem.

Elin's phone rang. "Hello?"

"Hi, Elin, it's Carl." She could hear traffic noise in the background; was Carl standing on a street somewhere?

"So can you talk now?"

"Yeah, thanks. You know, I can definitely help you analyze those phone numbers."

"Awesome." But why hadn't he said so in the first place?

"The only problem, though, is that I'd need to use my own software."

"And...?" She didn't give a rat's ass who'd made the tool, just as long as it worked.

"Well that means the transaction wouldn't be done through the company IT Experts Support."

So that's what he was getting at. "I see. So what do you suggest we do?"

"Well, you'd have to pay me directly."

"Well that's really not a problem, Carl. But if you want to be paid under the table, I wouldn't get an invoice – which would make it problematic to post the expenditure in our accounting system."

"No, I wouldn't need to be paid illicitly, you'd definitely get an invoice. I have my own company now."

"Well that would be just fine, then. How much would you charge?"

"Five thousand."

Elin swallowed – she hadn't seen that coming. "Well that's kind of steep, you know. I'm pretty sure it's not going to take you more than ten minutes to import and analyze the data."

"Yeah, but developing that software was a ton of work. So I need to be compensated for all the time I put in. It's like a licensing fee."

Elin hesitated. This was no piddling amount that Carl was asking for. And shouldn't she first discuss the matter with Tobias, or at least with Lars? But she desperately needed Carl's help, otherwise she'd never be able to analyze the data.

"Okay, I see your point," she said slowly. "So I'll pay you the five thousand – but you've really got to be quick."

"Absolutely. If you send me the data now, you'll have the results after lunch. I'll e-mail you from my own account and then you can send me the data and confirm the order and the fee. Okay?"

"That's fine. Let's do that." She felt kind of uneasy about placing this order with Carl without consulting anyone else about it first. "So how will this play out in the future? Will you be doing some of the work for us via your own company?"

"I'm not really sure yet. I might just quit my current job so that I can focus on my own company. But I haven't completely made up my mind yet. And it's not official yet either. So if you could keep this to yourself, I'd appreciate it."

"Absolutely. I'll send you the file as soon as I receive your e-mail."

They said goodbye to each other. Elin shook her head inwardly. Carl undoubtedly had a surprise up his sleeve. If he really was serious about this new company of his and if she would need to go see him at his apartment or in an office, the place would undoubtedly look even worse than his current office did. Just thinking about it gave her the willies.

***

Elin pointed to the phone numbers that she'd marked with a yellow highlighter on two lists. Lars looked at them eagerly.

"This number was in each case logged in to the same tower as Patrik's number. At the *Huvudsta* subway station here in Stockholm, both numbers are in the same segment according to the triangulation. I'll bet that this Natalia person lives somewhere around here, in an apartment where Patrik visited her. I checked, and Patrik was in fact here at least twice a week over a period of several months. And this number that I believe is Natalia's was in this same location every day, mainly in the evening and at night."

"Is that the only number that appears concurrently with Patrik's at this location?" Lars said, looking dubious.

"Well no, of course not. But this number also shows up along with Patrik's in Norrland. I can't triangulate there, though, because only one tower is accessible from the cabin they rented. Which is why I have such a long list for that location – half of Östersund is logged on to this tower. But this number's the only one that appears on the list in both Stockholm and Norrland at the relevant points in time. That's how I was able to identify them."

"Wow, how'd you do that? Did you go through the numbers one by one?" Lars gave her a doubtful look.

"Yeah, well I had some help." Elin was being cagey because she felt insecure about broaching this subject. "Well, as it turns out, Carl has a little software tool. But as it also turns out, it wasn't cheap."

"That's okay, it's part of our expenses."

Elin breathed a sigh of relief.

"That's terrific," Lars said. "What are we going to do with this number? Do we know where the phone is located?"

"Well, yes and no. The number's been deactivated since this past 5 July – I suppose because Natalia removed the SIM card. Timewise this is consistent with the week during which Patrik rented the cabin and could be the day of the accident."

"I see. But what's the deal with the yes and no – I only understand the no part."

"Well, I've gone a bit further. As you can see here in the list, you can actually glean additional information about the number. Not only where it was located, and which conversations were held, but also the identity of the actual phone that the SIM card was in. You can also see the make of the phone here – in this case a Samsung Galaxy S7 – and the so-called IMEI number, which is the ID number for this phone." Elin paused to see if Lars was following, and when he nodded, she continued with her explanation. "You can use this number to search for new activity. And as you can see here, this phone was used a few days later in Jönköping, with a new SIM card." Elin pulled two additional lists out of her pile of papers and pointed to the marked phone number. "But interestingly, the activity occurred only from early July to early September and then abruptly stopped. And now that same phone's using a different SIM card again and has been logged on in Göteborg ever since."

"The lady does get around, doesn't she?" Lars interjected.

"Seems like it," Elin said, nodding. "The good news here is, though, that she spends most of her time in two locations in Göteborg. She spends a few hours beginning early in the morning in this office building in the downtown area, and she spends most of the remainder of her time in this residential area in the Johanneberg neighborhood. To all appearances, the address that comes into play here is Eklandagatan 42, which I presume is where she lives."

"Well that's simply awesome," Lars said enthusiastically. "What do you say we pay that address a little visit, right now?"

Elin was pleased to see that Lars was on the same wavelength that she was. She also felt that they needed to act quickly, because Natalia could take that phone somewhere else at any time. "I've checked out the building. It has six floors each of which contains two or three apartments. But of course there's no record of anyone named Natalia currently residing there."

"Well we'll just have to go and see, she might be subletting."

"Well we could call up each of the apartments and ask to speak to her."

"Not a good idea, because maybe the people who answer the phone will lie and Natalia will be scared off. And then she'd just be gone in a flash. I think we should head over there tomorrow."

"I agree. What we could do before going there, though, is search the apartment here in Stockholm. It's located at Jungfrudansen 72-76 in Solna.

However, it's an eight-story building, so it won't be easy."

"Plus it's been more than three months since Natalia actually lived there. So this is going to be a tough one. Let's stick a pin in this for the moment, given that the trail in Göteborg is still fresh. 'Cause we might not only find leads there, but maybe, if we're lucky, we might even be able to locate this Natalia person."

"Well yeah, assuming the phone is still being used by the same person. Natalia could have given it to someone as a gift or thrown it away. And maybe someone found it and is happily using it."

"Well let's keep our fingers crossed that that isn't what happened." Lars looked at the lists of numbers with a smile on his face. "Because if it is what happened, all your work will have been for naught. We're going to operate on the assumption that this Natalia person lives in Göteborg and feels safe there. Let's head over there tomorrow. I'll pick you up at around 10, okay?"

"Is there rice in China? Of course I'm coming. Something's happening at long last." Elin wanted to jump for joy.

22

No way, Natalia thought, as she froze in terror. She was just about to get off the bus when she spotted him. It was Stanislov, she was absolutely certain, his huge frame was unmistakable. He was standing diagonally across the street from her apartment, smoking in the entrance next to a small store called Kiosk. If she hadn't taken this bus, which stopped on her side of the street, she probably wouldn't have spotted him.

Natalia went back to her seat on the other side of the bus. As other people were also getting off at this stop, she luckily hadn't been standing right at the door when it opened. Otherwise, he might well have spotted her. What the hell was that bastard doing here anyway? She simply had to face the fact that he'd managed to track her down. But how?

After doing the pregnancy test, she'd decided to leave Stanislov. And she'd done a good job of laying the groundwork. She'd emptied out one of Patrik's bank accounts so that she wouldn't be making any withdrawals that Stanislov could use to track her down, as he also had access to this account. She'd also gotten a new SIM card for her phone, another prepaid card. And then she'd packed her backpack and had gone to Göteborg, where she'd rented a room and had even found a job as a cleaner. She'd been here in Göteborg for six weeks now. During the first two weeks she'd been quite anxious and was always looking around apprehensively to see if Stanislov might be following her and might suddenly appear behind her. But over the ensuing four weeks she began to feel increasingly safe – and now there he was, waiting for her to come home. What should she do? All her belongings were in the apartment, along with most of her cash. But if Stanislov was watching the building, there was no way she'd be able to get into the apartment.

The bus continued down the street, putting distance between her and Stanislov. Natalia breathed deeply. How on earth had he managed to find her? He didn't know a thing about computers and hacking, which just weren't his thing. What he was all about were fistfights and manipulating people. But she knew full well that he had ties to folks who knew how to do these things. She'd never met them, and he'd always been secretive about them. But she knew that they gave him loads of information about potential victims – information that would otherwise be quite difficult to obtain. She'd thought at first that these dudes were pals of his that were doing him a favor or getting him information on a quid pro quo basis. But she'd since come to believe that these men were from the world of organized crime – a world that Stanislov was part of as well. This also jibed with what she'd found out and with what had made her decide to leave Stanislov. She'd overheard a conversation in which Stanislov was receiving instructions. They had to do with young women named Galenka and Anastasia, who Stanislov evidently "cared for" and with whom he was probably pretending, as he was with her, that he wanted to build a life together. She still couldn't understand why she'd fallen for him in the first place. What an idiot she'd been! But he looked so sweet sometimes, with those big dark puppydog eyes. And she'd probably wanted to believe in him too.

Natalia thought it over. She couldn't stay in Göteborg. She needed to somehow get her stuff and her money and disappear. She'd call her roommate Britta and ask her to bring her things surreptitiously. Britta would surely be pleased if, instead of just vanishing into thin air, Natalia paid this month's and next month's rent. Plus, she was a really nice person, and they'd gotten along really well. Natalia was even a little sorry to have to leave her. But she had no other choice. She'd never be able to hide from Stanislov now that he'd tracked her down.

She already had an idea about where she could go. She'd found an old friend from the children's home, on Facebook, through which they'd been communicating regularly via Messenger for the past few weeks. Her friend, whose name was Lyudmila, had made a life for herself in Budapest. She appeared to be doing well there, even though she was kind of cagey about how she earned her money. Probably something you wouldn't want to shout from the rooftops – Natalia already had a pretty good idea about her friend's source of income. Be this as it may, she would surely be able to stay with Lyudmila for a while and hide out from Stanislov. Budapest was a long way away, though, so she decided to go part of the way by train and try to hitchhike the rest of the way. Flying there was too risky, as her name would likely turn up on some list or other and Stanislov would undoubtedly be apprised right away. And besides, her European Union visa had long since expired, and if her passport was checked at the airport she might be deported to Russia.

Anyhow, at least she had a plan now and was gradually calming down. She took out her phone, text-messaged Lyudmila and then dialed her roommate's number.

23

Elin opened the passenger door and got out of the car. Lars had found a parking space right in front of the building. The drive from Stockholm had gone quickly; they'd made it to Göteborg in just under five hours.

They went to the building's entrance, which was a few steps down, below street level. Elin scrutinized the 18 intercom buttons and the names next to them. There were no names for three of them, and Elin checked the remaining names against the list of residents that she'd printed out.

"Unfortunately, there's no name here that isn't on the list."

Lars nodded. "I'd figured that's what we'd find. Natalia probably isn't all that interested in having visitors. I think we'd be better off looking at the mailboxes."

"Yeah, but to do that we need to get into the building."

"So I guess we should either ring all the bells, or else wait until someone enters or leaves."

Elin checked the time on her phone; it was just after 3. "Well I guess at this time of day we won't have to wait all that long until someone comes in or out, don't you think?"

"Yeah but it's not a very good idea for us to hang around the door to the building. Too noticeable." Lars looked up and down the street. "There's a small pizza place down there on the left, why don't we just mosey on over there and have a cup of coffee."

Elin looked at the place – the small restaurant was only a few doors down. All of the buildings were set back from the street the same amount below street level, but there was a small wall and a small recess between each of the entrances.

"But if someone comes, we won't be able to get to the door in time. It's too far."

"Well I can't, with my lame knee. But you're a good sprinter," he said with an encouraging laugh.

Elin looked closely at the distance again and shook her head. "It's over 30 feet, plus I'd have to go up a set of stairs and back down again. I'd never be able to do that before the door closes."

"Well not if someone's leaving, but when you see someone approaching the building, you can get into position sooner."

"Well, maybe." Elin still had her doubts. "Why don't we just sit in the car? Then we'll be a lot closer."

"Because there's no coffee in the car," Lars said with an impish smile. "And I absolutely need coffee – after all I did all the driving to get us here." He began walking toward the pizza restaurant.

"Well why didn't you say so in the first place!" Elin said, following behind Lars. "But don't blame me if we miss the next opportunity to get into the building."

"No worries. I'm sure that door's going to be opened more than just once over the next two hours. So let's go get some coffee first, shall we?"

On a lawn in front of the pizza place there were three small tables, which were not in use, owing to the chilly October temperature. However, this didn't prevent Lars from sitting down at the first table and dragging a folding chair over to it. "I'll go inside and get us some coffee. What should I get you?"

"A large latte, please. And maybe a cinnamon bun or something."

"I'll see what they have." Lars disappeared into the restaurant.

Elin sat down on the opposite side of the table, which had a view of the entrance to no. 42. She kept a close eye on the building until Lars returned. He was carrying a small tray containing a cup, a large glass and two *kanelbullar*.

Elin picked up the glass containing her latte. "Aha, I see they had cinnamon buns. Awesome."

Lars sat down and sipped his coffee. Elin was reaching for one of the *bullar* when she spotted a young woman coming out of no. 42. She got up, but then froze. "Oh damn. The door'll be closed before I even get to the curb. I hope that's not Natalia."

Lars turned around. "Blond, middle thirties. It could conceivably be her."

Elin had already stood up, with a *bulle* still in her hand. "Should I go after her?"

"Nope, easy does it. We need to proceed in an orderly fashion. By which I mean, first we need to ascertain whether Natalia even lives there, and secondly we need to identify her – and then we can approach her."

Elin sat back down. "Yeah, but what are we supposed to do with her? Hand her over to the police?" She took a bite out of her *bulle* and swallowed a big gulp of coffee.

"Look, we'll cross that bridge when we come to it. Let's just talk to her first and try to pressure her a bit. And then what we do will depend on what she tells us and whether or not we believe it. And ultimately we also have to find out what Christina's take on all this is."

"Do you think we should abduct her and take her to Stockholm?"

Lars shook his head. "Look, Elin, we don't do things the way you're accustomed to doing them from your past cases. We're not the police and we don't break the law. Which is why I'd be very very reluctant to abduct her."

"Okay, then let's wait until we gain access to the building and can have a look at the mailboxes. If I see Natalia's name there, then we'll press the buzzer of the relevant apartment. But what happens if it's the same with the mailboxes as it was with the doorbells, i.e. no name that's registered there? Are we really going to sit here all evening and wait until someone materializes who might be Natalia?"

"Well, there is another way." Lars scratched the back of his head. "Wasn't there a single elderly lady on the list of residents?"

Elin looked through her list again; the date of birth of each resident was indicated next to their name. "Wait a sec. Yeah, here she is. Marta Sjöblom, born 1935, so she's 81; her birthday's in April." Elin gave Lars a questioning look. "How come?"

"Elderly folks tend to live in the same apartment for a long time and are home most of the time. Which means they also tend to notice everything that's going on around them in the building. Some of them are in the habit of keeping an eye on what their neighbors are up to. And so we might well get the information we want from this lady – providing that we act all nice and friendly and come across as being trustworthy. What we should do is concoct a believable cover story as to why we're looking for this Natalia person."

Elin reflected for a moment. "Well, I could say that Natalia's a friend of mine and that I wanted to visit her. And that I came all the way from Stockholm especially for this purpose, and so on."

Lars nodded. "Yeah, that'll work. But then you should ring her bell alone. That would be best in any case. If the two of us show up at her door she might be even more scared than if it's only you."

"Particularly with a huge dude like you standing behind me. Okay, I'll do it."

While they studiously drank their coffee, Elin kept her eye firmly on the building entrance. Lars had shifted his chair slightly so that he was facing away from the restaurant and could keep an eye on the street.

Elin had just finished her *bulle* when Lars gestured toward the sidewalk with his head and whispered quietly, "Hey look, seems like there's a man over there who's headed for our building."

And indeed, a middle-aged male wearing a dark coat and carrying an attaché case was over there. He stopped in front of the steps of no. 42, rummaged in his trousers pocket and seemed to be about to enter the building.

"Okay, here goes." Elin set down her glass, stood up and climbed the steps to the sidewalk. The man appeared to have found his key and was making his way down the stairs to the entrance. Elin quickened her step. Just as she got to the steps, the man had opened the door and had entered the building. Elin scampered down the stairs and leaped to the entrance, catching the door just before it closed. Boy, that was a close one, she thought.

Elin kept the door slightly jar and waited until the man had disappeared up the stairs. She then darted through the doorway and turned her attention to the mailboxes, which were arranged in three superimposed rows consisting of six mailboxes each. She compared the names on the mailboxes with the names on her list, checking off the names as she did so. The two last mailboxes had no name on them, just like the doorbells, and were probably there as a backup. Unfortunately, the names on her list and those on the mailbox matched up perfectly, there was no name on a mailbox that didn't appear on the list – and there was certainly no Natalia. Which meant that she was going to have to talk to the elderly lady, hoping against hope that she was in the right building – otherwise she'd have to go through this all over again in the neighboring buildings. But somehow Elin was certain she was in the right place, as the triangulation had been very precise.

In a small glass box next to the elevator there was a list of the building's tenants, where Elin could see that Marta Sjöblom's apartment was on the second floor. Elin took the stairs. Marta's apartment was on the right, and in the center of the door there was a sign with the name Sjöblom on it, in large letters. Elin pressed the buzzer; she could hear a shrill sound coming from inside the apartment. She waited a few moments and was just about to press the buzzer again when she heard light footsteps.

The door opened a crack and she could see that the security chain was still attached. A wrinkled face framed in white curly hair was looking out at her suspiciously.

"Yes?"

„*Hej,* Marta. I hope I'm not disturbing you. I'm not a door to door salesperson or anything like that. I'm looking for a friend of mine named Natalia, who I understand lives in this building. But unfortunately, her name isn't on any of the doorbells and I've been unable to reach her on her cellphone. Do you think you could help me out?"

The elderly lady, who, like Elin, was on the short side, looked Elin up and down. Then she said, in a squeaky voice, "You say she lives in this building?"

Elin nodded emphatically. "Yes, she gave me this address, Eklandagatan 42. I just arrived from Stockholm and was planning to visit her for a week. As far as I know, she rents a room in an apartment here."

"Aha, so I guess you're referring to a young blond number?"

Elin smiled. "Yeah, that's her. Have you seen her by any chance?"

The lady nodded. "Yes, I've seen her quite often in the building, although she moved in only a few weeks ago. I don't know her name. Britta told me that she rented a room to her."

"Oh terrific, that's very helpful. Could you tell me which apartment Britta is living in?"

"She lives right above me; her last name's Lilja."

"Thanks a million. I'm going to go up there right now." Elin bid the lady goodbye and the door closed. Should I go up there and ring her bell right now? she wondered. No, she thought, I'd best call Lars first. She keyed in his number as she slowly ascended the stairs.

"Hello?"

"I've found her, Lars. The elderly lady has spotted her on a number of occasions and describes her as a young, blond number. She also told me where she lives – she rents a room from someone called Britta Lilja who lives on the third floor. I'm at the door to that apartment as we speak. But here too, all I see is the name of this Britta person. Should I ring the bell?"

"No, hold off a bit. Let's discuss how best to proceed. Could you open the front door and let me in?"

Elin went down the stairs and opened the door for Lars and brought him up to speed in a hushed tone.

"Good work," Lars said, with an approving nod. "You know what? I think we should stick with the cover story we concocted. You go up there and ring the bell alone. But I'd like to eavesdrop, so I'll go stand on the landing just below."

They then did as they'd planned, but Elin came up empty-handed – and even after she'd rung a third time there was no answer. She could hear the doorbell, but there appeared to be no one home. She consulted her list again. As Britta was 41, she probably had a job, but hadn't come home from work yet.

They decided to go back to the pizza place and have something to drink. Lars got spring water for them, and they sat down at the same outdoor table again. The sky was turning murky and the temperature was dropping. Elin zipped her jacket all the way up.

"We're getting close now, aren't we?" This was the kind of work that she really enjoyed – particularly when something came of it. But she also had to admit that Lars had really good ideas, such as talking to the elderly lady; that had been a bull's-eye. Plus, she'd once again learned a valuable lesson.

"I sure hope so."

"When should we try again, do you think?"

"Around five, I suppose."

Elin checked her phone. "That's a good hour from now. You don't really want to sit here all that time and freeze our asses off, now do you?"

"Nah, let's go inside. I have to make a call."

They picked up their glasses and headed into the restaurant, where it was nice and warm. They sat down next to a window, from which, though they couldn't see the entrance to no. 42 very well, they at least had a clear view of the sidewalk in front of the building. Lars took out his phone and dialed a number, while Elin checked her Facebook Messenger. Still no response from Maja to her good-morning message. So either Maja had stopped checking her Messenger, or she was deliberately ignoring her. Last night had been pretty much the same as every other night, though. Maja had been glad to hear that Elin had a new case.

They then ordered another pizza, which they shared, and then Elin went to the car. She got in and didn't have to wait long until she saw a woman making her way toward the building from across the street. Elin got out of the car, and this time had no difficulty getting to the door before it closed. After waiting a few moments for the woman to disappear into the elevator, she signaled to Lars and they mounted the three steps to the building. Lars waited, keeping out of sight in the recess, while Elin rang Britta Lilja's doorbell again.

This time someone was home; right away she could hear footsteps moving toward the door. When it opened, Elin realized that this was the woman she'd just seen enter the building. She had taken off her coat and shoes and was wearing an elegant pants suit with a beige blouse. She had dark, shoulder-length hair and was wearing glasses with black frames. She gave Elin an inquisitive look.

"Hi, my name's Elin and I'm looking for Natalia – who as I understand it is living in your apartment."

"What do you want with her?" Evidently, Britta was distrustful.

"I'm a friend of hers from Stockholm and I was planning to pay her a visit."

"Well, your timing's off. Didn't she tell you anything?"

Elin was disconcerted. "What do you mean? I've been trying to call her cellphone, but she doesn't pick up."

"Natalia moved out yesterday."

Elin was dumbfounded. "What? Yesterday? What'd she do that for?"

The woman gave Elin a penetrating look. She appeared to be pleased with this outcome, because she then said, "Why don't you come in for a moment so that I can tell you more." She took a look around the staircase as she said this.

This was of course not so good for Lars, as he wouldn't be able to eavesdrop on their conversation. But Elin couldn't very well say no, because then she might not find out anything further. And if she now revealed the existence of Lars, the whole business about wanting to visit Natalia would be exposed for the lie it was. So she entered the apartment. She followed the woman to the end of a corridor, where she opened a door.

"This was Natalia's room."

Elin entered the room, which was quite small, less than 30 square feet, and contained a bed, a night table, a chair and a clothes closet. There were no personal effects, and the room appeared to have been recently cleared out.

The woman looked at Elin. "I packed up her things myself – she didn't have much. It all fit in a small suitcase and a sling bag."

Elin was confused. "Why did you do that? Couldn't Natalia have done it herself?"

"Yeah, it was kind of weird. She called me yesterday afternoon and asked me to bring her stuff to the train station. When I got there, she paid me a month's rent and then vanished."

"But then why did she have me come all this way from Stockholm without telling me she was leaving?" Elin shouted, pretending to be upset in order to keep up the pretext about visiting Natalia. "Did she by any chance tell you why she had to leave so suddenly?"

After looking Elin up and down again, the woman said, "She told me that some guy from her past had appeared and that she had to get out of Göteborg. She seemed very distressed when I saw her at the train station. She kept looking around. Which is why I didn't want to talk to you in the staircase either."

What a mess! Elin simply couldn't believe it. She'd missed Natalia by a few hours.

"Did she by any chance tell you where she was headed?"

The woman shook her head. "Nope, no idea. I had the impression that she wanted to keep me in the dark. So I don't really know much. But she was super distressed, that's for sure."

Elin stared at the woman. Did she really not have any other information?

"She lived here for a few weeks, right? I don't get it, not at all," Elin stammered.

"Right, she moved in during the first week in September. She paid two months' rent in advance, and just now she paid me another month's rent, though October isn't over yet. It's such a shame, we got along really well and she was a terrific roommate. Clean and quiet. Unlike the girl I had here before. That one had a constant stream of visitors and played loud music. I kicked her out after three months, but I would have loved to have Natalia around for longer than that."

"Well how on earth am I going to find her now?"

The woman shrugged. "No idea, sweetie, I really can't help you. All I have is her cellphone number. If you can't reach her at that number, you'll just have to wait until she contacts you."

Well there was no way Natalia was going to be doing that! Elin asked Britta to compare the phone numbers; it turned out to be the exact number that Elin had identified and that had brought her here. After thanking Britta and saying goodbye to her, Elin went down the stairs to Lars, who gave her an inquisitive look. Elin just shook her head and kept on walking downstairs. She was really frustrated, having missed Natalia by a hairsbreadth – that was super bad luck.

An hour later Lars and Elin were driving down the highway and passed by the entrance to Liseborg, Göteborg's renowned theme park. Elin looked at the Ferris wheel and the AtmosFear. Formerly known as the Lisebergtornet tower, it afforded park visitors the opportunity to experience a free fall from a height of well over 300 feet. She'd been here many years ago on a class trip – four days in Göteborg, one of which was spent at Liseberg. Back then she'd really loved the rides; but the AtmosFear didn't exist yet and the tower was used solely as an observation platform. But what she'd liked most of all was the roller coaster.

As for her case, Göteborg had been a total washout. After discussing what to do next, she and Lars had decided to dial Natalia's number. They'd actually expected it to be disconnected. Then when Elin got back to Stockholm, she'd been able to resume her search for the IMEI number in the hope or locating Natalia's phone. But that wasn't the worst of it. A man had picked up the phone who was very difficult to understand and presumably inebriated. And to top it all off, after some back and forth and the guy at the other end hanging up on them twice, the guy had let on that he'd found the phone in a trash can at the train station the day before. He also said that he'd tried unsuccessfully to hack the PIN code, and that the battery was almost dead. But he could still pick up incoming calls – and fortunately was still able to do so. They'd offered him a thousand kronor for the phone and had then agreed on 1,200. The man had handed over the phone to them at the train station. He was an older homeless guy, rather heavy set, with a gray beard and dressed in several layers of worn clothes and a wool cap. The man reeked of alcohol, cigarette smoke, and sweat, and had three full to bursting plastic bags in one hand and the phone in the other. He was evidently very pleased to get the money, and as he headed out, Elin had no illusions as to what he was going to use it for. She had connected the phone to her laptop immediately, but the phone appeared to have been wiped clean before she'd gotten to it. Which meant she now had no way of contacting Natalia – who this time had not only gotten a new SIM card but had gone so far as to throw the phone away. Thus, there was now no way to track her down. And if none of the phone data could be recovered, they didn't have information about Natalia or her whereabouts either. They'd come up completely empty-handed.

And so, Elin and Lars didn't exchange a word during the entire five-hour drive home – which didn't help to improve the mood. And to top it all off, it was raining cats and dogs. Elin just wanted to get home and enjoy a nice bottle of red wine; hopefully Maja would be in a good mood.

NOVEMBER 2016

24

She was on the tram, pleased that she'd been able to get a seat – which was often problematic nowadays, as people were packed in like sardines. Natalia was on the way home – home still being her room at Lyudmila's. Rooming with Lyudmila had turned out to be a real stroke of luck. She was a real sweetheart, and had taken Natalia under her wing, like a sister, and had even helped her find a job. Since then, Natalia had been working as a server at a restaurant near Buda Castle. It was super stressful being on her feet for ten hours at a stretch – but she liked working there nonetheless.

Most Hungarians were really nice, and she was particularly fond of her boss. She'd always gotten along well with people, and with men above all. Okay, she knew she was pretty – but she also had a disarming smile, which, strangely enough, women found seductive as well. She was courteous and friendly with the customers, and they were polite and respectful with her in return. The only problem was the language barrier. Hungarian is a difficult language, though she'd already picked up a few useful phrases. Many older Hungarians had learned Russian in school, but none of them had any desire to speak it. Which was understandable as the Russian occupation hadn't exactly made the natives well disposed toward the Soviet Union. It was lucky that she knew English, because oftentimes that was the only way she could make herself understood. She also spoke English with most of the customers at the restaurant, as it was mainly frequented by tourists.

Natalia liked Budapest, which was divided into two parts, called Buda and Pest, by the Danube. Buda, which was hilly and green, had more upscale residential districts, whereas Pest consisted of a flat expanse dotted with some high-rises. From the restaurant where Natalia worked, there was a magnificent view of the Danube and of Pest, whose banks were dominated by the Parliament building and its numerous towers. She loved this view and enjoyed just perching on a chair and gazing at it. She did this whenever there was a brief lull – which was unfortunately rarely the case as the restaurant was very busy and she was kept occupied pretty much all day. When she first came into the restaurant for her job interview, she was overcome with shyness – the decor and the view immediately made her feel like she was in a very upscale restaurant where she, as an illegal immigrant, wouldn't be allowed to work. But her boss-to-be, whose name was Csaba, had noticed her and waved to her. He was expecting her, and apparently Lyudmila had praised her to the skies, as he'd hired her after asking only a few perfunctory questions. And the fact that she had neither a visa nor a work permit didn't seem to bother him a bit. He paid her off the books, which was apparently advantageous for him. She'd recently asked him whether someone could run afoul of the law in Hungary for employing illegal immigrants. Csaba had merely laughed, saying that no one would be checking him, as he was on excellent terms with people in many high places, including the police and the tax office. In Hungary, everything depended on who you knew, just like at home in Russia. And bribes also helped to grease the wheels of human relationships, though no one ever said so openly.

Natalia often found herself wondering how Lyudmila had managed to make such a good life for herself in Hungary in such a short time. Lyudmila had told her her story in dribs and drabs. She'd come to Hungary on a visa and had married, and then divorced, a Hungarian. This had enabled her to obtain a residency permit and start her own business. Lyudmila had gotten an exclusive escort service up and running – a business that meshed well with the restaurant in Buda that Csaba owned, along with a small hotel in Pest that he co-owned with his sister. The guests of this hotel were apparently good customers of Lyudmila's escort service. Natalia still wasn't sure whether Lyudmila worked as an escort, or if her role was confined to that of manager. Nor did she care which was the case, that was strictly Lyudmila's affair – she was just so grateful that Lyudmila had made her feel so warmly welcome in her home. She knew that Lyudmila had at least a dozen girls working for her full time, plus a few that went on dates intermittently. Lyudmila's income was probably off the books, and thus tax-free, for the most part. This stood in stark contrast to Sweden, where all businesses pay high taxes and are kept under the watchful eye of the tax authorities. And anyway, most payments in Sweden are made by credit card, which makes it virtually impossible to cheat the tax man. Natalia had been under the impression that this was also the case in all European Union countries – but at least in Hungary it was still quite common to pay in cash, even for relatively large purchases.

The tram bell sounded, and it came to a halt. Natalia stood up, as she'd reached her stop. The only disadvantage of working near Buda Castle was that the commute back and forth to work was relatively long. Getting to Pest was quick and easy with the M2, one of the two subway lines that traverse the Danube. But when she got to the end station, Örs vezér tere, *she had to take the tram five stops to* Szugló utca. *All told, this took upwards of an hour. Which is why she'd thought about renting a room in Buda. But on the other hand, she was also trying to save money, as she wasn't sure how long she'd be able to work until she got so pregnant she'd have to stop. Plus, once her baby was born, she wouldn't be able to work full time. And anyway, she didn't really know how she was going to manage all this. But Lyudmila had told her that it would all work out and that she'd be there for her – which reassured her.*

Upon reaching the building, she mounted the few steps to the entrance and opened the front door. Then she climbed the stairs to the third floor. As the apartments all had cathedral ceilings, three floors added up to a lot of stairs.

Natalia was already out of breath by the time she reached the first landing and thought, as she had many times before, that these steps were going to pose a real problem during her third trimester – and unfortunately the building had no elevator.

Upon reaching the third floor, she put her key in the lock and turned it. The key always got stuck a little, and you had to push upward to the left while turning it. In the rather dimly lit hallway, Natalia could hear Lyudmila's voice coming from the kitchen. She hung her jacket in the closet, admired the ceiling's stucco embellishments for the umpteenth time, and went around the corner.

"Priwétik *Natalia,*" *Lyudmila shouted, rushing toward her. She had an apron tied around waist and a cooking spoon in her right hand and was wearing her long blond hair in a ponytail. She put her left arm around Natalia and kissed her on the cheek.*

"Hi Lyudmila," Natalia said with a smile. Then she greeted the two men in the Hungarian manner:

"Szia Sándor, szia *Gábor.*"

Sándor, who had been Lyudmila's boyfriend for nearly two years, lived two floors above her, on the top floor. Gábor, Sándor's brother, lived and worked with him. They owned an online store that had its ups and downs economically. Depending on how the store was doing, Sándor was either very busy or spent much of his time in Lyudmila's apartment. As it happened, the store was currently experiencing a dry spell. Natalia was fond of the two of them – honest dudes, with muscular builds and a smattering of tattoos. Sándor was a bit taller and had shaggy hair, whereas Gábor had short hair. Both Gábor and Sándor tended to laugh a lot and were always ready to lend a hand. Natalia had often asked Lyudmila why she didn't just move in with Sándor. But Lyudmila liked her independence and was evidently happy with the situation as it was. Sándor usually slept over at her place and they often spent the weekends together, if Sándor wasn't working. At first, Natalia was worried that she might be disturbing them, but the apartment was spacious, and her room was on the other side of the living room and even had its own bathroom.

"Your timing's impeccable, sweetie," Lyudmila said. "Dinner's almost ready." As this happened to be the one night in the week that Natalia had off, she'd come home early. On other nights, she ate at the restaurant.

She took an envelope out of her purse. "This is from Csaba," she said, handing the envelope to Lyudmila, who nodded and laid it on the dresser next to the corner seating unit. The kitchen, which was also spacious, offered more than enough space for cooking and for a table that seated eight.

Natalia didn't know what was in these envelopes, one of which she gave Lyudmila each week. She assumed they contained cash, but she wasn't completely sure. Nor did she much care, so long as these deliveries weren't implicating her in some kind of illicit activity. Being pregnant had altered her view of things. In the past, she'd been up for just about anything that brought in some money – but now her first thought was always for her child. She wanted to be a good mother – an exemplary one even. She'd done plenty of bad things while she was with Stanislov, but she wanted to leave all that behind her now and had promised herself that she'd never get involved in anything like that again.

Lyudmila heaved the large saucepan onto the table. "We're having pörkölt *this evening, at the behest of these two Hungarian gentlemen."*

Natalia sat down – and suddenly realized that she was famished. Hungarian goulash was really going to hit the spot, she thought. She looked around at her dining companions, all of whom were in an upbeat mood – and hungry. Gábor served her some goulash, and Sándor, who'd sliced the bread, handed her a chunk. Natalia could scarcely believe how great her life was right now. At long last she could relax and feel safe – it was almost like being with her Babushka.

25

Lars, who was running late, rushed into the office and opened the door to the conference room. Christina and Elin, who were already seated at the table, both said "Hi" to him. Christina was dressed all in blue and was wearing an orange silk shawl. As she had an appointment near the detective agency, she'd decided to come in for a wrap-up meeting.

Lars sat down, and noticing that there were documents on the table said, "Elin, has the meeting already started?"

"No, I was waiting for you. We haven't been talking about anything special."

"Great." Lars sighed, this meant that he would have to convey the bad news – as he was in fact the case manager. Lars looked over at Christina. "I'm afraid we haven't been able to make much headway. I would have liked to be able to tell you that we've solved the case, or at the very least that we've found some trace of Natalia. But we appear to have run into a brick wall. Our investigation thus far has centered around three things. First, the bank transactions; second, Natalia's apartment here in Stockholm; and third, we've tried to track her down. Elin, why don't you talk about the accounts and Natalia's phone."

Elin nodded and took a document out of the stack of papers in front of her.

"Okay, I'd like to say this right off the bat. Concerning the international debit transfers, we haven't been able to find out anything more than the police did. The funds were transferred to accounts in Switzerland and Luxembourg – though we haven't been able to identify any of the account numbers. As you know, these transfers didn't begin until the month before Patrik disappeared. But he then withdrew the entirety of his savings, which amounted to nearly two million kronor. And he'd previously deposited these assets in various investment funds that paid good interest. How did he come by such a large amount of money?"

"Well there's no mystery about that," Christina said dryly. "He inherited a small condo from his aunt who died over ten years ago and who had a very special relationship with Patrik. She had no children of her own, and so Patrik got the condo, which he then flipped. The apartment, which was near Karlstad, sold for around 1.5 million. I suppose the rest consisted of savings and interest."

"Well, that explains it," Lars said.

"I find it interesting, though," Elin said, "that as early as this past January, Patrik started making cash withdrawals far larger than any he made last year. He withdrew eight thousand kronor once a month.

Obviously, his monthly salary didn't cover this – which is why in March, for the first time, he sold some of his investment fund shares – but not many of them, only 50,000 kronor worth. But that was enough to finance the cash withdrawals until June. We also think that we've found out what Patrik did with the money. In February he began renting a small one-room apartment in Solna that cost 6,000 kronor per month. We believe that he rented this apartment for Natalia."

"He did this back in *February*?" Christina shook her head in disbelief. "How did you find out about this?"

"Through the triangulation data from his second cellphone. He was in the habit of going there – there being Jungfrudansen – three or four times a week, which made it quite easy for us to figure out which building it was. It happens to be a huge apartment high-rise with hundreds of residents. But its property management company was extremely helpful – and was in fact instrumental in our finding out exactly which apartment he'd rented. Patrik cancelled the lease at the end of June. We spoke with some building residents, but none of them had ever seen Patrik or knew anything about him. But some of the residents we spoke to had run into a blond woman in the elevator – though none of them appear to have had any contact with her."

"So does that mean that he met this woman in January and then rented her an apartment right away?"

"No, we believe that they actually got to know each other last year. The number 15 in the Natalia15 password probably stands for 2015. In any case, Natalia had her own phone, which she'd also been using in Norrland since last November. And it was at this juncture – in fact the very same day – that Patrik bought his second phone. So we presume that he bought both phones and SIM cards. Our theory is that they met last fall, that Patrik fell for her, and then arranged for them to communicate in secret before renting them a love nest – i.e. the apartment in Solna. I'm so sorry, Christina, but these are the facts."

Christina looked at Elin sadly, but calmly. "I see."

Lars truly felt sorry for her, but he didn't see how he could have made this news any more palatable for her. He could well imagine what she must be thinking right now. How could she not have noticed anything? He decided to change the subject.

"We were able to track Natalia to Göteborg, however. Although she switched SIM cards twice after her stay with Patrik, she kept the same phone. And so we were able to localize it, and found out that she'd moved to Göteborg."

"She'd been in Jönköping during the previous five weeks," Elin interjected. "While there, she replaced her SIM card again, before continuing on to Göteborg."

"Thanks, Elin, I forgot to mention that. In any case, as we'd hoped to be able to meet with Natalia in Göteborg, we went there last week. We found her building and then the room she was renting, but we missed her by a day. She'd moved out the previous evening and had apparently left Göteborg. At any rate, the trail went cold at the Göteborg train station." Lars then told Christina about Natalia's phone and the woman she'd rented a room from.

"We carefully analyzed her phone, but we couldn't extract anything else from it," Elin added. "All the data had been deleted – which means that there's no possibility of tracking her down via the phone."

"Isn't there any other way, though?" Christina asked.

Lars looked skeptical. "I'm afraid not. But we did get her last name, by phone, from the woman she was renting a room from. Her full name is Natalia Serimanov – assuming that's not an alias, of course – and she's Russian." Lars had pretended to Natalia's former landlady that he was from the tax office and was gathering information about rental income. And while interviewing her, he'd slipped in a question about the tenant's name and nationality. This was a ploy that often worked, given people's deferential attitude toward tax officials. "And then of course we googled this name and did a Facebook search for it – but we came up empty-handed. And if there's no mention of this Natalia person anywhere online, or if she doesn't materialize, I'm afraid our chances of finding her are nil."

"I think she's probably left Sweden," Elin interjected. "She told her landlady that someone from her past had showed up. The landlady said she seemed very anxious. Natalia's from Russia, so presumably she went back to her homeland."

"Quite possibly," Lars said. "Which makes it even less likely that we'll be able to track her down." He spread out his hands. "As I said, we would have liked to have been able to tell you that we'd found a clue to her whereabouts, but that simply isn't the case. All of the clues lead to a dead-end. And having carefully weighed all the facts, we recommend that you consider this case closed. We believe strongly in giving our clients something in return for their money, and we doubt that's going to happen if we keep investigating this case. Not to mention the fact that I really have no idea where else we should look. We made it clear from the outset that we couldn't guarantee results. But despite this, I had truly believed that we'd be able to come up with more than we have – but unfortunately we were unable to. For which I am sorry."

Christina leaned back and sighed. "Yes I'd also thought you'd come up with something, otherwise I wouldn't have put you back on the case. But I'd nonetheless like to thank you for your efforts. I'm impressed at the wealth of information that you have been able to find. I had hoped that the police would be this committed to solving the case, but they apparently have more important things to do. That said, I now at least have an inkling of what happened to Patrik – even if it's not at all to my liking. I guess I'll just have to accept that I'll never know everything and that this Natalia person has simply slipped through our fingers." She seemed calm.

"I'm also quite frustrated that we've hit a brick wall," Elin said, apparently unable to resist jumping in. Lars knew that this failure to solve the case was bothering her. "And we were so close, too. If we'd gotten to Göteborg a day sooner, we would have found her."

"Well I guess it just wasn't meant to be," Christina said, shrugging in resignation. She stood up. Lars had the impression that Christina had shed a few pounds, as her suit was rather loose around the hips. Was it grief that was eating away at her?

They shook hands, and Christina left the office.

"So what now?" Elin asked peevishly.

"Well, we move on to the next case," said Lars. "You know, this investigation of the two Eriksson employees. Don't take it so hard. You can't expect every single case to be solved. It seems to me that we did pretty well, all things considered. And you played an instrumental role in helping us get as far as we did."

Elin gathered her stack of papers together and looked at him skeptically. "You mean like a marathon runner who quits after eight miles and whose trainer says, 'Congratulations for getting this far, you did a great job.'?"

Lars had to laugh in spite of himself. "Oh, come on, this has nothing to do with our endurance or how we handled the case. We didn't have enough to work with to solve the case. It's as simple as that."

Elin shook her head. "I don't know. Somehow I have the feeling that we overlooked something. If only I knew what it was."

"Yeah, but you said that last week too, and I gave you three days to come up with something. There's nothing to be found, take my word for it."

"I'm not so sure."

"In any case, it's over and done with now. Elin, I beseech you, just let it go, put it behind you. We're not being paid any more, so we're going to cease all work on this case. You do get that, don't you?"

Elin turned on her heels and left the room. "Yeah, yeah, yeah," was all that she said as she left. He sympathized with her frustration, but there was nothing he could do about it. And anyway, he had a completely different problem on his hands that made this situation with Elin pale in comparison. Lisa hadn't calmed down, and instead of making up, they'd had yet another argument over the weekend. She was apparently going to divorce him if he didn't promise to quit his job. Lars couldn't understand why she insisted on putting so much pressure on him. Plus, he really liked his job – and anyway what else was he supposed to do? Get a job as a security guard? He couldn't imagine anything more monotonous, plus security guards often have to work nights – he'd go batshit crazy if he had to do that, he was sure of it. But he didn't want to get divorced either. So they'd have to reach some kind of compromise. He needed to talk this through with someone, and he'd already thought about inviting Elin out for a beer. But maybe she was too young to give him advice – plus she seemed far too frustrated with the outcome of the case to even have such a conversation with him. He of course had a few buddies, but they knew Lisa and he wasn't sure that they'd side with him. He definitely didn't want to see his relationship with Lisa become fodder for gossip among their friends and acquaintances. Should he perhaps give Martin a call? They'd always gotten along well, and Lars had given him some advice when he got interested in Liv. Lars felt that Martin would be a good listener and would maybe even give him some sound advice. And as he lived in Berlin, there was little chance that anyone who lived around here would be gossiping about the situation. Yeah, that was a good idea. He decided to give it a try – preferably before Martin left his law office for the day.

26

Maja inserted the key in the lock of her apartment door and walked in. Elin checked the time; it was just a little before 8.30.

"Hi Maja."

The response was a barely audible "*Hej.*" Elin stood up and went to the hallway. Maja was standing in front of the clothes closet taking off her black high boots. Elin still had no idea what the matter was – but Maja certainly was acting strangely nowadays. Though there were times when she was almost like the "old" Maja – for example when Elin had recently come home from Göteborg.

On that occasion they'd opened a bottle of wine and had drunk the whole thing. Elin had told Maja about her day, and Maja had been interested in all of it – and afterwards they'd discussed the Natalia case at length. Then they went to bed, and though they didn't have sex, they fell asleep in each other's arms. But now Maja was back to being extremely standoffish. And this is how it was all the time now, she'd be cheerful one minute and then all withdrawn the next.

Elin went over to Maja and hugged her, and after a brief hesitation, Maja hugged her back – and even kissed her on the mouth. But she didn't look happy at all.

"Had a stressful day?"

"No, everything's fine," Maja said, avoiding Elin's glance.

Then she turned around, went into the bathroom, and closed the door behind her.

It had been this way lately every time Elin asked Maja how she was doing. And though Maja would always assure her that everything was peachy keen, she felt that something was amiss. She'd asked Maja if she was still mad at her mom, but Maja had said she wasn't.

Elin went back to the living room, where the dinner that she'd made – vegetarian lasagna with green-pepper salad – was already on the table. She'd also opened a bottle of red wine, in the hope that Maja would let herself be seduced. Elin sat down and waited. She decided that tonight she wasn't going to be all mellow but would instead try to bring things to a head. Something was eating at Maja and she intended to get to the bottom of it. If it had to do with her, then she absolutely had to find out what it was, because otherwise she couldn't do anything about it. If not, well great, but then she wanted to find out how she could help Maja – and in many cases just getting a problem out in the open was the first step toward solving it. And the fact that thus far they hadn't been able to thrash out the problem – whatever it was – was really bothering her. They were in the habit of talking about absolutely everything, and Elin couldn't understand why Maja was being so secretive now. Which would appear to indicate that the root cause of whatever was bugging Maja was Elin herself – and that worried her a lot.

When Maja finally came back into the room, her expression brightened.

"Wow, you made dinner. It smells really good."

"Yeah, I was waiting for you to come home, hungry though I was."

As Maja taught evening classes, she mostly came home around this time. Elin usually ate earlier because she was often too hungry too wait.

"Would you like some wine with that?"

Maja, who had just helped herself to some salad, looked up, arched an eyebrow and said, "Yeah sure, why not. A glass of wine won't do me any harm. Plus it'll go well with the lasagna."

Elin poured them both some wine and they began tucking into the food. She'd been intending to refrain from doing what she usually did – namely blurt out her questions – and instead give Maja time to settle in. She wanted to create a relaxed atmosphere that she could use as a springboard to a serious and substantive conversation.

So she encouraged Maja to rattle on about her classes. She almost always had funny stories about her students' antics – and tonight was no exception. During a judo class, one of her advanced students, who was always trying to get everyone to notice how adept she was, had tried to throw Maja to the mat. But the woman had seriously miscalculated, and without Maja needing to do much of anything, had herself ended up flat on her back, to her great surprise. Maja had nearly burst out laughing, and the other students had gotten a kick out of it too.

When they'd finished the lasagna, Elin placed a tray with crackers and cheese on the table, and Maja let herself be talked into a second glass of wine. Now, Elin thought, is the right moment to have *the conversation* with Maja. It had already been hard for her to wait so long, which had made her quite anxious.

Elin looked at Maja. "Tell me, babe, what's going on? You know, I can tell that something's eating you."

Maja stared into her wine goblet. "What do you mean? Everything's fine, really."

Maja made as if to rise from the table, but Elin laid her hand on her arm to keep her from standing up.

"Come on, Maja. I'm not blind. It's been obvious for weeks now that something's up with you. At first I chalked it up to the disastrous dinner with my parents, but you've said repeatedly that you're over it. So then, what's the matter? Is it something to do with me? Or have you perhaps met someone else?"

Maja flinched, as if she'd been stung by a wasp. "No, it's nothing like that. Oh lord, Elin, I'm so sorry, I didn't want you to get that impression. Really, it's got absolutely nothing to do with you."

This was a great weight off Elin's shoulders – whatever it was couldn't be as bad as she'd feared. Maja stood up and gave her a big hug.

"Really and truly, that wasn't my intention at all. I was sure I could get through this without you noticing anything."

"Yeah, but have you perhaps forgotten that your girlfriend's a detective? Of course I noticed."

Elin pushed Maja back a bit so that she could see her facial expression.

"But then, what's going on? You really can tell me."

Maja nodded, and swallowed. Whatever it was, she was evidently having difficulty talking about it. But what could it be? Every conceivable scenario went racing through Elin's mind. She knew that Maja had gone to the gynecologist a few weeks ago for her regular checkup – but she hadn't asked Maja about it, and had simply assumed that everything was fine, as always; for after all Maja was still in her early thirties. So had the doctor maybe found something? She felt chills go down her spine.

"Are you ill? Is that it?"

Maja shook her head. "No, I'm in perfect health. Where'd you get that idea?"

"Well dammit, you're not telling me anything, so I'm reduced to guessing." Elin was beginning to feel that Maja's behavior was over the top. Why didn't she just come out with it?

Maja swallowed again, and finally blurted out, "It's got to do with my job."

So that was it. But that couldn't be all that bad, could it? There was always a solution in such situations. So why was she making such a federal case out of it?

"Okay, why don't we sit back down, you have a big gulp of wine, and then tell me everything from the beginning. I want to hear every single detail. 'Cause you know, I love you, babe."

Maja's shoulders slumped, but she nodded and sat down. Once she had gamely had a gulp of wine, she finally began talking.

"It seems like I'm about to be kicked out of my studio. I talked to my boss and she gave me an ultimatum. I haven't found a new place yet, but I don't want to move too far away because then I'll lose all my clients. I just don't know what to do."

Elin still had no idea why Maja had been so secretive about this, but she sensed this wasn't the opportune moment to broach the subject. Right now, she just wanted to hear the whole story.

"I see. Well then, what happened between you?"

"It was my fault. I offended her."

Now that Maja had gotten started, the words just came tumbling out of her – so much so that Elin had difficulty understanding what had actually happened. Apparently, it had started with little teasing remarks between Maja and Brigitta, who was the owner of the studio. At first Maja had meant these comments as jokes, but they soon took on a more serious cast – and they weren't funny any more. For example, Brigitta had blamed Maja for the flood at the studio, because she'd failed to notice that the radiator was dripping in her classroom. And then she'd had the nerve to ask Maja, with a straight face, to go halves on the deductible. For Maja, this had been the last straw and she'd called Brigitta a "menopausal bitch." This latter insult was undoubtedly what had caused the conflict to escalate – because Brigitta, who was pushing fifty, was at an age where menopause might well have set in – but she went to great pains to create the very opposite impression. But in any case, Brigitta had countered by calling Maja a "lesbian slut" and both women had gone their separate ways feeling very aggrieved. And as the argument had occurred in the presence of a number of colleagues, it was impossible to make like nothing had happened. Maja had tried to apologize, since she'd been the one to hurl the first insult – but Brigitta had rebuffed her. So her boss had informed her that November would be her last month in the studio.

Maja had looked at some other spaces since then, but either there was nothing available, or the approach wasn't to her liking, or the place was too far away. So she was starting to panic, as time was running out.

"What do your colleagues think about all this?" Elin asked.

"Well, they tell me in private that I'm in the right, but none of them are willing to take my side, because they're afraid they'll be kicked out too." Maja looked at Elin despairingly.

"But Maja, would it really be that bad if you took a month or two off? Something's bound to open up soon."

"Yes, but I need the money. As you know, I used up all my savings paying off the mortgage on the condo."

"Yeah, I know, but we can certainly live on my money for a while, 'cause after all I earn a pretty good salary."

"Yes, but I don't want to be a financial burden for you."

"Oh come on. If you don't feel good about it, then you can pay me back later. But after all, we're life partners aren't we? It's almost like we're married."

Maja nodded.

"So there's nothing wrong with me helping out in an emergency situation like this. And anyway the very same thing could easily happen to me. Just think about the situation I was in last summer. Tobias was on the verge of firing me. I was just lucky that Lars went to bat for me, because otherwise last June I would have been in the same pickle that you're in now. And for sure you would have helped me out, right?"

"Yeah, you're right," Maja said sheepishly.

"We'll figure it out, I guarantee. If all else fails, you can just open your own studio."

"Yes, but I'd need money for that too," Maja said, looking at her almost defiantly.

"Yeah, and so what? I have some savings, your parents will pitch in for sure, and you can always get a bank loan – after all, banks want to earn interest."

"Well, maybe. But for the moment, I'm going to keep looking. Maybe I'll find something after all."

"Now that's more like it." Elin took a deep breath. But now she simply had to ask Maja this, even though doing so might get her hackles up: "But really, Maja, what kept you from talking to me about this in the first place? I could have helped you out much sooner – looking around for studios and keeping my ear to the ground about possible vacancies. But what do you do instead? Fret the live-long day and fill me with anxiety every time I lay eyes on you, 'cause I have no idea what's up with you. Why the hell didn't you say anything?"

"Yeah, you're right, I shouldn't have done that. But you had too much else on your plate. The tough child molestation case this past summer, and then taking care of Ebba, which is also a psychological strain. And then you were upset about the verdict. And then there was the Patrik case, which preoccupied you so much but ended up leaving you feel frustrated. And to top it all off, the whole thing with your mom, which hit you really hard and for which I'm partly to blame. If I hadn't pressured you to come out to your parents, this problem never would have arisen. Therefore, I don't feel that I have the right to lay my own shit on you."

Elin stared at her. She had to admit that Maja wasn't exaggerating and that all these things had in fact been weighing on her. She often discussed these matters with Maja, who was an unfailingly good listener and was understanding and always tried to lift her spirits. But it was now dawning on her that she'd been so preoccupied with her own troubles that she had failed to notice what Maja was going through – and Maja hadn't wanted to make Elin's burden even heavier than it already was. Elin lowered her head. Shit, she'd really screwed up this time.

"I'm so sorry. I never wanted you to feel that I was only capable of dealing with my own problems."

"But Elin, you can't do anything about this, because none of your problems are your own fault. You just had too much on your plate, that's all. Which is why I wanted to spare you all this crap. And as my relationship with Brigitta deteriorated, the right moment to talk to you simply came and went, and I felt guilty about not talking to you about it. See what I mean? I'd been hoping to find a new studio quickly, and then I would have come to you and would have told you the whole dumb story in one fell swoop and would have explained how everything had worked out okay in the end. And then that wouldn't have been an additional burden on you. I meant well...you know...the best laid plans of mice and men and all that. And now I guess you're mad at me."

"No, not at all. I'm angry at myself. I want things to go well for you. Plus you always help me with my problems. So I want you to always feel that you can confide in me, no matter what I happen to be going through. I don't want to be shielded from the bad stuff – after all I'm your girlfriend, not your baby sister."

"God, you're such a sweetheart. You're so cute when you're mad."

Maja stood up, put her arms around Elin, kissed her and held her tight. Elin felt as if a huge burden had been lifted from her shoulders. Maja wasn't angry at her and her problems would, and could, be dealt with. Plus, she was sure that this discussion had done them both a world of good. Because now, Elin would be more aware of what was going on with Maja and would never again fail to notice that something must be bothering her. She wanted to be sure that Maja never again felt that she couldn't confide in her and tell her what was bothering her.

But for now, she intended to bask in the glow of their reconciliation. Maja caressed her in a place that provoked completely different feelings in her. She sensed that they'd need to repair to the bedroom real soon – but not to sleep.

27

She leaped off the tram. Another day at work done with, thank god. Though the sun had set, here on Nagy Lajos király útja *everything was lit up like a Christmas tree and the street was lined with stores. It was different when she walked down the side streets – but she'd only been afraid at the beginning, and now she felt safe.*

Natalia had adjusted well to life in Budapest and had even learned some Hungarian, which wasn't easy as it was a difficult language. She felt better than she'd felt since her Babushka had passed away. She was also showing now, but that didn't bother her a bit. Plus, Lyudmila had already started preparing for the final weeks of Natalia's pregnancy and for after the baby arrived. She sensed that Lyudmila was also happy about the impending birth of a baby. Natalia found herself thinking about Patrik quite often, and time and again castigated herself for not having had the courage to run away with him. She missed him terribly. But she had to let go of these regrets and turn her thoughts to the future. She would try to make up for what she had done to Patrik with this child, the fruit of their love. For this, she was prepared to do everything within her power.

She had arrived at the building and was on the staircase. She paused for a moment on the second-floor landing to take stock of the situation. She heard loud voices that appeared to be coming from above her. She looked up to where the apartment was. Was Lyudmila having an argument with Sándor? Should she perhaps come back later? She went up to the third floor and listened at the door. She heard Russian being spoken. But wait, it wasn't just Russian, it sounded like Stanislov's voice. She froze. Had he tracked her down? Her first impulse was to turn around and get the hell out of there as fast as she could. But then she heard what sounded like a slap, and Lyudmila screaming. No, she couldn't abandon Lyudmila to her fate. But on the other hand, she was powerless to stop Stanislov. She needed to get help, and she prayed that Sándor and Gábor were home. She climbed the stairs to the fifth floor, as quickly and quietly as she could. She could see through the opaque class on the apartment door that the lights were on – a good sign. She rang the doorbell. She heard steps and breathed a sigh of relief. Gábor opened the door.

"Szia Natalia. What's up?" he said, looking at her in amazement.

"I...I...Is Sándor home? Lyudmila needs your help," she said – though she was so upset, and out of breath from climbing the stairs, that she could hardly speak.

"How come? What's wrong?"

"Come quickly. My Russian ex is downstairs and he's beating her up."

"What the hell...? That's horrible," Gábor said, turning around and shouting into the apartment. "Sándor!"

Sándor peeked out from behind a door, and Gábor said something to him in Hungarian. He then ran over to the door.

Natalia could see that both men fully intended to go downstairs. "He's dangerous," she said.

Sándor paused and turned toward her. "Is he armed?"

"I don't know, I didn't go into the apartment, I just recognized his voice."

Sándor ran back into the apartment and came back a moment later with a baseball bat in each hand and handed one to Gábor. The two men then dashed down the stairs, and Natalia sat down on the top-floor landing. She didn't dare follow them downstairs. Instead, she held her face in her hands and listened to the sounds coming from below. The key turned in the lock, the door opened, she heard loud voices. Then there was silence. What was happening? Now she could hear people moving around in the stairwell.

"You never come back!" *she heard Sándor shout. Someone ran down the stairs. Had they thrown Stanislov out? Now someone was coming up the stairs; paralyzed, her gaze fixed on the landing, she held her breath. It was Gábor, still holding the baseball bat. She exhaled with relief.*

"Come on," he said, gesturing to her to come down.

She stood up. "Is he gone?"

Gábor nodded and went back downstairs, with Natalia following behind hesitantly, taking the steps very slowly. Gábor was waiting at the door to Lyudmila's apartment and looked at her.

"What happened?" she asked.

Come on in," Gábor said, pointing to the door. She went in, then down the hallway to the living room, from which she could hear voices. Lyudmila was sitting on the couch, and Sándor had his arm around her; his baseball bat was on the floor. Lyudmila was sobbing, tears streaming down her cheeks. Natalia rushed over to her.

"What did he do to you? God, I'm so sorry, it's all my fault."

Lyudmila looked at her with moist eyes, her face smeared with mascara. "That asshole beat me. But I didn't say anything."

"What did he want?" Natalia asked, though she was pretty sure what the answer would be.

"He wanted to know your whereabouts."

Natalia shook her head. "I don't understand how he could have found me. I bought a new SIM card, and a new phone."

"He hacked your Facebook account."

"That fucker!" Natalia could hardly believe her ears. "Did he tell you that?"

"He sure did," Lyudmila said, nodding.

Natalia sank into an armchair. She'd intentionally used an alias for her Facebook account – Babushka's Sweetheart, she'd called it. Stanislov must have found out about this name while they were living together.

"I'll delete the whole account immediately."

"Well it's too late for that, he's already been here," Sándor said.

Natalia grimaced. "I'm so sorry. Really and truly."

"We already know that," Lyudmila said peremptorily. "I imagine you're the last person who wanted him to be here."

"But now we've got to figure out what to do next," Sándor interjected.

Natalia nodded in agreement. "I'll get the hell out of Dodge." She didn't at all relish the prospect of being on the run yet again – and she'd been feeling so safe here.

"No, there's no need to pack your bags just yet, we'll find a solution," Lyudmila said.

Sándor looked at her skeptically. "I think we need to talk this over. We can't run the risk of something like this happening again. Maybe the next time he'll show up with a buddy or two and give you a really good beating."

"Well one thing's for sure, I can't stay here." Natalia was dead serious. "Either he'll find me, or he'll let loose on you. We simply can't take that risk. You don't know what he's like. He's capable of anything."

Lyudmila stood up. "Well, right now I'm going to go into the bathroom and assess the damage – and repair it as best I can."

As Natalia watched Lyudmila leave the room, she realized that this girl was not easily intimidated. She placed a hand on the slight swelling in her abdomen. God knows what would have happened if she'd fallen into Stanislov's clutches. Wasn't there anyplace where she would be safe from him? He was ruining everything, yet again.

DECEMBER 2016

28

Lars was sitting in his car watching the building across the street – its front door, to be specific. This was yet another one of those monotonous surveillance sessions during which little or nothing actually happens, and that are unlikely to yield anything of interest. The client, a company, suspected a woman in its employ of using her working hours to take care of personal matters – or at least that was the official version. Lars presumed, though, that the company was just looking for an excuse to fire her.

He'd been sitting out here since 9 a.m., and in the two ensuing hours nothing at all had happened. But that could potentially change now that lunchtime was approaching. Perhaps the lady would go on an errand that would extend past her allotted lunch break, and that would give her employer at least some evidence of misconduct.

He'd used the time he'd spent sitting in his Volvo twiddling his thumbs to reflect on something that was preoccupying him – namely the Lisa situation. Lars had phoned Martin ten days ago to ask him if he'd be willing to help him with a personal problem. Martin had immediately said yes and had listened attentively to what Lars had to say. In telling Martin about the ringer he was being put through with Lisa, Lars had been totally open, for after all he had nothing to be embarrassed about – apart perhaps from Lisa's irrational behavior. They'd discussed the matter for quite a while, during which Martin had given Lars some genuinely sound advice.

Most of the cases that Martin's firm handled were settled out of court. Oftentimes, they involved situations where the positions of both sides had become so entrenched that any kind of dialogue was simply out of the question. In such cases, Martin would get the parties to stop trying to persuade their adversary to see things their way, so as to allow time for the parties to reconsider their positions. Plus, a deadline would be set by which the parties were required to come up with a compromise solution. Of course, both parties would then come up with self-serving proposals. But that didn't really matter, because what actually allowed the stalemate to be broken was that both parties were forced to review the facts of the case – which more often than not paved the way for reaching a settlement.

Martin's advice was rooted in this very principle – namely agreeing with Lisa on a deadline by which the parties would have to come up with a compromise solution and would then discuss it with each other or possibly with an outside party, who would act as a kind of referee or mediator. For this role, Martin had proposed a marriage counselor – but that wasn't a deal-breaker and could be done at a later stage. Martin had proposed a three-week hiatus, which would give Lars a respite and would give Lisa time to see reason – and would hopefully allow for negotiations that centered mainly on substance, not emotions. For after all, Lisa could hardly expect Lars to just abandon a career that he found quite satisfying and magically pull another one out of a hat. The main advantage of such an arrangement would be a genuine cease fire during the hiatus – that is, no discussions or arguments about the contentious issues, concerning which both Lars and Lisa would reflect.

Lars had also thought that last weekend would have been an opportune moment to talk to Lisa, as both kids were away, and Lisa appeared to be in a rational frame of mind. So he'd told her, as gingerly as he knew how, that he very much wanted to find a solution that was good for all concerned – and then proposed the idea of a hiatus. Lisa had been skeptical at first, saying that she already had a solution and didn't need to mull things over any further. But Lars had appealed to her sense of fair play and had beseeched her to give him time to reflect on her demands and come up with proposals. She'd finally agreed to this and they had made January 15 the date by which they would reflect on their respective positions. This relatively lengthy hiatus had a positive side effect, in that it ensured that family peace would reign during the Christmas holidays – which would be beneficial for all of them, the kids in particular.

Once they'd reached an agreement on this, Lisa was like a different person, in that she went along with their pact not to bring up the subject of Lars's job – and thus there were no arguments. The atmosphere at home was much more pleasant, and even the kids felt the difference as they'd of course noticed that as a rule, peace and harmony did not exactly reign in their home.

Lars was well aware that the can of contention had merely been kicked down the road. If, by the appointed deadline, he didn't come up with a good – and above all feasible proposal – then Lisa's nagging would probably start all over again. And Lisa would be unlikely to agree to a second hiatus.

And there lay the crux of the problem: Lars wasn't even a smidgen closer to coming up with a solution – despite the fact that he'd carefully considered how he could alter his position, but he kept going around in circles. He had never been able to imagine working as a security guard, and the only other kind of job he was qualified for was being a cop. The police were in fact desperately looking for personnel and were only too pleased to have ex cops rejoin the force. The problem with this solution was that he wouldn't be getting his old job back, which he'd really enjoyed, as it had involved active work outside the office. He'd likely not be allowed to take up such a position owing to his leg injury – plus Lisa felt that this solution would leave her and the kids worse off. So that left a police desk job. He'd already done a stint in that capacity and hadn't liked it a bit. Plus taking a job as a cop would involve a considerable cut in salary relative to what he was earning working for Tobias – and that prospect didn't appeal to him at all, and Lisa would also probably thumb her nose at it.

So that left only one option, namely making his work safer. This in turn meant working as a security guard or at a desk job, the option he found most distasteful of all. And yet, it was the aspect of his work that was dearest to his heart that Lisa found most objectionable – the part where he had to use his instincts, when things really happened, and he could really help someone, as had occurred in the previous case with Elin. It was basically a vicious circle. Lisa simply couldn't accept what he really wanted, and the very thing he hated she found awesome. There was no room for compromise.

Lars suddenly noticed that the woman he'd been watching out for was just leaving the building, apparently by herself – and was easy to spot, as she was wearing a bright red parka. Lars immediately took a picture of her; the date and time were automatically added. The woman turned right toward the employee parking lot and headed toward a, likewise red, Toyota Prius that was hooked up to a charging station. She got into the car, after disconnecting the charging cable. Lars started his Volvo, put it into gear, and followed the woman's vehicle at a safe distance. The company was located in Bromma and the woman headed east, toward Solna, where she turned into the parking lot of a popular mall called Solna Centrum. Lars parked there too and walked quickly so that he wouldn't lose sight of the woman. He came up close behind her at the revolving door and followed her inside, the red parka like a lantern before him. She entered the foodmarket, where she met up with a man, apparently for lunch. As far as Lars could tell, they were having Italian food. Lars bought himself a sandwich, still keeping his eye on the subject and her companion, and then sat down at a small table a bit further away, from which he could continue surveilling the red parka. At first nothing special happened – it was just two acquaintances having lunch together.

He found himself thinking, once again, about his problem with Lisa. He failed to understand why she was so intractable. She was in such a rage all the time that it was impossible to even talk to her – and that wasn't even like her. Sure, they'd had their disagreements, but they'd always been able to at least talk about things. Actually, when he stopped to think about it, it was he, not she, who usually gave in. For instance, when they were looking to buy a house, he would have preferred one in the south as he would have had less of a commute. But they'd ended up living in the northwest, which was Lisa's stomping ground. And when they'd been looking at schools for Stina, Lisa's preference had also prevailed. It wasn't like he had a problem with this decision – but if he'd had his druthers, he would have opted for a different school. Did he give in too often? Had Lisa become too used to getting her own way all the time?

He understood her concern about his being away from home working on cases that put him in jeopardy. But now she was making a federal case out of the fact that Elin was his partner. Should he perhaps let Elin go just because his wife went ballistic every time he so much as mentioned her name? And anyway, only Tobias could fire her – plus as far as Lars was concerned, she was a brilliant detective. She had good instincts, good ideas, outstanding computer expertise, and loads of energy. When she'd first started out, she had too much of a tendency to act on her own; but he hoped that they'd gotten past this – she was now a much better partner than she'd been before. Sure, she still had a lot to learn, but she was a quick study. Plus, more often than not she was in an upbeat mood – and even if some of the stupid sayings she came out with got on his nerves, her sunny disposition was contagious. In other words, he was loathe to do without her.

So, he asked himself, is there a way out of this pickle? He knew one thing for sure – he didn't want to be alone with Lisa during this upcoming post-hiatus discussion. Even if the next few weeks might help her to calm down and see things more rationally, he doubted that she'd suddenly become Miss Ready to Compromise. This was going to become a particularly knotty problem if he couldn't come up with a different solution. He for sure didn't want to embark on a different career. The only change he was prepared to make was to try to be more open with Lisa – which meant letting her know what types of cases he was investigating, and his whereabouts during these times. The problem was, though, that in her current frame of mind, Lisa wouldn't regard this as a solution – and he strongly doubted that this was going to change by the time January rolled around. So he needed someone who'd act as a mediator, who'd help smooth things out during the meeting and who'd keep the discussion on track. If only Lisa could put herself in his shoes. At the moment, the only people she was talking to about her marriage were her mother and her girlfriends – who were apparently taking her side, rather than acting as devil's advocate. So he decided to look for a good marriage counselor, in the hope that Lisa would agree to allow such a person to act as mediator.

It was a tricky situation, one that he didn't like one bit. But he didn't want to lose Lisa, and he was prepared to go to great lengths to save his marriage. In other words do a lot – but still, there were limits. Because after all she had married a cop and she couldn't very well expect him to morph into a bookkeeper at a moment's notice.

Lars checked his watch. It had been 40 minutes since the woman had emerged from her office, and even if she left the restaurant right now, she wouldn't be able to get back to her office by the end of her 45 minute lunch hour. And at the moment she didn't look like she was going anywhere, as she and her companion were engaged in an animated discussion as they sipped their coffee. For the woman's employer, this would probably count as a strike against her. Not that Lars enjoyed getting other people into trouble, particularly for such trivial infractions. He'd always disliked this – alas unavoidable – aspect of sleuthing. But as it was totally safe, Lisa was all for it.

29

She was on the Metro on her way to Budapest's Nyugati Pályaudvar *train station. She'd been thinking long and hard about what she should do. She'd been staying in Csaba's hotel for the past two weeks and he'd often given her a ride to the restaurant in his BMW X5 – which was very convenient for her. But the Metro was also really easy. She only had to change once, at* Deák Ferenc tér; *the trip didn't take much longer than if she was driven – and they invariably ended up struck in traffic.*

Lyudmila had convinced Csaba to let her stay in the hotel for a pittance, because Lyudmila didn't want Natalia to leave Budapest – and Natalia had agreed to this arrangement. But they had to be extremely careful when they met up, and despite all their precautions Natalia was worried the whole time that Stanislov was going to suddenly materialize. And he had in fact turned up again, but at Lyudmila's building, not Natalia's hotel. He hadn't threatened her that time, but she'd spotted him more than once hanging around in front of her building, and he'd also followed her on several occasions. This evidently didn't faze Lyudmila a bit, and she enjoyed leading Stanislov on wild goose chases – though Natalia found these incidents disquieting. She knew that Stanislov would never give up, and that he wouldn't be content with just watching for very long. It was only a matter of time before he found out about Lyudmila's connection with Csaba – which would lead him to the restaurant and then her hotel. And where was she supposed to go if they crossed paths again? She wasn't so sure that she'd be able to escape his clutches like the last time.

So she realized that she'd simply have to get out of Budapest. But where could she go? She was out of options. If she went back to Russia, it would be even easier for Stanislov to track her down – and he'd already proved that he could do so in Sweden. Her pregnancy was slowly but surely making her situation even more difficult. Sure, she could get by on Patrik's money for a while longer, but it wouldn't last forever, and once she had her baby, she didn't want the little tyke to lack for anything, and she had no idea how she was going to manage that. Things had gone super well here in Budapest thanks to Lyudmila's help, but all that was over now. Natalia was afraid that Stanislov would corner Lyudmila – someplace where no one could come to her aid – and get her to tell him where Natalia was. Such a situation could end very badly for Lyudmila, and she'd probably end up disclosing Natalia's whereabouts. So the best course was to disappear without telling Lyudmila where she was going.

In other words, she'd given a lot of thought as to what she should do. She'd realized that there was only one option, and that her chances of coming out of this unscathed were slim. And above all, she needed to consider the baby she was carrying. She absolutely did not want its childhood to be anything like hers had been, and what befell her was secondary. So she at least wanted to give it a try.

As the Metro was pulling into the stop for the train station, Natalia stood up, held onto a strap as the subway train came to a stop, and exited the car along with a dozen other passengers. She got on the long up escalator. She knew that this train station had payphones, which was a rarity nowadays as everyone had a cellphone. Although a phone call from a payphone could be traced to Budapest, and even the number was transmitted so that someone could call back if they wished to, the payphone number would lead to the train station, not her. In light of her experience with the cellphone that Stanislov had evidently been able to localize in Göteborg, she'd decided to foreswear cellphones, even though she could have purchased a burner phone. And maybe she would in fact buy one, depending on how this call went. If she was going to make any more phone calls, she needed to find a more convenient solution than having to go all the way to this train station.

When she arrived at the top, she turned right into a corridor and saw three blue phones hanging on the wall, with instruction signs above them. Natalia had purchased a phone card – the number she'd found online. Her heart was pounding as she dialed the number. So much depended on this call. She needed to express herself well – but feared that she'd be too frightened to say anything at all.

After three rings, someone picked up and said, "Hello?"

Natalia swallowed. She tried to say something, but the words wouldn't come. She hung up. She needed to breathe deeply. Should she really do this? She began to feel overcome with doubt.

She'd thought about this long and hard, and she just had to at least give it the old college try. She took a few large gulps from a bottle of water she had with her.

She then pressed the redial button. Someone picked up after the first ring. "Who's this?" a woman asked.

"Hi, my name's Natalia..." Natalia finally managed to say.

Silence on the other end. Then Natalia began talking...and talking.

30

Liv cleared the table and the kids loaded the dishwasher. Martin was watching the news on TV.

"Can we go upstairs?" Hampus asked.

Liv looked around. The dishes had been taken care of, and there was nothing on the table but an Advent wreath, in the middle. She preferred wiping down the table herself; the kids always made such a mess of it anyway.

"Okay, put the bread in the bread box – and Saga take your school bag upstairs with you, I don't want you leaving it here in the kitchen. Apart from that, you're done."

After doing what their mother had asked of them, the two children scampered upstairs. Liv was wiping down the table with a damp cloth, when the land phone rang.

She set the cloth down on the sink, dried her hands, and picked up the receiver.

"Liv Ulldahl," she said.

"Hi, Liv, it's Christina."

"Hi there. How are you doing?" Liv was aware of what Lars and Elin had discovered during the second phase of their investigation, as Christina had told her all about it over the phone two weeks previously. Had something new come to light, perhaps? But this was unlikely, as Christina had told her that Lars and Elin had closed the case.

"Well okay, I guess, but I'm kind of discombobulated at the moment."

"Because of stress at your office?"

"No, actually it's because of Patrik."

"How come? Has anything new come to light? I thought that Lars and Elin had closed the case."

"Right, it's not from them. I... Liv, can you keep a secret?"

"Absolutely." What's up? she wondered. This sounded intriguing.

"Great. Well, guess what – that woman called me up."

"Which woman?"

"That Natalia person – the one Patrik had a fling with."

"No way! Why on earth did she call you? Have you got a new lead?"

"Don't need one. She wants to come visit me."

Liv was dumbfounded. Who would do such a bizarre thing? First the woman vanishes without a trace, and then decides to contact Christina just like that? "Okay, so tell me. What exactly does she want?"

"The whole situation's pretty complicated. But I think she's telling the truth. The problem is, though, that she's being stalked by Patrik's murderer. Yes, he was murdered, his death was no accident. I'd suspected this all along, and now this woman has confirmed my suspicions. Isn't that simply awful? And apparently Patrik wasn't the only victim. She had a scam going with her partner, where she'd flirt with men and milk them for as much money as she could, and then her partner would off them."

"That's horrible. And she just came out and told you all that?"

"Yeah, she said she fell for Patrik and didn't want to see him killed. She's sorry for what she's done and wants to change her life."

"And you're supposed to help her do this, is that it? Sorry, I don't get it. Isn't that asking a bit too much?"

"Yes, and that's not all." Christina fell silent for a moment, and Liv could hear her breathing. "The lady's pregnant," Christina said. "With Patrik's child."

"Oh god no!" Liv said, sitting down on the chair next to her. This was becoming crazier by the second.

"Yeah, she's 100 percent sure it's his child. And now she wants to have the child and give it a good start in life."

Liv swallowed. "And I suppose you're the good start? Now don't tell me you plan to go along with this."

"Well I've given it a lot of thought. She called me yesterday afternoon, and I hardly got any sleep last night. At first I thought to myself, why should I concern myself with her problems? But then I thought, well, it is Patrik's child – which would mean I'd at least have something of his. And perhaps that would give me a fresh perspective. You know, after Patrik passed away…"

Liv could hear Christina sobbing. "Yes, I can see this must be very hard for you. You're on your own all of a sudden, and I know that you miss Patrik, despite what he did. But what does this woman want from you? Money?"

Christina blew her nose. "No, she wants to give me the child. She wants me to adopt it and raise it."

Liv was stupefied. Was this Natalia completely insane? First she steals Christina's husband and has an affair with him. And as if that weren't enough, in the final analysis his death was her fault; and now she wants to pawn off her kid on Christina. "Christina, you can't seriously be thinking of going through with this! How can this woman possibly expect you to do anything for her?"

"She's desperate. She ran away from her boyfriend, but this guy keeps tracking her down. He just did it again – found her in Budapest, where she apparently has a friend. She's afraid that he'll kill her, and the baby she's carrying. She wants to at least save the child."

"What did you tell her? You didn't agree to anything, did you?"

"No, and she wasn't expecting me to either, at least not right away. I just said I'd think it over. She's going to call back."

"So are you going to do as she asks? Is that what you've decided?"

"Yes," Christina said hesitantly. "I simply cannot expose Patrik's child to this kind of danger. And even if the two of them managed to escape this monster's clutches, what kind of upbringing would this kid have? Constantly on the run. With a single working mother. Without the benefit of kindergarten and a good education. I'm sorry, but I can't let that happen."

"I hope you know what you're about to saddle yourself with. After all, you're single too, and you have a career – not to mention the emotional strain that bringing up this child would entail."

"Yeah, but I live in Sweden – a welfare state par excellence. I get paid maternity leave, and there are kindergartens here that will look after the kid all day. And if need be, I can take time off from work; I've saved enough money to finance that."

"Well I can see that you've made up your mind." Liv still had her doubts.

"Maybe it's hard for you to understand where I'm coming from, Liv. And sure, the whole situation's surreal – but this is probably my last chance to have a kid. Plus, this might give my life new meaning. Maybe it'll help me put this whole thing behind me and let go of Patrik for good."

"Don't you think you're being a bit naive? Because the little tyke might constantly remind you of these difficulties and might prevent you from putting them behind you."

"Could be. But I don't think so. I think having Patrik's child in my life will help me. You've got two kids, Liv, and you probably know better than I do how a child totally changes your life and how much love you get in return."

Liv had to admit the truth of this. But there was no getting around the fact that it was different with a child you've given birth to. An adopted child, even one fathered by an ex, wouldn't be at all the same thing. But it seemed like she wasn't going to be able to talk Christina down from this particular ledge.

"Well, yes, I suppose you're right. So what now?"

"Thanks for being so understanding, Liv. Natalia has to stay somewhere. Ideally, I'd like to have her stay here, but I'm afraid that her ex might manage to find her here too. We need safe haven that has no connection to Natalia's past – or me for that matter."

Was Christina perhaps thinking of Liv's and Martin's apartment in Berlin? Liv girded herself for this eventuality – which there was no way she was going to allow to happen.

"So I wanted to ask you something," Christina said. "Don't you own a cabin in Småland? Could I rent it from you, for the duration of Natalia's pregnancy? Is the place winterized?"

Liv breathed a sigh of relief. This was quite feasible. She'd inherited the cabin from her grandmother, and it was vacant pretty much all the time. So it wasn't such a bad idea if someone took care of it for a time. Plus, she always felt guilty about neglecting it. During their vacation in Stockholm they hadn't even managed to take the trip up there. It was just too far away, more than a four hour drive from Stockholm. Though the distance wasn't really the problem: she dreaded the prospect of setting foot in the cabin. And yet, she was loathe to part with it, as she had such fond memories of the many wonderful summers she'd spent there with her grandmother. Even though the events of the previous year had catastrophically clouded this picture – it was in this very cabin that Liv had been assaulted and kidnapped. She definitely had no intention of ever going up there alone.

"Would that work for you? If not, I can of course rent a different cabin. So feel free to say no."

"Yes, I think that would be okay. The cabin is winterized, and it even has central heating and a fireplace. It'll be warm and cozy in there."

"That would be awesome. Do you need to think it over some more?"

"I need to talk to Martin about it, but I think it'll be fine."

"Thanks, Liv. But please, don't say a word to anyone – and make sure Martin doesn't either."

"Of course," Liv said. "How about Lars and Elin? Wouldn't it be wise to bring them in? I'm sure they'd be more than willing to have a little chat with this Natalia person. And I'll bet you anything that, Lars, being an ex-cop, would be able to get something out of her."

“No, I think it’d be better if she comes here first and I can meet with her. Because I want to make sure her pregnancy goes off without a hitch. That’s my main concern right now. Which is why everything has to be kept under wraps for the moment. I want to, as much as possible, minimize the risk that this killer might get wind of our plans.”

“I see. I sure hope you’re doing the right thing. You’re embarking on what sounds like quite an adventure.”

“Yes, I know. I really appreciate your being so honest with me. It’s done me a world of good talking to you about this.”

They said goodbye to each other. Liv remained seated for a moment. What a weird situation! She was eager to find out what Martin would say about it. He’d probably show Christina far less understanding than she had.

She got up and went into the living room; the news was almost over; the weather report was on. Rain for the next few days, typical December weather in Berlin.

Martin looked over at her. “Who was that, honey?”

“It was Christina. And

you’ll never believe what she told me.”

31

Christina was waiting at the Trelleborg ferry port, so early in the morning that it was pitch dark – though the landing pier was lit up like a Christmas tree. She was waiting for Natalia, who was supposed to be arriving on the next ferry from Rostock, Germany. In the two phone calls they'd had before her arrival, Christina had had the impression that they both had similar concerns. Natalia had made it clear that if this whole thing was a trap, she'd refuse to give her child up for adoption and would make sure that Christina never laid eyes on it. And though Christina had no intention of involving the police, Martin had told Liv that he was concerned that the reverse might be the case – namely that Natalia might be setting a trap for her. Maybe it was all a pack of lies and Natalia and her cohort were just trying to milk her for even more money. Christina doubted that this was the case, but just the possibility was upsetting to her. Which is why she kept checking out the other people who were waiting for the ferry to arrive – but she couldn't really tell if any of them had bad intentions. And in any case, it seemed to her that no one was paying her particular attention. Liv had advised her against going to meet Natalia at the ferry by herself –

but then who could she have brought along? She desperately wanted to keep the whole business secret; and Liv and Martin, the only people who were in the know, hadn't been able to be with her today. Not to mention the fact that Natalia had insisted that Christina come to the ferry terminal unaccompanied, because otherwise she wouldn't be able to trust her. It was a classic catch-22 situation. Which was why she was standing her all by herself feeling downright queasy. But it wasn't the concerns Martin had expressed that were making her feel uneasy, but rather the fact that she'd now have to deal with Natalia and this totally sticky situation, the likes of which she'd never imagined she could ever find herself in. For one thing, that Patrik would ever have dreamed of leaving her for another woman. But the fact that she was about to meet his lover, who was also partly responsible for his death – and in order to figure out what would be best for Patrik's child; well that was just off the charts as far as she was concerned, and she wasn't the least surprised that Liv had her doubts. She'd had some misgivings of her own, though she hadn't admitted this to Liv – and yet she felt that she really owed it to herself, and Patrik, to forge ahead. Plus, if she turned Natalia down, she'd probably regret it till the day she died.

Natalia had told her she'd be easily recognizable as she'd be wearing a bright red cap – which Christina was now looking out for. She was angry at herself for not having asked Natalia to say exactly what kind of cap it was: a baseball cap? a pom-pom hat? or perhaps some other kind of head covering?

The passengers were now disembarking from the ferry through an illuminated and glassed-in gangway and were either carrying or wheeling their suitcases. Christina spotted a red baseball cap, which set her pulse racing, only to realize that the cap was emblazoned in white letters with the word "Berlin," and its wearer was a small, heavy-set man.

The ferry disgorged its passengers for what seemed like an eternity to Christina; but she hadn't seen anyone who could have been Natalia. She checked her watch; passengers had been disembarking from the ship for 15 minutes. Had she perhaps missed Natalia? Or had something gone wrong, and maybe Natalia wasn't on the ferry at all? She checked her phone: no messages, no missed calls. Unfortunately, Natalia had Christina's phone number, but Christina didn't have hers. During her last phone conversation with Natalia, she'd asked how she could reach her, and Natalia had said that she was going to leave both her phone and her SIM card in Budapest because she planned to buy a new prepaid phone when she arrived in Sweden. And now here she was, waiting for Natalia as planned – but there was no Natalia to be seen. The stream of passengers had petered out and there appeared to be no more of them on board; it had been at least a minute since anyone had come down the gangway. What should she do? She checked the time again. Her only option was to stand here and wait until the disembarkation was definitively over with – or maybe even until passengers began boarding for the return trip; then she'd be absolutely sure that something had gone sideways. Which would mean she'd simply have to wait until Natalia contacted her again. Or maybe just forget the whole thing. Although she didn't relish this prospect one bit, she'd spent a huge amount of time mentally debating the pros and cons, had finally come to a decision, had made all the arrangements for Natalia's stay, had driven here to meet Natalia at the ferry – and she'd even been kind of looking forward to seeing the child. Had this really all been for naught?

As she stood there feeling hopeless and with all these thoughts racing through her mind, she suddenly heard the sound of approaching footsteps that sounded like high-heeled shoes. And sure enough, someone was coming down the gangway, she could already see the person's legs. Brown high-heeled boots, and next to them a suitcase with wheels. Now a beige coat and dark brown shawl came into view, followed by a long blond mane and an elegant, light red wool cap. This must be her, Christina thought. Her heart was in her mouth. She took another look around, but she was completely alone and was relieved to see that Natalia was coming toward her without anyone in tow.

As for Natalia, she, too, gave the immediate environs the once-over, and appeared to be afraid that someone might try to do her harm. So at least they had this fear of the unknown in common. Christina took a good look at Natalia, who was indeed attractive: slender but not emaciated, as far as this was discernible under her coat. She had a pretty, small-boned face, thin with a turned-up nose, high cheekbones, full lips and large green eyes that Christina was now looking into: Natalia was standing right in front of her.

"Hi," she said, almost shyly. "Are you Christina? I'm Natalia."

Christina was overcome with emotion, she felt totally confused, and very warm and her eyes filled with tears. The tension had been too much for her, and now the moment that she'd been waiting for had arrived. Unable to say hardly anything, she looked for a hanky.

"I'm so sorry...I'm just...I also don't know...this is all too much for me." She rummaged around in her coat pockets.

Then Natalia took a step toward her, placed one hand on Christina's arm, and with the other handed her a hanky, which Christina gratefully took.

"It's okay, I understand what you're going through. I find the whole situation weird, too."

Christina blew her nose and looked into Natalia's eyes. Natalia smiled at her – a really friendly smile that made her face even prettier; a look that men would surely characterize as smoking hot.

"You okay?" Natalia asked, encouragingly, and Christina nodded. They left together, with Natalia's hand still on Christina's arm – a sensation Christina found to be very agreeable. What was this chick doing to her? She'd flashed her one itty-bitty smile, and now she felt totally comfortable with her? It began to dawn on Christina the kind of effect Natalia must have had on Patrik.

Christina showed Natalia where her car was parked, and they got in. The two women exchanged glances. Then Natalia took off her cap and shook out her blond mane.

"So tell me. Are you still willing to do what I proposed – or do you perhaps have something else in mind?" Natalia asked.

Christina searched within herself – but opposition to Natalia's plan there was none. "No, I'm good," she said. "I was having doubts – but now that I've met you in person, I'm absolutely sure that I'm doing the right thing. Even though I don't know you yet and should actually detest you with every fiber in my being."

Natalia lowered her eyes and nodded. Then she met Christina's glance, opened her large eyes wide, and flashed them at her. "That's so kind of you. I promise you that you won't regret doing this. I won't give you any trouble."

Christina placed her hand on Natalia's, which was soft and warm. Had Natalia perhaps triggered some kind of maternal instinct in her? She herself didn't understand what was going on, but it didn't matter now – because now they needed to get to Liv's cabin and then they'd have the whole day to talk.

***

Christina closed the front door and showed Natalia in. The cabin was warm and cozy – Christina had arrived last night and had slept over. Otherwise she would have had to drive all night in order to meet the ferry in Trelleborg at 5 the following morning. Also, this way she was able to get everything in readiness and switch on the heating. She'd found the key in its hiding place under a stone in the front yard, exactly where Liv had said it would be.

She noticed that Natalia was looking around. "How do you like it?"

"I love it. It's so spacious. And so well decorated." Natalia seemed to be totally taken with the place.

"So you think you'll be able to survive staying here for a while?"

"For sure. I'm going to make this space a real nest for myself."

"This cabin's pretty secluded, but I guess that's what you wanted."

"You're right – this way no one can find me."

"The town's a few miles away, but there's no bus. We can go shopping today so that you can stock up on the things you need. But if you run out of something and I'm not around, you'll have to take a taxi into town."

"No problem. I don't need much in any case." Being in such a secluded place didn't seem to faze Natalia in the least.

Christina went upstairs with Natalia and showed her the bedroom, which she'd gotten all ready for her – though she herself had slept in the other bedroom that was normally Liz's. The only appurtenance on the second floor, apart from the two bedrooms, was a bathroom. Natalia placed her suitcase on the bed and opened it.

"Is it okay if I hang my clothes in the closet?"

"Of course. This is your home now." Liv had cleared the way for Christina and Natalia to make untrammeled use of the cabin – to which end she'd hardly left any of her things behind and the closets were almost empty – and stocked the kitchen and living room with a full complement of amenities.

Once Natalia had unpacked, she and Christina sat down for coffee. Christina asked her what she liked to eat and made a shopping list. She noticed that Natalia spoke excellent Swedish and rarely had to search for a word – which would come in handy for situations like food shopping. Of course, Natalia had a strong Russian accent, but Christina didn't mind that at all.

They got in the car and drove to Tensta, which was the nearest town and had a large supermarket. They did the shopping together, stuffing the shopping cart full to the brim. It was Saturday and Christina had decided to take Monday off, so that they'd have almost three days to get acquainted. She planned to go shopping with Natalia again early Monday morning, so that she'd have enough supplies to last her to the following weekend. Christina intended to come up here on the weekends in order to make sure Natalia's pregnancy was going smoothly – and also to spend time with her and get to know her better. She also needed to find healthcare for Natalia, who was not registered in Sweden and thus was not entitled to avail herself of the country's medical services. But Christina knew of a gynecologist in Jönköping who accepted private patients.

Christina's dealings with Natalia had been nothing but pleasant thus far, and she particularly appreciated that Natalia wasn't demanding, and was also down to earth and a genuinely nice person. Any doubts she might have had about the undertaking with Natalia had fallen away, and she was definitely going to help her during the prenatal and postnatal periods – and would then adopt the child. And if Natalia wanted to be involved in raising the child, that was perfectly okay with her – but then Natalia would have to obtain a residency permit and Christina had no idea how to go about doing that. Also, Natalia needed to put her past firmly behind her. Christina hadn't yet asked her for any further details, but the threats from her Russian ex that Natalia had told her about over the phone were evidently still all too real. But Christina was confident that this secluded cabin in Småland would be an ideal safe haven for Natalia – and she found it hard to imagine that her ex would still be trying to track her down six months from now. Everything was going to work out for the best, she was sure of it – surer than she'd ever been of anything.

32

Natalia warmed her hands on the coffee mug. She was sitting on the deck behind the house and looking out over the small expanse of lawn that abutted the woods. The temperature was barely above freezing, but this deck was sheltered from the wind and the sun was out. So in her warm hat and heavy coat, she felt quite comfortable. She turned her face toward the sun, so as to derive the maximum warmth from it.

She loved the total peace and quiet here, surrounded by nature – it reminded her of her Babushka's cabin, which had also been in the woods. Maybe living here would give some people the creeps, but she loved these digs. Also, this had gone down in exactly the same way as when Patrik had rented the cabin in Norrland, where they'd been completely on their own and had gone on magnificent walks. The only problem was that she'd had this fucking sword of Damocles dangling over her the whole time. She'd known full well what Stanislov had in mind and she'd tried to talk him out of it – but in the end the subject hadn't even been considered, since he wasn't content with just withdrawing money with her cash card; he wanted everything. She'd offered to relieve Patrik of his other credit card, but Stanislov had realized that Patrik would have immediately deactivated it. Plus, they hadn't been able to access the Swiss savings accounts that Patrik had transferred all his money to. So she'd realized what would happen. She'd been too much of an idiot to recognize what a great opportunity being with Patrik would have been for her; and she'd been too much of a coward to stand up to Stanislov – though doing so might not have made any difference. And then what had she ended up doing to poor Patrik? Couldn't she have at least alerted him to the impending danger? He might have even forgiven her, and they could have put their heads together and found a solution. When Patrik tumbled down the cliff, her heart almost stopped. Completely dazed, she had staggered to his car with Stanislov by her side, and it had been hours before she could think straight again. And then Stanislov had smacked her really hard for not answering his questions. That's good for everything, he'd always say. And in fact, his slap had brought her back to reality – a reality without Patrik that was the very opposite of her heart's desire. But she'd continued functioning, as she had before. Except now, the loathing she felt for Stanislov, that was new, and it had never subsided. A mixture of hate and distrust. This distrust had made her more vigilant – and she'd come to realize that Stanislov was getting other women to engage in undertakings similar to the ones he'd assigned her. If she'd known that before, for sure she would have acted differently.

She had told Christina the whole story, first in its broad outlines by phone, and then in minute detail over the past few days. Christina wanted to know everything, and Natalia could understand that. She had feared that Christina might take her to task for what she had done. At first Christina had cried, but then had become very calm – and had even said that she could forgive Natalia. Natalia hadn't been expecting this, and so she in turn broke down in tears, sobbing as she hadn't done since her grandmother passed away. Christina had taken her in her arms and comforted her – the very woman who'd stolen her husband away from her. She was awed by Christina's magnanimity – she'd never experienced anything like it before. And yes, she really liked her. Christina was so warm-hearted and understanding, and Natalia couldn't understand how Patrik could have simply up and left her. Though of course Christina wasn't all that pretty and was on the plump side – and Patrik had let on that they didn't have sex any more. But still, she was a truly amazing person.

Natalia and Christina had hit it off from the very start – and after their conversation that first evening, they'd become fast friends. Together, they had made dinner, listened to music, put wood in the fireplace and lit a fire. This had made them feel even more secure in each others' company, and the smell of burning wood had reminded Natalia of her Babushka's cabin. The kitchen there contained only a wood stove and the living room had a fireplace – unlike her current digs, which had radiant heating and where the fireplace was mainly for atmosphere, not heat.

Christina had left yesterday, which had genuinely saddened Natalia – though she'd only be gone a few days and would be back Friday evening. Natalia was very much looking forward to that. But in the meantime, she'd be just fine. She had a TV and a shelf full of books, most of which were romance novels. Though she wasn't really into reading books, she'd actually found one that sounded really good, called Gränslandet : en kärleksroman *("The Frontier: a love story") by Ingrid Tollgerdt-Andersson. It was about three generations of women who are seeking happiness but are having difficulty finding it. Which isn't surprising, given that the story is set in the 20th century, when things were pretty tough for women. The first one, Christine, wants to start a new life, and her daughters would like to break down barriers. Natalia identified with these characters and was curious to see if the book might be able to help her.*

Natalia really wanted to talk to Lyudmila and hoped that Stanislov wasn't causing her any problems again. She would have liked to tell her how well things were going for her here. But she dared not contact Lyudmila. She was afraid of leaving any trace of her presence, as there was no way of telling what resources Stanislov had at his disposal. When she'd taken leave of Lyudmila in Budapest, all she'd told her was that she was leaving Hungary. She had decided not to contact Lyudmila at all, either by phone, via social media, or in any other way. Natalia fervently hoped that a time would come when she would be able to see Lyudmila again. But for now, she would just have to wait.

She had drunk all her coffee, and now a massive cloud was obscuring the sun and was robbing her of the warmth of the sun's rays. She began to shiver and decided it was time to go back inside. It would be nice to light a fire and read, as in any case the sun would be setting in just two hours; the days were very short in Sweden at this time of year. But when it was dark outside, the cabin was so nice and cozy with a fire blazing in the fireplace.

33

Lars was in his office, writing a report about the surveillance of an employee that had yielded no results. He'd had the impression from the outset that the man hadn't done anything wrong, and the surveillance had borne this out. To all appearances, he was a model employee who was always on time and observed all the rules, regulations and policies of his company. But Lars couldn't, of course, rule out the possibility that someone had warned the employee that he was being watched. This sort of thing happened from time to time, especially when too many people were in the loop. Conceivably, one such person might have felt that his loyalties lay with the employee in question, and not with his company. Such incidences were virtually impossible to prove, but they of course made surveillance utterly pointless – not to mention a total sleeping pill for the detective. Though the fee was exactly the same as for surveillance that yielded actual results.

Lars had just finished writing the report when his phone rang – a German number. Martin perhaps? He picked up.

"Hi, Lars, it's Liv. I'm worried about Christina." She sounded agitated.

"Hi, Liv. What's up?"

"I can't reach her, and she didn't show up for work this morning – and didn't call in sick or the like. She's never done anything remotely like that before."

"Yeah, I know, she's the very picture of conscientiousness. But you know, glitches do happen, even to the best of us. Maybe she forgot to take her phone with her, and now she's stuck in traffic."

"I fear it's not that simple. There's something going on right now that's got me really worried about my not being able to reach her. We'd agreed to talk on the phone early this morning, before she left for work.

But she didn't call and isn't picking up either her cell phone or her land phone. So then I called her at work, and her colleagues were also surprised that she hadn't turned up."

"I see. But what's this 'something' that's going on right now? I really have no idea what you're talking about. We haven't had any contact with Christina for weeks now."

"Well...um...I'm...afraid...I can't really say anything about that right now. I promised Christina I'd keep it a secret. But, say, could you maybe swing by her house and see if everything's okay? I'll pay you for your time. I don't know anyone else that I could ask."

Lars didn't like this a bit. Liv was unwilling to bring him up to speed, but he was supposed to find out what was going on in Täby?

"Please, Lars, trust me. I'd tell you more if I could. Just take my word for it when I say that something untoward might be afoot there. If Christina's safe and sound when you find her, I'll ask her to bring you up to speed. But if you don't find her, call me right away."

This "safe and sound" made Lars even more suspicious. "So are you saying that it might be unsafe for me to go there? Shouldn't I take some backup along with me?"

There was a moment's silence on the line. Then Liv said in a serious tone, "Yes I think you should take someone with you – proceed with extreme caution once you're there."

Lars swallowed. What kind of craziness was afoot *now*? But on the other hand, could anything that terrible really happen? He'd stop by and take Elin with him. The place was in a row-house development in Täby, so it shouldn't pose a big problem. Or could it? But anyway, he wanted to do Liv a favor – which maybe would lead to a new case.

"Okay, Liv. We'll go check it out."

"Thanks a million, Lars," Liv said, exhaling audibly. "And please, get over there right away, okay?"

"Will do."

Elin would jump at the opportunity to do something different, as she was currently doing boring surveillance.

Just under 45 minutes later, Lars and Elin were at Christina's front door. Elin had grilled him about the reason for this trip – and even though Lars insisted that he was just as much in the dark as she was, Elin didn't buy it. Even now, she was giving him an extremely skeptical sideways glance.

Just as Lars was about to ring the doorbell, Elin said, "Hey, look, the door's open". She grasped the doorknob and pulled the door open – toward the outside as is customary in Sweden.

"Wait a sec," Lars whispered. "We need to be careful."

Again this skeptical look. He'd already told her everything Liv had told him, including the bit about "safe and sound" and "be careful." But she'd nonetheless unsheathed her truncheon and pulled it all the way out – she seemed to have grasped that this was serious. Lars was holding a can of pepper spray – which, in Sweden, private individuals are not allowed to use. But it is extremely effective when it comes to warding off an attacker, which is why Lars had a few cans on hand, in case he needed it for a hazardous mission like this one.

Lars and Elin inched their way down the hallway to the living room, where they were met with a very strange sight. The room was normally very neat and tidy, but now the coffee table was askew, a drinking glass was knocked over, and papers were scattered all over the floor. Had there perhaps been a break-in?

Lars signaled to Elin to follow him, and they moved slowly and carefully from room to room, and finally to the second floor. No one seemed to be in the house, and nothing seemed to be amiss. No trace of Christina, and her cellphone was nowhere to be found.

They then went back to the living room, and Lars called out, "Is anyone home?" No answer.

Elin looked at him inquisitively. "So will you now finally tell me what the hell's going on here?"

"Look here, Elin. How many times do I have to tell you? I've really and truly told you everything I know. Liv told me she couldn't fill me in because she'd promised Christina to keep this thing secret – whatever it is. I have no idea what's going on here. I can't make heads or tails of it either – but maybe

Christina started a risky relationship or is otherwise involved with shady characters, how the hell should I know? But one thing is clear: this place looks suspicious. It's not like Christina to leave her living room in this state and to leave the front door ajar. If she still can't be reached and doesn't call work to explain her absence, then all things considered, there's good reason to be worried."

He spread out his arms, uncertain what he should do next. Just then, the land phone that was on a dresser next to the couch rang. They looked at each other.

"Should we answer it?" Elin asked.

"Sure, why not? Maybe the person on the other end will think you're Christina and we'll get a lead." Lars pressed the speakerphone button and nodded to her.

"Hello?" Elin said uncertainly.

"Christina, is that you? Thank god I've finally reached you." It was Liv for sure.

"No, sorry," Lars said. "It's only me and Elin. We've just looked through the whole cabin. Christina's not here, and neither is her phone. Plus the living room is kind of a mess," he said, and described how it looked.

"That doesn't sound good," Liv said in a worried tone. "But tell me, how did you get in?"

"Yeah, that was weird, too. We found the front door ajar and just walked in."

They could hear Liv gasp. "Oh no," she finally said.

"Liv, something's definitely amiss here. Don't you think it's about time you brought us up to speed?"

"Yeah, you're right. But I need to talk to Martin first. I'll call you back later, okay?"

Lars was about to say something, but Liv had already hung up. He shook his head – she'd left him no choice. He looked at Elin. "Okay then we'll just wait until we get further information. And what do you say we kill the time with a nice coffee break."

Elin grinned and went into the kitchen. Now, at least, she was convinced that Lars was just as much in the dark as she was.

***

They had drunk almost all the coffee when Lars' phone rang. Martin's number flashed on the screen. Lars picked up.

"Hi Martin."

"Hi there, Lars. I just got finished talking to Liv about you-know-what." Martin sounded as mellow as ever.

"Yes, Liv told us to drop by Christina's house, and something's definitely wrong here. But Liv didn't want to tell me what this is all about, so we're of course curious to find out more."

"Yeah, well, that's why I'm calling."

"Okay, then I'll put you on speakerphone so that Elin can listen in. Okay, then here goes."

"You need to understand that Liv is in kind of a bind here. She solemnly swore to Christina that she'd keep this whole matter under wraps. But now it seems that something's happened to Christina – and so I think it's okay to break the promise now."

"I see." Lars could hear Martin's inner lawyer speaking – but he didn't care, so long as he was finally going to spill the beans.

"However, it doesn't make sense to bring you into the loop unless you're prepared to take on a new case. It concerns helping Christina, and to do that you'd need to go somewhere, right now, that's a few hours' drive from Stockholm. Do you have time today and tomorrow to work on this case?"

Lars looked at Elin, who nodded in excitement. She seemed to be totally stoked about taking on such a case, as was Lars, despite a voice in his head that said, "Hey wait a minute there, buddy" – a voice that reminded him of his wife's. But he decided to pay no attention to it just now.

"Yes, that works, we can do it. Though of course it depends on what the whole thing's actually about. I don't want to end up buying a pig in a poke here."

"Sure, I can understand that. Okay, it's kind of a bizarre story that has to do with Christina's late husband. As you have no doubt gathered, he was having an affair with a young woman, who, as far as we know, is from Russia and who's name is Natalia.

She recently called Christina and made a truly unusual proposal. You need to know two things, though. First, her ex is trying to track her down, and she says if he finds her, he might try to kill her – or at least do her serious bodily harm. The other thing is that she's pregnant, and she claims that Patrik is the father."

Lars and Elin looked at each other, and Elin rolled her eyes. Lars still didn't see where all this was going.

"Christina made a deal with Natalia to the effect that Christina will adopt the child and will provide Natalia with a safe haven during the pregnancy."

"Unbelievable!" Elin said. "But how can she be sure that Patrik really is the father? And even if he is, why on earth does she want to adopt the child? I mean after all, Patrik abandoned her."

"Yes, we had the same concerns, and Liv of course conveyed them to Christina. But we don't need to discuss all this right now, you know. The fact is that Christina intends to go ahead with this, and, with Liv's permission, she's stashed Natalia in the cabin in Småland. That was last weekend. But in the event Christina's been kidnapped, then the perpetrator will undoubtedly turn out to be Natalia's ex, the Russian – in which case it's only a matter of time until he heads for that cabin. In fact, he might well be on his way there now. So we would like you to drive up there and make sure that everything's okay."

"You mean the cabin that Liv was kidnapped from?"

"Yes, that's the one. I'll send you the address."

"Can't we just phone the cabin?" Elin asked.

"Afraid not. Liv has had the phone turned off, and we don't have a number for Natalia."

"I see." Every possible scenario was racing through Lars's mind. "Why not ask the police to check it out?"

"Well, we'd considered that possibility. But for one thing, this wouldn't be in Christina's interests, since the whole business would come to light; plus I don't have much faith in the Tensta police. My experience with them when Liv was kidnapped from there last year was none too positive. But if you don't want to make the trip, then I suppose that would be our only option. But Lars, really, we'd be eternally grateful to you if the two of you would drive up there right now."

"Just a sec," Lars said, as he muted the phone and looked over at Elin. "Well? You in?"

"Absolutely. The whole thing sounds totally wild, but at least something's finally happening. And it might be super exciting. I just need to get my gear from home, and then I'm good to go."

As for Lars, he still had his gear in his car, and it would surely be better to spare Lisa the details of this case. He decided to text her, rather than going home.

He took the phone off mute. "Okay, Martin, we're in. We're heading out the door right now. Send us the address and anything else we might need – and then we'll give you a call once we're on the road, if need be."

"Thanks a million, Lars, I owe you one," Martin said, sounding relieved.

They hung up the phone and left the house.

"I hope we're not too late," Elin said.

Lars nodded. "Well I suppose that depends on how much resistance Christina puts up. Anyway, it hasn't been all that long since she disappeared. But we really need to step on it!"

34

Christina was in the trunk of the car, stark naked, with her hands tied behind her back with cable ties that cut into her flesh at the slightest movement. Her ankles were also tied, and a piece of duct tape was plastered diagonally over her mouth. She was nothing but a bundle of pain. Her face was swollen and hurting from the beating she'd gotten. Her body was one giant dull ache, and her thigh was burning like hell. But the duct tape was the worst. She'd sobbed quietly as the trunk of the car was slammed shut. Crying so much had left her with a stuffed nose, so that she had to struggle desperately for air, and it was only after several panicked minutes that her nose was clear again – but she still felt like the tape was suffocating her. The car was moving, and the noise of the engine would drown out her muffled cries for help – which in any case the driver wouldn't hear if she died a wretched death back here. Plus, the driver couldn't have cared less what happened to her.

When the doorbell rang that morning, she was just getting dressed. She wondered who could be wanting something from her so early in the day, but her suspicions weren't aroused. Peeking through the window next to the front door, she saw a tall man carrying a pile of magazines, and assumed he was going to try to sell her a subscription. Which was, no doubt, what she was meant to surmise. She opened the door just a crack, but the man pushed his way in. She immediately let go of the door and fled to the living room, in a panic. The intruder grabbed hold of her there and threw her to the floor. As she fell, she bumped into the coffee table, causing a glass to topple over and a pile of papers to fall to the floor. She was unable to put up a fight, because before she knew it her attacker was on top of her, holding her arms together, tying her up and putting duct tape over her mouth. He then dashed through the house and appeared to be checking out the whole place. Christina had thought that he was looking to steal her money and valuables, but when he came back, as far as she could tell he'd taken nothing but her cellphone. But then she almost fainted in terror upon hearing him say to her, in a strong Eastern European accent, that he was going to take her along with him, "so that we can have a little chat" – because now she knew who he was, and that Natalia was in danger too.

The man grabbed hold of her and dragged her to the front door, where he watched the street for a time before pushing her over to a car that was parked in front of the house. He tossed her into the back seat and sat down next to her. Another man was sitting in the driver's seat, and the engine was running. She could hardly see outside, because the rear windows were darkened. Then a bag was pulled over her head; immediately she was terrified that she would suffocate, and her heart began racing. But she managed to collect herself, because she needed to figure out where the car was going. At first, she could follow the car's route quite well and could figure out which direction the car was going in by its right and left turns. However, when the car began moving straight ahead at a steady speed, she assumed they were on the highway – and there were no more clues to be had.

At one point she screamed and sobbed loudly behind the duct tape in order to draw attention to herself, but the man sitting next to her slapped her on the head and shouted at her to keep quiet. The two men didn't talk much, only a few brief remarks in Russian – or at least that's what she thought it was. Every possible scenario went racing through her mind.

One of the men was probably Natalia's ex, who must have found out somehow that Christina was in contact with her. How he'd managed this was a mystery to her; she racked her brains, but for the life of her, she couldn't figure it out. She decided the wisest course would be to deny everything and act dumb, and she used the time in the car to think up as many plausible and coherent answers as she could. But at that juncture, she had no idea what awaited her.

Christina couldn't tell exactly how long they'd been driving. It had seemed like an eternity, but she figured that they'd been in the car for no more than 30 minutes. She had been lying next to the guy, with her legs pulled up and her head leaning against his hip. He had kept putting his meaty hand on her head or shoulders, which made her shudder in fear every time. But nothing happened to her while they were driving – the bad stuff didn't begin until afterwards. She'd figured they were going to take her someplace where they wouldn't be disturbed – which is what happened.

When the car finally came to a stop, the bag was removed from her head. She was standing outside a small cabin, around which nothing but a forest was to be seen; so, she surmised, we must be pretty far from Stockholm. Surely, they're going to remove the duct tape and start interrogating me now, she thought. But they didn't. They tied her hands in front of her and left the tape on her mouth. No sooner was she inside the cabin than the men were all over her. First, they slapped her face, and when she tried to fend them off with her arms, they punched her in the stomach and for a moment she could hardly breathe. She ended up collapsing on the floor, where she held her arms in front of her face as the blows and kicks rained down upon her. Then it was over, and she was a whimpering bundle of pain, curled up on the floor. Her attackers lifted her up and set her on a chair, with her hands and feet tied to it. She hurt everywhere, and the pain had obliterated all semblance of thought. A blow to the kidneys had been particularly painful, and she felt like she'd been stabbed in the lower back.

When they finally removed the duct tape, she began to sob uncontrollably. The two men stood there waiting for her to regain at least a modicum of composure – but then immediately asked her about Natalia's whereabouts. She told them that she didn't know anyone named Natalia, which earned her a slap on the face. And this time she couldn't protect herself, as her hands were tied to the armrests of the chair. This back and forth went on for quite some time, always the same question with Christina giving pretty much the same answer every time. The slaps were violent, but Christina had made up her mind that she wouldn't betray Natalia. She also feared that the men would kill her once she'd told them what they wanted to know, because then they'd have no further use for her – and this strengthened her resolve.

When the two Russians realized that they were getting nowhere, they briefly conferred in their native language, whereupon the driver nodded and left the cabin. His confederate taped her mouth shut again, and for a second or two Christina thought they'd believed her and were going to take her home. But the Russian who was guarding her picked up a pair of scissors and began cutting off her clothing – first her pants, then her blouse, and finally her bra and panties. Christina tried to break free, but she couldn't really defend herself. Now she was totally nude, except for her socks. How humiliating it was to be sitting here stark naked, at the mercy of this violent guy, with her breasts completely exposed. She couldn't even close her legs, as her feet were tied to the chair legs. Christina looked down at her body, whose corpulence she found embarrassing. This sitting position made her look chubbier: her stomach stuck out, her large breasts laid almost on top of it, she had a sizeable spare tire around her hips, and her thighs resembled the folds of an accordion. But why the hell was she worrying about her appearance? She had other problems on her hands right now – the little matter of life and death, for example.

What else did this violent scumbag intend to do to her – was rape next, perhaps? But what actually happened was far worse.

Her Russian guard had settled into an armchair and wasn't even watching her any more. All Christina could do was wait, and her breathing gradually returned to normal. But she was starting to feel very cold. The cabin was unheated, and the outdoor temperature went down to zero at night. After a time, the Russian put his jacket back on that he'd taken off before he began brutalizing Christina; but he continued to ignore her and instead fooled around with his phone while Christina began shivering.

The driver finally returned – though how long he'd been gone Christina couldn't tell – carrying a metal box with a handle on it. Christina shuddered at the thought of what they might do to her next. Were they planning to really torture her?

The Russian guy got up from the armchair and took off his jacket. The shit was about to hit the fan – again. He planted himself in front of Christina and said, "Now we're going to show you what we can do with you and then believe me, you'll talk."

The other guy placed the box on the floor, opened it and took out a metal object that resembled a jug with a holder under it, a handle on its side, and a straight, open-ended tube on top. He turned a wheel on the tube, which emitted a hiss, and then lit a lighter and held it up to the tube – and a jet of flame came shooting out of it. Christina opened her eyes wide, in sheer horror.

The Russian standing before her spoke again. "Maybe you've never seen one of these before, but it's a blowtorch. The temperature of the flame is more than 1000 degrees. My buddy here's going to show you what this little baby can do."

He then said something in Russian, and his confederate picked up what looked like a very thin aluminum plate. He tensioned the plate in a small holder, which he placed on the floor. He then pointed the flame at the plate and adjusted the flame with the little wheel, until the flame turned blue. The plate quickly started glowing, and when the guy pulled the flame back, Christina could see that it had burned a hole in the plate. She swallowed, staring at her torturer, who merely said, "And now we're going to show you what real pain feels like. At first he's going to be real nice about it and only hold the flame on you for a second – but if you don't talk, he'll be more than happy to extend the treatment."

He nodded to his confederate and gave him a command in Russian. The man turned toward Christina, blowtorch in hand, and drew nearer to her. She emitted a muffled scream under the duct tape and shook her head violently back and forth. Goddammit, they had to at least give her a chance to talk. But her captor paid no attention to her gesticulations and pointed the flame at her right thigh. Already feeling the heat of the torch, Christina squirmed around in the chair and tugged on her shackles in desperation – but the flame reached her skin and a horrific pain spread through her whole leg. She screamed under the gag, and then everything went black.

When she came to, her thigh was still burning like fire; it looked horrible and smelled of charred flesh. Desperate and in agony, she sobbed. After removing the duct tape, all the Russian said to her was, "Talk."

Christina's resolve was broken, she couldn't take any more – so she talked. At first, she couldn't say a word, but after they gave her a glass of water, she told them the whole story, from the beginning. At one point she faltered when they asked her for the address of the cabin; but a slight wave of the torch was enough to get her talking again. Once she'd told them everything and answered all their questions, they bandaged her thigh, put the duct tape back on her mouth, dragged her to the car, and put her in the trunk.

She assumed that their next stop would be Liv's cabin, and that her captors had taken her along so that they could interrogate her again in case it turned out that she'd been lying. Plus, they wanted to make sure that she wouldn't sound the alarm. Christina had no illusions about what they would do with her once they got hold of Natalia. Because then she'd just be a superfluous witness – collateral damage that needed to be gotten out of the way. She was so done in that she found herself hoping that her death would be quick and painless. She just wanted it to be over, longed to be put out of her misery. She was past hoping that she'd ever get out of this situation alive. No one knew that she'd been kidnapped, and Liv and Martin were the only ones who knew about Natalia and the cabin. And they were far away, in Berlin. No, there was no way out. She'd seen, and felt in her own body, that these men would stop at nothing. She now realized that Natalia hadn't been exaggerating a bit and that her anxieties had been totally justified.

Natalia would have little chance of escaping unscathed, as she had no idea what was going to be arriving at her front door before very long. Chances were that the two of them were going to share the same fate. But Christina was tormented by the fear that Natalia's death would be anything but quick and painless, as this Russian seemed to harbor a deep loathing for her. Given that he'd been tracking her for months all over Europe and had spared no expense in doing so, he would no doubt exact a high price from Natalia.

Christina cursed herself inwardly for having been clueless about what she was getting into and having been absurdly naive and overconfident. And for this, she was going to pay with her life. In killing her, this Russian bastard would be eliminating all traces of Patrik, of her, and Natalia – as well as Patrik's child.

35

Elin was happy to see that they had almost reached their destination, having just passed Tensta, and now finding themselves driving through the woods. As the GPS hadn't found the address, she'd keyed its coordinates into the device. Elin had already investigated the cabin and its environs using the satellite view on Google Maps. The house was on a road that passed through a large forest, and there weren't any other houses for miles around. Behind the cabin was a yard and a garden shed, and in front of the entrance were two parking spaces. Liv and Martin had both called during the trip up here and had given them a wealth of information. They had recommended that in order to reach the cabin without being noticed, they shouldn't park there, but should instead take a narrow path that led from the road, a short distance before the cabin, directly through the forest to the rear property line.

Lars had driven as fast as he could, up to 150 km per hour where it was safe to do so, thus probably saving them around 30 minutes' driving time. Elin prayed that they wouldn't arrive too late. All the information they had about this Russian guy had been conveyed to them indirectly and consisted of Natalia's take on him that Liv and Christina had relayed to them. But there could be no doubt that he was a dangerous fellow indeed. And if he'd invested all this time and effort into tracking down Natalia, it was unlikely it was just to have a nice chat with her. The worst-case scenario was that Natalia and Christina would already be dead when they finally arrived, with nary a sign of the Russian. Then the whole mission would have been for naught.

They had just turned right when Lars said, "This must be the place."

And in fact, on the opposite side a wider road branched off into the forest – but after a few meters grew narrower. Lars made a U-turn and turned down this road. Just behind the bushes on the edge of the road he found a small parking space that his Volvo fit into perfectly. He could remain here without being noticed from the road.

"So here we go." Lars gave Elin a serious look. "As I said, we're not going to storm the cabin SWAT-style. First we need to do some reconnoitering."

"Copy that." Elin had realized that Lars was right, because they had no way of knowing what they'd find. She had been assuming that as it would be the two of them against the Russian, they could start the operation immediately. But as Lars had pointed out, they had no way of knowing whether the Russian was alone – or armed. Plus, Lars wanted, at all costs, to avoid a situation where the Russian could take the women hostage and escape with them, because then they would have gained nothing.

"Shouldn't we take our gear with us anyway?"

"Absolutely. We need to be prepared for any eventuality – plus time is of the essence."

Lars grabbed his backpack from the back seat. Elin had a small bag in front of her, from which she took her truncheon and binoculars. Her knife was already attached to her belt. They put on their jackets, which were dark green and thus served as camouflage in this terrain; luckily there was no snow on the ground.

They made their way down the forest path, which was about a yard wide and curved through the trees. The path was muddy in places, but apart from that, the walk was easy. Elin led the way, with Lars behind – but soon he slowed down, as his knee seemed to be bothering him. Elin reached the end of the path first – and as Liv had said it took less then ten minutes to get there. Elin took up position behind a tree and scanned the surroundings. Because she had ended up next to the property, she had a good view of the whole scene. She had a side view of the cabin – both the driveway and the yard behind it were well within her field of view; but the garden shed was for the most part obscured by the cabin. Total calm reigned, and there wasn't a car to be seen. Either they'd gotten here before the Russian, or he'd already left. She of course hoped that they'd gotten here first, because then they'd be able to rescue Natalia. But unfortunately, Natalia had never laid eyes on them and would have no idea what they were doing here in the first place – and probably wouldn't be all that willing to come with them.

Lars arrived and positioned himself behind her. "What's the situation?"

"I haven't seen a thing – no movement, no people, nada. Do you think we should approach the house?"

Just then she heard a car engine and saw a car driving down the street.

Lars had heard it too. "Let's wait till the car drives by."

But instead of driving by, the car turned into the driveway of Liv's cabin. The doors were opened roughly, and two men burst out of the car – one was tall and well built; the second man was stocky and brawny, and was bald. The driver, who was the taller of the two, ran around the house carrying a longish object in his hand that Elin assumed must be a crowbar. The smaller man took up position at the entrance.

Lars pulled Elin farther back into the bushes.

"Shit," she whispered. "Why couldn't they have arrived five minutes later?"

"Nothing we can do about that now. Do you see Christina anywhere?"

Elin picked up the binoculars and trained them on the car, which was a large Audi, probably an A6 sedan.

"I don't see her. Maybe they've got her tied up on the back seat."

Lars placed a hand on her arm. "Well, whatever – the fact is we've got ourselves a really dangerous situation here. We're facing two guys with really bad intentions. I'm going to call the cops."

"Good idea."

"I'll go back into the forest a ways so that they can't hear me talking on the phone – you stay here and keep watch, okay?"

"Copy that."

"And Elin, don't even *think* about making the slightest move until I get back."

Lars knew from past experience that Elin hated just sitting around and watching – but she nodded anyway. Lars disappeared down the path.

Just then she heard a crashing sound from the rear of the house – the tall guy had apparently forced the back door open. Elin couldn't see the deck and instead was keeping her binoculars trained on the stocky guy, who was supposed to be guarding the front entrance, in case Natalia tried to make a run for it. But this didn't happen, because less than a minute had elapsed when the tall guy called out to his confederate in what sounded like Russian. The stocky guy took off like a shot and ran around the house to the back door.

Where the hell has Lars gone? Elin wondered. She turned around but could neither see nor hear him. This was the perfect opportunity to go over to the Audi and see if Christina was inside. If she could bring her to safety, that would be a major accomplishment.

Assuming of course that she was still alive, and the Russians had taken her with them.

She looked around again. No sign of Lars. What the hell was taking him so long? All he had to do was make an emergency call. She looked over at the Audi again, which stood there, invitingly, with its doors wide open. The Russians were in the house, probably dealing with Natalia. Elin decided to check whether Christina was in the car. She cautiously moved through the cover provided by the bushes and trees, until she reached the road and looked for the Russians again. The coast was still clear. Ducking, she crept down the driveway, and then inched forward so that she could peer into the car. No one inside. On the back seat there were some soda cans and a couple of bags of chips – but no sign of Christina. But she hadn't checked the trunk yet. Elin stealthily crept to the rear of the Audi, checking the whole time for any Russian who might suddenly materialize. She pressed on the button that opened the trunk, and the lid swung open. Elin recoiled in horror, unable to recognize the shapeless white thing that she saw. It was only on second glance that she realized that what she was looking at was a corpulent, naked woman with her hands tied behind her back and her legs tied together, covered in bruises, a serious burn on one thigh and a bandage on it that was soaked in blood. The woman's face was red and swollen, and a wide piece of duct tape covered her mouth. Her large eyes stared back at Elin. The woman was alive, and conscious. Could this be

Christina? Elin couldn't tell for sure – and so, with a swift movement, she removed the duct tape and placed her index finger over her mouth.

"Quiet."

Yes, it was in fact Christina. Elin cut the cable ties with her knife. Christina's skin was extremely cold to the touch, and she was shivering all over – not surprising in this freezing cold weather. Those scumbags could have at least covered her. Gingerly, she helped Christina out of the trunk – who stood there unsteady on her feet. Elin took off her jacket and draped it over Christina's shoulders. It was of course much too small, but it would have to do for the moment.

"Can you walk? I want to get you out of here and bring you to safety."

Christina made a rasping sound, cleared her throat twice and then said, "I'll stay here. You need to help Natalia, they're going to kill her."

Elin reflected for a moment. Was that a smart move? Well, bringing Christina over to Lars's car would take almost half an hour, and Natalia might be dead by then. Plus, the heat was on in the Audi, as the engine was still running.

"Okay, then, get in the driver's seat, lock the doors, and take off if you see either of the Russians. Think you can manage that?"

Christina nodded and took a few steps. After checking to make sure the coast was clear, Elin slowly guided Christina to the driver's door and helped her get in the car. Then she closed both doors as gingerly and quietly as she could and waited until Christina had locked them. After giving Christina the thumbs-up, she headed toward the rear of the cabin. Looking back one last time, she saw that Christina had picked up a can of soda and was drinking thirstily from it. Well that seems to have worked out pretty well, Elin thought. She crept over to the right corner of the house and looked around – the coast was clear. As she knew that there was a window on this side of the cabin, she wanted to reconnoiter there first. Ducking down, she crept over to the window, below which there was a pile of flowerpots. She put her feet in the spaces between them. Slowly she straightened up, only to be confronted with a horrific sight. She had a clear view of the whole living room, in the middle of which a blond woman was standing – or rather hanging – stark naked, and who for sure was Natalia. In the area leading to the deck, the living room had a high peaked roof with a large pillar going through it. The men had tied Natalia to it, with her arms raised, and her toes just barely touching the floor. The tall Russian was standing in front of her wielding a belt that he was using to whip Natalia mercilessly. With each blow, her body swung a bit in the opposite direction and she emitted such a loud scream that Elin could hear her through the triple-glazed windows. Shit, she really needed to do something. But how? It was her, by herself, against two men. She'd have to wait for Lars. And what had become of the short stocky guy? She didn't see him in the living room – but maybe he was sitting in a corner out of her field of view and was enjoying the show.

The tall guy walloped Natalia yet again with the belt, and must have hit an especially sensitive place, because Natalia shrieked in pain. Elin, recoiling in horror, kicked over a stack of flowerpots, two of which shattered with a loud crash. Shit, hopefully they didn't hear anything, I need to get out of here, she thought. But it was too late, she heard someone shouting, and the stocky guy came dashing around the corner, a cigarette dangling from his mouth. He'd probably been standing on the deck, smoking – what a rotten break! Elin had no choice but to gird herself for the impending confrontation. The stocky Russian had seemed rather short next to his buddy, but Elin now noticed that he was still taller than she was.

As this powerhouse of a guy was heading toward her like a cannonball, Elin feinted at the last second and stuck out her left leg. The stocky guy tripped and ended up sprawled on the ground – but immediately turned over on his back. In a flash, Elin threw herself on him – she simply had to neutralize him. She sat on him, pummeling his face, but her blows didn't seem to faze him in the least. He just grinned and grabbed her hands – first one, then the other. So there she was, wrists gripped in his vice-like paws. The guy was really strong. They met each other's gaze. Elin frantically tried to decide how she could use her feet; but then the guy suddenly turned over with all his might, dragging her along with him – then she was on the bottom, and he on top. And boy, was he heavy. The stocky guy slid up to her hips and pressed her left arm down on the floor. Then he let go of her right wrist and placed his left forearm across her neck, using all his weight to press on her windpipe and cutting off her air supply. He was staring down at her. He reeked of cigarette smoke and had horrendously bad breath. She tried to strike him with her free right hand but was unable to reach a vulnerable part of his body, as his shoulder was in the way. Plus, he had turned his head away, so she couldn't try to gouge his eyes. She could move her legs, but that was no help, as being kicked in the back didn't bother this guy at all. With his weight on her, she felt like her hips were being mashed into the floor, and with her left arm immobilized, she was completely at his mercy. She began to panic – she needed air. She knew it wouldn't be long before she fainted. There was only one way out of this. She felt for her belt, found the leather sheath attached to it, and opened it. She pulled the knife out, grasped the handle tightly, and stabbed her attacker as hard as she could. She had apparently hit the bulls-eye, as the full length of the blade pierced his torso right between two ribs, entering his thorax. Her attacker twitched and froze, and then collapsed on her – and the pressure on her neck was finally gone. With great effort, she rolled the Russian's heavy body off of hers and took a deep breath; her neck was throbbing with pain. That sure was a close one, she thought.

Just as she got up to see if the man was still breathing, she heard rapid steps behind her. She turned around, but the tall Russian was already upon her. The last thing she saw was his boot connecting with her temple. Then she passed out.

36

Lars was outraged – he'd never experienced anything like this before. These emergency calls could normally be accomplished in two minutes, tops. But this one, he realized after checking his watch, had taken more than ten minutes.

First, he'd landed in a queue – for an emergency call, no less. Was the whole police force perhaps at a Christmas buffet and only had backup personnel manning the phones? The call-taker was one of those people who asks you for every last detail, thrice over. Lars tried to keep his cool, but he ended up yelling at the call-taker that the life of two women was hanging in the balance and that every second counted. The call-taker then explained calmly that he simply had to have every last detail in order to assess how many men needed to be dispatch to the scene. Lars then said that he needn't figure out anything of the sort, because as an ex-policeman, Lars knew that he needed four armed cops and an ambulance in this particular situation. And though the call-taker thanked Lars for pointing this out, another difficulty arose. All police precincts in Sweden were in the process of being consolidated – which meant that, especially in the north, the catchment area of a single precinct often comprised hundred of square kilometers. The Tensta precinct was now only manned on Tuesdays and Thursdays – and today was Wednesday. And if a patrol car didn't happen to be near the scene, the Jönköping police would have to be dispatched, and it would take them at least half an hour to arrive.

And given the fact that for the moment, Lars and Elin were left to fend for themselves, Lars made his way down the path back to the house as quickly as he could. When he arrived at the edge of the forest, Elin was nowhere to be seen. What the hell, Lars thought. He'd instructed her to do absolutely nothing and to wait here for him to return. Couldn't this chick *ever* do as she was told? It was always the same story with her. He picked up the binoculars and trained them on the car, whose doors were now closed, and there appeared to be someone in the driver's seat. Was it the stocky Russian? There was no sign of Elin. He shifted the binoculars in the other direction, toward the rear of the cabin. Wait a sec, he thought, there's something on the ground there. He zoomed out the field of view. Yup, someone was lying on the ground, motionless. But it wasn't Elin, who was small and delicate; this person's body was almost completely round. Was it the stocky Russian? If so, what the hell was he doing there? What had happened to him? And if it was him, who the hell was in the car? He'd just have to go check it out. But first he needed to go to the car, because if the Russian was in there, he'd spot Lars walking across the lawn.

Lars crept along the edge of the forest towards the road, trying not to make a sound. When he got there, he'd be able to more easily see who was in the car. It was neither Russian, that was for sure; and it was a female, that was also for sure; but was it Christina? It couldn't possibly be Elin. Lars slowly approached the car. Yup, it was Christina, badly battered, but Christina all the same. She spotted Lars and opened the window a crack.

"What happened?" Lars whispered. "Where the hell is Elin?"

"You've got to help her, otherwise they're going to kill Natalia," she said hoarsely, indicating the right side of the cabin. "The last I saw of Elin, she was at the corner of the house, back there. But I haven't laid eyes on her since."

So once again Elin had acted on her own initiative – and of course without consulting him. The nerve of that girl!

"You alright?"

Christina merely nodded and indicated with a wave of her hand that he should go to the cabin. Well, okay, he in any case needed to have a look at the corpse that was lying there.

Crouching down, Lars made his way along the side of the cabin to the lifeless body. Yup, there he was, the stocky Russian guy, lying on his back. Lars took the pepper spray out of his chest pouch, just in case, but the man didn't move, and as far as Lars could see, he wasn't breathing. What had gone down here? Lars kneeled next to the lifeless man, the pepper spray at the ready, and felt for a pulse in the man's carotid artery. Nope, no pulse, dead as a doornail. But what – or who – had killed him? At first, Lars couldn't find any obvious injuries – that was, until he leaned over the body and saw the knife sticking out of the man's chest cavity. Though there was little blood, the knife had apparently gone right into the man's heart. This appeared to be Elin's doing – Lars was pretty sure it was her knife. But then why hadn't she removed it, instead of leaving it stuck in the body? Something was definitely amiss here.

Lars turned around toward the cabin, where he spotted a side window that would enable him to see what was going on in there. Perhaps Elin had taken care of the other Russian too, and so the crime scene was now secure – the kind of handiwork he'd come to expect from Elin. But her leaving the knife behind – that wasn't like her.

Under the window, he now noticed, there was a stack of flowerpots – but one of them was tipped over and two were broken. Lars gingerly positioned himself next to them and peered in the window from the side. Though he had a clear view of the whole living room, at first it was hard to take in everything at one glance. A young woman was suspended in the middle of the room – stark naked and with streaks of blood on her. Judging from the size of her stomach, she was very pregnant. The Russian was in the process of walloping her with a belt, but the woman didn't seem to be reacting – perhaps she'd passed out. Lars realized that he had to do something, because if he didn't, this woman wasn't long for this world – and that unborn child was clearly getting the worst of it, as the Russian wasn't making any allowances for the woman's pregnancy. But where the hell was Elin? He looked around the living room and finally spotted her lying in a corner on the floor, with her back to the room and apparently tied up. Fuck, so the tall guy had caught her after all. This Russian guy, Lars thought, must detest Natalia so much that he couldn't even think straight – because otherwise he would have realized that he'd been caught red-handed committing a crime and would have fled the scene. Or did he perhaps really believe that Elin had come here on her own? Well anyway, the small stocky guy was out of the picture, so now it was going to be Lars against the tall Russian. Lars himself was about six feet tall, and he figured that the Russian was about the same height. But the Russian was really ripped, though Lars had pretty muscular shoulders. So that meant the Russian had more bulk – he was built like a tank, with bulging muscles. But Lars was sure he could take him on. After all, he had the element of surprise going for him, plus his combat implements. He removed his knuckle-duster from his belt, put it around the fingers of his right hand, and grabbed the pepper spray with his other hand. He could really feel the adrenaline shooting through his veins now – the time for action had come. He went to the back of the cabin and checked the deck. As he'd expected, the coast was clear. He could see that the door had been forced open and that the crowbar used for this was lying on the deck. Which meant that he didn't have to worry about how he entered the cabin; the door was only open a crack. Through it, he could hear the woman being whipped and her quiet whimpering – so she wasn't unconscious after all. Lars briefly considered taking the crowbar along with him, but he decided it was too unwieldy for close combat and felt more secure with the pepper spray and the knuckle-duster.

Another blow with the belt, followed by a scream – it was now or never. Lars went over to the door and opened it. The Russian was about to wallop the girl again, but froze and wheeled around to face Lars, who rushed at the Russian before the guy knew what was happening, brandishing the pepper spray. But the Russian had quick reflexes and managed to shield his eyes with his right arm before Lars could press the button on the pepper spray. Lars tried to punch the Russian with his right hand, but the Russian was quicker and clobbered him in the stomach. Lars couldn't breathe and felt like he was going to pass out. Pressing his advantage, the Russian wrested the pepper spray away from Lars and threw him to the floor. Before Lars could so much as brace himself, the huge Russian jumped on top of him. Lars felt a stabbing pain in his chest and heard a cracking sound. The Russian had his meaty paws around his neck and was trying to strangle him. Fuck, thought Lars, this guy is strong and fast – a deadly combination. Lars punched the Russian in the side with his knuckle-duster, aiming for the kidneys. The Russian flinched but continued trying to throttle Lars. Lars feverishly thought about what his options were in this situation. Two words came back to him from his training at the police academy: eyes and scrotum. But unfortunately, the guy was astride him, so the scrotum was out of the question – so Lars tried for a punch to the face. But this proved impossible, as the Russian kept turning his head back and forth. The pressure on his neck was becoming unbearable, and Lars couldn't breathe. There was only one vulnerable place left. You couldn't dislodge the hands of such a strong guy, though that's what most people try to do in such situations. And yet, each hand has a pinky, and if you manage to grab them and pull them outward, the pain is unbearable and in most cases your attacker will let go. Lars grabbed hold of both pinkies and wrenched them sideways as hard as he could. The Russian screamed in pain, and let go of Lars's neck, in order to free his pinkies. Lars could breathe again, and he inhaled deeply. But his respite was short-lived. The Russian slammed his knees into Lars' forearms and began trying to throttle him again. Lars desperately tried to free his arms, but the guy had them pinned down, with all his weight. Lars felt the pressure on his windpipe – but this time he couldn't really fight back. Then he saw something move right behind the Russian. Was it Natalia? It was indeed – and she had been able to get her battered body swinging back and forth. Was she trying to come to his aid? Lars saw her swing backwards and then come flying at the Russian at top speed, feet first. Lars managed to arch his torso enough to line up the Russian with Natalia's rapidly approaching feet, whose heels caught the guy on the side of the head. Whereupon the pressure on his neck eased and Lars was able to flip the Russian off him. He quickly got up and gave the Russian a good swift kick in the side. But he just shook it off and was already on all fours. Just as Lars was about to hit the guy with his knee, he turned and pulled Lars to the floor. Lars could hardly believe it – this guy was on top of him yet again.

The Russian punched him in the face and grabbed for the belt that he'd dropped during the fight. With a swift movement, he wrapped it around Lars's neck, and as he began to pull on it, Lars knew he was a goner. There was no way to prevent the belt from tightening around his neck. The Russian had him pinned down and he couldn't reach any vulnerable part of his adversary's body. He began to feel weak. Natalia couldn't help him now either; the last rolling movement on the floor had placed them out of her reach. Lars hit the Russian, but his blows grew increasingly feeble, and he wouldn't be able to put up a fight for much longer. So was this it for him, then? Was he going to die, here in Liv's cabin, in a fight with this criminal? He could feel the fog of unconsciousness invading him. But just when he was about to pass out, he heard a dull thud, and then something heavy landed on the floor next to him. The Russian collapsed on him and the tugging on the belt ceased. With his last bit of strength, Lars loosened the belt and air began flowing into his lungs again – and slowly he regained full consciousness. What had happened? He rolled the Russian off him, removed the belt from his neck and rubbed his throat. The crowbar lay behind him. When he turned around, he saw Christina standing behind him, wearing a jacket that was several sizes too small for her and one of whose sleeve seams had burst. Her stomach hung down in folds, and under the jacket she was stark naked, and had a bandaged thigh and blood running down her leg. Her hands hung at her sides – she was clearly at the end of her tether and sunk to her knees. Lars stood up, gasping for breath. Just as he was about to rush to Christina's aid, he heard Elin, who, having turned around, cried out, "The Russian first, Lars. You need to tie him up before he comes to."

Lars shook himself; first he needed to be able to think straight. Elin was right, tying up the Russian was urgent, otherwise the fight might start all over again – and he had no way of knowing how hard Christina had hit him. He took the cable ties out of his pants pocket and tied the Russian's hands behind his back, using two ties, just to make sure. Then he tied the Russians ankles together, bent his legs and attached the Russian's hands to his feet, so that he would be completely immobilized. Lars noticed that on the back of his head the Russian had a pretty serious wound that was bleeding profusely – so he'd probably be down for the count for quite a while.

He turned toward Christina, who had crawled over to Natalia and was stroking her legs. Lars stood up and was just about to go over to her, when Elin said, "Untie me first, Lars, and then I can help too."

Elin's hands and feet were tied. She had a lacerated left temple, the side of her face was completely caked with blood and her neck was very reddened – but apart from that, she seemed to be alright.

Lars nodded. In a daze, he staggered over to the kitchen counter for a sharp knife. He then freed Elin, who rubbed her wrists and immediately got up.

"Let's free Natalia," she said, springing over to the two women in the middle of the room. Lars followed behind. Each intake of air triggered a stab of pain in his chest cavity, and he feared he had a fractured rib.

Elin gently put her arms around Natalia, to steady her body.

"Sever the cord, Lars!"

Being relatively tall, Lars could reach Natalia's hands, though his ribs hurt when he stretched out his arm. After Lars cut the cord, Elin grabbed hold of Natalia, and the two of them carried her over to the couch, with Christina crawling behind them.

They carefully set down Natalia, who whimpered at every movement and was a mess. Her face was swollen and smeared with blood, and she was also bleeding from the mouth. Her attacker had probably knocked out a few of her teeth. She had long striations all over her body, and she was bleeding from the wounds where she had been struck by the belt buckle, whose tongue had penetrated deeply into her flesh. Christina slowly hoisted herself onto the couch, and Elin helped her to sit next to Natalia. Lars was in awe of Christina, who was in almost as bad shape as Natalia, but whose only thought was to help her.

"Thanks. You know, Christina, you saved my life," he whispered hoarsely.

She looked at him, with her swollen face. "Bullshit," she said feebly, "if you two hadn't showed up, both of us would be dead by now. I'm the one who should be thanking you. What brought you here?"

"Liv sent us. She was worried because she couldn't reach you. But now we need to patch you up and find you something to wear." Lars had difficulty talking, and his chest hurt with every intake of breath.

"Our things are upstairs," Christina said, putting an arm around Natalia.

Elin came from the hallway carrying dressing material. "I found this stuff in the bathroom – there's a medicine cabinet in there. Should we use them, or would you rather we waited for the ambulance? How long till it arrives?" Elin had washed the blood off her face and had wrapped her head in a damp towel.

"How's your injury?" Lars asked.

"My head's buzzing a little, but it's not too bad," she said, smiling cheerfully. "What's the story with the ambulance?"

Lars checked his watch. He'd called 20 minutes ago. "Hopefully, they'll be here within about ten minutes. I suggest that we put adhesive bandages on the flesh wounds and let the doctors do the rest. But we need something comfortable for the women to wear. Could you have a look upstairs?"

"Sure," Elin said, smiling at him; she appeared to be in a state of near euphoria. Elin handed Lars the dressing material and ran upstairs. Lars ripped open some of the packages, covered the worst of Natalia's wounds with pieces of gauze and then attached them with adhesive bandages. He avoided putting the bandages right on the wounds, since the doctors were for sure going to remove them immediately, which could be painful. As he was tending to an abdominal wound, he felt something move under the skin – the child in Natalia's womb shifting position.

"Your child's alive," he said to Natalia, who nodded and smiled wanly, as she'd felt it as well.

"Thank god," Christina murmured, with tears in her eyes.

Elin came back downstairs with the clothes. "Here you go, a jogging suit and a bathrobe. Plus panties and thick socks." She gave the women the clothes and helped them to put them on. Lars watched Elin, who was still flowing with happiness. Did she know that the stocky Russian was dead? Why was she in such a jolly mood? Lars got two glasses of water from the kitchen.

Once Christina and Natalia had gotten dressed and had made themselves comfortable on the couch, glasses of water in hand, Lars took Elin aside.

"Are you on something? Why this newfound giddiness?"

Elin shook her head, smiling. "No, but I feel like a newborn babe. We've all come through this alive, and I'm so happy that we got here in time and could rescue the two of them. Or rather, the two and a half of them."

"Well, it was a close call, and the whole thing could have gone sideways. Tell me, though, why didn't you wait for me as we'd agreed?" He gave her a reproachful look.

"Well it took you forever – what were you doing all that time?"

"The call-taker was a disaster – kept me on the line for ten minutes."

"I couldn't wait any longer, Lars. The stocky Russian had vanished into the cabin, and I simply had to see what was happening with Christina. And by the way – what's the story with that guy?"

"He's lying out there, dead as a doornail. You stabbed him right in the heart."

"Oh my," Elin said, swallowing. "That wasn't my intention, but it really was a desperate measure, in self-defense, otherwise he would have throttled me."

She looked at him beseechingly with her green eyes, seeking his approval.

"Oh, I believe you. But you're going to be facing an extensive police investigation. Just so you know."

"Well actually, I'm looking forward to it," she said grinning at him – her sunny mood was apparently unshakable. "And how about you, how are you doing? Were you hurt? That huge guy was pretty close to doing you in, it seems."

"Seems like I've got a couple of broken ribs and some bruises. But that's about it."

They could hear sirens wailing in the distance.

"Sounds like the cops are finally here. Typical, now that the situation's under control. Elin, I think you'd better stand by the front door – or even better on the road, so that you can waylay the cops before they step onto the property. Raise your arms over your head so that they can clearly see you and tell them that they needn't do any SWAT-like maneuvers, as the perpetrators have been neutralized. What we really need right now is medical assistance."

She nodded. "Will do," she said and dashed to the front door.

Lars looked around the room. Natalia's clothes that the Russian had ripped from her body were lying on the floor. Plus the crowbar – and next to it the Russian, who was still dead to the world. Lars placed the crowbar off to one side, as he didn't want the cops thinking it was a weapon that could be used against them and reach for their guns. It would certainly be grimly ironic if, having overpowered the perpetrators, they ended up being killed by a trigger-happy cop.

The two women were cuddling on the couch, with their eyes closed – so for the moment, he couldn't do anything further for them. He sank stiffly into an armchair – everything hurt, especially his ribs. And now the sixty four thousand dollar question: What the hell was he going to tell Lisa? She'd probably file for divorce lickety-split. The cease-fire had officially collapsed, and he might as well cancel the appointment with the marriage counselor right away. Lars sighed.

37

Martin had just come home. The kids were playing upstairs. They were evidently too busy to come down and had merely shouted "Hi" from the top of the stairs. So Liv had come over to him immediately, and he saw that she'd been crying.

"There's news from Sweden," she said giving him a serious look.

"Is it bad?" he asked, in a distressed voice. After the phone conversations with Lars that morning, he had been wondering what was going on there; but he'd had wall to wall appointments for the rest of the day and hadn't gotten around to calling either Liv or Lars. He'd spent the afternoon in court, and cell phones weren't allowed there. On his way home, he'd still been thinking about the court session, and what was unfolding in Sweden today had completely slipped his mind. The whole matter had occurred to him only now.

"Well, yes and no. You should sit down, though."

That didn't sound too promising. Martin set down his attaché case, took off his coat, and sat down at the kitchen table.

"So tell me, what happened?"

Liv pulled up a chair next to him at the table, sat down and turned her face toward him.

"Well, the good news is that they're all alive."

"Good," Martin said, waiting for more.

"But they're also all in the hospital." Liv began to cry. Martin put his arm around her and stroked her shoulder.

"Honey, how bad is it?"

Liv reached into her sleeve and pulled out a hanky that seemed the worse for wear. Martin rummaged around in his jacket pocket and took out a fresh package of tissues.

Liv blew her nose.

"They beat Natalia to within an inch of her life, but she'll be alright, and the child too." Liv sniffled and took a deep breath. "As for Christina, those scumbags tortured her, with a blowtorch, no less; can you imagine?"

"Oh no. That's simply awful. How's she doing?"

"She's the one who called me. She was very weak and just gave me a very brief rundown of the salient points. She has third degree burns on her thigh, but apparently the pain's gone. But her face is in worse shape – they slugged her there too. But she thinks it'll heal."

Liv burst out crying again. "How can people do something like that," she said through her sobs.

"How about Lars and Elin? How are they?"

"Christina says they weren't seriously injured, but they had to fight like lions and got hit a lot."

Martin swallowed again – what she was saying sounded so dramatic!

"Lars wants you to call him as soon as possible."

"Sure, I'll do it right now. Did Christina tell you anything else?"

"Nope." Liv shook her head. Martin tried to hug her, but she pushed him away. "Not right now. Just call Lars, I want to know the details."

"Okay, whatever you say."

Martin took his phone out of his pocket and switched it on. He hadn't turned it back on after court, and had three missed calls, all of them from Lars. Martin pressed on Lars's number and switched to speakerphone. Lars picked up immediately

"Hi, Martin."

"Hi, Lars, I just got home. I was in court. Liv gave me the broad outlines about what happened; she's listening in. How are you doing? Were you injured?"

"Yes, but I'm basically alright. The guy broke three of my ribs, plus I have a whole bunch of bruises, and a shiner."

"How about Elin?"

"She got a bad cut on her temple that needed stitches. Apart from that, she's okay – plus she's really ebullient, despite her having killed someone today – but in self-defense of course."

"Wow, that really was a dangerous mission, wasn't it?"

"You can say that again, dude. All three of us came within an inch of our lives. There were two Russians.

One of them overpowered Elin and tied her up. He had Natalia at his mercy and gave her a terrible beating. When I intervened, it was touch and go for a while – but the other guy was a lot stronger than me and he got the upper hand. If Christina hadn't stepped in, I would have been killed. As far as I'm concerned, she's a real hero. She herself was tortured, was kept in the trunk of a car for hours, stark naked and tied up, in freezing temperatures – and was still able to find the strength to fight back. She cracked the Russian over the head with a crowbar – he's in the hospital in a coma right now and has a fractured skull."

"Wow, you've really been through the ringer, haven't you? How are Christina and the young woman doing?"

"Well not too bad, under the circumstances. Christina's one tough gal, and I think she'll bounce back real soon. She's got a really bad burn, but luckily it's not very large. Her face is in really bad shape, but the doctor says it'll heal, and she won't need any further treatment. Natalia's worse off, though – the guy broke her jaw and knocked out some of her teeth. She was operated on this afternoon and the surgery went well. She'd also got a bunch of wounds – none of them life-threatening, though, and they'll heal. But there will probably be some scarring. Luckily nothing happened to the baby, and the doctors say it's fine. Those two gals, Christina and Natalia, have a really close connection to each other – which, considering their history, is kind of hard to understand. But I'm convinced that what they went through today will really cement the bond between them. It'll probably take everyone involved quite a long time to get past what happened today – it was really tough, I'm telling you. Elin will have to deal with some PTSD eventually, I think. It's not so easy to get past having killed someone. Plus, the police investigation isn't going to make things any easier. They're probably going to ask us to stay here until they've got to the bottom of all this. I'm also afraid that we're going to have to talk to them about the whole business with Patrik and Natalia. I doubt they'll believe us if we say that the Russians did all this just for the fun of it. There's no way this whole thing can be kept under wraps, whether Christina likes it or not."

"I see. But I strongly advise you to get yourselves a good lawyer."

"Already in the works. Christina knows one and she's already given her a call."

"Great. But does this mean that we did the right thing by having you go there? Or should we have taken a different tack? I mean we're terribly, terribly sorry that the two of you were in so much danger and were injured to boot."

Lars cleared his throat. "Really, it's no problem. Such risks go with the territory. Elin thought it was great, and she's totally grateful to have had the opportunity to let off some steam again. Well, I only wish I could have stood up better to this guy – but thanks to Christina it all turned out well. The only fly in the ointment – and it's a major one, believe me – is my wife. I mean, look, your idea of taking some time out worked well up to this point, but she's going to crucify me for what went down today. I haven't even dared call her yet. I mean, what can I say to her? She is going to go ballistic."

Martin also had no idea what he should advise Lars to do. It was of course perfectly understandable that Lisa would take a very dim view of all this.

Liv broke in, having regained her composure.

"Hi, Lars, Liv here. Martin told me about your problem, but scout's honor, no one else knows about it – we haven't breathed a word to anyone. If you don't mind me putting in my two cents, I think you really do have to give her a call, like right now. And you need to tell her the naked truth, without pulling any punches. And tell her how important being a detective is to you and that you simply don't want to give it up – dangerous missions included. She'll simply have to make a choice. If she really loves you, then she'll learn to live with the inherent hazards. And if she doesn't, well, then it's moot, you'll lose her anyway."

After a moment of silence, Lars said, "Is that your take on it too, Martin?"

"Yeah, Lars, I think Liv's right. It's the only way – you know, the best defense is a good offense."

"Okay thanks, to both of you, for being so honest with me. I think I'll do it. But I definitely need a good strong glass of whiskey to give me courage – and of course there's not a drop of alcohol to be had in this whole damned hospital."

"Best of luck, Lars. We'll be keeping our fingers crossed."

They said goodbye to each other.

Liv looked at Martin. "What have we done? How could we have let Lars and Elin get mixed up in this?"

Martin shook his head. "Honey, we did the right thing, we had no other choice. Because otherwise Christina and Natalia would have been killed. And then we really would have had good reason to flagellate ourselves. And Lars and Elin have pulled it off again. Luckily neither of them was seriously injured, and they'll make a full recovery."

"True. Except...all of this is even worse than what we went through last year. Torture, brutal beatings, and a life and death struggle – why did it have to come to this?"

"Well it seems to me that this Natalia person simply got mixed up with the wrong people, and you have to tread very carefully in such situations. Once you get involved with people like that, it's almost impossible to extricate yourself. Assuming, of course, that this Natalia person is as nice as Christina says she is. For her sake, I sure hope so."

"I have great confidence in her, you know, and I doubt that she could be so mistaken about someone."

"Yeah, but, honestly, didn't she have even the glimmer of an idea of what Patrik was up to?"

"Oh come on, that's totally different – husbands are a tough nut to crack," she said with a mischievous smile.

Martin had to laugh, in spite of himself. "I admit defeat, I'm powerless before such compelling feminine logic. Come here, you sexy thing."

He stood up and pulled her up, so that he could embrace her. She snuggled up to him, her head resting on his shoulder. Martin knew what was going on inside her at the moment. Something bad had gone down yet again at the Småland cabin – the very dwelling that was such an integral part of the bond between Liv and her grandmother. Liv's kidnapping last year, today a life and death struggle. It would be a long time, if ever, before she could get these images out of her head. Up till today, Liv had been reluctant to go to the cabin – and with all that had happened, he realized that she'd probably never want to set foot there again. It would probably be best to sell the place, grandma or no grandma. That decision was totally up to Liv, of course, but he was definitely going to suggest it to her. Only not today. She needed time to process all this.

He pressed her to him, and then asked her, "Do we have anything to eat? I'm famished."

EPILOGUE

MARCH 2017

She held out her plate to the woman at the food counter for a second helping. Ladling the food onto her plate, the woman winked at her, for she knew that Natalia could use the sustenance. On Thursdays they served the classic Swedish dish for this day of the week – pea soup with bacon bits, and pancakes with jam for dessert.

Natalia carefully carried her tray from the counter to her table and slowly lowered herself into a chair; moving was problematic in this, her third trimester. As usual, she ate with Melly and Kicki, who she'd become friends with. Friends came in very handy in prison, and Melly and Kicki were really special. Melly was small and powerfully built, with tattoos all over her body, including her face – colorful tattoos with every imaginable motif. All the inmates claimed to be "totally innocent," except for Melly, who made no bones about the fact that she'd deliberately offed her boyfriend by knifing him. This earned her the respect of the other inmates, none of whom dared mess with her. Kicki, on the other hand, was tall and slim, had only one tiny tattoo on her upper arm, and was currently the only inmate who had her kid with her. He was now three months only, and she'd been incarcerated for six months here at Färingsö, the women's correctional facility located west of Stockholm. So Kicki was a good person for Natalia to talk to, as she was due in two weeks. When the time came, she would immediately be taken to a nearby hospital – for which the day-release form was already filled out and signed. Afterwards, she and the baby would be returning to her cell at Färingsö prison, where the child would be living under the same conditions as her. As Natalia's lawyer had explained to her, Swedish prisons do not have separate cell blocks for women with children. Children are allowed to remain with their mothers for as long as the mother wishes, and provided that the Department of Child Protective Services and the prison administration adjudge this arrangement to be in the child's best interests. In most such cases, children remain with their mothers for only a few months, and for up to two years at the most. Natalia had already agreed with Christina that she would take the child after it was weaned, whereupon Christina would become the child's foster mother pro temp. They had decided to do the formal adoption later on, as the child was automatically granted Swedish citizenship by virtue of Patrik being its father. This status of her child would also support Natalia's citizenship application after she was released from prison.

"Crappy Thursday grub," Melly said, pushing the plate of food away.

Melly was always complaining about the food, whereas Natalia quite liked it; such healthy and hearty casseroles were common fare in Russia and were also good for you. But anyway, she was finding just about any food to her liking just now and was hungry all the time.

"Can I finish yours?" she asked.

"Sure, knock yourself out," Melly answered. "But I want the pancakes," she said, grinning.

Kicki's little girl started crying.

"What's up with her?" Natalia asked.

Kicki lifted up the girl and sniffed her behind.

"I need to change her diaper, it's soiled again."

"Oh come on, can't you wait until I'm finished eating so that I can do it?"

Natalia tended to jump on any opportunity to take care of Kicki's baby, as she wanted to learn how to change diapers so that she wouldn't be a total beginner when her own child arrived. She was expecting a boy, and she and Christina had already settled on a name for him – Patrik, of course. She was pleased as punch about this.

She'd completely recovered from her injuries. Her jaw was all better. Her face had cycled through every color of the rainbow, from blue to green to yellow and she now had a good, healthy complexion. As for the scar on her cheek, she simply hid it with concealer. The wounds on her body had healed, and she could live with the few scars that remained. All that was still missing were the five teeth she'd lost, but the dentist had advised her to do the implants after the baby was born, as the procedure would require a number of visits.

Natalia was eating her pea soup, and Melly's too, and now turned to her pancakes. She adored pancakes with jam and proceeded to slather them accordingly. And with a dollop of cream on top, it was the perfect dessert.

She'd been convicted of three counts of fraud and being an accessory to murder and had been sentenced to eight years. Her lawyer advised her to only plead guilty to the charge involving Patrik, but Natalia had wanted to have a clean slate, and for her past life to be over and done with so that she could move forward – something she felt she couldn't do if she only copped to a portion of the charges against her. The DA and judge had taken this into consideration in setting her sentence, and with time off for good behavior she'd be out on parole in two years. But Melly and Kicki, who'd gotten life, wouldn't be so lucky – although most such sentences are reduced.

"Coming?" Kicki said, as she got up from her chair.

"Yup."

Natalia followed Kicki back to her cell, where they changed the diaper together. Kicki told her how to go about changing the diaper and showed her how to get almost all the feces to stay in the diaper. The baby's mood instantly turned sunny and she was very playful with the two women.

Then Natalia went back to her cell, which was small and simply furnished, as one would expect in a prison. But this was fine with Natalia, who was in any case accustomed to making do with little.

Christina would be visiting her this coming Saturday and came at least once a week. Natalia looked forward to these occasions like a child waiting for Santa to arrive. For her, Christina was like her Babushka – not as old of course, but with the same warm-heartedness. She had the feeling that her life was now coming full circle and that she'd returned to her native soil. Christina was her new home – they'd decided to live together when Natalia was released, and of course with Patrik Jr. This was in fact her fondest wish.

She was thrilled that Christina had gotten better so quickly and was now looking really good. But she also realized that the effects of the events on that fateful December day would haunt Christina for the rest of her days. Christina didn't want to talk about it and was always soft-pedaling it – though she had admitted to Natalia that she was seeing a therapist once a week in order to put all that trauma behind her.

Natalia's friend Lyudmila had visited her a few weeks ago, and they'd burst into tears as they fell into each others' arms. Lyudmila had wanted to know all the details, and they'd put their heads together to piece together the puzzle of how Stanislov had managed to track her down. Stanislov and a buddy had waylaid Lyudmila's friend's brother Gábor and made him talk. But of course Gábor could only tell them what he knew – which was that Natalia had left Budapest, that she was pregnant with Patrik's child and that she intended to have the baby. Gábor felt terrible about having betrayed Natalia – but they'd threatened to cut off his balls if he didn't talk. Luckily, they'd been satisfied with getting this much out of him and had let him go. Afterwards, Stanislov had apparently put two and two together. He knew that Natalia had run out of people she could turn to – and that she was going to need help if she was going to have the baby. Then, Stanislov or a buddy of his had hacked into Christina's phone data, a list of which the police had found in his Audi. And when he saw that Christina had received numerous calls from Budapest, he realized what was up and had proceeded to kidnap Christina.

Natalia fervently hoped that Stanislov, who was still in a coma, would never wake up. Christina had really clobbered him, and she was eternally grateful for that too. And even if Stanislov did wake up, he'd be tried for three counts of murder, kidnapping, aggravated assault, and attempted murder. He would surely get life, but most such sentences are reduced to 18 years after ten years have been served – which would mean that Natalia would once again have to be watching her back all the time. And she was sure that Stanislov would seek revenge, even after all those years. So hopefully he'd never, ever wake up from that coma.

Natalia was the only one to be convicted of a crime. The charges of aggravated assault against Christina and manslaughter against Elin had been dropped, as the police and the DA ended up accepting that they had acted in self defense – although establishing this had required a number of interrogation sessions. Natalia felt this was as it should be and was happy about this outcome. She would have felt horribly guilty if one of the people who'd come to her aid ended up getting into serious trouble for doing so.

Natalia reached over to her night table and picked up the book that Christina had brought her last week. The cabin in Småland had been a crime scene for quite some time, and so had been cordoned off by the police. When the cordon was removed, the owner had decided to sell the cabin and had cleared it out. The book that Natalia had begun reading back then had ended up in Christina's possession, and now Natalia could resume reading it. She was now on the third generation of strong, independent female characters from Gränslandet : en kärleksroman *("The Frontier: a love story"), and the book gave her courage. Like those women, she would never give up and would do everything within her power to make a success of her new life. And she wasn't alone – she had Christina by her side.*

THANKS TO THE READER

I am thrilled that you have chosen my book.

I am even more thrilled that you have read it to the end. I especially hope that you liked it. If so, I would like to ask you for a small favour: take a few moments of your time and rate my book on Amazon.

If you didn't like something about the book, please tell me directly! Your feedback is extremely important to me – this way I get the chance to consider the preferences of my readers.

contact@christertholin.one
www.christertholin.one

My heartfelt thanks
Christer Tholin

ABOUT THE AUTHOR

The author is originally from Schleswig-Holstein in Germany and has lived for many years with his family in Stockholm / Sweden, where he works as an independent management consultant.

He is a great fan of Swedish crime literature and had been planning for a long time to make his own contribution. That has already come to fruition with his first book, VANISHED? which is also the first book of the *Stockholm Sleuth Series* introducing Elin and Lars. SECRETS? is their second case, MURDER? their third, and GUILTY? their fourth.

www.christertholin.one

VANISHED?

Stockholm Sleuth Series, Book 1
By Christer Tholin
2016, Stockholm

She: a very hot 30 something Swedish woman. ***He:*** a native of Berlin, on vacation in rural Sweden, seeking solace for his broken heart. They meet. He finds her irresistible. But before their relationship can get off the ground, she vanishes mysteriously, having apparently been abducted. So Martin sets out to rescue Liv from her captors, with the aid of two Swedish detectives in a race against time – and across Sweden. In so doing, Martin and his intrepid detective duo put their very lives on the line.

https://www.amazon.com/gp/product/B071KYQ2XZ/

SECRETS?

Stockholm Sleuth Series, Book 2
By Christer Tholin
2017, Stockholm

In the crime novella SECRETS?, fledgling private investigator Elin Bohlander takes on what looks like an easy assignment — at first: to determine if her client's boyfriend is having an affair with another woman. To do this, Elin follows him to a secluded cabin in the woods, where she soon discovers that what's actually transpiring is stranger than anyone thought. Having ventured too far, she's stumbled upon a hornet's nest and put her life at risk. But it's too late. Can Elin win the unequal fight against a gang of brutal child molesters?

https://www.amazon.com/gp/product/B075VWXGHN/

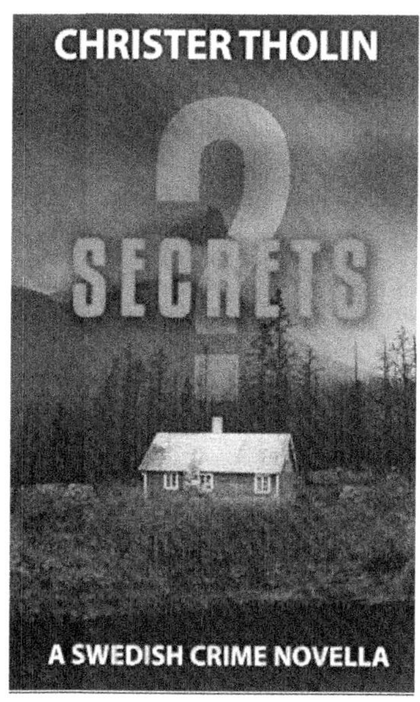

GUILTY?

Stockholm Sleuth Series, Book 4
By Christer Tholin
2020, Stockholm

Stockholm: From one day to the next, 16-year old Hanna just vanishes without a trace. Her worried parents ask the detectives Lars und Elin to find their daughter. The two of them do just that and very quickly. However, Hanna's problems are far from over – she is trapped in the clutches of a "loverboy". Just a few months later, the two private detectives are hired once again: Hanna is in serious trouble. This assignment pushes everyone involved to their limits ...

Printed in Great Britain
by Amazon

23717568R00189